All the Kingdoms of the Earth

I hear a Sovereign talking in my arteries
Reversing, with His Promises, all things
That now go on with fire and thunder.
His truth is greater than disaster
His Peace imposes silence on the evidence against us.

—Thomas Merton, "Senescenti Mundo"

ALL the

KINGDOMS

of the EARTH

*Israelite Prophecy and International
Relations in the Ancient Near East*

Norman K. Gottwald

Lowry Professor of Old Testament
Andover Newton Theological School

HARPER & ROW, PUBLISHERS

New York, Evanston, and London

To Linda Sharon and Lise Carol

Grateful acknowledgment is made to New Directions for permission to quote from "Senescenti Mundo" from THE SELECTED POEMS OF THOMAS MERTON, copyright 1944, © 1959 by The Abbey of Gethsemani, Inc.

FIRST EDITION

LIBRARY OF CONGRESS CATALOG CARD NUMBER: 64-19499

I-O

Contents

v

III. ISRAELITE PROPHECY AND INTERNATIONAL RELATIONS IN THE EIGHTH CENTURY

IV. ISRAELITE PROPHECY AND INTERNATIONAL RELATIONS IN THE SEVENTH AND SIXTH CENTURIES

V. Israelite Prophecy and International Relations
in the Ancient Near East

List of Maps

Abbreviations

AASOR Annual of the American Schools of Oriental Research

AJSL   American Journal of Semitic Languages and Literatures

ANEP   J. Pritchard, ed., *The Ancient Near East in Pictures Relating to the Old Testament*

ANET   J. Pritchard, ed., *Ancient Near Eastern Texts Relating to the Old Testament*

BA   Biblical Archaeologist

BASOR Bulletin of the American Schools of Oriental Research

BJRL   Bulletin of the John Rylands Library

BZAW Beihefte zur Zeitschrift fuer die alttestamentliche Wissenschaft

CBQ   Catholic Biblical Quarterly

ET   Expository Times

HTR   Harvard Theological Review

HUCA Hebrew Union College Annual

HZAT Handbuch zum Alten Testament

IB   The Interpreter's Bible

ICC   The International Critical Commentary

IDB   The Interpreter's Dictionary of the Bible

IEJ   Israel Exploration Journal

JAOS   Journal of the American Oriental Society

JBL   Journal of Biblical Literature

JBR   Journal of Bible and Religion

JCS   Journal of Cuneiform Studies

JNES   Journal of Near Eastern Studies

JPOS   Journal of the Palestine Oriental Society

JQR	*Jewish Quarterly Review*
JR	*Journal of Religion*
JSS	*Journal of Semitic Studies*
JTS	*Journal of Theological Studies*
KS	A. Alt, *Kleine Schriften zur Geschichte des Volkes Israel*
KZAT	*Kommentar zum Alten Testament*
LVTL	L. Koehler, ed., *Lexicon in Veteris Testamenti Libros*
LXX	Septuagint
MT	Masoretic Text
OS	*Oudtestamentische Studien*
PEQ	*Palestine Exploration Quarterly*
PJ	*Palaestina Jahrbuch*
RB	*Revue Biblique*
RHPR	*Revue d'Histoire et de Philosophie Religieuse*
RSV	*Revised Standard Version*
TZ	*Theologische Zeitschrift*
VT	*Vetus Testamentum*
ZAW	*Zeitschrift fuer die alttestamentliche Wissenschaft*
ZDMG	*Zeitschrift der deutschen morgenlaendischen Gesellschaft*
ZDPV	*Zeitschrift des deutschen Palaestina-Vereins*
ZTK	*Zeitschrift fuer Theologie und Kirche*

Preface

This inquiry has two immediate aims: first, to canvass the prophetic references to international relations in the light of recent substantial gains both in historical knowledge of the ancient Near East and in theological exegesis of the Old Testament; and, second, to draw some theoretical conclusions about the nature of the political outlook of the prophets, particularly their view of international affairs.

Throughout the study I have been overwhelmed by the number and variety of skills which a biblical interpreter must have to do his work properly. Professional modesty has cautioned me not to paint so large a canvas as I have here attempted. It is not so easy, after all, to be an "authority" on all of the prophets as on one—or, even better, on one aspect of one prophet. But I have chosen the scope and method of the study with deliberation.

Anyone who surveys Old Testament studies since World War II will be impressed by the astonishing rate of publication. In most studies of late there has been a conscious effort to overcome the fragmentation of the textual units which resulted from too rigid literary-critical canons in the earlier stages of biblical research. A half-dozen significant theologies of the Old Testament have synthesized the richly detailed results of linguistic, form-critical, and historical research into a grand design, or at least into a number of reasonably well-integrated fundamental themes. One can only be profoundly indebted to these efforts, which in some instances have produced brilliant results.

Yet the communication between exegetical and theological studies is by no means as full and free as is desirable. In my judgment what is most needed at present is for exegetical studies to become more integrated and for studies on select topics to be pursued in connection with related topics instead of in splendid "thesis-like" isolation. A too pedantic and restricted mood in exegesis cannot be rectified merely from the side of broader theological construction, for then the gulf between material and conclusions is only widened. The exegete and the historian must pursue their constructive, integrating course until they come closer to the theologian and can present him with well-thought-out conclusions, even when those conclusions must admit to unsolved problems and to contradictions and tensions in the material. We cannot expect the theologian to make up for unventuresome and narrow-visioned exegesis.

In this framework, I saw my task to be a working-through of the prophetic allusions to international relations, from earliest times to the restoration of the Jewish community to Palestine in 538 B.C., in the light of our ever-enlarging knowledge of ancient Near Eastern history, and particularly of diplomatic practice. At the same time I have recognized that several topics have significant connections with international relations: religious universalism, the mission of Israel, eschatology, and the concept of world peace. Each of these has been reckoned with insofar as international relations have influenced their prophetic formulation. Accordingly, I have drawn into this study, especially from Isaiah onward, passages of a broader nature—in particular socalled eschatological passages—whenever I was convinced they would illuminate the manner in which the religious outlook of the prophet and his orientation in foreign relations tended to interact and to cross-fertilize each other.

Most of the intensive research was done at the Hebrew University in Jerusalem, Israel, in 1960–61, where I was privileged to work as a Fulbright Research Scholar and also as the beneficiary of an American Association of Theological Schools faculty grant. Not least of the contributions to this study was the author's firsthand experience of the topography and climate of ancient Palestine and his contact with those elements of biblical life which survive archaeologically in the ruins and in the museums and sociologically among the Jewish and Arab populations. That experience has sometimes compelled reassessment of the established conclusions of literary-historical criticism. If there is occasional salutary questioning of old positions in this book, I think it is due above all else to the liberating and profoundly instructive experience of living for a year in the land of the prophets.

The translation of the Old Testament is my own. In the Bible translations, brackets enclose explanatory interpolations and transliterations of the Hebrew, whereas parentheses indicate additions for smoother reading. In quotations from non-biblical texts, I have retained the punctuation of the sourcebooks. In a large majority of cases the non-biblical quotations are taken from James Pritchard, ed., *Ancient Near Eastern Texts Relating to the Old Testament,* who regularly uses brackets to indicate restorations in a broken or obscure text, parentheses to supply interpolations intended to improve the reader's understanding, and italics to designate a doubtful translation of a known text. The maps are drawn from my *A Light to the Nations: An Introduction to the Old Testament.*

And now to award credits. The chronology employed follows W. F. Albright for the kingdoms of Israel, except as otherwise noted; S. Pallis for early Mesopotamia; P. Van der Meer and A. Poebel for Assyria; W. S. Smith for Egypt; and O. R. Gurney for the Hittites. Portions of the manuscript have been read by three faculty members at the Hebrew University: Dr. Abraham Malamat in Jewish History, Dr. Hayim Tadmor in Assyriology, and Dr. Shemaryahu Talmon in Bible. Each made corrections and valuable suggestions. I have often revised or sharpened my position in response to them. Some sections of the last chapter were presented at a Hazen Group discussion in New Haven in the spring of 1962, and for the final writing I have had the benefit of numerous suggestions made on that occasion.

A persistent larger interest has motivated this study. What contribution can the Hebrew prophets make to international relations today? Is there anything in their outlook which is pertinent either for the church and synagogue or for the state in our age? I have, however, deliberately avoided reference to this interest, except on the last page, because I wanted to pursue my examination of the prophets with the fullest possible objectivity. Only in this way could I be assured of presenting results which deserved serious consideration by political scientists, government officials, ethicists, theologians, and concerned Jews and Christians. Elsewhere I plan to state what I believe to be the modern implications of my study. In the meantime, this book may serve as a starting point for others to develop their own conclusions.

Newton Centre, Massachusetts   N. K. G.
July 1, 1964

Map 1

THE ANCIENT NEAR EAST 3000–500 B.C.

BLACK

Troy

ASIA MINOR
ANATOLIA

•Hattusa
(Khattushash)

HATTI

Kanish

AEGEAN
SEA

Cilician Gate

Taurus Mts.

SY

Ala

Ugarit

Han

CAPHTOR
(CRETE)

KITTIM
(CYPRUS)

Byblos

Dam

MEDITERRANEAN SEA

Tyre

Tanis - Avaris - Ramses

Sais

Jerusalem

Gaza

Bubastis

Memphis

LOWER
EGYPT

SINAI

SCALE OF MILES
0   50   100   200

El-Amarna

TO SO.
ARABI

RED SEA

UPPER EGYPT

Thebes

URARTU

chemish
aran

ASSYRIA

Nineveh

Ashur • Nuzi

Mari

BABYLONIA

Ecbatana

Median Gates

PERSIA

AKKad
Babylon

Susa

ELAM

Nippur • SUMER

Erech

ur •

TO INDIA

PERSIAN
GULF

ARABIA

• Tema

CASPIAN
SEA

Euphrates R.

Tigris R.

Diyala R.

---------- MAJOR ROUTES

CHAPTER I

Imperialism and International
Relations in the Ancient Near East

Our Western reading of history, so heavily indebted to Greece
and Rome, normally begins with the presupposition that political
life in the Near East prior to Alexander lay under the curse of
tyranny. Aristotle's political writings gave credence to the notion,
and there was little basis on which to contradict him until the remarkable recovery of ancient Near Eastern civilization in the last
150 years.

Of the three possible types of government known to Aristotle
(monarchy, aristocracy, democracy), he found monarchy the
least satisfactory.[1] Plato's dream of the ideal philosopher-king
was for him without embodiment since the disappearance from
the earth of the legendary "heroic" kings who had founded the
city-states of Greece. The only kings known to Aristotle were
Spartan kings and Oriental kings. The former he found distaste-
ful to his sense of freedom and the latter he found abhorrent both
to his sense of freedom and to his cultural pretensions. Aristotle
judged Oriental kingship to be virtual tyranny, an observation
based largely upon his acquaintance with the late Persian kings.

[1] Aristotle, *Politics* (Loeb Classical Library, English trans. by H. Rackham,
1932), Book III; cf. G. H. Sabine, *A History of Political Theory*, 3rd ed.
rev., 1951, pp. 90–101.

The true king rules by consent and is protected and supported by his citizens. The tyrant represses his subjects with the aid of mercenaries. Even though Aristotle admitted that the Persians had at least the form of monarchy, he treated the substance as tyranny.[2] Their mentality being a slave mentality, the Asiatics have received the oppressive rule they deserve.[3] Everywhere in this conception operates the controlling notion that the Greek city-state is normative. The empirical content of the judgments on Near Eastern kingship is so thin as to be virtually nil and quite at odds with the passion for factual study typical of Aristotle's painstaking study of some 158 Greek city-state constitutions.[4]

It is precisely this empirical lack in Aristotle's assessment of Asiatic kingship that has been supplied in the last century and a half. (Furthermore, we no longer feel quite the same compulsion to elevate Western political institutions at the expense of Eastern.) In particular, Aristotle's claim that the city-state flourished only among the Greeks is flatly contradicted by ancient Mesopotamian records. The true nature of Near Eastern kingship is visible in a wealth of fascinating detail, and its strengths and weaknesses, its similarities and dissimilarities to Western political forms can be permitted to unfold without unfair forcing of the evidence.

[2] His uncertainty as to how to characterize Oriental government is apparent in the following: ἔχουσι δ' αὗται τὴν δύναμιν πᾶσαι παραπλησίαν τυραννίσιν, εἰσὶ δὲ καὶ κατὰ νόμον καὶ πατρικαί. ("The power possessed by all of these [barbarian kingdoms] resembles that of tyrannies, but they govern according to law and are hereditary.") *Politics* III. ix. 3.

[3] Although what evidence he had militated against the conclusion, Aristotle judged Oriental rule to be practical if not formal tyranny: διὰ γὰρ τὸ δουλικώτεροι εἶναι τὰ ἤθη φύσει οἱ μὲν βάρβαροι τῶν Ἑλλήνων οἱ δὲ περὶ τὴν Ἀσίαν τῶν περὶ τὴν Εὐρώπην, ὑπομένουσι τὴν δεσποτικὴν ἀρχὴν ουδὲν δυσχεραίνοντες. Τυραννικαὶ μέν οὖν διὰ τὸ τοιοῦτόν εἰσιν, ἀσφαλεῖς δὲ διὰ τὸ πάτριαι καὶ κατὰ νόμον εἶναι. ("For because the barbarians are more servile in their nature than the Greeks, and the Asiatics than the Europeans, they endure despotic rule without any resentment. These kingships therefore are for these reasons of a tyrannical nature, but they are secure because they are hereditary and rule by law.") *Politics* III. ix. 3 Cf. comments of S. Smith, "Kingship in Early Semitic Kingdoms," in S. H. Hooke, ed., *Myth, Ritual, and Kingship*, pp. 22–24.

[4] Sabine, *op. cit.*, p. 88. Unfortunately, only Aristotle's discussion of the Athenian constitution has survived (*Athenian Constitution*, Loeb Classical Library, ed. H. Rackham, 1935).

From City-State Through Kingdom to Empire

Frequently when Near Eastern political institutions are examined, attention focuses upon the New Kingdom of Egypt with its Asiatic Empire or upon the imperial achievements of the Assyrians, Neo-Babylonians, and Persians. Thutmose III, Sargon, Nebuchadnezzar, and Cyrus are the exemplary empire-builders in pre-classical antiquity whose dominions extended over Palestine and consequently elicit the special interest of biblical students, who have so often determined the direction and emphasis of Near Eastern studies. Yet this selective emphasis is misleading for it too easily overlooks the fact that the high political accomplishments of the Egyptians in the late second millennium B.C. and of the Mesopotamians in the first millennium were in turn built upon at least 1,500 years of previous political accomplishment. *The later empires were in fact the products of an elaborate political syncretism which can only be fully appreciated by a consideration of the earlier Egyptian kingdoms and the preceding Sumero-Akkadian city-states and quasi-empires.* Our method will be to consider first the pre-Assyrian political development in Mesopotamia, next to turn to the Egyptian political history in its antecedents and culmination, then to survey Hittite imperialism, and to conclude with the Mesopotamian political zenith from Assyria to Persia.

The Early Mesopotamian Heritage

The city-states of the lower Tigris-Euphrates Valley (see Map 2), in which high civilization first emerged in Mesopotamia about 3000 B.C., were relatively self-contained agricultural units composed of walled cities with surrounding fields and villages. The prevailing ethos of these city-states was that of man as the servant of the gods, who owned the land. The multiplicity of the gods found its counterpart in the many city-states, each with its patron deity. A fundamentally religious outlook was translated into a priestly theocracy in which the temple and its personnel administered government and economy.[5]

The city-state was ruled by an assembly of leaders who reflected the divine pantheon. Originally a body of free citizens
with an executive arm of elders, the assembly by the dawn of
the historical era was apparently dominated by priests. This assembly theoretically sought a common mind but in practice it
selected one man to serve as ruler. He is variously known as
patesi, ensi ("governor") or *lugal* ("great man"). He stood as it
were at the head of the human pantheon just as Anu stood at
the head of the divine pantheon. In principle he could not act
willfully although in practice strong *patesis* were often at odds
with the assemblies they represented. The workings of this political system are imperfectly known but they do accurately reflect
the fact that ancient Sumerian monarchy was a limited theocratic monarchy; it could even be called a type of "primitive
democracy."[6]

As representative of the god the *patesi* discharged primary responsibilities for the entire community.[7] He was responsible for
the maintenance of the canal system. In the temple storehouses
he received all the produce of the realm. He controlled all crafts
and commerce. Temples were his to build and to maintain, and
he officiated in the cult as the high priest. Administration of
justice was in his hands. He served as judge and appointed
judges. Legal precedents, not yet "codes" in the Western sense,
were gathered by him and declared exemplary.[8] Armies went
forth under his command.

[5] A. Deimel, "Die sumerische Tempelwirtschaft zur Zeit Urukaginas und
seiner Vorgaenger," *Analecta Orientalia* 2 (1931), 71–113, and S. Pallis,
The Antiquity of Iraq, pp. 488–96.

[6] T. Jacobsen, "Primitive Democracy in Ancient Mesopotamia," *JNES* 2
(1943), 159–72. S. Kramer proposed the term "politocracy" to describe this
tightly knit theocracy (*Some Sources of Intellectual and Social Progress in
the Ancient Near East,* 1942).

[7] In addition to discussions of *patesi* in Deimel, *op. cit.,* and Pallis, *op. cit.,*
see also H. Frankfort, *Kingship and the Gods,* 1948, chap. 16, which traces
the persistence of the Sumerian concepts of *patesi* (petty king) and *lugal*
(king with imperialist pretensions) in the later Mesopotamian forms of
kingship.

[8] T. J. Meek, "The Origin of Hebrew Law," *Hebrew Origins,* esp. pp.
53–58.

Nothing was spared to give the *patesi* the communal resources needed to serve in his calling as the god's deputy to govern the body politic. He alone held private property. To him was given a considerable administrative staff to expedite his religious, economic, judicial, and military tasks. It is easy to see that the central authority vested in the *patesi* was a necessity for maintaining the level of corporate action needed to sustain civilized life in ancient Mesopotamia. It is also easy to understand that, with the elaboration of civilization and the clash of rival political groups, power would tend to accrue to the *patesi* beyond that originally granted by the assembly.

With the development of military skills, the increase of population, and growing territorial ambitions, city-state began to lord it over city-state. Although of the same language and culture, the Sumerians did not form a political confederation. Eannatum of Lagash (c. 2400) defeated several neighboring city-states and even asserted his control over Elam to the east of the Delta.[9] About a century and a half later Lugal-zaggisi (2313–2289) subjugated all of Sumer from his capital at Erech. To give a rationale to the dominance of one city-state over others, the Sumerians developed the conception of the choice of one *patesi* by the gods to rule over all the others. This was expressed as election by Enlil, the god of Nippur, who in historical times, as the god of civilization, had become the most beneficent of the deities. The favor of Enlil was thought to circulate among the city-states as he chose now this ruler and now another to hold political ascendancy.[10] Sometimes the rejection of one ruler was explained by the anger of the gods because of his misbehavior. Sumerian civilization had found a means for giving coherence to the political fragmentation of the city-states and to the shifting balance of power among the several states.

In the classic city-state period of ancient Sumer it is not possible to speak clearly of a kingdom which was any more than an aggregation of separate city-states. At the most it was a feudal

[9] A. Poebel, "Der Konflikt zwischen Lagaš und Umma zur Zeit Enannatums I und Entemenas," *Paul Haupt Anniversary Volume*, 1926, pp. 220–67.

[10] Frankfort, *op. cit.*, pp. 216–17.

arrangement in which the *patesis* of the subject city-states served as feudal barons in their separate realms. It was an extremely loose arrangement that disintegrated whenever a strong conquering ruler produced a weaker son.

The Semites, who developed a powerful state at Agade (Akkad) in the middle Tigris-Euphrates region (see Map 3), were heirs of the Sumerian political apparatus as well as of much else in Sumerian culture. Sargon of Agade (2242–2186) asserted that Enlil had chosen him, and he favored Nippur by making it the cult center of his kingdom.[11] The old city-state divisions of the lower valley, were retained. The major innovation was that Sargon undertook to assert his authority by taking a direct hand in the choice of *patesis*. This was a blow at the old hereditary principle, but whether Sargon carried it through logically by installing Akkadians in all the Sumerian city-states or chose from among rival local dynasts is unknown. Akkadian hegemony was asserted northward along the Tigris and Euphrates rivers as far as northern Syria. This was primarily economic hegemony; owing to the sparseness of population in northern Mesopotamia and the vast distances involved, no continuing political control could be asserted. Nevertheless the expanding horizons of Mesopotamian empire did lead the Akkadian monarch to style himself "King of the four quarters of the world." *If the great economic hegemony of Agade is in mind, Sargon's kingdom may be designated an "empire"; but the term is clearly inapplicable in its standard political sense since only middle and lower Mesopotamia were integrated into the kingdom and then only haltingly by a combination of old city-state units ruled by royal appointees.*

With the passing of the Akkadian kingdom, a renascence of Sumerian political independence occurred. The Third Dynasty of Ur under Ur-Nammu (2044–2027) asserted its sovereignty over a region nearly as vast as that of Sargon's realm (see Map

[11] T. Jacobsen, "The Assumed Conflict between Sumerians and Semites in Early Mesopotamian History," *JAOS* 49 (1939), 485–95, stresses that, in the defeat of Lugal-zaggisi by Sargon, "what the sources show is not a racial grouping: Semites with Semitic gods against Sumerians with Sumerian gods, but a purely political fight: two city-states, Agade and Uruk, bidding for hegemony in Babylonia," of which the most dramatic example was Sargon's submission to the Nippur shrine's pan-Mesopotamian religious hegemony.

4). The Sumerians had clearly profited by the practical administrative and commercial genius of the Akkadians, as is tacitly admitted in the title adopted by these neo-Sumerian rulers, "King of Sumer and Akkad." In fact the early Sumerian tendency toward theocratic concentration of power in the priesthood and governor was now combined with political hegemony to produce a marked centralization of power in the city-states, notably Ur and Lagash, which by turns held the ascendancy. At this period the deification of kings emerged explicitly in a manner never repeated in Mesopotamia, especially in the veneration accorded Dungi (or Shulgi) of Ur (2026–1979).[12] It is inaccurate to attribute this royal deification to the Semitic Akkadian element, for the later more Semitized dynasties of Sumer, especially in Larsa and Isin, employed the deification of the king only sporadically, and the later Semitic kingdoms resisted all tendencies to make the king into a god. It seems to have been a special development rising out of cultic and imperial needs. The king was called a "god" insofar as he served as the bridegroom of the goddess at a state festival, and he was customarily addressed as a "god" only by persons in vassal city-states, not by his own subjects.[13]

The dynasties of Larsa (2026–1762) and Isin (2022–1797), which preceded the rise of the Amorites and gradually gave way before them, seem to represent the further Semitizing of the social and political institutions of Sumer. Akkadian became the common language and the original Sumerian was reserved for religious purposes. Decentralization of power reversed the tendency of the previous period in Sumer. Perhaps most significant for future social and political developments was the extension of private property into the Sumerian city-states.[14] This was anti-

[12] T. Fish, "The Cult of King Dungi during the Third Dynasty of Ur," *BJRL* 11 (1927), 322–28.

[13] Frankfort, *op. cit.*, chap. 21, esp. pp. 299, 302, based in turn on Frankfort, Lloyd, and Jacobsen, *The Gimilsin Temple and the Palace of the Rulers at Tell Asmar*, 1939; cf. C. Jeremias, *Die Vergoettlichung der babylonisch-assyrischen Koenige,* who sees evidence for the deification of kings in offerings to kings' statues which Frankfort interprets as merely temporary cultic sanctification of the king.

[14] Pallis, *op. cit.*, pp. 510–11.

pathetic to the original Sumerian theocracy. It seems probable that the Semitic builders of the Akkadian kingdom introduced the concept of private property into lower Mesopotamia. In imitating the political success of the Akkadians the successors of the earlier Sumerians also copied the institution of private property. The development of trade seems to have produced a class of merchants who were not content to be entirely beholden to priest and king.

The existence of a propertied class in Mesopotamia was of utmost importance to the second great Semitic kingdom, namely, the Amorite dynasty of Babylon (1826–1526) (see Map 6). Hammurabi's "code" shows that one of his chief functions as king was to secure the rights of land and of capital. This meant in one sense that the state was increasingly secularized; private ownership instead of theocratic ownership became normative. A tax system was introduced and even temples paid taxes to support the government instead of receiving taxes for the god and his retinue as they had formerly in Sumer. In this way an internal social and economic differentiation was recognized and encouraged.[15]

At the same time a political autocracy was developed and the state in the person of the king was given functions of social cohesion throughout the realm that had hitherto been granted only to the religious representatives or to the *patesis* as deputies of the local gods. Priestly theocracy gave way before royal autocracy, which secured itself, not through unbridled despotism, but through its success in welding together the varying social and economic drives of the populace and in holding at bay the previously inordinate demands of the cultic apparatus. All this is well expressed in Hammurabi's bold assertion, "I am the king exalted above the city kings."

In the administration of his realm, Hammurabi (1724–1682) abolished the old Sumerian term *patesi* as well as its Akkadian equivalent *issakkum*.[16] This was imperative because the Sumerian office was in fact abolished, and governors or prefects in charge of taxation, trade, and the militia took their place. All were di-

[15] *Ibid.,* chap. 10.
[16] *Ibid.,* pp. 521–23.

ectly responsible to the court at Babylon. A large civil service was recruited to care for the increased correspondence, the oversight of state slaves, and the raising of the army levy. Hammurabi strove mightily to integrate the former city-states, conceived no longer as subject feudal kingdoms but as administrative units answerable directly to him through his appointees. In this respect the Amorite reign from Babylon may be called the first Near Eastern "empire." Yet a true provincial system was not evolved, even in Sumer. As for northern Mesopotamia and Syria, they were as imperfectly governed by the Amorite dynasty as they had been by the Akkadian dynasty.

The novel element in the Amorite dynasty was the successful increase of central royal power, not by the deification of the king, but by a process of practical secularization working to the mutual advantage of king, merchant, and landowner, who asserted their respective rights over against the priesthood.[17] The continued cultic glorification of the state by the elevation of Marduk as the chief god of Babylon and his fusion with Enlil of Nippur should not obscure the fact that political institutions were actually disengaged from religious controls. The process, of course, was never carried through theoretically or institutionally, for the political leaders never gave up religious forms of thought. Mesopotamian rulers from Hammurabi on, nevertheless, learned how to separate religious forms of thought from a total religious institutional control of society and the state. A pragmatic secularism flourished while theocracy remained the ideology of Mesopotamian civilization.

International relations in Hammurabi's age are brilliantly illuminated by diplomatic correspondence found at Mari (see Map 6), consisting mainly of letters addressed to Zimri-lim,

[17] *Ibid.*, pp. 520–28, documents the new status of the classes by reference to Hammurabi's code. F. M. T. Boehl, *King Hammurabi of Babylon in the Setting of His Time* (about 1700 B.C.), pp. 23–26, thinks that the absence of palace remains from Hammurabi's dynasty demonstrates, in sharp contrast to the lavish court at Mari, a diversion of resources from royal monopoly to the immediate economic needs of the free citizens. His bestowal of royal properties on free citizens, especially military colonists, is discussed by C. Koehne, "Die Bevoelkerungspolitik in der Gesetzgebung Koenig Hammurabis," *Zeitschrift fuer Soziale Wissenschaft* (1918), pp. 46 ff.

king of Mari, by foreign rulers and Mari officials in the foreign
service.[18] One of the corresponding kings is Hammurabi of Babylon. For the greater part of his reign, Hammurabi headed one of
several contending states which struggled by diplomacy and war
to gain the upper hand in Mesopotamia. Among the rivals of
Babylon were Larsa, Mari, Eshnunna, Qatanum, and Yamhad.
Assyria was in a period of decline after the vigorous Shamshi-
Adad I (1744–1724) and was not influential in international
politics.

By means of coalitions, the stronger states sought to tip the
balance of power in their favor. The coalitions shifted frequently
as smaller states threw their weight toward this king or that in
the hope of gaining advantages with the eventual "winner." It
was in fact a period of military stalemate marked by feverish
diplomatic activity, well expressed in the letter of an official of
Mari to his king: "There is no king who, of himself, is the strongest. Ten or fifteen kings follow Hammurabi of Babylon, the same
number follow Rim-Sin of Larsa, the same number follow Ibâl-
pî-El of Eshnunna, the same number follow Amût-pî-il of
Qatanum, 20 kings follow Yarim-lim of Yamhad."[19] The stalemate was broken in the late reign of Hammurabi when he defeated Assyria, Larsa, Assyria (a second time), Mari, and Eshnunna in succession and extended his suzerainty the length of
the Tigris-Euphrates Valley.[20]

*Of particular note is the convincing evidence of highly de-
veloped rules of diplomacy, which must already have had centuries of tradition behind them.* Protocol held sway in all matters
of diplomatic exchange, recognition, and negotiation. Sizes of
delegations and amounts and types of gifts subtly expressed the
ranking of states within the international hierarchy. To stop sending gifts was tantamount to breaking off diplomatic relations.

Although we do not possess the texts of treaties from the Mari

[18] This correspondence is appearing in transliteration and French translation in A. Parrot and G. Dossin, eds., *Archives Royales de Mari,* 1950——.
An extremely valuable systematic analysis of the diplomatic documents is
that by J. M. Munn-Rankin, "Diplomacy in Western Asia in the Early
Second Millennium B.C.," *Iraq* 18 (1956), 68–110.

[19] *Ibid.,* p. 74.

[20] Boehl, *op. cit.,* pp. 13–14.

age, the ethos and procedure of treaty-making are abundantly
reflected in the correspondence. *The vassal treaty, familiar from
the age of Hittite domination in north Syria some three hundred
years later, is already a fully established form of international relations in Amorite Mesopotamia.* Vassal states subordinated their
foreign policies to the suzerain, but in domestic affairs they had
virtual freedom as long as they sent tribute and supplied the
prescribed quota of troops for coalition campaigns. In fact, the
services of the suzerain were frequently offered to settle disputes
between vassals by arbitration.[21] In general it seems that treaties
between equals were said to establish *aḫûtum,* "fraternity,"
whereas treaties between unequals were said to express the
abûtum, "paternity," of the suzerain and the *marûtum,* "son-
ship," of the vassal, who owed to his suzerain *wardûtum,* "service." A general term for international treaties was *salîmum,*
"friendship." It seems, however, that these expressions had not
yet acquired the status of technical terms and were, therefore,
used with some fluidity so that the exact category of the treaty
cannot invariably be concluded from them.[22]

Treaty ceremonies included a written contract in the presence
of the gods of the participating states, who witnessed the oaths,
the sacrifices, and other ritual acts. A knife or finger was apparently drawn across the throat (*lipit napištum,* "touching of
the throat") or an ass was killed in order to express the fate of
the one who would break the treaty.[23] A vassal who concluded a
treaty was said "to seize the hem of the garment" of his suzerain.
Breach of treaty was called *qullultum,* "sin." The great majority
of the treaties reported concerned mutual defense or offense, but
neutrality pacts are attested, and such international problems

---

[21] Munn-Rankin, *op. cit.,* pp. 95–96.

[22] *Ibid.,* pp. 76, 84, contra G. Dossin, *Mélanges Syriens,* II, 90, who sees
greater technical precision in the use of covenant terms than does Munn-
Rankin.

[23] Munn-Rankin, *op. cit.,* pp. 89–91. *Lipit napištum* may have referred to
strangulation (Dossin), but probably cutting the throat is intended (A.
Falkenstein). Munn-Rankin notes the survival of the ass-slaying ceremony
in eighth-century Syria when Ashurnirari V of Assyria and Barga'yah of
KTK concluded treaties with their vassal, Mati'ilu of Arpad. It is not clear
whether the sacrifice of the ass and the symbolic throat-slitting of the treaty
partners were performed alternatively or simultaneously.

as interterritorial theft and brigandage, abduction of women, and extradition of fugitives were dealt with by treaty. Frequently treaties were sealed by dynastic intermarriages which had the intent of bringing two ruling houses together in complete good faith.

Diplomats were apparently of various ranks, although no clear hierarchy can be discerned. Those conducting delicate negotiations were high officials, but routine exchanges were frequently handled by lower persons. Members of the foreign service presented credentials and were tax exempt in the host country. Permanent representation seems not to have existed, but protracted negotiations might keep ambassadors at a foreign court for many months. When traveling, diplomats were provided safe conduct by armed escorts, in certain instances supplied by the host country. The ambassador presented and interpreted his country's policies. He was able to comment on a written message but had to adhere to its contents. Although presumably allowed a specified latitude in negotiations, in an impasse, or faced with new terms, he had to refer matters to his own ruler for new instructions. Sometimes extremely close liaison developed between foreign kings and ambassadors, as, for example, the ties between Hammurabi of Babylon and Zimri-lim's ambassador.[24]

The Egyptian Heritage

Egyptian monarchy sprang up at the dawn of history with a startling completeness. The type of central royal control of a vast river valley that was not achieved in Mesopotamia until Sargon's reign was fully formed by Menes at a time when Sumer was still a congeries of city-states.

Geography had much to do with this early political accomplishment. The Nile Valley was protected from outside disturbances, and the navigable river afforded a ready means of communication.[25] Yet there was much in the setting to breed division

[24] Ibâl-pî-El says, "Whenever Hammurabi is turning over a matter in his heart he sends word to me and wherever I am I go to him. Whatever the matter that he is turning over in his heart he tells me of it" (Munn-Rankin, *op. cit.,* p. 104).

[25] Frankfort, *op. cit.,* chap. 1; S. Passarge, *Die Urlandschaft Aegyptens*

and complacency: the intense heat, the dependability of the Nile's rising, the great length of the land, the contrasts between the broad delta and the narrow band of the river valley, and the host of regional customs, claims to power, and dialects.

Menes (c. 3000) unified Egypt under the rubric of "the two lands," his own Upper Egypt and the Delta or Lower Egypt (see Map 2). The symbols and mythology of the kingship ever afterward preserved a clear sense of the two component regions. It is not probable that Menes unified two strong kingdoms, for Lower Egypt was at this time in the hands of rival rulers and it is not even certain that Menes or his predecessors had long ruled supreme in Upper Egypt. When central rule lapsed at various periods in Egyptian history, generally not two but many regional authorities asserted themselves. The reality of "the two lands" was apparently more cultural and religious than political, reflecting both the stark physical contrasts between the two regions and the Egyptian tendency to perceive reality in complementary or opposing pairs.[26]

In a remarkable manner the plethora of local deities and symbols was brought to bear upon the person of the single ruler. Variety served to enforce unity. Pharaoh was the very epiphany of the gods on behalf of human society. He was not a man selected to serve the gods, nor was he a man deified at the time of coronation. He was a god by birth, publicly recognized as such at his accession and coronation.

The absolute claim of deity for the Egyptian ruler did not make of him an arbitrary despot, for it was the genius of his work as a god among men that he support the order of justice and custom upon which god and man depend. It is true that the deliberative assembly of Sumer seems entirely absent from historical Egypt. At most there was an advisory court council which the pharaoh consulted at will. Yet he was held in the grip of convention even more powerfully than was a Mesopotamian

---

und die Lokalisierung der Wiege der altaegyptischen Kultur (Nova Acta Leopoldina, N.F. IX, 58), 1940.

[26] Frankfort, *op. cit.,* pp. 19–20, and E. Drioton and J. Vandier, *L'Égypte,* pp. 162–63.

king. In practice he was the executor of a body of traditions and conventions which he could at most modify. Such changes as he introduced would have been effected with subtlety and with a sense of their correspondence with justice.

In practice the Egyptian king carried out the same tasks as the Mesopotamian king. He was high priest, chief justice, commander-in-chief, and steward of the state economy.[27] Much of his work was delegated to officials, who in the Old Kingdom were generally of the royal house. Closest to the king stood the vizier with far-reaching responsibilities of adjudication and administration of public works and foreign relations. At first the vizier was of the royal family. Later he was a hereditary officer in a noble family. Finally he was a noble chosen specifically for the task at the discretion of the king.[28] The state treasurer directed the collection of taxes in kind and their storage and distribution. Since all land was theoretically the god's, it was also the property of the pharaoh, the divine son. Actually private property was recognized on a broad scale down to the New Kingdom.

Internal administration, apart from immediate high officers, is not well known. Provinces or nomes were ruled by independent princes during the Old Kingdom (2680–2565), perhaps as part of the price that Menes had to pay for establishing the dual monarchy. In the Middle Kingdom (2052–1786) the princes were replaced by governors appointed by the king. This action represents a centralizing tendency similar to that of the direct royal appointments of local officials by Sargon and Hammurabi.

Until the New Kingdom the army mustered for foreign campaigns was composed of disparate elements drawn from the provincial militia, the temple troops, and the frontier guards. In emergencies they were mustered and equipped by the pharaoh for battle. At the utmost the standing army of the king was small.[29] Such a system was adequate for defense and for warfare

---

[27] Frankfort, *op. cit.*, chap. 4; G. Steindorff and K. C. Seele, *When Egypt Ruled the East*, chap. 9.

[28] K. Sethe, "Die Einsetzung des Vezirs unter der 18. Dynastie," *Untersuchungen zur Geschichtes Aegyptens*, 1909, pt. V. 2.

[29] R. O. Faulkner, "Egyptian Military Organization," *Journal of Egyptian Archaeology* 39 (1953), 32–33, believes that even in the Old Kingdom a

with the more primitive peoples of the Upper Nile and Sinai, but a large standing army had to be organized when Egypt launched an Asiatic empire.

Egypt's "empire" may be said to have begun with the Middle Kingdom's expansion for hundreds of miles up the Nile into Nubia and to the borders of Punt (see Map 5).[30] The physical and cultural achievement of subduing this region and civilizing it was no small one. Administratively Nubia was formed into a single district attached to the southernmost province of Egypt and ruled by an official entitled "Prince of Kush (Nubia) and Overseer of the Southern Lands." The Egyptianization of Nubia was so thorough that in later centuries a Nubian dynasty would rise up to give political leadership to Egypt when there was none to take the throne in Memphis or Thebes.

After the creation of the dual monarchy, the really decisive event in Egypt's political history was the invasion by the Hyksos, their two-hundred-year domination, and their slow expulsion (see Map 6).[31] Formerly Egypt had been politically introverted. During the New Kingdom (1570–1085) she turned outward as a matter of self-protection and with a thirst for conquest. Formerly all foreign contacts had been commercial in intent—to secure wood from the Phoenician coast, copper and turquoise from Sinai, and ivory, cattle, and slaves from Nubia and Ethiopia. *Now there was an impulse to dominate Asia as Asia had dominated Egypt.* An imperialistic impetus was felt in the Egyptian soul compounded of the bitter memory of national humiliation and the lure of the exotic in distant Asia. Patriotism and adventure linked arms.

The imperialistic vitality of the New Kingdom was astonishing. The national effort to expel the Hyksos spilled over into a deep penetration of Palestine and Syria (see Map 7). A large standing army was created with a core of native Egyptians supplemented increasingly by mercenaries. Divisions of approximately

---

small but strong standing army must have existed. Otherwise the pharaoh could not have asserted his authority against the monarchs who possessed well-equipped militias.

[30] Steindorff and Seele, *op. cit.*, pp. 19–23.

[31] *Ibid.*, chap. III.

five thousand men each were named after chief Egyptian deities.[32] Chariotry, introduced by the Hyksos, greatly facilitated campaigns to distant lands. Garrisons and royal commissioners were located at strategic points in Palestine and Syria, but no provincial organization was attempted. The loyalty of local princes was secured by the twin inducements of trade with Egypt and military pressure. Since the tribute and occasional imposts levied on the subject states were likely to be greater than the trade benefits, a strong army was the only way to maintain the Asiatic empire.

At home Egypt was changing. The long-standing theoretical possession of all land by the state was now more rigidly practiced.[33] Taxes increased. Chief beneficiaries were the temples, whose lands were made tax free and to whom pharaohs gave large tracts of land and other gifts in gratitude for their services. Perhaps as much as one-third of the lands came under temple control. The governmental bureaucracy swelled in size and the old hereditary prerequisites for office gave way to personal ambition and influence. The army became a problem to provision and to pacify when not on campaigns, and the seeds were sown for the later mercenary uprisings. With the growth of "big government" in Egypt came a new culture. There was a love of luxury and ornamentation and fascination with novel foreign styles. Most influential of all was the influx of foreigners, as slaves, traders, and diplomats opened Egypt to a cosmopolitanism she had never known.[34]

The New Kingdom expanded into Asia in two great waves, the first, in the fifteenth century, spearheaded by Thutmose III (1504–1450) and the second, in the thirteenth century, directed by Ramses II (1301–1234). The first wave receded because of internal Egyptian weakness culminating in the Amarna revolution when Akhenaton (1380–1363) was more interested in religion and domestic policies than in foreign affairs.[35] The second wave

[32] Faulkner, *op. cit.,* pp. 42–45, notes also that the subunits seem to have been 50 and 200 (under Ramses IV, 250).

[33] E. Meyer, *Gottesstaat, Militaerherrschaft und Staendewesen in Aegypten,* and W. F. Edgerton, "The Government and the Governed in the Egyptian Empire," *JNES* 6 (1947), 156–59.

[34] Steindorff and Seele, *op. cit.,* chap. 10.

[35] J. A. Wilson, *The Burden of Egypt,* 1951, chap. 9.

reached its high-water mark when it met the Hittite kingdom of Asia Minor expanding southward. After an indecisive battle at Kadesh, the two empires agreed to co-exist and signed a "non-aggression pact" (see Map 8).[36] Yet both empires were swept out of Asia by the eruption of the Sea Peoples from the Mediterranean, among whom were the biblical Philistines (see Map 9).

At its zenith the Egyptian New Kingdom was the equal of Hammurabi's empire, but in certain respects it was a monumental failure. Instead of holding the various segments of the domestic population in balance, the New Kingdom grossly favored the priesthood and the army. The eventual effect of this favoritism was to undermine the royal power and to undercut all future attempts to repeat the glorious conquests of the New Kingdom.[37]

The consequences are written everywhere in later Egyptian history. For more than one hundred years Egypt was ruled by priest-kings of Amon from Thebes (1085–950). They were followed in turn by Libyan kings, who took advantage of the great power exercised by Libyan mercenaries in pharaoh's service (950–730) (see Map 10). When this line was exhausted the scepter passed for a century to Nubian rulers (751–671). Thereafter Egypt was invaded by Assyria (671, 663), ruled for seventy-five years by Saite kings, who made a last major effort to reassert Egyptian greatness (663–524) (see Map 11), and then dominated by Persia and Greece.[38]

The verdict upon Egyptian empire-building is that as long as it was undertaken within the Nile Valley and in nearby Sinai and Libya it was a success, but the enormous effort to carve out an Asiatic domain caused the state to overextend itself. The price paid in strengthening the priesthood and the army was not only to undermine the foreign holdings but to strike at the very heart of Egypt. The result was that Egypt was eventually ruled by

[36] Both the Egyptian and the Hittite versions of the treaty are translated in full in *ANET*, pp. 201–3.

[37] Meyer, *op. cit.*

[38] For the Saite and Persian periods of Egyptian history see F. C. Kienitz, *Die politische Geschichte Aegyptens vom 7 bis zum 4 Jahrhundert vor der Zeitwende.*

kings from lands she had once conquered and was humiliated again and again by Mesopotamian and Greek armies.

It appears that Egypt learned few lessons from her attempts at empire-building, that she did not in fact have the resourcefulness and flexibility to recover from the mistakes in her one great bid for Near Eastern empire. Yet that does not tell the whole story, for Mesopotamian empire was growing apace and, when Egypt under the Saites had a last opportunity, the power balance was already hopelessly tipped against her. It is not to be forgotten either that Mesopotamian empire-building received fresh infusions of blood and technique from many sides during centuries when Egypt remained mostly to herself with little political stimulation.

The Anatolian Heritage

The Hittites of Asia Minor developed a strong feudal kingdom from about 1750 B.C. on, analogous to the Hurrian and Kassite regimes in Mesopotamia (see Maps 6 and 7). For three centuries they were a significant imperial power in northern Syria and Mesopotamia, c. 1500–1200 B.C. (see Map 8). Hittite kingship seems to have arisen, like the Sumerian, from an assembly of free citizens or noblemen with a deliberative body of elders. The struggle for power between king and nobility was centered on the problem of succession to the throne. Civil strife and court intrigue were common in the early kingdom. By 1650 under King Telepinus (1525–1500) definite succession rules were promulgated, and thereafter the council drops from view and the kingship becomes a fixed hereditary office with centralized powers. Also like his Sumerian counterpart, the Hittite monarch was pre-eminently the high priest of the state.[39]

By a stroke of fortune, our knowledge of ancient Near Eastern

[39] The Hittite monarchy is treated by A. Goetze, *Das Hethiter Reich,* and O. R. Gurney, *The Hittites,* chap. 2, and the relation of the king to the assembly or assemblies is fully discussed by R. S. Hardy, "The Old Hittite Kingdom: a Political History," *AJSL* 58 (1941), 177–216. Hardy finds two assemblies: the *tuliyas* with judicial powers over the king but no advisory functions, and the *pankus* with judicial power over citizens and advisory functions with the king.

political treaties is largely supplied by Hittite texts from the fifteenth through the thirteenth centuries, i.e., at the height of the Hittite empire. Treaties with states in northern Syria and southern Anatolia, as well as with Mitanni and Egypt, supply a rich body of materials.[40] Roughly speaking, there are "parity" treaties and "vassal" treaties, but this classification does not do justice to the varieties of form and language in the treaties. It seems that each treaty was formulated on an individual basis and the conventional patterns were modified to meet special needs.[41] Some states, such as Aleppo and Carchemish, were incorporated in the empire and ruled by royal princes for whom no stipulations are given but whose fealty is asserted. Others, although actual vassals, such as Kizzuwatna, were treated with the appearance of equality perhaps because of their sensitivity as formerly powerful states. In drawing Kizzuwatna into the Hittite fold, the suzerain counters Mitannian objections by insisting that it is strictly a matter of self-determination and he further claims that, in a similar situation, Mitanni had taken over a Hittite-oriented state in spite of Hittite remonstrances.[42]

Most of the vassals were placed on the throne by the Hittites and owed personal allegiance to their suzerain. Civil strife often tore the vassal states and made it necessary for the Hittites to support sympathetic local rulers. Occasionally a dynasty went over to Hatti voluntarily, as in the case of the house of Aziras[43] at Amurru, and remained faithful through several generations, but more often the Hittites had to support a faction within the state and later elevate its leader to the throne. The treaty texts

[40] The Hittite political treaties have been published by E. F. Weidner, *Politische Dokumente aus Kleinasien*, and J. Friedrich, *Staatsvertraege des Hatti-Reiches in hethitischer Sprache* (*Mitteilungen der vorderasiatisch-aegyptischen Gesellschaft* 31.1 [1926]; 34.1 [1930]). They are discussed in a systematic, critical manner by V. Korošec, *Hethitische Staatsvertraege. Ein Beitrag zu ihrer juristischen Wertung.* The relevance of these treaties for an understanding of the biblical notion of covenant has been developed by G. E. Mendenhall, *Law and Covenant in Israel and the Ancient Near East* and D. J. McCarthy, *Treaty and Covenant.*

[41] Gurney, *op. cit.,* pp. 76–77.

[42] *Ibid.,* pp. 78–79.

[43] *Ibid.,* p. 74; the treaty of Mursilis with Duppi-Tessub, grandson of Aziras, is translated in *ANET,* pp. 203–5.

are lavishly expressive of the peculiar intimacy between suzerain and vassal.[44] They regularly contain a preamble reminding the vassal of the favor of his Hittite lord and of his solemn obligation to fealty. A treaty of Suppiluliumas (1380–1340) with Mattiwaza of Mitanni followed the defeat of Mitanni as an imperial power. It is cast in the manner of a vassal treaty, but in actual fact the Hittites were not sufficiently strong to exert control beyond the Euphrates. The treaty may have been chiefly a pledge of Mitanni not to interfere in Hittite territories to the west of the Euphrates. This alone would have greatly solidified Hittite power in northern Syria and freed it to face the growing Egyptian threat from the south.[45]

An outstanding example of the parity treaty is the pact between Ramses II and Hattusilis concluded c. 1293–1270, sixteen years after the indecisive battle of Kadesh. This treaty sealed the realities of the power balance according to which Egypt held southern Syria and Palestine and Hatti held northern Syria (see Map 8). Of particular value is our possession of both the Egyptian and the Hittite versions of the treaty.[46] They agree in substance, but, since the Egyptian version was inscribed on the temple wall at Karnak where it was constantly available to the public, it is a more tendentious account and represents Hattusilis as suing Ramses for peace. The covenant terms are described in the Egyptian account as "the good regulations of peace and brotherhood."[47] The Hittite version has "treaty . . . for establishing [good] peace [and] good brotherhood [worthy of] great [king]ship forever."[48] The articles provide for respect of each other's territories, reaffirmation of a former treaty (or treaties) which had been effective in earlier times (but neglected more recently by Muwatallis, according to the Egyptians), a defensive

[44] Korošec, *op. cit.,* analyzes the chief structural elements of the treaty; his work is helpfully summarized by Mendenhall, *op. cit.,* pp. 32–35.

[45] The text of the treaty between Suppiluliumas and Mattiwaza is translated in *ANET,* pp. 205–6 and the historical introduction on p. 318. The historical significance is clarified by I. J. Gelb, *Hurrians and Subarians,* pp. 75–81.

[46] See note 36.

[47] *ANET,* p. 199, col. 2.

[48] *Ibid.,* p. 202, col. 1.

pact by which the parties agree to help one another when attacked, and extradition of political refugees.

Normally a copy of the treaty was engraved in metal. Unfortunately none of the originals have survived, and we possess only the less valuable clay copies. The metal originals were displayed publicly at the state sanctuaries. Periodically the treaty text was read with the intent of reminding leaders and peoples of their obligations and of incorporating successive rulers and generations in the original covenant. The relevance of this conception for understanding the Old Testament covenant ideology and forms has been explored with valuable results, but the similarities do not prove that the Hebrews borrowed directly from the Hittites.[49]

It is not easy to answer the question: How far were the Hittite treaties typical of ancient Near Eastern treaties at large and how far were they the products of a special Hittite tradition? No conclusive comparison with the Mari age treaties is possible, chiefly because we have no actual treaty texts from Mari but only references to them. Certain features in the Amorite and Hittite treaties agree: the written contract, the witness of the gods, the subordination of the vassal in foreign policy and his relative freedom in domestic policy, and extradition of fugitives. Yet there are differences: vassal dynasties were frequently in-

---

[49] Mendenhall, *op. cit.,* p. 35, was impressed by the fact that the Hittite-type vassal treaty of the period before the time of Moses "is not attested for any other subsequent period." Thus he felt justified in concluding that formally the Yahweh-Israel covenant was derived from the Hittite suzerainty treaties. Since then, however, an Aramaic suzerainty treaty of the same type has been found from the eighth century (between the suzerain Barga'yah of KTK [?] and the vassal king of Arpad, apparently Mati'ilu). A. Dupont-Sommer, "Une inscription araméene inédite de Sfiré," *Bulletin du Musée de Beyrouth* 13 (1956), 23–41, has noted the parallels to the earlier Mursilis-Duppi-Tessub treaty, e.g., the clause "(if you do such things), you act in disregard of your oath." Accordingly, the Hittite suzerainty treaty may have influenced Israel at a time later than Moses since it survived in north Syria and Mesopotamia for centuries (cf. J. A. Fitzmyer, "The Aramaic Suzerainty Treaty from Sefire in the Museum of Beirut," *CBQ* 20 [1958], 444–76; see also note 75). That such treaties were also known in Palestine is not impossible. For Hittite influences in Palestine, cf. E. O. Forrer, "The Hittites in Palestine," *PEQ* 68 (1936), 190–209; 69 (1937), 100–115. D. J. McCarthy, *Treaty and Covenant,* 1963, throws some doubts, however, on comparing the secular treaty-form with the biblical covenant-form.

stalled by the Hittites whereas the Amorites seem to have worked largely with the dynasties at hand; also, the historical preamble to Hittite vassal treaties giving the background for the present intimate bond between suzerain and vassal and the periodic public recitations of the treaty text are not alluded to in the Mari period.

Some or all of the differences may be explained by the lack of Amorite treaty texts and by the dissimilar historical situations. The Amorite powers in the Mari age were struggling with one another more or less as equals, whereas the Hittites had a hegemony in northern Syria. The latter were in a better position to dictate terms and to enforce their will; the contending Amorite states had to appeal more to self-interest and to offer a better arrangement than their rivals unless they had a momentary preponderance of strength.

The Later Mesopotamian and Iranian Heritage

Between the fall of the Amorite dynasty of Babylon and the rise of Assyria lay several centuries of political lag in Mesopotamia. During this time the major imperialists were the Egyptians and the Hittites. Southern Mesopotamia was ruled from Babylon by a long line of Kassite kings (c. 1500–1200) and in northern Mesopotamia the kingdom of Mitanni held sway (c. 1500–1370) (see Map 7). Both were feudal kingdoms with a ruling class of Indo-European origin superimposed upon local petty kingdoms. The Kassites seem to have contributed little to Mesopotamian culture, whereas Hurrian social practices did have considerable influence on the Mitannian population.[50] Neither kingdom was strong enough to overcome the other or to stand effectively against Egypt or Hatti. They were, however, of sufficient standing to enter into diplomatic relations with the larger powers seeking to win their favor as dependable allies. It was common in the fifteenth and fourteenth centuries for Egyptian pharaohs to

[50] On the Kassites, cf. A. Scharff and A. Moortgat, *Aegypten und Vorderasien im Altertum,* pp. 332–39, and on the Hurrians, *ibid.,* pp. 340–48, and R. T. O'Callaghan, *Aram Naharaim.*

accept Mitannian and Kassite princesses as wives for their sons.[51]

The Assyrian empire developed slowly, since it was challenged and closely confined by its neighbors for many centuries, only breaking out of its heartland along the upper Tigris when led by particularly strong rulers: Ashur-uballit I (1362–1327), Tukulti-Ninurta I (1242–1206) (see Map 8), and Tiglath-pileser I (1114–1076). Only in the ninth century was its influence steadily felt in southern Mesopotamia and in Syria-Palestine, under Ashur-nasirpal II (883–859) and Shalmaneser III (858–824) (see Map 10). Then, after a half-century of decline, the glorious neo-Assyrian empire was advanced from the Persian Gulf to the Nile Valley (see Map 11) by an unparalleled succession of military and administrative masters: Tiglath-pileser III (744–727), Shalmaneser V (726–722), Sargon (721–705), Sennacherib (704–681), Esarhaddon (680–669), and Ashurbanipal (668–633). The eclipse of this empire at the end of the seventh century was as abrupt as its rise in the middle of the eighth.[52]

Although their brutality in war has been celebrated in the dubious company of Attila's Huns and Hitler's SS troopers, *the Assyrians were direct heirs of the Sumero-Akkadian-Amorite political heritage. To this heritage they added a practical genius for achieving more permanent results from their conquests than had any previous Near Eastern empire.*[53]

Monarchy in ancient Assyria seems to have arisen along the lines of monarchy in early Sumer. A leader was selected from a body of noblemen, perhaps even on an annual basis. The eponym or *limmu* lists of officials who gave their names to the years seem to attest to an early practice of rotating the leadership of state among several competent leaders.[54] Throughout Assyrian history

---

[51] Steindorff and Seele, *op. cit.,* pp. 108–11, and *Cambridge Ancient History,* II, 1924, 232–35.

[52] The standard work on the Assyrian empire is A. T. Olmstead, *History of Assyria* (cf. esp. the maps on pp. 46–47, which show the course of Assyrian empire under her strongest kings), but the book is not well documented and is seriously outdated in many respects. For later developments cf. Pallis, *op. cit.,* pp. 577–635, and H. Schmoekel, *Geschichte des Alten Vorderasien,* pp. 93–105, 187–212, 247–89.

[53] Olmstead, *op. cit.,* Preface, chaps. 46, 49, esp. pp. 606–11.

[54] Smith, S., *op. cit.,* pp. 54–64.

the reigning monarch was designated the eponym for the first full year of his rule, but thereafter the eponym lists were open to qualified officials who shared the honor.[55] Ashur, the original political center of Assyria, remained the site of the king's coronation. The ancient god of that city and of the land was Ashur, whose primacy was never shaken by the Sumero-Babylonian deities. Every Assyrian monarch referred to "my lord Ashur" as his protector and benefactor, and the theocratic foundation of the state remained clear in the continuing convention of treating imperial tribute as payment to the god Ashur.

Yet it is clear that to achieve an empire of such scope the Assyrian monarchy underwent a process of centralization and secularization. The role of subordinate officials was reduced; powerful governors were demoted or had their powers curtailed.[56] While the king remained obligated to the cult and was hedged about by omens of all sorts, his growing power as the head of a great empire allowed him to grant favors to certain gods and cities through tax exemption and temple-building.[57] Tensions between priest and king were bound to develop, and, without openly rejecting the cult, the king had various means of suasion, especially patronage, for keeping himself relatively free from priestly control.

In one sense this monarchic autocracy was the legacy of the Amorite dynasty, for the Assyrian monarchs were seeking to balance the many agricultural, commercial, religious, and social interests within the kingdom, and only a strong ruler could hope to do this rather than to be crushed by them. Yet there were distinct Assyrian contributions to this process. *The Assyrians conquered and administered an empire on a scale that dwarfed any empire heretofore organized. This achievement was made possible by advances in military technology, but the maintenance of such an empire was possible only if corresponding political forms could be created to keep it closely bound to the Assyrian home-*

[55] For the eponym lists for the years 882–688 see the fold-out diagram opposite p. 6 in E. Forrer, *Die Provinzeinteilung des Assyrischen Reiches.*
[56] Olmstead, *op. cit.,* pp. 203–4.
[57] *Ibid.,* pp. 206–7, 525–29.

land. The Assyrians' successes in this regard were uneven but of sufficient novelty and scope to distinguish them as the most successful imperialists of antiquity prior to the Persians and thus not only among the best fighters in antiquity but also among the most skillful administrators.

The military base of the Neo-Assyrian empire in the period 745–612 B.C. was a standing army of infantry, cavalry, and chariotry supplemented by siege units with battering rams and sapping commandos, which enabled them to capture virtually any city in antiquity if given enough time.[58] With Sennacherib there began to occur a massive shift in this army from free Assyrian citizenry to the incorporation of captured troops and the employ of mercenaries on an increasingly large scale.[59] The manpower needs of the empire began to tell, and the army became less and less dependable and eventually collapsed from within. In its heyday, however, this military force was impressive in its ruthless efficiency.

The administrative resources of the Neo-Assyrian empire were equally impressive if not quite so efficient as the military. Subject peoples were deported and colonized in various parts of the empire with a view to breaking up incipient revolts and making use of native skills for economic and political purposes. Conquered lands were incorporated into the empire either as vassal kingdoms ruled by native princes loyal to Assyria or as provinces headed by Assyrian appointees.[60] The latter system tended to replace the former but a total shift to provincial organizations was never at-

[58] W. Manitius, *Das stehende Heer der Assyrerkönige und seine Organisation,* 1910; J. Hunger, *Heerwesen und Kriegführung der Assyrer auf der Höhe ihrer Macht* (Der *Alte Orient,* 12:4), 1911; and helpfully illustrated accounts of troops, weapons, and strategy by G. Contenau, *Everyday Life in Babylon and Assyria,* 1954, pp. 141–57 and by Y. Yadin, *The Art of Warfare in Biblical Lands,* II, 1963, chap. VII.

[59] Manitius, *op. cit.,* pp. 11–21, 88–92.

[60] A. T. Olmstead, "Assyrian Government of Dependencies," *American Political Science Review* 12 (1918), 63–77, admirably discusses the political and human significance of the Assyrian provincial and vassal system. E. Forrer, *op. cit.,* is the definitive treatment on the composition and administration of the provinces, although our knowledge has been considerably enlarged since he wrote.

tempted. An element of pragmatic flexibility dictated various policies from country to country and there must have been as much of a shortage of able imperial administrators as of dependable soldiery.

For periods earlier than the mid-ninth century the records are so incomplete that the provinicial system cannot be descried. Shalmaneser III seems to have ruled over as many as twenty-six provinces which tended to be smaller along the northern and eastern frontiers in order to form a secure bulwark against the mountain peoples.[61] Palace officials were heads of provinces, beginning with the *turtanu* (equivalent to the Egyptian vizier) who was governor of Haran, but their administration must often have been nominal. Tiglath-pileser III, who had been governor of Kalhu, realized the dangers inherent in the large provinces in that their administrative posts offered too great a scope to scheming rebels. He broke up the provinces into smaller units so that their number was doubled.[62] The diminished importance of the governors is apparent in their infrequent appearance on later eponym lists. All ranks of officialdom were reduced in personal authority and linked more directly to the will of the king. The time-honored practice of eponym officials in setting up their memorial steles in the venerable city of Ashur was abolished. The Neo-Assyrian empire was achieved at the price of increased royal autocracy.

Neo-Babylonian imperial practice is not nearly as well known as the Assyrian and Persian.[63] Insofar as can be judged, the Chaldean dynasty which revived Babylon as the center of an empire (see Maps 11 and 12) made use of Assyrian imperial practices. The provincial divisions worked out by the Assyrians were probably taken over with little purposeful change. Nebuchadnezzar (604–562) concentrated on beautification of the capital city and strengthening of the Marduk cult. He ruled throughout his empire with the familiar Assyrian-style military campaign, during the course of which he punished rebels and encouraged

---

[61] Forrer, *op. cit.*, pp. 7–8; *Olmstead, History of Assyria*, pp. 146–47.
[62] Forrer, *op. cit.*, pp. 49–52; Olmstead, *History of Assyria*, pp. 203–4.
[63] E. Unger, *Theologische Literaturzeitung*, 50 (1925), 481; *Babylon, die heilige Staat*, 1931, pp. 282–88.

wavering provinces and vassal kingdoms to continue their tribute. Yet in many respects his grip was not as firm, for he did not seem to relish military action as the Assyrians had. The deportations he carried out seem not to have been programmatic. Exchanges of population were not involved; rebels were punitively detained and might at some later time be released. This significant difference between the Assyrian deportation of Samaria and the neo-Babylonian deportation of Judah may account for the continuing Jewish hope of restoration which persisted in spite of an exile of more than half a century.[64] Later Chaldean kings were even weaker in their imperial policies.

The actual goal of the Aramean-Chaldean dynasty was not succession to the Assyrian empire so much as revival of the ancient Babylonian synthesis of Mesopotamian peoples and culture achieved by Hammurabi and posited on the Marduk cult.[65] Military considerations were clearly secondary to political and cultural concerns. When the "neo-Babylonian" inspiration waned with Nebuchadnezzar's successors, the basis of the dynasty was undercut. Nabonidus (555–538) awakened internal jealousies because of his preference for Haran instead of Babylon, and his opening up of the Arabian trade during his long stay at the oasis of Tema in north Arabia was purchased by neglect of his imperial responsibilities in the Crescent proper.[66]

The Persian empire represents in especially clear form the awkward union of two conceptions of kingship which we have seen at work in the Sumero-Akkadian-Amorite phase of Mesopotamian political history and in the Assyrian phase: *(1) kingship as the limited rule of a leader designated by equals and (2) kingship as autocratic rule by one whose will and genius suit him for world dominion.* The Cyrus Cylinder shows the fusion of these two concepts. The Indo-European Persian kingship was that of a

[64] A. Alt, "Die Rolle Samarias bei der Entstehung des Judentums," *KS,* 1953, II, 325–29.

[65] Scharff and Moortgat, *op. cit.,* pp. 444–48.

[66] Our previous data on Nabonidus, exhaustively treated by R. P. Dougherty, *Nabonidus and Belshazzar. A Study of the Closing Events of the Neo-Babylonian Empire,* 1929, have lately been supplemented by C. J. Gadd, "The Harran Inscriptions of Nabonidus," *Anatolian Studies* 8 (1958), 35–92.

chief chosen by the leaders of seven clans which formed a tribal group. Cyrus of the clan of Anshan was king among the Persians who formed one tribe within the great Median empire that had joined with the Chaldeans to destroy Assyria. Swiftly he became ruler of the Median empire, but specifically Median political forms are not in evidence in his reign.[67] Once he had conquered all the former domains of the Medes and Chaldeans, Cyrus celebrated his descent from a royal family in Anshan, "a family (which) always (exercised) kingship," *and* simultaneously his succession to the long line of Mesopotamian political leadership, which he expresses by the adoption of the venerable royal titles "king of the world, great king, . . . king of Babylon, king of Sumer and Akkad, king of the four rims (of the earth), . . . whose rule Bel and Nebo love, whom they want as king to please their hearts."[68]

Although Cyrus (538–530) and his successors presented themselves to their Indo-European subjects as devout Zoroastrian worshipers, they were hailed throughout the Fertile Crescent as autocratic rulers who beneficently upheld the ancient cultural heritage of Mesopotamia. Yet the dimensions of this empire were staggering; it stretched from the Indian frontier to Egypt and Asia Minor (see Map 13). Such a domain could be held in check only by an improved road system and systematic administration. In this Cyrus showed an inventiveness that profited by Assyrian strengths and weaknesses. He formally abolished the vassal kingdom and turned the entire empire into twenty provinces or satrapies, each of which was of vast size.[69] In fact Babylon and Syria-Palestine (the greater part of the former neo-Babylonian empire) formed one satrapy. Each satrap had a large staff of officials in what amounted to a miniature court. This hereditary office, as

[67] Our knowledge of Median political beliefs is sketchy. The theory that the Medes alone in antiquity thought of the king as completely separate from his subjects and embodied in the various government offices which were filled not by his servants but by his corporate members is conjectural. Cf. F. W. Buckler, "The Oriental Despot," *Anglican Theological Review* 10 (1928), 238–49.

[68] *ANET*, p. 316.

[69] A. T. Olmstead, *History of the Persian Empire*, p. 59; C. F. Lehmann-Haupt, "Satrap," *Real-Encyclopaedie der classischen Altertumswissenschaft* (ed. Pauly-Wissowa), 1921, III, 82–84.

well as other high positions in the satrapal administration, was staffed by Persian and Median noblemen. To counteract temptations to revolt, certain key officials in each satrapy (the secretary, chief treasurer, and commander of the capital garrison) were directly appointed by the king and reported to him. A secret police corps, known as "the king's eye," checked the loyalty of the satrapal officials annually.

Wherever possible, concessions were made to local political practice, and the bureaucracies of important cities such as Babylon were incorporated into the new regime.[70] *The strong hand of Persian rule coupled with a generally tolerant attitude toward local feelings and practices made for considerable stability in the empire.* There were disturbances nonetheless, and the empire even threatened to break up within two generations when at the death of Cambyses the succession to the throne was bitterly contested until Darius (522–486) established himself.[71]

The Persian empire seemed destined to prevail far longer than it did, and we should not overlook the fact that its decision to attack the Greek city-states played no small part in the eventual unification of all Greece under Alexander, who himself turned upon Asia and overthrew the Persian tormentor. Beginning with a dynamic compound of persuasion and force, the Persian rulers relied increasingly on force. The effect of a waning Mesopotamian culture debased their tastes and judgments, and the higher motivations of Zoroastrian religion which they officially acknowledged were betrayed by a late Sumero-Babylonian love of luxury and autocratic conduct.

It was the kings of the last half-century of Persian rule who were best known to Aristotle and who moved him to conclude that Near Eastern kingship was sheer tyranny. He had little appreciation of the advantages which an empire such as the Persian offered its subject peoples or of the gratitude which led them to consent to it. He could see only the servility. He could not understand that the Persian empire was the culmination of a long and complex history in which force and persuasion had united to create a political order that brought some measure of stability

[70] Olmstead, *History of the Persian Empire,* p. 71.
[71] *Ibid.,* pp. 92–93.

through the balancing of internal interests and through the conquest of a hostile environment.

Even if our assessment is finally more negative than positive, we cannot avoid recognizing that the history of ancient Near Eastern politics, and especially of its imperial aspects, was a morally mixed and pragmatically complex self-expression of these ancient peoples. They were not willfully enslaved; they chose to barter the chaos of smaller independent political units for the security of larger units. They were also in part willing and in part forced to sacrifice the freedom of the former type of political order for the orderliness of the latter. They considered it on the whole a worthwhile bargain.[72]

International Relations in the Ancient Near East

From the point of view of the specialist in one particular culture or period, the ancient Near East appears as a tremendous mélange of social and political institutions contributed to by the numerous peoples who pressed into the Fertile Crescent from all directions. Yet it is also true that in international relations, as in many other fields, a distinctive Near Eastern tradition had developed in Mesopotamia at least by the Amorite period (and probably much earlier) and, while supplemented and elaborated, it remained dominant down to the coming of the Greeks. This continuity is striking in that successive waves of outsiders adapted themselves with surprising uniformity to the protocol of international conduct worked out by the first part of the second millennium B.C. Even the proud Egyptians bowed to the conventions of western Asia, as symbolized in their use of the Semitic Akkadian language as the diplomatic tongue—especially surprising when they corresponded with vassals in nearby Palestine.

The Hebrews, who came relatively late upon the scene of Near Eastern history, entered also upon this heritage in international relations.[73] David was a shrewd practitioner of the diplomatic

[72] E. A. Proosdij, "Der sogenannte orientalische Despotismus," *P. Koschaker Festschrift*, 1939, II, 235.

[73] K. Galling, *Die israelitische Staatsverfassung in ihrer vorderorientalischen Umwelt.*

and military skills, and several of the later Hebrew kings were nearly or actually his equal—although curbed by external factors which did not hinder David. Increasingly, international relations became the determinative factor in the history of the Hebrew people as, successively, the Assyrians, neo-Babylonians, and Persians brought them into their spheres of influence. The Hebrew states had constantly to make fateful decisions with respect to international relations for they stood in one of the most exposed positions in the Fertile Crescent. On these critical decisions the prophets brought their searching minds and keen consciences to bear in warning and admonition. In the summary which follows it is the intent to focus upon our knowledge of international relations in the world of the prophets. Against this background we shall then be in a position to judge to what extent issues of international relations are treated by the prophets, from what point of view, and with what results. Emphasis will fall upon the empires contemporary with the prophets, but, wherever needful, the older and determinative periods will be cited.

War was a recognized instrument of foreign policy in the ancient Near East and was resorted to in situations generally understood to involve breach of treaties or implicit standards of international behavior. Among the causes of war were hostile acts of troops in plundering the countryside or investing cities, i.e., "aggression"; hostilities against an allied state; withholding of tribute by a vassal; assassination or deposition of a loyal vassal; and maltreatment of nationals, e.g., ambassadors or merchants, by imprisonment, abuse, or non-recognition.

Armies of imperial powers generally began as levies of free citizens but tended increasingly to employ units from conquered troops or to depend upon mercenaries. Beyond a certain point imperial commitments became greater than native manpower could meet, and with each increase of foreign dependence the vitality of the empire was sapped. In Egypt, Libyan mercenaries eventually became a decisive political factor which led to the long Libyan dynastic rule. The Saites were so dependent upon Greek mercenaries that they were easy prey for the Persians. Sargon built a standing Assyrian army which included crack units from the forces of vanquished or deposed kings. This was initially successful but soon the criteria for selection of foreign units grew looser and the commitment of Esarhaddon to capture Egypt proved too much for the overtaxed army.

Treaties were entered upon for many purposes: to impose loyal vassalage (Hittite treaties with north Syrian city-states; Ashurnirari V with Mati'ilu of Arpad in 754),[74] to obligate vassals in advance to a king's chosen successor (Esarhaddon's treaty with his eastern vassals in 672 binding them to Ashurbanipal),[75] to recognize an existing "balance of power" and to agree to non-aggression and non-interference (the Hittite Hattusilis and the Egyptian Ramses II divided Syria; Shabaka of Egypt and Sennacherib recognized a stalemate at the border of Egypt),[76] to secure trade benefits (Ahab of Israel and Ben-hadad of Damascus [I Kings 20:34]; Esarhaddon of Assyria and Baal of Tyre),[77] to join forces against a common enemy (Cyaxares the Mede and Nabopolassar the Chaldean),[78] to agree to neutrality in quarrels between states (the Amorite states in the Mari age), and to treat extraterritorial crimes such as brigandage and abduction (the Amorite states).

Intermarriage between royal houses was a frequent diplomatic device, best illustrated by the marriage of several Egyptian pharaohs of the New Kingdom to Mitannian princesses.[79] The higher rank of Egypt is tacitly assumed in the arrangement, for never does the king of Mitanni request an Egyptian princess. It was otherwise, however, with the Kassite Burnaburiash, who boldly insisted that the pharaoh could break custom and give an Egyptian princess to him if he really wished to show himself a "brother."[80] A daughter of the Hittite king Hattusilis was given to Ramses II after their famous treaty and was elevated to the

[74] Olmstead, *History of Assyria,* pp. 172–74.
[75] D. J. Wiseman, "The Vassal-Treaties of Esarhaddon," *Iraq* 20.1 (1958).
[76] Olmstead, *History of Assyria,* p. 309.
[77] *Ibid.,* pp. 506, 533.
[78] C. J. Gadd, *The Fall of Nineveh,* p. 33. The reference to the late-seventh-century treaty employs language familiar from eighteenth-century Mari: "[The King] of Akkad and Cy[axar]es at the city met one with the other. Friendship (*sulummuu*) and alliance (*aḫameš*) they established together" (1. 29, B.M. 21, 901).
[79] See note 51.
[80] Steindorff and Seele, *op. cit.,* pp. 111–12.

highest position as "great Royal Wife."[81] Sennacherib's daughter was married to an Egyptian by the name of Sheshonk, apparently from the pharaoh's court.[82] Esarhaddon's daughter married Bartatua, the Scythian, a clear sign of the growing importance of the Indo-European tribes from the north.[83] After the capture of Ashur, the Medes and Chaldeans cemented their alliance by the marriage of the crown prince Nebuchadenezzar to Amyitis, daughter of Cyaxares.[84]

Ancient Near Eastern empires enforced submission upon conquered territories chiefly through loyal vassals and provincial governors supported by force or the threat of force. A genuine provincial system was first developed by the Assyrians but never fully established by them. The Chaldeans inherited the provincial structure of the Assyrians but governed over a smaller region and in a more desultory fashion. The Persians perfected the provincial administration by a division of the vast empire into twenty regions, each similarly administered by a tightly knit bureaucracy that was subject to certain direct checks by the king.

Permanent military occupation was a physical impossibility owing to lack of manpower, the nature of the terrain, and technological backwardness. If dependence on treaty oaths and inducements by ambassadors or resident governors did not secure compliance, conquerors resorted to *periodic military campaigns which during the height of empire might be annually undertaken,* as, for example, by Thutmose III during the Egyptian New Kingdom[85] and by Assyrian monarchs from Shalmaneser III to Ashurbanipal.[86] Since, however, great distances were involved and no single region of the empire would be visited for many years

---

[81] *Ibid.,* pp. 251–52.

[82] Olmstead, *History of Assyria,* p. 309.

[83] *Ibid.,* p. 424.

[84] *Ibid.,* pp. 636–37; according to Eusebius, *Chron.* 29.35, who cites Berossus.

[85] Steindorff and Seele, *op. cit.,* chap. 7.

[86] W. Hallo, "From Qarqar to Carchemish: Assyria and Israel in the light of New Discoveries," *BA* 23 (1960), 38; Olmstead, *History of Assyria,* pp. 648–49, minimizes the extent of the Assyrian wars and the losses suffered in them. He notes that many of the annual campaigns were simply defensive operations by provincial troops against Arab, Aramean, or Median raiding parties.

in succession, the control of an empire was always tenuous at best and depended in large measure on the psychological suasion of a strong ruler and a sense of economic and political stability to offset the burden of subservience and the cost of tribute.

Imperial payments of several types are discernible in the diplomatic records and are especially plentifully attested in the Assyrian administration.[87] There were outright gifts to secure good will or commercial concessions, which the Assyrians tended to misrepresent as "tribute" when, for example, Egypt and Cyprus meant only to recognize Assyria's influence in the area and to secure favorable commercial conditions.[88] Tribute was regularly imposed upon conquered peoples and was to be paid per annum in Assyria. Indemnity for unsuccessful uprisings was always far heavier than the tribute.[89] Extraordinary levies of materials were demanded when an army was passing through a vassal's territory. The last placed a heavy burden upon the north Syrian states; in fact, the faithful vassal prince Panammu of Samal died while assisting his Assyrian suzerain in the siege of Damascus.[90]

Deportation of subject populations was practiced on a limited scale by the Hittites,[91] *but the Assyrians first made of it a deliberate policy of political and economic imperialism.* Tiglath-pileser III introduced deportation as a systematic exchange of populations with a view to deterring revolt and to employing the economic skills of new colonists.[92] Seldom, if ever, was the entire population of a conquered territory removed, for such an

[87] W. J. Martin, "Tribut und Tributleistungen bei den Assyrern," *Studia Orientalia* 8 (1936).

[88] Olmstead, *History of Assyria,* pp. 533–35.

[89] *Ibid.,* pp. 128–30.

[90] Bar-rekub tells the fate of his father Panammu: "Moreover my father Panammu died while following his lord Tiglath-pileser, king of Assyria, in the camp, also . . . and his kinsfolk bewailed him?, and the whole camp of his lord the king of Assyria bewailed him, and his lord the king of Assyria took . . . his soul, and set up for him a ? on the way, and brought across my father from Damascus to (this) place (?)" (text and translation in G. A. Cooke, *A Text-book of North Semitic Inscriptions,* 1903, p. 174.)

[91] Hardy, *op. cit.,* p. 194, gives examples from the Old Hittite kingdom. Movement of populations during the Hittite empire are noted by A. Malamat, "Doctrines of Causality in Hittite and Biblical Historiography," *VT* 5 (1955), 3.

[92] Ashurnasirpal and Shalmaneser III had deported populations on a limited scale (cf. D. J. Wiseman, *Iraq* 14 [1952], 25–27; and Shalmaneser's

operation would have been a superhuman task; instead, politically influential and economically productive groups—courtiers, soldiers, priests, artisans, and merchants—were normally transplanted.

Rebellions against imperial authority were constantly brewing and frequently breaking out, even under the Pax Persiana of the Achaemenids. It was the expected thing that the death of an imperial ruler should awaken widespread revolts, especially if his successor failed to use a firm hand immediately. Two great revolts are known to have engulfed virtually entire empires, one following the death of the Assyrian Shalmaneser III[93] and the other after the death of the Persian Darius the Great.[94] *The congenital weakness of monarchy in securing succession to the throne was never satisfactorily corrected in the ancient Near East.*

It was not uncommon for an emperor, however, to have to put down at least one revolt during each year of his reign. Troops were dispatched after each revolt and, while en route to deal with the immediate crisis, would put on "a show of force" for wavering vassals. Rebels counted on the laxness of the imperial will and the hope of awakening revolts in several regions of the empire at once. These hopes were not always ill founded, but rebels had as much trouble in joining their forces as did the imperial power in keeping down all revolts. Of course not all revolts were on a wide scale or fully concerted. During the Amarna age in Palestine the authority of the Egyptian New Empire slowly withered away through a combination of invasion by semi-nomadic outsiders and rivalry among the city-states nominally acknowledging Egypt. It is evident from the small detachments of troops requested by Egyptian vassals in Palestine (normally less than 100) that the struggles were in the nature of skirmishes.[95]

Treason was normally punishable by death, although there are

---

annals, 85–91), but Tiglath-pileser was the great architect of Assyria's deportation policy (cf. Olmstead, *History of Assyria,* pp. 188–89).

[93] Olmstead, *History of Assyria,* chap. 12.

[94] *Ibid.,* pp. 92–93, 107–16.

[95] J. A. Knudtzon and O. Weber, *Die El-Amarna-Tafeln,* 1907–15, is the standard transcription, translation, and commentary. S. A. B. Mercer, *The Tell el-Amarna Tablets,* 1939, is less reliable. Twenty-eight of the more

instances of exceptional leniency, even by the Assyrians, who in such cases apparently felt that the cunning rebel could be reformed to the empire's advantage.[96] Sennacherib and Ashurbanipal promised rewards for rebels captured, the one silver and the other gold to equal the weight of the informer.[97] *Intrigue among one's enemies was widely practiced in order to find a weak spot to exploit.* The Assyrians employed spies to good effect during Sargon's expedition to Musasir at the headwaters of the Upper Zab[98] and during Esarhaddon's invasion of Egypt.[99] The weapons of intrigue and espionage were well used against the Assyrians by the wily Chaldean prince Merodach-baladan.[100] At Shupria in the reign of Esarhaddon a rebellious state drew to itself a number of defecting Assyrian officials up to the rank of governor.[101] The great Babylonian revolt against Ashurbanipal was supported by some Assyrian governors and looked upon indifferently by others, although this was more in the nature of civil war since the rebels rallied around the king's brother Shamash-shum-ukin.[102] Master of intrigue in the ancient world was Cyrus, who at the same time managed to impress historians with his innocence. Illustrative of his ability are the accounts of his winning of friends in the camp of his enemies, e.g., Harpagus the Mede; the king of Cilicia; and Gobryas, governor of a Babylonian province. His empire was achieved at every key turning point by the help of a formal enemy.[103]

Balance of power politics were vigorously prosecuted in the ancient Near East. When radical shifts in the balance were threatened, sudden realignments of states were likely to occur. Toward the end of the Assyrian empire two centuries-old enemies

historically interesting letters are translated in *ANET,* pp. 483–90. The historical and political import of this correspondence has been reassessed by E. F. Campbell, Jr., in "The Amarna Letters and the Amarna Period," *BA* 23 (1960), 2–22.

[96] Olmstead, *History of Assyria,* p. 378.

[97] *Ibid.,* pp. 292, 456.

[98] D. D. Luckenbill, *Ancient Records of Assyria and Babylonia,* 1927, II, 169–72.

[99] *Ibid.,* pp. 554–59, 561–64.

[100] S. Smith, *The Cambridge Ancient History,* 1925, III, 62–66.

[101] Olmstead, *History of Assyria,* p. 365.

[102] *Ibid.,* chap. 34.

[103] S. Smith, *Isaiah XL–LV,* pp. 33, 129.

came to Assyria's assistance, Haldi to the north and Egypt to the southwest. Both attempted to shore up failing Assyrian power in order to gain for themselves an advantage in a new entente.[104] By the same logic, Medes and Chaldeans united to defeat Assyria. At first hostile toward Assyria, the Scythians joined her in alliance under Esarhaddon but reverted to enmity and united with the Medes and Chaldeans in the overthrow of Haran.[105] Obviously they wished to share in the spoils and could point to an earlier opposition to the Assyrians to justify partially their belated decision. *The advance of an imperial power sometimes had the effect of creating regional defense alliances composed of partners who, left on their own, were rivals.* Such coalitions were formed in north Syria and in south Syria against Assyria in the ninth century, and Israel was one of the states participating in the southern alliance. In the eighth and seventh centuries a Babylonian-Elamite coalition against Assyria was formed. It did not prove sufficient to overthrow the empire without the Medes but was a very serious drain upon Assyrian strength.

Strategic and economic control of Syria-Palestine was constantly sought by the strong states in the Egyptian-Mesopotamian-Anatolian triangle. Hegemony in this region, both for its resources of timber and stone and for its crucial significance in maritime and inland trade, always created an advantage which tipped the balance of power noticeably. *The truly powerful empires of antiquity—the Egyptian New Kingdom, the neo-Assyrian empire, the Chaldean empire, and the Persian empire—were at their height only when they securely held the Syria-Palestine land corridor.*

Assimilation of peoples and cultures in the ancient Near Eastern empires was never undertaken as a policy. A genuine totalitarianism did not exist in the sense that all inhabitants of an empire were under pressure to live a single type of life. For the most part the kings were content with cultural toleration, which produced a syncretism affecting the conqueror as well as the conquered. Atrocities against captives were apparently not ethnically or culturally motivated but directed as punishment to

[104] Cf. Gadd, *Fall of Nineveh*, p. 33.
[105] *Ibid.*

rebels and as warning to prospective rebels. There is, for example, no evidence for anti-Semitism before the Greek period and even during that period it was primarily a cultural animus.

Probably the greatest integration occurred in the late Assyrian period, when extensive deportations produced widespread social upheaval.[106] Even then the point was not to produce a single Assyrian type but rather to secure the political and economic foundations of the empire. As long as polytheism was the intellectual basis of human life, it was possible to combine the worship of the imperial god—Amon-Re, Marduk, Ashur, Ahura-Mazda—with recognition of innumerable national and local deities. Plurality was intellectually respectable as long as the hierarchy of religious loyalties gave room at the top to the current imperial deity. *Before Alexander we cannot discern a "Semitizing" or "Aryanizing" or "Egyptianizing" imperial program to correspond to the goal of "Hellenizing." For the ancient Near East mankind existed as a cosmic rather than a cultural or a political fact.* Alexander was the first in the Near East to conceive it as a cultural reality to be furthered or retarded, and thus the proper goal of imperial policy.

It is noteworthy to find such an elaborate network of diplomatic relations among the states of the ancient Near East. Clearly they were governed by rules of no recent date. *International relations had long since left the plane of simple attainment of goals by force without further ado. All relations, even those at heart deceptive, had to proceed along certain lines. There was a public sense of what was right and what was wrong in the conduct of states.* "Right" sometimes seems to mean no more than "appropriate" or "convenient," since open pursuit of power was too blunt and "undiplomatic" for man to tolerate. The intricacies and nuances of diplomatic relations gave scope to man's ingenuity, appealing not only to his cunning but also to his love of sport. Intertwined with these factors, now looming more or less prominently, was a sense of moral obligation expressed in the treaty provisions and sanctions, behind which stood the full force of the gods.

[106] Olmstead, *History of Assyria,* chap. 39.

Map 2

THE NEAR EAST IN 2600 B.C.

Euphrates R.

Tigris R.

Eshnunna

SUMERIANS ?

Nippur

Erech

Larsa

Lagash

Ur

Eridu

Memphis

PYRAMIDS OF GIZEH

Nile R.

Thebes

Syene

EGYPTIAN OLD KINGDOM, 2700-2200
SUMERIAN CITY-STATES, 2800-2400

Map 3

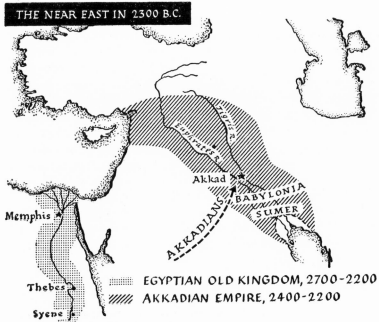

THE NEAR EAST IN 2300 B.C.

Tigris R.

Euphrates R.

Akkad

BABYLONIA

SUMER

AKKADIANS

Memphis

Thebes

Syene

EGYPTIAN OLD KINGDOM, 2700-2200
AKKADIAN EMPIRE, 2400-2200

Map 4

THE NEAR EAST IN 2050 B.C.

Tigris R.

Euphrates R.

GUTI

Herakleopolis

Nile R.

Ur

Thebes

▓▓▓ EGYPTIAN FIRST INTERMEDIATE PERIOD, 2200~2000
▨▨▨ THIRD DYNASTY OF UR, 2100~1950

Map 5

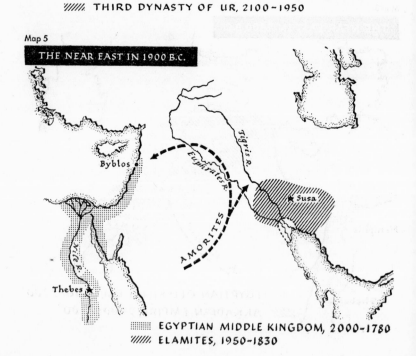

THE NEAR EAST IN 1900 B.C.

Byblos

Tigris R.

Euphrates R.

AMORITES

Susa

Nile R.

Thebes

▓▓▓ EGYPTIAN MIDDLE KINGDOM, 2000~1780
▨▨▨ ELAMITES, 1950~1830

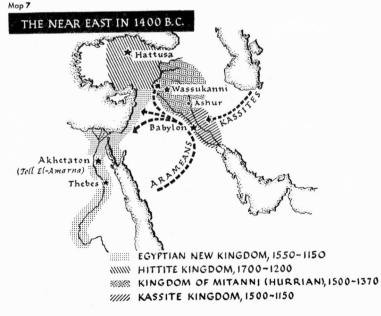

Map 6

THE NEAR EAST IN 1700 B.C.

HITTITES

★ Hattusa

HURRIANS

HYKSOS

Mari
• Ashur

★ Babylon

Avaris

▦ EGYPTIAN SECOND INTERMEDIATE PERIOD,
HYKSOS EMPIRE, 1780~1550
▨ OLD BABYLONIAN KINGDOM, 1800~1550
▧ HITTITE KINGDOM, 1700~1200

Map 7

THE NEAR EAST IN 1400 B.C.

★ Hattusa

★ Wassukanni
• Ashur

★ KASSITES

Babylon ★

ARAMEANS

Akhetaton
(Tell El-Amarna) ★

Thebes ★

▦ EGYPTIAN NEW KINGDOM, 1550~1150
▨ HITTITE KINGDOM, 1700~1200
▩ KINGDOM OF MITANNI (HURRIAN), 1500~1370
▧ KASSITE KINGDOM, 1500~1150

41

Map 8

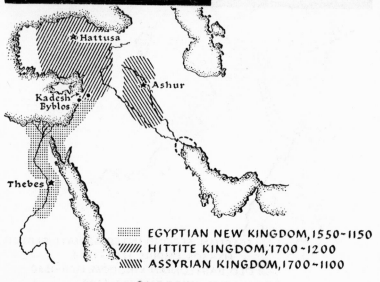

THE NEAR EAST IN 1225 B.C.

Hattusa

Ashur

Kadesh
Byblos

Thebes

```
▒▒▒▒  EGYPTIAN NEW KINGDOM, 1550~1150
//////  HITTITE KINGDOM, 1700~1200
\\\\\\  ASSYRIAN KINGDOM, 1700~1100
```

Map 9

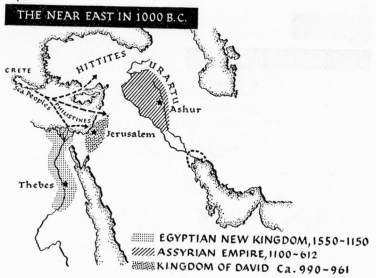

THE NEAR EAST IN 1000 B.C.

CRETE   HITTITES   URARTU

Sea Peoples   Ashur

PHILISTINES

Jerusalem

Thebes

```
▒▒▒▒  EGYPTIAN NEW KINGDOM, 1550~1150
//////  ASSYRIAN EMPIRE, 1100~612
▓▓▓▓  KINGDOM OF DAVID  Ca. 990~961
```

Map 10

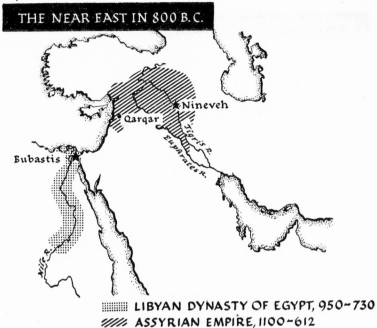

THE NEAR EAST IN 800 B.C.

Nineveh

Qarqar

Tigris R.

Euphrates R.

Bubastis

Nile R.

▓▓▓ LIBYAN DYNASTY OF EGYPT, 950~730
▨▨▨ ASSYRIAN EMPIRE, 1100~612

Map 11

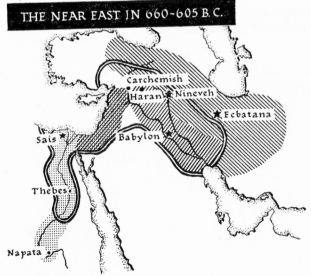

THE NEAR EAST IN 660~605 B.C.

Carchemish

Haran • ★ Nineveh

★ Ecbatana

Sais ★

Babylon ★

Thebes

Napata

〰️〰️ ASSYRIAN EMPIRE AT ITS ZENITH, Ca. 650
░░░ SAITE DYNASTY OF EGYPT, 663~525
▨▨▨ HELD BY EGYPT, 609~605
\\\\ MEDIAN EMPIRE, 612~550
▨▨▨ CHALDEAN OR NEO~BABYLONIAN EMPIRE, 612~539

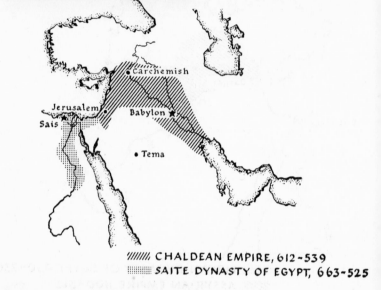

Map 12

THE NEAR EAST IN 580 B.C.

- Carchemish
- Jerusalem
- Sais
- Babylon ★
- Tema

▨ CHALDEAN EMPIRE, 612-539
▨ SAITE DYNASTY OF EGYPT, 663-525

Map 13

THE NEAR EAST IN 500 B.C.

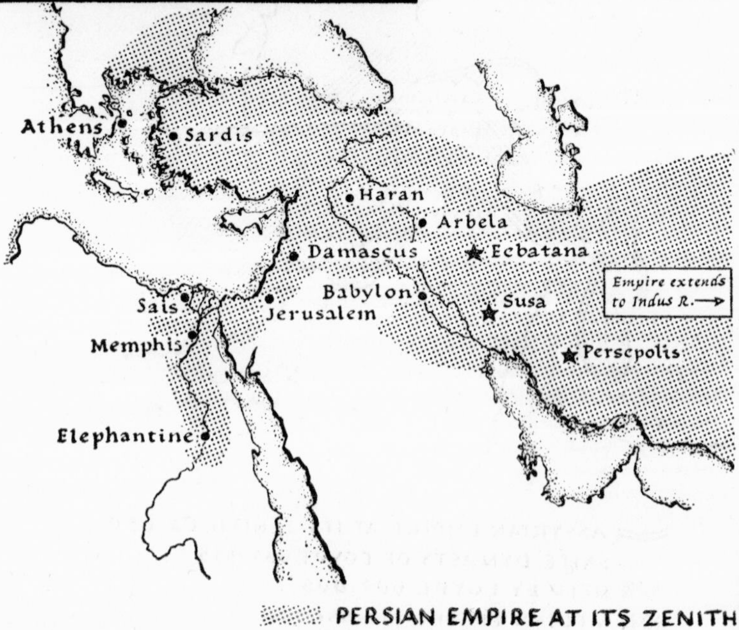

- Athens
- Sardis
- Haran
- Arbela
- Damascus
- Ecbatana ★
- Babylon
- Susa ★
- Jerusalem
- Sais
- Memphis
- Persepolis ★
- Elephantine

Empire extends to Indus R.→

▨ PERSIAN EMPIRE AT ITS ZENITH

CHAPTER II

The Political Prophecy of Early Israel

Hebrew prophecy arose as a political as well as a social phenomenon. The prophet advised rulers in decision-making in all matters of state. Prophetic counsel was explicit, but it rested in turn upon certain broad considerations of policy. The prophet was a living oracle who supplemented and finally replaced the inert oracles of lot and omen divination.

The same was true of non-Israelite prophecy as we meet it in eighteenth-century Mari, tenth-century Byblos, and eighth-century Syria (see Map 1). In the former city-kingdom, and in surrounding regions, a functionary described as "man of the god Dagan" carried messages to the king. These prophets announced, for example, victory over hostile Benjaminites[1] or they recommended offerings for the dead Jahdun-lim (an official?).[2] At Byblos "the god seized one of his"—i.e., the king's—"youths and made him possessed," with the result that he instructed the king

[1] G. Dossin, *Revue d'Assyriologie* 42 (1948), 125 ff.

[2] A. Parrot and G. Dossin, eds., *Archives Royales de Mari*, 1950, vol. III, no. 40. These and other texts from Mari have been translated and commented on by the following: A. Lods, "Une tablette inédite de Mari, intéressante pour l'histoire ancienne du prophétisme Sémitique," *Studies in Old Testament Prophecy Presented to T. H. Robinson*, 1950, pp. 103–10; M. Noth, "History and the Word of God in the Old Testament," *BJRL* 32 (1950), 194–206; and W. von Soden, "Verkuendigung des Gotteswillens durch prophetisches Wort in den altbabylonischen Briefen aus Mari," *Die Welt des Orients* 5 (1950), 397–403.

to give audience to the Egyptian ambassador Wen-Amon, whom he had formerly refused to grant diplomatic reception.[3] In the early eighth century King Zakir of Hamath, set upon by a league of seven (?) kings headed by Barhadad of Damascus, reports on a dedicatory statue inscription: "Be'elshamayn [spoke] to me through seers and through diviners. Be'elshamayn [said to me]: Do not fear for I made you king, and I shall stand by you and deliver you from all [these kings who] set up a siege against you."[4]

This is not to say that kings invented prophecy, for it was an independent shamanistic activity that arose in certain persons and could not be confidently restricted to hereditary lines. Kings realized the great need for contact with the religious forces which governed their actions and thus they drew prophetism into the court.[5] Yet these same or similar prophets doubtless had a large place in the life of the populace, who sought to penetrate the inscrutable future and to avert the dark powers. Prophecy and divination were closely linked, the former probably emerging out of the latter as the personal endowment of the interpreter allowed for innovation within the fixed mechanism of dream and omen interpretation.[6] It cannot be said that the final separation of prophecy and divination ever occurred on non-Israelite soil. Only the tendency existed. The kings thus supported the organs of divine-human communication, who tended by that very circumstance to bend their interests in a political direction.

[3] Published by W. Golenischeff, *Recueil de travaux relatifs à la philologie et à l'archéologie égyptiennes et assyriennes* 21 (1899), 74–102; translated in *ANET*, pp. 25–29, in which J. Wilson observes that "the determinative of the word '(prophetically) possessed' shows a human figure in violent motion or epileptic convulsion" (p. 26, note 13). The text is discussed by W. F. Albright, "The Eastern Mediterranean about 1060 B.C.," *Studies Presented to David Moore Robinson*, 1951, I, 223–31.

[4] Published by H. Pognon, *Inscriptions sémitiques de la Syrie, de la Mésopotamie et de la région de Mossoul*, 1907, pp. 156–78, translated in *ANET*, pp. 501–2, and commented on by C. C. Torrey, *JAOS* 35 (1915–17), 354–60; by A. Haldar, *Associations of Cult Prophets among the Ancient Semites*, 1945, pp. 74–75; and, at greatest length, by M. Noth, *ZDPV* 52 (1929), pp. 124–41.

[5] Haldar, *op. cit.*, pp. 63–70.

[6] A. Guillaume, *Prophecy and Divination*, 1938, pp. 37–53, 107–33.

Israel's Earliest Contacts with Prophecy

Balaam, summoned by Balak of Moab to frustrate the Israelite invasion, was a politically valuable prophet similar to those at Mari and Byblos (Num. 22–24). He came presumably from Pethor on the upper Euphrates,[7] not far from Mari. His prophecy was accompanied by sacrifice and divining procedures similar to those of the Babylonian *baru* priests (23:1–6, 13–17; 29).[8] Yet he transcended the *baru* ritual, for in his third and fourth addresses "he did not go, as at other times, to meet with omens, but set his face toward the wilderness" (24:1). It is admittedly difficult to assess the historical accuracy of the dominating JE conception of Yahweh's providential use of a foreign prophet against his will. Even allowing, however, for a considerable later theological bias, there are many historically convincing features in the Balaam oracles.[9]

No allusions in the four prophecies of Balaam require that they be dated as late as the united monarchy, although it is easy to see why the prophesied victories over Amalek, Edom, and Moab (24:17–18, 20) were treasured as allusions to David's conquests.[10] In fact, the Kenites of 24:21–24 are only to be referred

[7] The Pethor of the Hebrew text is generally identified with Pitru, near Carchemish, on the bend of the Euphrates in northern Syria, although not too much can be made of this identification. Some interpreters regard north Syria as too distant to send for a prophet. It is true that the versions are not unanimous in reading Pethor. The Samaritan Pentateuch and LXX state that Balak sent "to the land of the Ammonites." The Syriac and Vulgate may have read *happōthēr*, "the dream interpreter," instead of a place name.

[8] This point was first extensively argued by S. Daiches, "Balaam— a Babylonian *baru*," *Hermann Hilprecht Anniversary Volume*, 1909, pp. 60–70, who found several parallels: a morning sacrifice presented by the diviner and the offerer, the offerer remaining beside the sacrifice while the diviner consulted omens and undertook certain magical acts while walking (in Num. 23:3 he understood $w^{e'}\bar{e}l^ekh\bar{a}h$ as a ritual act and *wayyēlek šephi* as "he went by pace or step by step" after Assyrian *šēpu*), the importance of the diviner's seeing his omina with unhindered vision, and his falling down during the ceremony. Daiches acknowledged that in 24:1 Balaam abandons divination, but he insists that even here Balaam describes himself by the terms descriptive of a *baru* priest (24:3–4).

[9] W. F. Albright, "Oracles of Balaam," *JBL* 63 (1944), 207–33.

[10] *Ibid.*, p. 227.

to a time when they had not yet been absorbed into Israel, i.e., before the time of David.[11] And even so purportedly late a passage as 24:23–24 may be connected, not with Roman or Greek invasions, but with the incursion of the Sea Peoples in the twelfth century from Cyprus (Kittim) and their consequent threat to northern Mesopotamia (Ashur) beyond the Euphrates (Eber).

Probably the speeches are not verbatim from the prophet Balaam. It is psychologically difficult to explain how Israel could have come into possession of such speeches, and, most of all, the pervading sense of the élan of Israel is not very likely on the lips of a foreign prophet.[12] It is more likely that they are Israelite speeches from the days of the judges.[13] For our purposes, the real importance of the Balaam tradition and his prophecies, quite apart from their exact connection, is that they underline the early link between Israel and Near Eastern prophecy. *They serve to substantiate the recollection that Israel's earliest forms of prophecy were similar to those of surrounding peoples.* Even though the JE writers have sought to stress chiefly the uniqueness of Balaam's break with his own methods of divination, they serve inadvertently at the same time to underline the historicity of the Hebrew dependence upon non-Hebraic prophecy.

Such an interpretation of the Balaam materials is borne out by the so-called Taunt Song against Heshbon (Num. 21:26–30). This brief outcry has all the earmarks of an Amorite song of victory over Moab.[14] Israel has no place in the song. The invasion described is from the north rather than from the south, as we should expect if the song originally referred to Israel's attack on Moab (see Map 14). The normally Moabite city of Heshbon is called "the city of Sihon," from which he and his

[11] *Ibid.*

[12] A. H. Van Zyl, *The Moabites,* pp. 10–12.

[13] *Ibid.,* p. 12.

[14] M. Diman (Haran), "An Archaic Survival in Prophetic Literature." *Yedi'oth hahebrah lehaqirat Eretz-Yisrael we'atiqotheha* 13 (1947), 7–15 (Hebrew). G. E. Mendenhall, "The Hebrew Conquest of Palestine," *BA* 25 (1962), 81–84, offers the plausible suggestion that this taunt song over Moab by Sihon "may be taken as illustrative of the process by which the pre-Mosaic traditions were preserved," i.e., when the population of Sihon's kingdom was converted to Yahwism, the Amorite taunt song was transplanted into the body of Hebrew traditions.

Amorite army launch attacks deeper into Moabite territory. Israel has somehow come into possession of this song, perhaps by converting some of Sihon's subjects to Yahwism, and applied it rather awkwardly to the Israelite thrust into Moab which, in fact, followed the Amorite attack by some decades.

It may thus be claimed with probability that the form of the oracle against the foreign nation was one of the earliest, if not the earliest, form of Hebrew prophecy and that the style and motifs were taken over from non-Israelite prototypes; in some cases the actual foreign compositions were used.[15]

Inasmuch as these earliest prophetic recollections come from trans-Jordan it is not accurate to limit Israel's knowledge of prophecy to Canaanite forms.[16] Prophecy was not exclusively tied up with Canaanite baalism but existed rather in various forms which were not all determined by orgiastic nature religion.[17] The practical consequence is that Israel probably brought some form of prophecy with her into Canaan and thus it was possible from the beginning for a strongly pro-Israelite and pro-Yahweh political prophecy to exist in opposition to the religious and political claims of Canaanites. From the point of view of that ancient Yahwism, prophecy did not require naturalization to an Israelite ethos. Having been derived from Israel's contacts with trans-Jordan peoples, prophecy was remembered as one of her most ancient elements and could even be regarded as part of the Mosaic heritage (Num. 12:6; Deut. 18:15, 18; 34:10; Hos. 12:14).[18] There is, in fact, one tradition that pictures Moses as

[15] The general thesis of Israelite dependence on Near Eastern literary types is illustrated with a wealth of detail by A. Bentzen, *Introduction to the Old Testament*, 1952, I, esp. 113–18, and by A. Weiser, *The Old Testament: Its Formation and Development*, 1961 (trans. from the 4th German ed., 1957), pp. 11–68.

[16] As is done, for example, by G. Hoelscher, *Die Profeten*, 1914, pp. 140–43; S. Mowinckel, *Psalmenstudien*, 1922, III, 14–16; and J. Pedersen, *Israel, III–IV*, 1940, pp. 111, 115 f., 125, 142.

[17] T. J. Meek, *Hebrew Origins*, pp. 155–56.

[18] Halder, *op. cit.*, pp. 109–11, opposes the rigidity of the theory of the exclusively Canaanite origin of Hebrew prophecy although he grants that the Cannaanite environment mediated older and general Semitic influences. In addition to the observation that the Hebrew prophet has affinities with the Babylonian *maḫḫu* priest who was an ecstatic functionary (pp. 21–29), he notes that "it is equally possible that ecstatic priest-prophets were to be

the leader of group prophecy (Num. 11:16–29). In spite of some late features in this tradition, the primitive conception of ecstatic prophecy reflected in the account argues for its historicity.[19]

The Judges as Prophets

On first thought, the omission of prophets from the stories of the judges is puzzling. It becomes understandable, however, when we consider that the judges themselves in a sense fulfill the prophetic function as well as the political. They rally the loyalties of the people to the God of Israel. Deborah is in fact expressly called "a prophetess" in the later prose account, although her function in this regard is apparently understood as that of adjudication (Judg. 4:4–5). The Song makes it clear, however, that it is as the leader of the people of Yahweh in battle that Deborah had her chief distinction. Gideon's rallying cry of "the sword of Yahweh and of Gideon" shows quite clearly (7:20), as do his skillful tactics in battle (7:4–22), that this Yahweh-enthusiast conceived of himself as directly moved by the deity. One finds also that the idea of spirit possession is applied to these early judges (6:34; 11:29). Jephthah's war with Ammon is presented as a struggle

---

found in the half-nomadic tribes that—starting from the East—entered Palestine later" (p. 110). In other words, all of the waves of Hebrew settlers in Palestine could have known prophecy beforehand, either from the Babylonians or from the desert tribes.

[19] The narrative appears to be primarily E and seems to be related (though not a parallel recension) to the accounts of the appointment of judicial assistants by Moses in Exodus 18 and the specification of elders in Exodus 24 (note especially the rare stem *'tsl* in Exod. 24:11 and Num. 11: 17). The basic account is similar to Numbers 12:1–6 in that Moses is superior to all other recipients of the divine revelation, in that even the seventy receive their portions of spirit (*rûaḥ*) from his *rûaḥ*. The conception that Moses' experience of *rûaḥ* was ecstatic and the belief that he did not condemn independent prophetism (vss. 24–30) are striking and seemingly ancient features of the story (cf. G. B. Gray, *A Critical and Exegetical Commentary on Numbers, ICC,* pp. 115–16). Admittedly the belief that all of Yahweh's people would receive the spirit found particularly vigorous expression in the post-exilic age, when prophetism was faltering and its ideas were undergoing a sort of "democratization" (e.g., Joel 2:28–29; Isa. 4:4; Zech. 12; and cf. discussion in A. Jepsen, *Nabi. Soziologische Studien zur alttestamentlichen Literatur und Religionsgeschichte,* pp. 32–33), but it cannot be concluded from that fact that there was no pneumatism in the Mosaic period or that it was confined to Moses.

in which Yahweh gives his decision in the matter of a territorial dispute in trans-Jordan, and he who leads Israel's forces also expresses Israel's confidence in the judgment of Yahweh (11:27).

As long as the leadership of the tribes was on a charismatic basis, militant prophets were not encouraged to give tribal leadership. The judges themselves, with their spontaneous gifts of morale-building and military direction, did most if not all of the specialized work of the first Israelite prophets. In this respect the distinguishing mark of early prophetism, namely, its defense of Yahwism against all compromises, was superbly embodied in the fanaticism of some of the judges. Samson was a Nazirite who shared many of the early prophetic misgivings about civilization, and Barak had Deborah for a prophetic counselor. Doubtless other judges were influenced by prophets, and to this period should be assigned the awakening religious nationalism reflected in Balaam's Oracles and the Blessing of Moses (Deut. 33).[20] It is nevertheless clear that the judges were a mixed lot[21] and often failed to maintain Yahwism in its cultic purity and in its moral demand. This meant that Israelite prophetism, which endorsed the judges, was in fact in danger of interpreting itself as anti-foreign rather than pro-Yahweh.[22]

Saul and "the Sons of the Prophets"

With the monarchy a new situation developed which required the presence of prophets alongside the political leaders. Kingship became hereditary from David on, and no longer could it be assured that the head of the people would also have the necessary prophetic gifts; this danger could be felt both by those who wished to limit the monarchy religiously and by those who wished to invest it with religious symbolism.

In this regard Saul represents the transition from judge to king,

[20] Albright, "Oracles of Balaam," *JBL* 63 (1944), 207–33 and F. M. Cross and D. N. Freedman, "The Blessing of Moses," *JBL* 67 (1948), 191–210.

[21] W. Eichrodt, *Theology of the Old Testament*, 1961 (trans. from 6th German edition, 1959, with revisions), I, 306–9.

[22] For a valuable discussion of the ethnocentric character of Yahwism, according to which Israel's enemy was Yahweh's enemy also, cf. H. Schmoekel, *Jahwe und die Fremdvoelker*, pp. 36–60.

but he is still nearer to the former. He is appointed as *nāgîd* (prince) at the express initiative of Yahweh and with Samuel's wholehearted support; at least such is the witness of the early tradition (I Sam. 9:16).[23] The purpose of the choice is to win deliverance from the encroaching Philistines, and the method is to imbue Saul with military strength by his participation in the prophetic group ecstasy. It is as one of the *benê han-nebî'îm* (sons of the prophets) that Saul acquires strength to expel the Philistines (10:1–13). The prophets appear in a band; they play musical instruments in order to induce or, more probably, to accompany their collective prophesying. While the result was emotional excitation, perhaps to the accompaniment of a dance, there is no evidence that the prophesying here described was merely gibberish.[24] It may well have produced a simple catchword or refrain which was repeated rhythmically, or even a kind of hymnic praise from which developed the nationalistic poetry so richly preserved in the Psalms and in the early historical books.[25] "Ec-

[23] There is general agreement among scholars that the stories about the rise of kingship in Israel come from at least two sources. The late source includes I Samuel 7:2—8:22; 10:17–24; 12, although it is uncertain whether it is basically D as A. R. S. Kennedy thinks (*The Books of Samuel* [The New Century Bible], 1905, p. 16), or E as K. Budde thinks (*Die Buecher Samuel,* 1902, pp. xix–xx). The early source includes 9–10:16; 11:1–11, 15, but has been further subdivided with some justification by A. Lods into a "seer source" (13:3–5, 23; 14:1–20, 23a, 24b, 25–30, 36–46) and a "Jabesh source" (11; 13:2, 3a, 17 f.; 14:15, 21 f., 23b, 24, 31–35). The inconsistencies in the early source are real enough but they do not seem resolvable by Lods's partition ("Les sources des récits du premier livre de Samuel sur l'institution de la royauté israélite," *Études de théologie et d'histoire* . . . *en hommage à la faculté de théologie de Montauban,* 1901, pp. 259–84, and criticisms by R. H. Pfeiffer, *Introduction to the Old Testament,* 1941, pp. 344–45).

[24] The parallel story of 19:18–24, which seems to indicate that the prophesying of these bands was a wild ecstatic dance, is so anti-Saul in its bias that its historical value is doubtful (G. B. Caird, *IB,* II, 988). Jepsen's analysis of *hithnabbē'* (hithpael) and *hinnābē'* (niphal) falls into three phases: (1) about 800, when both meant "to rave"; (2) between 750 and 550 B.C., when the former meant "to rave" and the latter "to preach"; (3) after 550, when both meant only "to preach" (*op. cit.,* pp. 5–9). Although suggestive, this analysis is inconclusive, especially in the too sharp separation of ecstatic speech and normal speech and in the too confident dating of the literary contexts in which the terms occur.

[25] This point has been well supported by H. Junker, *Prophet und Seher in*

stasy" in early Israel is, therefore, not necessarily the free play of incoherent bodily movements and vocal sounds. It is at any rate clear that prophesying and military prowess are of one piece, for from this experience Saul receives the Spirit of God (11:6) and delivers the oppressed city of Jabesh-gilead (11:7–11).[26] The Philistine foreigners are merely the oppressors to be defeated, and prophecy is the ready instrument in the struggle.[27]

While the initial impression given by these early prophets is crude and primitive, it is likely that they had already separated themselves rather sharply from religious functionaries who used omens and lots. At the close of his rule it could be said of Saul that "Yahweh did not answer him, either by dreams, or by Urim [i.e., sacred lots], or by prophets" (28:6). The prophet was thought of as bringing a different mode of divine communication from that received by dreams or by the consultation of an oracle. *Socially prophets were indeed uncouth but religiously they represented a reaction to dependence upon mechanics in favor of a freer and more direct message from deity.* The content of that message we may assume to have been, as with the judges before them, the upbuilding of Israel by the defeat of threatening enemies.

Court Prophecy from David to Baasha

The prophets of the kingdom from David (see Map 15) to the Omri dynasty (see Map 16) were likewise directly involved in politics. They were in some cases court advisers who intervened in affairs of state on behalf of the national God. The Deuteronomist who records their words has, to be sure, shaped the stories in such a fashion as to stress their cultic concerns, and he

---

Israel, and gives an important counterbalance to the view that all such *Heilsprophezeiung* came from a common Near Eastern court setting (cf. H. Gressmann, *Der Messias,* and Schmoekel, *op. cit.,* pp. 28–35).

[26] One of the signal discrepancies in the early source, according to Lods, is the identification of the national enemy exclusively as the Philistines in one stratum (the "seer source") and, at first, as the Ammonites in the other stratum (the "Jabesh source").

[27] Meek, *op. cit.,* pp. 156–57.

has occasionally smothered their original message in his own verbiage.[28] Nevertheless the old traditions shine through in most instances and permit us to see the concrete nature of the prophetic guidance.[29]

Gad advises David, while he is in hiding from Saul, to leave Moab and to return to his faithful men in Judah (I Sam. 22:5). Late in the king's reign, when a census initiated by David has angered Yahweh, Gad offers the king a choice of punishment: famine, banishment, or pestilence (II Sam. 24:13). Finally, Gad urges David to build an altar to Yahweh on the threshing floor of Araunah, which occupied the height to the north of the city of Jerusalem (II Sam. 24:18).

A second prophet of David's court was Nathan, who first favored David's plan to build a cedar temple for the ark and then opposed it after a specific protest from Yahweh (II Sam. 7:1–7).[30] He condemned David for the murder of Uriah and announced that Yahweh would spare the king because he had repented, but, since he had scorned Yahweh's known will, the baby born of the union with Bathsheba must die (II Sam. 12:1–14). Nathan joined other officials in support of Solomon against Adonijah as David's successor and, in leading the struggle, showed himself an expert in court intrigue (I Kings 1).

Ahijah of Shiloh appeared abruptly as the instigator of a revolt by one of Solomon's labor chiefs, Jeroboam son of Nebat. The prophet performed a symbolic action by tearing Jeroboam's robe into twelve pieces and giving him ten pieces as a symbol of the defection of the northern tribes from David's dynasty (I Kings 11:29–31). Later Abijah, the failing son of Jeroboam, consulted the prophet concerning the prospects of his health and was condemned to die (14:1–6). The first speech of Ahijah is patently

[28] The Deuteronomic displacement or obscuration of the original prophecy is most clearly seen in I Kings 11:32–9; 14:7–11, 16; 16:16—17:4.

[29] G. von Rad, *Studies in Deuteronomy*, 1953, pp. 78–81, has usefully listed eleven instances of prophecies and their fulfillments embedded in the Deuteronomic history; he believes that "these citations go back in most cases to genuine prophetic words" (p. 82).

[30] The tendency to find a historical kernel in this prophecy is well founded. Cf., e.g., Caird, *op. cit.*, pp. 864–65, 1082, and N. K. Gottwald, *A Light to the Nations*, 1959, p. 195.

Deuteronomic (I Kings 11:31–39)[31] and the·first half of his speech concerning Abijah is also Deuteronomic (14:7–11).[32] The prophet's original support of Jeroboam's dynasty, which later turned to hostility, is very probably historical and possibly represented sectional jealousy. When Jeroboam made Dan and Bethel sanctuaries of Israel, instead of Shiloh, Ahijah turned against him. It is at any rate noteworthy that Ahijah is not in the capital of Shechem or Penuel but in his own hometown when Jeroboam's wife consults him (14:4). Shemaiah, called "man of God," who urges Rehoboam not to try to force Israel into loyalty to the Davidic dynasty, is a historically doubtful figure (I Kings 12:21–24).[33] He may well be a duplicate of Ahijah;[34] at any rate his objection to the Davidic dynasty is essentially the same as Ahijah's: Solomon has compromised the religion of Yahweh by bringing in other cults for the satisfaction of his foreign wives. Yet his stress upon not fighting with one's "brothers" strikes a protest against internecine war which was characteristic of Hosea more than a century later; it is not, however, an emphasis likely to have been introduced at a much later time.

Jehu ben Hanani prophesied the downfall of Baasha's dynasty, but the particular quarrel of the prophet with the king is not given, since the weak generalizing Deuteronomic condemnation for nothern kings has displaced the historical issue (I Kings 16:1–4). According to II Chronicles 19:2 the same prophet rebuked Jehoshaphat for having taken part with Ahab in the attack on Ramoth-gilead. That will have been at least twenty-eight years later than the condemnation of Baasha. That the same prophet should have condemned an Israelite and a Judean king may cast some doubt on the later incident; but his condemnation, while

[31] Caird, *op. cit.,* pp. 109–10.

[32] J. A. Montgomery and H. S. Gehman, *International Critical Commentary on Kings,* 1951, p. 266, regard vss. 7–16 as "stoutly Deuteronomic," but there is, in fact, a noticeably more vivid style and absence of theologizing in vss. 12–13, 15, suggesting an original core which has been almost lost in rewriting.

[33] Montgomery-Gehman, *op. cit.,* p. 251.

[34] It is to be noted that in its long supplement after I Kings 12:24, LXX attributes the symbolic act of a torn garment to Shemaiah, which suggests that he may have been confused with Ahijah.

theologically biased against Ahab, seems to retain a distinction between the prophet's objection to the foreign policy of Jehoshaphat and his approval of the king's cultic policy. The Chronicler reports that a seer called Hanani condemned Asa for his alliance with Syria against Baasha of Israel (II Chron. 16: 7–10), and in so doing he serves as something of a forerunner of Isaiah of Jerusalem. This seer may have been the father of Jehu ben Hanani or even Jehu himself, and a supposed chronological objection to the historicity of the passage appears to have been removed by the discovery of the stele of Ben-hadad.[35]

Reflection on these prophetic words shows at once that they were very specific directions or declarations. The prophet at this period was not a general religious teacher or moralist. He was one who brought the religious traditions of Yahwism to bear upon state decisions. He advised for or against particular courses of action. Sometimes he declared what would happen as the consequence of violation of the Yahwistic traditions.

The chief concern of this early prophecy was the political destiny of Israel. In a sense cultic advice looms rather large in the prophetic words we have surveyed, but really only general concerns of the national cult are in question. The minutiae of cultic procedure are left for others to control. Morality is of concern to the prophet only insofar as it affects the foundations of the state, and this clearly was the case when David stained his hands with a man's blood in order to take that man's wife. *It was the state, its well-being and destiny under Yahweh, that encompassed the concern of the prophet, who saw the responsibility for Israel largely concentrated in the person of the king.*

These early prophets were not necessarily committed to a single dynasty. Ahijah condemned Solomon and favored a parallel northern dynasty, and later he rejected the king he had appointed in the north. Likewise Jehu rejected the dynasty of Baasha. If the dynasty departed from the purity of Yahwism as the prophets

---

[35] *ANET,* p. 501. W. F. Albright, "A Votive Stele Erected by Ben-Hadad I of Damascus to the God Melcarth," *BASOR* 87 (1942), 23–29, argues persuasively for only two Damascene rulers by the name of Ben-hadad. With necessary adjustments in the chronology of Kings, Albright places the invasion of II Chronicles 16:4 about 879 B.C., within the reign of Baasha and thus in keeping with the Chronicler's report.

understood it, they did not hesitate to favor another and to work actively for replacement. Unfortunately the prophetic words are not sufficiently detailed for us to know the exact content of their thought. It seems that foreign alliances, the admission of foreign cults by Solomon, and Jeroboam's neglect of certain sanctuaries, such as Shiloh, formed the basis for the objections recorded in Kings and Chronicles. The earlier criticisms of David's rule, which did not go so far as to necessitate his removal from office, were based on a sense of what was inappropriate to the earlier traditions of Yahwism, namely, probing into divine mysteries by counting the population, replacing a simple tent sanctuary by a permanent building, and royal murder and adultery.

Prophecy During the Omrid and Early Jehu Dynasties

The fullest accounts of pre-writing prophecy in Israel are those concerning northern prophets during the dynasties of Omri and Jehu. Notable among these prophets were Elijah and Elisha but others appear: Micaiah ben Imlah (I Kings 22:7–9, 13–23), Zedekiah ben Chenaanah (I Kings 22:11–12, 24), anonymous individual prophets (I Kings 20:13, 22, 35; II Kings 9:4), and bands of prophets at the court (I Kings 18:4; 22:6–7, 10–12) and in the countryside (II Kings 2:15; 4:38; 6:1). The prophetic traditions preserved in Kings are of a mixed literary and historical character, and the extent of the original sources and the dates of the events recounted therein—and even their true sequence—are not easily come by.[36] An element of uncertainty necessarily attaches to any historical reconstruction of the period. Nevertheless even a tentative reconstruction affords some significant insights into Israelite political prophecy in the ninth century.

The vigorous Omri dynasty initiated a new phase in the history of the northern kingdom (see Map 16). In brief, Omri

---

[36] As to the various attempts to delimit the Elijah, Elisha, and other "cycles" in I Kings 17—II Kings 13, no entirely satisfactory conclusions have been reached, since the lines of demarcation are nebulous on literary grounds; it is not always easy to know which of the prophets or kings mentioned in a story is the protagonist and thus whether the interests are primarily "religious" or "political."

sought to accomplish for northern Israel what David had accomplished for united Israel.[37] He built a new capital at Samaria
on a militarily defensible site surrounded by a rich valley and
with easy access westward to the coastal trade route.[38] He arranged a treaty of alliance with Ittobaal of Tyre and sealed it
by giving his son Ahab to Ittobaal's daughter, Jezebel. Athaliah
of the house of Ahab—whether his daughter or sister is not
certain[39]—was married to Jehoram, son of the Judean king Jehoshaphat. This was of utmost importance for it marked an end
to a half-century of internecine war between Israel and Judah
and allowed the two countries to concentrate their energies on
other problems. Israel recovered Moab and Judah conquered
Edom. The chief threat to Israel was Damascus on the northeast,
whose forceful ruler Ben-hadad had extracted trade concessions
either from Omri himself or, more probably, from an earlier
Israelite king.[40] Damascene merchants were quartered in a special
section of Samaria. It was to the struggle with the rival power of
Damascus that the Omri dynasty directed its chief attention until
the threat of a still more powerful enemy forced a fragile unity
between Damascus and Israel against Assyria.

Ahab is limned as a gross apostate by the book of Kings (I
Kings 16:29–33). His sins are said to have exceeded those of all
the rulers before him. Yet a careful reading both of the indictment and of the stories in which Ahab figures shows that a
blanket condemnation of the king will not stand.[41] Ahab permitted his wife Jezebel to introduce a temple in Samaria for the
worship of her god Baal Melqart or Baal Shemayim.[42] There is

---

[37] J. Bright, *A History of Israel,* pp. 220–25.

[38] Cf. the results of the Harvard excavation at Samaria in J. W. Crow-
foot, K. Kenyon, *et al., Samaria-Sebaste,* 3 vols., 1942–57.

[39] II Kings 18:18; II Chronicles 21:6 read "daughter of Ahab" whereas
II Kings 8:26; II Chronicles 22:2 read "daughter of Omri."

[40] Albright, *op. cit.,* p. 27.

[41] C. F. Whitley, "The Deuteronomic Presentation of the House of Omri,"
VT 2 (1952), 142; Pfeiffer, *op. cit.,* p. 404.

[42] The otherwise undesignated Baal of the Omrid dynasty is regarded by
W. F. Albright, *Archaeology and the Religion of Israel,* 2nd ed., 1946, pp.
156–57, 229, and "A Votive Stele . . . ," pp. 28 f., and A. Alt, "Der
Stadtstaat Samaria," *KS,* III, 227, as *Baal Melqart,* god of the underworld.
O. Eissfeldt, *ZAW* 57 (1939), 1–31, and Montgomery-Gehman, *op cit.,*
pp. 308–9, prefer to see him as *Baal Shemayim,* the Baal of the Heavens,

no evidence that Baal worship was introduced anywhere else in Israel than at the capital. The Baal shrine on Mount Carmel was an ancient non-Israelite holy place and not the work of Jezebel.[43] It is also apparent that Ahab did not intend to replace Yahwism with Baalism. It was rather the privilege of royalty to provide in their own territory for the worship of the gods of states with which they were joined by treaty. As long as relations were maintained by sporadic diplomatic missions, the need for a permanent chapel would not be so acute. When, however, dynastic intermarriage brought foreign wives into the court, it was a matter of diplomatic courtesy to replace portable shrines with a suitable temple, which was normally incorporated in the palace complex. All that Ahab intended was to supply this diplomatic privilege to his Phoenician wife.[44]

To be sure Jezebel is represented as seeking the lives of Yahweh prophets, but probably because of their hostility. In defiance of established international practice, the Yahweh prophets tried to reverse Ahab's authorization of Baal worship in Samaria. It is possible that acts of violence against Baal prophets had preceded Jezebel's murder of Yahweh prophets, for somewhat later Elijah did not hesitate to lead the Israelites in the slaughter of four hundred prophets of Baal on Mount Carmel (I Kings 18:40). Furthermore, there is no reason to believe that Jezebel launched a purge of all Yahweh prophets in Israel. Her wrath seems to have been confined to those court prophets who directly opposed her adherence to the Baal cult.

---

also mentioned in the Zakir stele from Hamath in central Syria and the Azitawadda inscription from Adana in northern Syria.

[43] This is quite clear from the simple account prefacing the prophetic narratives: "Ahab took a wife; Jezebel daughter of Ethbaal king of Sidon, and he served Baal and worshiped him. And he erected an altar to Baal in the house of Baal which he built in Samaria and he made the Asherah . . ." (I Kings 16:31b–33a). The account has wrongly attributed Baal worship to Ahab's initiative, but it correctly connects the marriage to a Phoenician princess with the introduction of her native worship *to Samaria;* it is not said that she introduced Baal worship elsewhere in Israel. Of course, it is probable that local Baal cults were encouraged by the Samarian cult and that the various local Baal personalities tended to be syncretized.

[44] Bright, *op. cit.,* p. 225. Roughly the same was true of Solomon, except that he was somewhat more eager to embrace the foreign cults because of his love of ostentation and pageantry. Cf. Montgomery-Gehman, *op. cit.,* p. 235.

Elijah

Elijah's opposition to Ahab may be regarded as typical of the general Yahwistic prophetic resentment. Nowhere does the prophet accuse the king of deserting Yahweh altogether in favor of Baal; but his sin is just as great, in Elijah's view, for he has authorized the worship of *two* gods: Baal and Yahweh. Ahab and the people he represents continue "to limp with two opposing loyalties" (I Kings 18:21). *Baalism is condemned not because it is idolatry in the technical sense but because it divides and compromises the honor of Yahweh.* There is only one *elohim* for Israel and it must be either altogether Baal or altogether Yahweh. Therefore neither the place nor the manner of worship is in question. Elijah himself erects or repairs a Yahweh altar on Mount Carmel with no sense of obligation to sacrifice only at Jerusalem. His enmity toward Ahab and Jezebel is not predicated on their determination to extirpate Yahwism, since that is not their intention at all. It is predicated on their introduction of a national cult which challenges Yahweh's honor and threatens to make Israel a polytheistic people—even though the majority of Israelites never practice Baalism. The mere existence of the Baal cult in the Israelite capital supported by the ruler of the people is enough to make it a dangerous threat to the sole lordship of Yahweh over Israel. It is rather Elijah, if anyone, who sought to extirpate the opposition by violence.

Unfortunately the most explicitly political word in the Elijah traditions cannot be legitimately connected with him. Having fled to Mount Horeb in the face of Jezebel's threat against his life, Elijah is told by Yahweh that he must return and do three things: (1) anoint Hazael as king in Damascus; (2) anoint Jehu as king in Israel; (3) anoint Elisha as his prophetic successor (I Kings 19:15–18).[45] The succeeding narrative, however, speaks only of his choice of Elisha. The designation of Hazael as the

[45] I Kings 19:17 has sometimes been regarded as an infelicitous intrusion, disturbing the continuity from vss. 16 to 18 (Montgomery-Gehman, *op. cit.*, p. 315), but the prophecy of the devastating swords of Hazael, Jehu, and Elisha certainly fits the belligerency of the rest of the section and is not syntactically impossible.

Aramean ruler and of Jehu as the Israelite king is left to Elisha (II Kings 8:7–15; 9:1–10). If Elijah did receive such a command his non-compliance with two-thirds of it is difficult to explain. The likely explanation is that the greater figure Elijah has attracted incidents connected with the lesser figure Elisha. Even so, we should have expected the editor to comment on the fact that the commands given to Elijah were only carried out by Elisha. The specific aim of 19:15–18 was apparently an inept attempt to justify the later extremism of Elisha in uprooting Ahab's house by claiming that such extremism had been endorsed by his master Elijah when in fact it had *not*. The section remains an enigma and offers no precise historical information.

The extent of Elijah's recorded pronouncements on political matters is limited to condemnation of Ahab's house and the prophecy of its eventual overthrow. The anti-royal animus of Elijah is strictly directed to the king's introduction of the Baal cult into Samaria and his callous murder of the Israelite Naboth, who is condemned by false witnesses so that his land may be expropriated by the king.[46] There is no evidence that Elijah himself fomented rebellion against the house of Ahab (excepting the above-mentioned and untrustworthy command of I Kings 19:15–16). This lack may of course be due to the sparseness of the Elijah legends. The reference to seven thousand who have not capitulated to Baal (19:18) is probably not intended as the total faithful population in Elijah's day but refers to the Yahweh zealots under Elisha who were ready to fight until Baal was removed.[47] This group will have included prophets, Rechabites, and court officials such as Obadiah (18:3–16). That the battle is to be carried beyond extirpation of the Baal prophets to extirpation of the house of Ahab was apparently not a strategy with which Elijah sympathized. It was Elisha who in the light of further Baalistic penetration of the court and in consideration of the

[46] It was customary for landowners convicted of major crimes, especially of sedition, to forfeit their property to royalty. Cf. K. Galling, *Die israelitische Staatsverfassung in ihrer vorderorientalischen Umwelt,* p. 35, and K. H. Henry, "Land Tenure in the Old Testament," *PEQ* 86 (1954), 10–11.

[47] Montgomery-Gehman believe the seven thousand "may be an authentic note of some census taken of the Zealots" (*ICC,* p. 315), but it seems more probable that it is a round number.

weak successors of Ahab felt that Ahab's house must be removed from Israel by means of prophetic agitation, and it is primarily that later mood which has been put on Elijah's lips in 19:15–18.

Elijah does not appear to have had any clear concern with foreign affairs as such. *Only to the extent that he contends for the Yahwistic purity of Israel does he have any strong convictions on relations with other states. By forbidding Israelite kings to recognize foreign gods and to provide reciprocal worship, the prophet forecloses the possibility of foreign relations among equal states.* In fact, the contest between Baal and Yahweh on Mount Carmel may have been a frontal attack upon the Israelite treaty with Tyre.[48] This treaty seems to have brought Mount Carmel and part of the plain of Accho into Israelite control, as it had been in David's reign; but with this acquisition of new territory came the mixed legacy of an active Baal cult and a lapsed Yahweh cult on the same peak. Elijah was not content to *revive* the Yahweh worship. On what was now Israelite soil he had to *extirpate* the Baal worship. Only as Israel conquers other states and imposes treaties upon them can she avoid diplomatic recognition of the foreign gods. That Ahab was involved in more than one alliance is attested by Obadiah's remark that the king has sought Elijah as a fugitive in foreign lands and has required the officials to give an oath that they do not know of his whereabouts (I Kings 18:10). Such an oath would be possible only within the framework of a treaty which included an extradition clause.[49] All the provisions of parity treaties for interdynastic marriages and diplomatic exchanges are abhorrent to the stern Yahwist.

[48] A. Alt, "Das Gottesurteil auf dem Karmel," *KS*, II, esp. 143–47. However, his division of the chapter into a trial tradition (18:17–40) and a rain-bringing tradition (18:2b–16, 41–46), originally entirely separate, is unnecessary since the story has reasonable coherence taken as a whole (Montgomery-Gehman, *op. cit.*, 135–36; D. R. Ap-Thomas, "Elijah on Mt. Carmel," *PEQ* 92 [1960], 146–55).

[49] This is well illustrated in Alalakh Texts No. 2:27–28 and No. 3.38–39. The latter is an extradition treaty between Idrimi of Alalakh and Pillia [of Kizzuwatna?] which reads: "In whatever city they proclaim a fugitive (to be), then the *hazannu* with five good men must declare the oath of the gods" (D. J. Wiseman, *The Alalakh Tablets*, 1953, pp. 27, 32, plates II, IV). The connection with I Kings 17:10–11 has been noted by A. Rainey, "Administration in Ugarit and the Samarian Ostraca," *IEJ* 12 (1962), 62.

On the other hand, he does not urge a program of Israelite imperialism, probably because he is no court prophet but a rural purist who struggles with the immediate crisis of a jeopardized monolatry.[50] It is his follower Elisha who enters more openly into political activity. Also, in theory Elijah should not have been opposed to treaties between the two Yahweh-worshiping states of Israel and Judah.

Anonymous Prophets

Several of the prophetic traditions in Kings are illuminative of the Aramean-Israelite wars during the Omrid dynasty. The theory that some or all of these stories should be transferred to the reigns of Jehoahaz or Joash under the Jehu dynasty only creates new problems while purporting to solve other, largely imaginary ones.[51] The stories remain best understood, either as stated or as implied, in the reigns of Ahab and Jehoram.

Chapter 20 of I Kings tells of an unsuccessful siege of Samaria by the Arameans and of a later victory over Aram in the following year at Aphek. In spite of legendary features, such as the enormous number of Syrian dead (vss. 29–30), the incidents can be placed in the reign of Ahab some months or years before the Battle of Qarqar in 853.[52] Until the successes of Israel against Aram at Samaria and Aphek, Omri and Ahab had been vassals of Damascus. With these successes Ahab was able to join the anti-Assyrian coalition with Damascus and Hamath as an equal partner.

Here and there political details show through the narrative. Ahab's "father" had been forced to cede cities (apparently in

[50] Elijah's severe claim for Yahweh's sufficiency is well expressed in his contemptuous retort to Ahaziah, "Is it because there is no God in Israel that you are going to consult Baal-Zebub, god of Ekron?" (II Kings 1:3).

[51] The arguments for shifting the stories from the Omrid to the Jehu dynasty have been presented, although with differing results, by A. Jepsen, "Israel and Damaskus," *Archiv fuer Orientforschung,* 14 (1942), 153–72, and Whitley, *op. cit.,* pp. 144–47. The essential outlines of the biblical data have been supported by Emil G. Kraeling, *Aram and Israel,* chaps. 6–9, and, more recently, by M. F. Unger, *Israel and the Arameans of Damascus,* pp. 70–74.

[52] So N. Snaith, *IB,* III, p. 166, and Unger, *op. cit.,* p. 67.

Bashan and Gilead) to Ben-hadad's "father," and the latter had established merchant quarters in Samaria as a part of the Syrian hegemony over the caravan traffic from Damascus to the port of Accho (vs. 34). If the passage is read literally, Omri is specified as the vassal, and, although this is seemingly inconsistent with Omri's expansion into Moab, the latter conquest would have been within Israel's vassal rights provided that the suzerain Damascus agreed. It is not impossible, however, that in this case "father" means loosely a predecessor, even of a different dynasty, and may refer to Baasha, who suffered considerable loss of territory to Damascus (I Kings 15:20); either he or Jeroboam may have been earlier humiliated by Tabrimmon or Hezion, father and grandfather respectively of Ben-hadad I.[53] If so, Omri may have retained the status of nominal vassalhood while expanding into Moab and arranging trade agreements with Tyre, biding his time for open revolt against Damascus.

Of particular interest in the account are the offhand references to the structure of the warring kingdoms. The attacking force of Syrians is said to consist of thirty-two kings headed by the king of Damascus (vs. 1). Aram was apparently a federation of local city-state rulers and chieftains who had been forced to accept the leadership of the strongest Aramean city in the region, namely, Damascus. The kings were not temporary allies or coerced vassals but representatives of the component units (city-states and tribes) of the Syrian kingdom, each leading a contingent of troops.[54] After the defeat of the Syrians, Ben-hadad reorganized his kingdom by replacing the kings with governors (vs. 24). The aim will have been to concentrate authority in his hands, especially to put the armed forces under a single command. External military pressure is thus seen to accelerate cen-

[53] Rezon, who is described as the leader of a successful Damascene revolt against Solomon, is probably to be identified with Hezion (I Kings 11:23; cf. I Kings 15:18). The incorrect form Rezon is probably a confusion with Rezin, king of Damascus in the eighth century (II Kings 15:37; 16:5; see Unger, *op. cit.*, p. 57).

[54] A. Alt, "Die Syrische Staatenwelt vor dem Einbruch der Assyrer," *KS*, III, 223–24, contends that the coalition of originally separate political units into a kingdom under the hegemony of Damascus alluded to in I Kings 20:1 was typical of Syria, for he finds the same pattern in Arpad and Hamath in the ninth and eighth centuries B.C.

tralization of a recently formed kingdom just as it earlier had affected Israel under Saul and David. By contrast, Israel is pictured as already centralized in a system of provinces (*medînôth*), each with its governor (*sar*), who had a select corps of trained soldiery, a knighthood (*ne'ārîm*) ready for instant service.[55] These are said to have numbered 232 and to have formed the elite unit directing the attack that broke the siege of Samaria (vss. 15, 17). The Samaria ostraca[56] show that in the late ninth or early eighth century the northern kingdom was already efficiently organized for the payment of oil and wine, either from crown land or from general taxation,[57] for the upkeep of the court at Samaria. It is possible that the produce from particular estates, villages, or fields was earmarked for the maintenance of specific officials. In any case, we can imagine that such an economic base for officialdom was at least partially a legacy of the Solomonic kingdom and that it was capable of supporting a sizable corps of civil and military officials.

Ahab's attitude toward Damascus was lenient but eminently prudent. He allowed the twice-defeated Syrian king to state his own terms of peace, with the clear understanding, of course, that he must offer concessions commensurate with his humiliating defeat. Ben-hadad accordingly stated minimal terms which were immediately accepted by Ahab: the return of the previously Is-

---

[55] The administrative officers of the kingdom, especially those in the provinces, are not clearly classified in the Old Testament; cf. Alt, "Der Anteil des Koenigtums am der sozialen Entwicklung," *KS*, III, 371–72. The term *sar*, for example, is used variously for heads of families or clans and for civil and military officers; cf. R. de Vaux, *Ancient Israel. Its Life and Institutions*, p. 69. In I Kings 20:14–15 *sar* is more likely to be a civil title (so de Vaux, pp. 69, 220, and Alt, p. 370) than a military one (so Montgomery-Gehman, *op. cit.*, p. 323, who point out that the provincial administrators are called *nitstsāvîm* in I Kings 4:7).

[56] The original publication of the texts was in G. A. Reisner, *Israelite Ostraca from Samaria*, n.d., and in revised form in Reisner, Fisher, and Lyon, *Harvard Excavations at Samaria*, 1924, pp. 227–46.

[57] The former proposal was made by M. Noth, "Das Krongut der israelitischen Koenige und seine Verwaltung. Die samarischen Ostraka," *ZDPV* 50 (1927), 211–14, followed by J. N. Schofield, *Documents from Old Testament Times*, 1958, pp. 204–6. The latter proposal, by Rainey, *op. cit.*, pp. 62–63, is regarded as a fresh and apparently feasible alternative to the "royal estate" theory by Y. Aharoni, "The Samaria Ostraca—An Additional Note," *IEJ* 12 (1962), 69.

raelite cities in the trans-Jordan and the grant of Israelite commercial quarters in Damascus. This did not necessarily require the expulsion of the Syrian traders from Samaria but rather more equitable terms for their continuation as a merchant enclave rather than as conquerors.[58] Such an enclave will have brought many commercial advantages to Samaria in the way of increased trade, and we can be sure that Ahab profited greatly from the tolls exacted from caravans passing through Esdraelon along the Damascus-Accho highway. *By any reasonable political and economic criteria Ahab had wisely handled the negotiations to the advantage of Israel for he had made a friend and profitable partner where he could not hope to be absolute master.*[59]

The attitude of the prophets toward Ahab's foreign policies, as described in I Kings 20:1–34, is sometimes characterized as unqualifiedly favorable in contrast to the hostile view of Elijah in I Kings 18–19, 21.[60] This, however, is a far too simple contrast. It is true that an unnamed prophet announced Ahab's victory over the besieging Arameans: "Do you see this great crowd? Behold I am giving it into your hand today so that you may know that I am Yahweh!" (vs. 13) and before the battle at Aphek a man of God declares that "because Aram claimed Yahweh to be a mountain God and not a valley God, therefore I will give all this great crowd into your hand so that you shall know that I am Yahweh" (vs. 28). Ahab inquires of the prophet as to the military means best suited to lift the siege: with which troops should he lead? and should he join battle at once or wait? The prophet here serves the purposes of military guidance formerly provided by the priestly lot (cf. I Sam. 14:19, 41; 23:9–13). The exclusive Judean control of the ephod and oracle led to the

[58] The existence of legally autonomous but militarily unsupported trading colonies in foreign lands is well illustrated by the Assyrian colonies in Asia Minor in the nineteenth century B.C., which are rather fully reported on in the Cappadocian texts from Kanish. Cf. G. Contenau, *Trente Tablettes Cappadociennes,* 1919; B. Landsberger, *Assyrische Handelskolonien in Kleinasien,* 1925.

[59] A. T. Olmstead, *History of Assyria,* p. 134; Unger, *op. cit.,* pp. 66–67.

[60] Snaith, *op. cit.,* p. 166. Jepsen, *Nabi,* pp. 90–91, concludes that the closeness of prophets to Ahab here related, and contradicted by chaps. 17–19, argues for the identification of the king in chap. 20 as Joash of the Jehu dynasty rather than Ahab.

emergence in north Israel of the *nābî'* as an actually more service-able oracle, and with this transfer went the ideology of the holy war formerly associated with the ark but now spiritualized as the fiery chariots and horsemen of Israel which only the prophets, or those they enlighten, are able to see (II Kings 2:12; 6:15–17; 13:14).

On the other hand, a third man described as "one of the sons of the prophets" bitterly excoriates the king for his failure to apply the rules of holy war in a thoroughgoing manner. When Ahab failed to execute the captive Ben-hadad, he forfeited the support of some of the very prophets who had promised him victory. *It is clear that the prophets were not consistently pro-monarchic or anti-monarchic. They championed the strict interests of the national god, and in the very military operations which they supported they could find reason to condemn a king who failed to follow out their wishes in all matters.* In fact, the prophets were not of a single mind on each issue; in a somewhat similar circumstance, Elisha favored sparing the lives of Syrian captives (II Kings 6:20–23). The reason for the differences of judgment in the two instances, however, is that Ahab's leniency with Ben-hadad may have resulted in a parity treaty between Israel and Aram, and thus a recognition of Aram's gods, whereas, in the release of the raiding party, there was no covenant involved.

How are these stories of the open activity of Yahweh prophets in the reign of Ahab to be reconciled with the Elijah traditions which show Yahweh prophets persecuted and in hiding (I Kings 18:3–4)? It is difficult to locate chap. 20 at the height of Jezebel's struggle against the Yahweh prophets in Samaria, but it may easily have preceded or followed Jezebel's attempted purge. If the intense Baal-Yahweh struggle for control of the state was concluded by Elijah's victory on Carmel in the early years of Ahab's reign, the Aramean-Israelite battles of Chapter 20 may reasonably be placed at a later date. Ahab will have called a halt to the open warfare between the two religious parties. The murder of a majority of the Baal cult personnel by Elijah will have left Baalism relatively weak. For the rest Ahab probably tolerated the Baal shrine in Samaria as the private chapel of his wife.

Yahweh will have been restored as the unequivocal national god. The Yahweh prophets were returned to royal favor and protection. In such an atmosphere of neo-nationalism the defeats of the Syrians were heralded by the Yahweh partisans.

Nevertheless the failure to apply strict principles of *ḥērem* and of non-alliance with foreign powers continued to irk some of the prophets. Probably Elijah shared essentially in this mixed viewpoint: satisfaction with the checking of Baal penetration and the victory of Israel over Aram, disappointment that the Baal cult was not wholly expunged from Israel and that alliances were permitted with Damascus and Tyre. *In sum, no sharp ideological difference between Elijah and the anonymous prophets of Ahab's reign can be confidently affirmed. At most we glimpse the difference between regularly consulted court prophets and rural free lances.*

Micaiah ben Imlah

The attack upon Ramoth-gilead in which Ahab lost his life seems to have come as a result of Ben-hadad's failure to return to Israel all or some of the trans-Jordan territories which he had promised.[61] According to the chronological note this attack occurred three years after the Battle of Aphek.[62] Between these events fell the Battle of Qarqar, in which Israel and Aram were allies. The sudden switches from Aramean-Israelite hostility to partnership and back to hostility seem abrupt but they are not without parallel in the shifting international tides of that time and place. After the Assyrians were repulsed from south Syria at Qarqar in 853 (see Map 16), they did not return until 849— which interval gave opportunity for old regional quarrels to flare up again. Ben-hadad perhaps relied on the recent Aramean-Israelite axis to atone for his failure to make full territorial restitution to Israel. In this hope he was mistaken, for Ahab decided to prod him with force.

Yahweh prophets encouraged Ahab in his righteous cause.

[61] Unger, *op. cit.*, p. 69.

[62] For attempts to place this date in the international chronology, see the bibliography in Montgomery-Gehman, *op. cit.*, p. 337 n.

They formed a four-hundred-voice chorus directed by Zedekiah ben Chenaanah: "Ascend to Ramoth-gilead and prosper; Yahweh will give it into the hand of the king!" The symbolic dance of Zedekiah with iron horns forecast and reinforced the victory of Israel for its strength will prevail over the enemy. No doubt we have a glimpse here of the circles which produced and preserved the nationalistic poetry of Balaam's Oracles, the Blessing of Moses, Jacob's Blessing, and Psalms such as 21–22, 61, and 83 (cf. the horn imagery of Deut. 33:17).[63] The prophetic chorus speaks only briefly here, but the terse story form has probably sacrificed the longer poetic declamations which normally celebrated such a preparation for battle.

Micaiah is not on the scene at the time for he does not share the general prophetic optimism, yet it is exceeding the evidence to regard him as one set apart from the court prophets in either position or rank. In all respects he is one of them, except that "he does not prophesy good concerning me [Ahab] but rather evil." As a result he sees only defeat for Ahab and decimation of a leaderless Israel, which he tersely casts in the imagery of a wandering flock without shepherd.[64] His vision of Yahweh's heavenly council and of a spirit who volunteers to lure Ahab to Ramoth-gilead would perhaps be clearer if we knew the ground of the prophetic attack upon Ahab. Unfortunately the basis of Micaiah's opposition to Ahab is not given.

If we were to conjecture, it probably lay in Ahab's refusal to follow through a total program of Yahwism by expelling Baal altogether and prosecuting an independent foreign policy of holy war and non-alliance. Micaiah may also have been deeply troubled by such inner Israelite breaches of covenant as the murder of Naboth. He was a political extremist who objected to compromise. He believed that if foreign powers were not defeated by an Israel unflinchingly loyal to Yahweh they would rise up to punish and to oppress a people only halfhearted in their

---

[63] *Ibid.,* p. 338.

[64] The relation of this vision to the call visions of other prophets, notably that of Isaiah, is important to note. Micaiah's vision may, indeed, have a kind of prototypical significance for later visions, as noted, for example, by I. Engnell, *The Call of Isaiah,* 1949.

dedication to him. As far as the story allows us to judge, Micaiah and the four hundred shared a considerable area of agreement, but the lone prophet was a rigorist in a situation where his colleagues were inclined to look upon Israel's military aspirations with somewhat uncritical favor. *All were "moralists" but they drew the line at different points.* The four hundred were willing to accept political vagaries and necessary deviations from the old Yahwism and to proclaim victory for the present Israel in the name of the ancient God. *Micaiah insisted that the ancient religio-political blessings entailed the ancient religio-political demands, that the one could not be invoked without submitting to the other.*

Elisha

Apparently at some time not long after the death of Ahab, Elijah passed on his historical task and religous authority to Elisha, who was almost immediately plunged into international affairs. Moab, which had been subservient to Omri and Ahab, revolted at the latter's death.[65] Jehoram, the son of Ahab, joined with Jehoshaphat of Judah in a campaign to reconquer Moab in approximately 849. Judah participated with Israel as an equal in the enterprise.[66] Jehoshaphat had a decided interest in keeping Moab in subjection to Israel inasmuch as he wished to maintain his own hold on Edom, and the trans-Jordan states tended to follow one another's example in compliance or in re-

[65] The apparent contradiction between the Moabite Stone's claim that Mesha revolted in the midst of Ahab's reign and the Old Testament's report that the revolt occurred after the death of Ahab (II Kings 1:1; 3:15) has been resolved in various ways, e.g., by assuming that the revolt actually began in the middle of Ahab's reign when he was occupied with Damascene and Assyrian affairs but that the withholding of tribute was not noticed by the biblical records until the time of his son Jehoram (Van Zyl, *op. cit.,* pp. 138–40), or by assuming that "Omri's son" in the Moabite Stone really means "grandson" and so refers to Jehoram rather than to Ahab (Bright, *op. cit.,* p. 228 n.) .

[66] If Judah was in an inferior position in Israel, it is surprising that Ahab should give his daughter Athaliah in marriage to Jehoram of Judah. Overlords did not customarily so honor their vassals. Furthermore, II Chronicles 17:2 pictures Jehoshaphat as fortifying garrisons not only in Judah but in Israel as well (cf. Bright, *op. cit.,* p. 222 n.).

volt. A rebellious Moab would inevitably weaken the Judean control of Edom. The king of Edom was impressed into the attacking force as the vassal of Jehoshaphat.[67]

The plan of attack devised was to skirt the Dead Sea to the south and to approach the Moabite capital of Kir-hareseth via the Wadi Zered (see Map 16). It was an arduous approach, requiring a steep descent into the Arabah and a difficult ascent onto the Moabite tableland.[68] It also involved logistic difficulties. The advantage of the plan lay in the factors of surprise attack and of Moabite vulnerability. Mesha had fortified his northern approaches in the region from the plains of Moab opposite Jericho to the Wadi Arnon,[69] but his southern flank was relatively undefended.

When the allied armies ran out of water within sight of the salt waters of the Dead Sea, they sought a prophet. Elisha was at hand, doubtless in somewhat the role of a military chaplain, much like the *baru* priests who accompanied Mesopotamian kings to battle. Elisha was contemptuous of Jehoram for he could not forgive him for being the son of Ahab. One wonders if the prophet had willingly accompanied the troops or was in fact a captive. Jehoram protested his belief in Yahweh in such vital matters of national security, but only the presence of Jehoshaphat persuaded Elisha to prophesy.[70] The prophet's unexpected friend-

[67] Any harmonization of what is said about the government of Edom in I Kings 22:47 and II Kings 3:9; 8:20–22 must remain problematic. If II Kings 3:9 is to be taken at face value, the following is probably the best reconstruction of events: As late as the reign of Jehoshaphat, Edom was ruled not by a king but by a governor appointed by Judah. This may well have represented a policy begun by David or Solomon. Late in Jehoshaphat's reign, at least by the time that Jehoram had come to the throne of Israel, a native prince was designated vassal king in Edom. A few years after that, in the reign of Jehoram of Judah, Edom revolted and either the vassal king or someone else was designated monarch. On the other hand, "the king of Edom" in II Kings 3:9 may be an anachronism when in fact it was still a Judean governor who was responsible for levying the Edomite troops that joined in the campaign. The former position is argued inconclusively by R. E. Murphy, "Israel and Moab in the Ninth Century B.C.," *CBQ* 15 (1953), 416–17.

[68] Some idea of the difficulty of travel through this region may be gained from D. Baly, *The Geography of the Bible*, 1957, pp. 31, 164–65, 238.

[69] Van Zyl, *op. cit.*, pp. 141–42.

[70] It is noteworthy that in two critical situations involving an alliance

liness toward the Judean king can perhaps be explained by the fact that Jehoshaphat was credited with Yahwistic religious reforms such as the removal of male cult prostitutes from Judah (I Kings 22:46). Furthermore, all of his foreign relations were either with the Yahwistic sister state of Israel or with states which he dominated, such as Edom and Philistia. Jehoshaphat, unlike several Judean kings before and after him, did not submit to any foreign power such as Damascus, and there were in fact no dynastic intermarriages to jeopardize Yahweh's sole position. The marriage of Ahab's daughter (or sister) Athaliah to Jehoshaphat's son, Jehoram, had not as yet borne the bitter fruit of Baalism in Judah and therefore, from Elisha's perspective, did not undermine the position of Yahweh as the only god of Israel and Judah. Elisha thus seems to have thought of Jehoshaphat as a reliable model of what an Israelite king ought to be: vigorous in the exercise of his powers but faithful to the old Yahwism.

Elisha directed the kings to dig trenches or cisterns in the wadi floor in order to trap the flash flood which he said would wash through it by morning (less likely with the intent of digging down to subsurface wells or streams).[71] Refreshed by the miraculous flow of water, the invaders, he insisted, would press on to capture the Moabite strongholds and to lay waste the countryside by cutting down trees, stopping up wells, and heaping stones on the fields. The water came as promised, probably rushing down from a localized cloudburst at the headwaters of the wadi. Nevertheless the campaign ended in frustration for the invaders, in spite of the lavish promises of Elisha. The Moabites were besieged in their capital. With a picked force the king tried to break through and escape to Aram,[72] but he failed to break the siege ring. He then resorted to the extraordinary measure of sacrificing his elder son

---

between Israel and Judah it is Jehoshaphat, the Judean, who takes the initiative in asking for a dependable Yahweh prophet (I Kings 22:5, 7, and II Kings 3:15). This certainly argues for the more discriminating piety of Jehoshaphat but does not necessarily indicate that Micaiah and other lone Yahweh prophets were from the south, as Guillaume, *op. cit.*, p. 143, seems to imply.

[71] Montgomery-Gehman, *op. cit.*, p. 361.

[72] Reading "Aram" in place of MT "Edom" in accord with the Old Latin, since MT ignores the fact that the king of Edom is among the besiegers.

in a ceremony on the city wall in the sight of the Israelites and Judeans. The impact of the deed upon the onlookers was so demoralizing that they could not press their advantage and, with that, "great wrath fell upon Israel," which probably refers to an invasion of Israel by the Arameans, who forced the disheartened Hebrews to withdraw from Moab.

The frank account of Elisha's brilliant success in divining the sudden flow of water and his gross error in prophesying Moabite defeat shows the struggle of the national gods Yahweh of Israel and Chemosh of Moab, which is reflected with equal naïveté in the victory stele of Mesha, probably written shortly before this campaign.[73] Although Chemosh is not named in the biblical account, it is taken for granted that the supreme devotion of Mesha in sacrificing his son had an adverse effect upon Israel. The reversal is described very interestingly in a neutral manner ("great wrath fell upon Israel") where one might normally expect that Yahweh would be described as the cause or agent of the wrath. In this account we see starkly reflected a henotheistic presupposition, even though it is not fully drawn. For the moment Yahweh is bested by Chemosh. Doubtless Israelite rationalization tended to explain the defeat as the consequence of Ahab's sins operative in the rule of Jehoram, and such may have been the motive of the Deuteronomist in reporting the story without comment. It is a story which shows quite clearly that while the Yahwism of these ninth-century prophets was an intensely practical monotheism, the power of Yahweh did not extend without hindrance into all lands. It was in the process of doing so, but the unexpected outburst of primitive religious feeling could evoke in an Israelite king and his army a frankly henotheistic experience, and the prophet was himself unprepared to cope with the savage power turned loose by a foreign deity.

Of particular interest is Elisha's intemperate summons to a scorched-earth policy, which accords with other allusions to the

---

[73] The Moabite Stone inscription was published by R. Dussaud, *Les monuments palestiniens et judaïques (Musée du Louvre)*, 1912, pp. 4–22. Competent translations are found in G. A. Cooke, *A Text-book of North Semitic Inscriptions*, pp. 1–14; *ANET*, pp. 320–21; and D. Winton Thomas, ed., *Documents from Old Testament Times*, 1958, pp. 195–98.

savagery of trans-Jordan warfare (cf. Amos 1:3, 13; 2:1). He calls for devastation of the countryside in disregard of the rule concerning conduct of holy war in Deuteronomy 20:10-20. All trees are to be felled, whereas Deuteronomy allows only the felling of non-fruit-bearing trees. The story of the Moabite campaign does not report the treatment of captives—whether they were spared whenever a city surrendered voluntarily (Deut. 20:10-11) or whether all males were put to the sword (Deut. 20:12-14). We may conclude from the Mesha stele that the ritual murder of captives was widely practiced in the Moabite-Israelite wars by both sides,[74] but whether it was always enforced cannot be determined. And whether Elisha was more or less lenient in his application of the code of holy war than other prophets or than prevailing custom cannot be easily judged. It is noteworthy that on a slightly later occasion he seems less extreme (II Kings 6:21-22), wheras the anonymous prophet who condemned Ahab for sparing Ben-hadad was stricter (I Kings 20:35-43), as Samuel had been in his insistence that Agag the Amalekite king must be ritually slaughtered (I Sam. 15:3, 32-33).

It seems that holy war entered Israel from its desert experience and was observed longer and more savagely in its wars with other semi-nomadic peoples, such as the Amalekites and Moabites, than with the more civilized peoples of Canaan and Syria. Increasingly the development of a professional army drawn from a civilian population led to an erosion of the homogeneous concept of a people at total war.[75] In this one respect at least the influence of Canaan had a humane effect upon Israelite culture. There was always, however, a tendency to relapse into the cruelties of holy war. The savagery of the wars and raids in trans-Jordan reflects apparently the surviving influence of the belief in holy war, according to which whole populations struggled with one another as the ritual combatants of deities and therefore deserved to live or to die as totalities. Even though both Israel and Aram had

---

[74] See esp. lines 15–19 of the Moabite Stone.

[75] The contrast between "a people under arms" and "a professional army" is well drawn by de Vaux, *op. cit.*, pp. 214–25, without oversimplifying the situation.

become heirs of the civilized methods and codes of warfare, when they struggled together they tended to fall back into their original semi-nomadic practices. It was this level of barbarism which especially shocked the prophet Amos, but which did not seem to have any fundamental effect upon the ninth-century *n*ᵉ*bîʾîm*, although they sought at times to mitigate its worst features.

The remainder of Jehoram's reign seems to have been occupied with wars against the Syrians, the latter taking the initiative in periodic raids and ambuscades (II Kings 6:8–23) and in at least one concerted siege of Samaria (6:24—7:20). The prophet continued to serve as a firebrand for Israel's cause against Damascus. His extensive contacts with prophetic guilds throughout Samaria supplied him with a ready-made communications system, which he exploited fully.[76] When Syrian raiding parties sought to ambush the king, Elisha had a way of hearing their whereabouts and warning Jehoram.

So unerring was the prophet's intelligence that the Syrians began to suspect they had an informer in their midst. Elisha was discovered at Dothan, which guarded the northern approaches to Samaria, and a band of troops was dispatched to capture him, but Yahweh struck them with blindness at the prophet's request. The party was led to Samaria where their sight was restored. The jubilant king was disposed to slay them on the spot, but Elisha reminded him of the terms of holy war, i.e., non-Canaanite captives are to be killed only when they belong to forces which have resisted an ultimatum to surrender (Deut. 20:12–14). Undoubtedly the prophet had the further motive of sparing the troop so that it could report at firsthand to the Syrian king concerning the power of Israel's God. At any rate it was no unmotivated act of mercy. Elisha adhered to the generally agreed-upon rules of war and sought at the same time to extract a psychological advantage from his generous act.

The siege of Samaria (apparently the "great wrath" of II

---

[76] Commentators have usually assumed that Elisha's clairvoyant powers are referred to in the narrative of II Kings 6:8–23 (cf., e.g., Guillaume, *op. cit.*, p. 307), but the simplest meaning of the text is that the prophet had intimate contact with a kind of "underground" that supplied him with quick information.

Kings 3:27) plunged the populace into such starvation that virtually inedible animal parts and products (such as an ass's head and pigeon's dung) were drawing exorbitant prices[77] and even cannibalism was resorted to.[78] Jehoram's frustration exploded in a rage against Elisha, who symbolized Yahweh's protection of Israel and who, as a stanch Yahweh partisan, insisted on holding out in the siege. The hardships of the siege and famine were laid at the prophet's door; impetuously, the king threatened to strike him down. Jehoram wanted to surrender, for he protested "this evil is Yahweh's doing and should I wait for him any longer?" (6:33). The prophet managed to persuade him that the siege would be lifted the very next day; meal and barley would be sold at a price many times less than the current price for an ass's head and a pigeon's dung.

Abruptly the Aramean army broke the siege and fled toward Damascus, leaving supplies and weapons scattered about. The circumstance is described thus: "the Lord caused the Syrians to hear the noise of chariots, the noise of horses, the noise of a great army, so that they said to one another, 'Behold, the king of Israel has hired against us Hittite kings and kings of Musri[79] to come against us.' " (7:6) It is difficult to know what credence to put in a detail which may be nothing more than a convenient legendary embellishment. The remark is suspicious in that normally at this period the former Hittite-dependent states of northern Syria were in sympathy with Damascus rather than at enmity,[80] but the alliances in this period were often transient, as is

[77] Plutarch, in *Artaxerxes XXIV,* reports that 60 drachmas were paid for an ass's head in time of famine. That would be about 15 shekels compared to the 80 (or 50 in LXX) in II Kings 6:25. During Ashurbanipal's siege of Babylon against Shamash-shum-ukin's revolt, grain on the black market sold for sixty times the regular price (Olmstead, *op. cit.,* p. 471).

[78] Cannibalism during sieges in the last years of the Assyrian empire is now well documented. Cf. A. L. Oppenheim, " 'Siege Documents' from Nippur," *Iraq* 17 (1955), 79 and n. 34.

[79] The location of Musri in northern Syria or Asia Minor is now generally accepted in place of its traditional identification as Egypt (cf. Alt, *KS,* III, p. 230; Montgomery-Gehman, *op. cit.,* pp. 227–28). For a recent defense of the traditional identification of Musri as Egypt, see H. Tadmor, "Que and Musri," *IEJ* 11 (1961), 143–50.

[80] E. O. Forrer, "The Hittites in Palestine," *PEQ* 68 (1936), 197, objected that the author of II Kings 7 was out of touch with historical reality for he

clear from the vacillation in Aramean-Israelite relations and in the later alliance of Damascus-led states against Zakir of Hamath.[81] It is possible that we have here a circumlocution for the report of an attack from the north which caused the Syrians to retreat hurriedly in order to protect Damascus. If so, the incident is an analogy to the "rumor" which Isaiah expected would cause Sennacherib to withdraw from Jerusalem (according to another of the prophetic narratives used by the Deuteronomist; II Kings 19:7). Yet for want of fuller knowledge of Syrian affairs at this time we cannot be more exact in our exposition of this intriguing allusion.

One of the strangest incidents in the prophetic tales is the audience of Elisha with Ben-hadad's officer, Hazael, in Damascus. *It is the sole instance of an Israelite prophet's addressing a foreign official in person on his own soil,* assuming of course that Jonah's appeal to the king of Nineveh is wholly legendary. The impression given by the story is that Elisha is in Damascus on his own business, perhaps as an itinerating healer visiting Israelite war captives or even on some mission of intelligence-gathering for the Israelite king. Ben-hadad, who had heard of Elisha's miraculous powers in healing his officer Naaman (supposing that incident occurred earlier, as reported in II Kings 5), inquired of the prophet whether he should recover from his own severe illness. Elisha answered with the weary perfunctoriness of Micaiah mumbling to Ahab, "You shall indeed recover!" but to Hazael he confided, "but Yahweh has revealed to me that he shall certainly die."

That which began as a simple intuition suddenly took on new significance when the prophet was overtaken by a trance which caused him to stare fixedly at Hazael, much to the officer's embarrassment, until the prophet gave vent to a flood of tears. Elisha explained that Hazael would bring terrible suffering upon Israel for "Yahweh has shown me that you are to be king over Syria." There is no evidence that Elisha advised Hazael to kill his ailing master or that he even so much as hinted at it. Perhaps

failed to realize that the "Hittite" states of north Syria were not grouped *against* Damascus at this time but *with* Damascus against Assyria.

[81] Montgomery-Gehman, *op. cit.,* p. 387.

while in Damascus he had heard of court machinations against the failing Ben-hadad. What concerned the prophet, however, was solely the effect of the new king's rule upon Israel. How the transition from Ben-hadad to Hazael would be effected did not interest him. It was Hazael who drew the conclusions and smothered his master. Elisha himself took no part in the cere-monial designation or investment of Hazael, for Yahwistic royal ritual would have had no meaning to an Aramean and the prophet would have refused any part in ceremonies invoking the Aramean god Hadad. To be sure, the impact of the prophetic vision with its weird demonstration of "concentration mysti-cism"[82] made a powerful impression upon Hazael so that, what-ever the prophet's actual intent, he did in fact prove to be a direct influence in the palace revolution. Hazael certainly found nothing in Elisha to discourage his own rising ambitions and much to inspire him to strike immediately.

The instigation of Jehu's revolt against Jehoram is attributed to Elisha in spite of the fact that the new king and the prophet do not directly meet in any of the biblical accounts. Elisha sent an underling to anoint one of the Israelite commanders at Ramoth-gilead, Jehu, as the next king. Only this simple proclamation ac-companied the act: "Thus says Yahweh, 'I anoint you king over Israel.' "[83] Elisha's own motivation in removing the Omrid dy-nasty is not stated. Jehu's attitudes are somewhat more fully alluded to. He objects that no peace is possible in a kingdom where "the harlotries [$z^e n\hat{u}n\hat{i}m$] and sorceries [$k^e s\bar{a}ph\hat{i}m$] of Jeze-bel are so numerous" (II Kings 9:22), which seems to refer figuratively to the queen's militant Baalism. The citation by Jehu of Elijah's earlier prophecy of doom over Ahab because of the king's complicity in the death of Naboth (II Kings 9:25–26; cf. I Kings 21:17–20) appears to be intrinsic to the narrative, as is

[82] This is the phrase of J. Lindblom, "Die Geschichte der Propheten," *Studia Theologica* 1 (1935), 7–28, which he contrasts with "absorption ecstasy," a totally non-Israelite phenomenon.

[83] In vss. 3 and 12, wherein Elisha first gives instructions to the prophetic anointer of Jehu and wherein Jehu reports to his fellow officers, only the short form of the designation formula appears. Thus, vss. 7–10a appear un-supported and take away much of the suspense of the succeeding story. Cf. Montgomery-Gehman, *op. cit.,* p. 400.

also the allusion to the prophesied death of Jezebel (II Kings 9:36; cf. I Kings 21:23). Whether I Kings 21 and II Kings 9 are from the same hand is problematic.[84]

Whether deliberately or otherwise, Jehu failed completely to understand the basis of Elijah's protest against the Omrids. Jezebel and Ahab had suborned witnesses to accuse Naboth falsely of cursing the king and thus to bring about his death. Naboth's coveted property then fell into the hands of Ahab since all property belonging to the heirless dead was subject to royal confiscation. Yet Jehu did not hesitate to represent himself falsely as a Baal worshiper in order to lure Baal devotees to their doom (II Kings 10:18–27). Nor did he shrink from the mass murder of all of Ahab's and Ahaziah's heirs in order to remove all possibility of blood revenge from the royal houses in Israel and Judah (10:1–17). In the establishment of a new dynasty the extirpation of the old was, of course, a frequent practice since the instability of dynastic succession was always a tormenting problem that required drastic measures. With what sincerity we cannot easily judge, but it is evident that Jehu publicized his new regime as the very embodiment of pure Yahwism; by means of his radical policies, Baalism was to be forever rooted out of Israel. Jehu invoked the prophecies of Elijah to justify his action against Ahab's house as the deserved judgment of Yahweh. In his own behavior, however, there was the inconsistency of indiscriminate slaughter of Ahab's partisans, including Yahweh worshipers and Baal worshipers alike. The fact that all the devotees of Baal in Israel could be easily gathered into the Samarian temple, itself probably not a large structure, shows that Ahab had indeed effectively checked the spread of Baalism and that it had remained simply an adjunct of foreign policy to meet the religious needs of the queen and her courtiers. It is hard to avoid the conclusion that Jehu either was blinded by his fierce fanaticism or was shrewdly employing the religious issue in a play for personal power. He was at any rate abetted in this by the prophets who first sponsored him and by the Rechabites who actually ac-

[84] D. Napier, "The Omrides of Jezreel," *VT* 9 (1959), 377–78, follows J. Skinner and I. Benzinger in regarding the two accounts as roughly contemporary but by different hands unfamiliar with each other's work.

companied him in his wild reign of terror (10:15–17).

By his wholesale assassinations, Jehu swept away the foreign alliances which entailed the danger of religious compromise; in this act he must have cheered many of the prophets. Israel stood alone now, without Tyre and Judah, and—more regrettably from a patriot's view—with Moab fully independent. But Israel could not dictate her own future apart from the other nations. The ignominy of foreign subservience could not be escaped indefinitely; it need not, however, have come as soon as it did. Early in his reign Jehu paid tribute to Shalmaneser III on his last campaign into southern Syria and thus, ironically, became the first Israelite king to be pictorially represented. He is shown on Shalmaneser's black obelisk[85] in the posture of submission before the Assyrian king, his face to the ground, accompanied by some of the finest products of Israelite craftmanship as tribute for his suzerain. The fact that other states in Syria—some considerably nearer to Assyria than Israel—did not submit to Shalmaneser at this time strongly suggests that Jehu made overtures to Assyria.[86] He sought, in other words, to find protection against surrounding states whom he had offended by his brutal rise to power. *If this natural interpretation of the evidence will stand, Jehu appears as a clever politician who used the prophetic objections to foreign alliances to establish himself, only to make such foreign alliances as he thought would best serve his own purposes.* In place of the Omrid dynasty's barter and limited struggle with equal or near-equal states such as Damascus, Jehu hoped to set up an Israelite hegemony in Palestine under the benevolent protection of Assyria.

Unfortunately for Jehu, his plan did not materialize. Shalmaneser made only one more strike at Damascus and it was indecisive (837). Thereafter he was occupied elsewhere than in Syria, and with his assassination in 824 revolt swept the empire. For about thirty-five years we hear of no Assyrian armies in the west. Hazael was free to press his designs on Israel. He attacked through the whole of trans-Jordan and conquered it as far as the Arnon in

---

[85] See the photographs of the obelisk in *ANEP*, pp. 120–22, and the translation of the inscription in *ANET*, p. 281.

[86] Olmstead, *op. cit.*, p. 141; Unger, *op. cit.*, p. 76.

Moab. By the time of Jehu's son, Jehoahaz, Israel was left with a pitiable force of only ten chariots, fifty horsemen, and one thousand men (II Kings 13:7).[87] Hazael was able to strike deep into Philistine territory, to attack Gath, and to gain control over the trade routes into Arabia (II Kings 12:17). Jehoash of Judah acknowledged his vassalage to Hazael by paying tribute (12:18). The plight of Israel was more desperate than it had been at any time under the rule of the Omrids.

One wonders at the silence of the prophetic traditions during this period. Stories of the avid partisanship of the prophets on behalf of Jehu are to be expected. The utter ineffectuality of Israelite arms against the rampaging Arameans may have driven them to silence, and yet, had they been as satisfied with Jehu's policies later as they were at the beginning of his rule, the deep plight of Israel would not have been enough to stop their mouths. The success of holy war did not depend upon numbers. The damaging factor must have been the increasing awareness that the "pure" Yahwism of Jehu's dynasty was not after all so unadulterated. All of his violence against Ahab's house and the Baal followers did not prevent the growing internal and external weakness of Israel. Capping it all was the recollection of Jehu's cynical summons to Assyria. Even Ahab had never submitted Israel to vassalage!

The only event to brighten prophetic hearts was the revulsion against Baalism in Judah which accompanied the overthrow of Athaliah and the installation of the boy-king Jehoash by the Yahweh priest Jehoiada. This incident is fully reported in a story, southern in origin, which knows nothing of the work of prophets in the uprising (II Kings 11).[88] It involved a popular national

---

[87] The MT reads "ten thousand infantry men," yet that same number contributed by Ahab to the coalition at Qarqar was as large as the contingent from Hamath. It is difficult to believe that such a large force of infantrymen would have been possible with a chariot force reduced to ten and a cavalry (or scouting) unit reduced to fifty; in short, the judgment that "the king of Syria had destroyed them and made them like dust at threshingtime" (II Kings 13:7b) seems grossly exaggerated in such a circumstance. Consequently, it seems best to assume that "one thousand" should be read in place of "ten thousand." Cf. Kraeling, *op. cit.*, p. 81, and Unger, *op. cit.*, p. 79, who depend in turn upon *Orientalistische Literaturzeitung* 1901, p. 144.

[88] A useful discussion of the character of this story and of the contrast

upheaval but was sharply distinguished from Jehu's uprising in that it signaled the return to the unbroken reign of the Davidic dynasty rather than the introduction of a new house. Consequently the bloodshed was limited to the execution of the usurping queen Athaliah and the chief priest of Baal Mattan. That no worshipers were executed suggests that Baal worship was limited to the immediate circle of the court and that all the princes who formally observed it under Athaliah's reign did so begrudgingly and only out of political necessity. Thus the deep internal scars inflicted on the northern state by the revolt of Jehu were avoided by the relatively bloodless coup of Jehoiada on behalf of the house of David.

Late in the reign of Jehoahaz, Adad-nirari III of Assyria carried out an attack upon Damascus (805), and thereafter the more frequent raids by Assyrian kings on Syria forced the Syrians to divert their attention away from Israel.[89] Jehoash was thus able to recover cities in trans-Jordan, aided by the death of Hazael, who was followed by a weaker ruler, Ben-hadad II.[90] The aged Elisha encouraged Jehoash in his wars of reconquest by directing the king to perform a symbolic act of arrow-shooting which the prophet explained as "Yahweh's arrow of victory, the arrow of victory over Aram!" (13:16). Yet even this prophetic boost was not unqualified, for the prophet expressed his disappointment in the king, who could have crushed Syria utterly but,

---

between the religious situation in north and south is given by Montgomery-Gehman, *op. cit.*, pp. 416–18.

[89] The anonymous "savior" of II Kings 13:5 by whom God delivered Israel from the Syrians is probably the Assyrian Adad-nirari III. If so, he is the first Assyrian king to be referred to in the biblical text (H. Schmoekel, *Geschichte des Alten Vorderasien*, p. 259 n.; B. Mazar, ed., *Views of the Biblical World*, vol. II, p. 272; and W. W. Hallo, "From Qarqar to Carchemish: Assyria and Israel in the Light of New Discoveries," *BA* 23 [1960], 42).

[90] There is no need to believe that the Ben-hadad of Baasha's reign (I Kings 15:18) was other than the Ben-hadad contemporary with the Omri dynasty (I Kings 20:1), whose throne name was Adad-idri (Albright, "A Votive Stele . . . ," and R. A. Bowman, "Ben-hadad," *IDB*, I, 381–82). The son of Hazael contemporary with Jehoash of Israel was thus Ben-hadad II, perhaps to be identified with the Mari of Damascus who paid tribute to Adad-nirari in 804 (R. de Vaux, "La chronologie de Hazaël et de Benhadad III, rois de Damas," *RB* 43 [1934], 512–18, and Montgomery-Gehman, *op. cit.*, pp. 436–37).

because of his little faith,[91] now would be able only to repel the
Syrians, not totally incapacitate them. With this incident, still reflecting the prophets' faith in the holy wars of Yahweh and their
simultaneous dissatisfaction with the wavering kings of Israel, the
prophetic traditions of the Omrid and Jehu dynasties come to a
close.

The Political Rigor of Ninth-Century Prophecy

*We have seen a fundamental tendency in the political outlook
of the ninth-century prophets. They were all sympathetic toward
the Israelite and Judean kings as the rulers of the people of Yahweh, whom they thought of as embracing the kingdoms of both
Israel and Judah.* There are no entirely clear instances of opposition between Israelite and Judean kings in these prophetic
narratives so we are unable to judge how they would have re-
acted to disputes between two Yahwistic states.[92] *The prophets
supported and some even incited and directed the kings in their
wars against foreign powers. They opposed alliances with foreign
states because of the danger of religious syncretism, which they
saw tragically exemplified in the encroachments of Baal in both
kingdoms.* Yet their intemperate opposition compelled them to
exaggerate the actually limited gains made by Baalism even under
Jezebel. They further objected to the formal acknowledgment
of foreign deities involved in the alliances with Tyre, Syria, and
Assyria.

The prophets were extremists in their insistence that Israel live
wholly by the ancient rules of holy war. Yahweh's power to deliver his people must be trusted even in the face of seemingly
hopeless odds. Yet the promise entailed certain responsibilities, for
there were Yahwistic cult and social rules to be observed by those
who wished to claim Yahweh's help. When Ahab took land by
false witness and murder, he invalidated himself as a true leader

[91] The refusal of the Hebrew king to take advantage of all the prophetic
resources in order to achieve victory or security is a feature which II Kings
13 shares with Isaiah 7; in the former case an omen is not fully exploited
and in the latter it is rejected altogether.

[92] But see the roles of Ahijah and Shemaiah in the split of the united
kingdom, *supra,* pp. 54–55.

of Yahweh's people. When Jehoram in his zeal attempted to impose *ḥērem* upon war captives in defiance of the established practice, he was cautioned for exceeding his mandate. But there seems to have been no single received body of rules so explicit as to exclude differing interpretations. An anonymous prophet condemned Ahab for failing to take the life of the Aramean king Ben-hadad when he came seeking terms of surrender, and Elijah executed the prophets of Baal, who were probably Tyrian nationals and should have had diplomatic immunity in Israel. It was the military weakness of Tyre, no doubt, which prevented that state from punitive action against Israel. Yet in his defense Elijah might well have argued that by intervening in local religious matters and proselytizing among Yahwists the Baal prophets had forfeited their extraterritorial rights.

Foreign relations were for these prophets entirely incidental to the welfare of Israel. Only as other states impinged directly upon the life of Israel were they thought worthy of consideration. This restricted outlook may explain the absence of any allusion in the prophetic traditions to the major imperialist of the time, Assyria. Such incentive as perhaps existed to refer to Assyria was cut short by the circumstances of Israel's relations with Assyria in the midninth century. Ahab entered parity alliances with several non-Yahwistic states, chiefly Damascus and Hamath, in order to repel Assyria, and Jehu callously submitted to Assyrian suzerainty in order to establish himself against the neighboring states. The one policy succeeded and the other failed, but in neither case did the prophets comment on what was to them a faithless action. Hazael's revolt in Damascus comes into the prophet's purview because that king served as an instrument for the threshing of Israel. Jezebel is of magnitude in the traditions because she imported her own religion and tried to make it the equal of or even the substitute for Yahwism.

As shapers of foreign policy the Yahweh prophets were thus of little practical help to kings. They presented a baffling contradiction of support and criticism which could not easily be translated into political policy. They wanted Israel to be great but not on the only terms which could have borne fruit in her situation, namely, by means of skillful alliance diplomacy. Although the prophets were powerful builders of morale who enabled Israelite kings to perform seeming wonders in extricating themselves from military disadvantage, they offered no basis for a long-range domestic and foreign policy. They were essentially negative in all that pertained to long-range policy. The indispensable ingredients of a successful foreign policy—ties with friendly neighboring states which would assure the acquisition of materials, commerce, and military assistance—were ideologically against their grain, unless these could be taken by force of arms in the name of Yahweh. Yet the latter course necessitated, from the prophet's point of view, a degree of Yahweh puritanism which no Israelite king was willing to embark upon and, from the king's point of view, superior resources of manpower which Israel did not possess as against the equally strong or stronger Aramean state at Damascus.

International relations for the ninth-century prophets meant largely either the sphere of Yahweh's effective power in enforcing the rule of Israel or the sphere of subtle and disastrous temptation to religious syncretism and compromise. The foreign power as the instrument of Yahweh's punishment is not nearly so evident a motif in these traditions as it is in the Deuteronomic outlook dominating the history as a whole. Nor is there any sign that foreign nations have laws which they are to observe because Yahweh has fixed them. At the utmost, individual foreigners, such as Naaman, could be won to belief in Yahweh and practice the Yahweh cult in his homeland.

In the clash between the practical political needs of the small Hebrew states and the grandiose schemes of religious faith arose the tension between king and prophet which continued in the period of the great classical prophets. This early delineation of the struggle between political responsibility and religious obligation was never wholly superseded, yet from Amos onward the issues were more openly joined and whole new dimensions of insight were achieved by the prophets—dimensions which only succeeded, however, in baffling even further the already confused Hebrew kings.

Map 14

OLD TESTAMENT PALESTINE

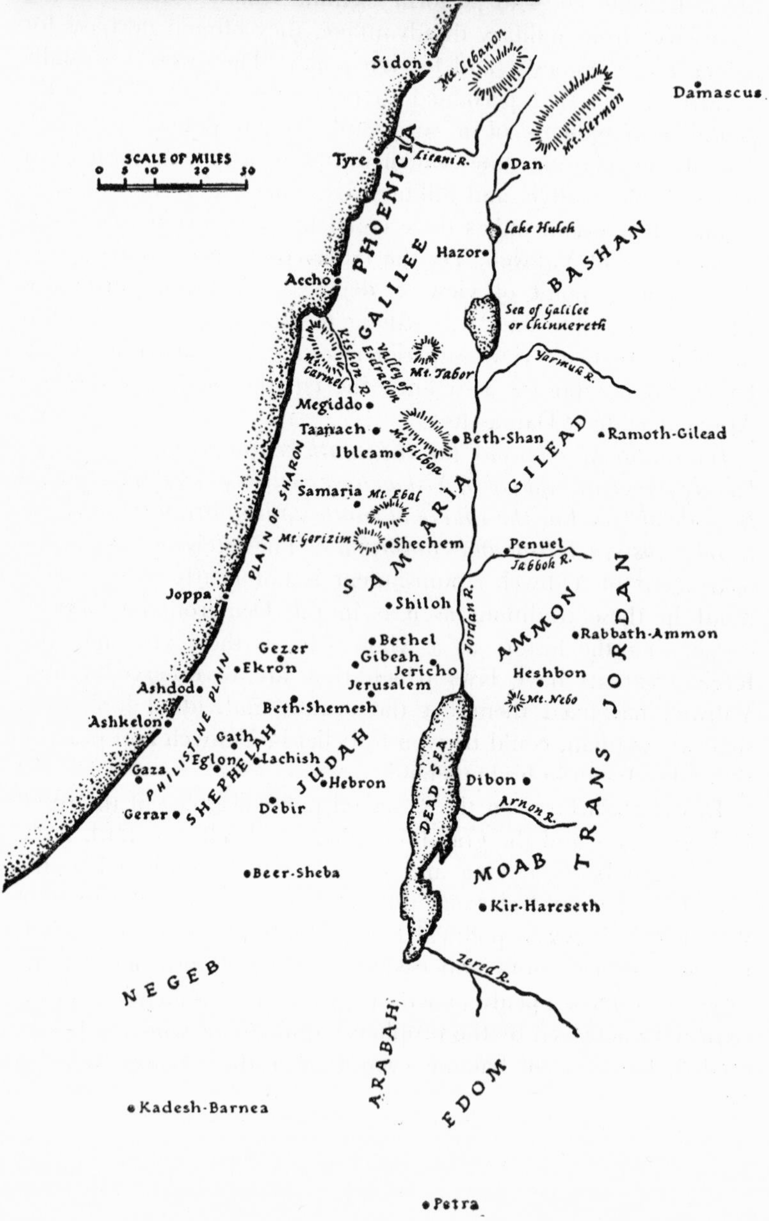

SCALE OF MILES
0 5 10 20 30
Sidon
Mt. Lebanon
Mt. Hermon
Damascus
Tyre
PHOENICIA
Litani R.
Dan
Lake Huleh
Hazor
GALILEE
BASHAN
Accho
Sea of Galilee or Chinnereth
Mt. Carmel
Kishon R.
Valley of Esdraelon
Mt. Tabor
Yarmuk R.
Megiddo
Taanach
Mt. Gilboa
Beth-Shan
GILEAD
Ramoth-Gilead
Ibleam
Samaria
Mt. Ebal
SAMARIA
PLAIN OF SHARON
Mt. Gerizim
Shechem
Penuel
Jabbok R.
Joppa
Shiloh
Jordan R.
AMMON
Rabbath-Ammon
Gezer
Bethel
Gibeah
Ekron
Jericho
Heshbon
Ashdod
Jerusalem
Mt. Nebo
Beth-Shemesh
Ashkelon
PHILISTINE PLAIN
Gath
Eglon
Lachish
JUDAH
Gaza
Hebron
DEAD SEA
Dibon
SHEPHELAH
Debir
Gerar
Arnon R.
TRANS JORDAN
Beer-Sheba
MOAB
Kir-Hareseth
Zered R.
NEGEB
ARABAH
EDOM
Kadesh-Barnea
Petra

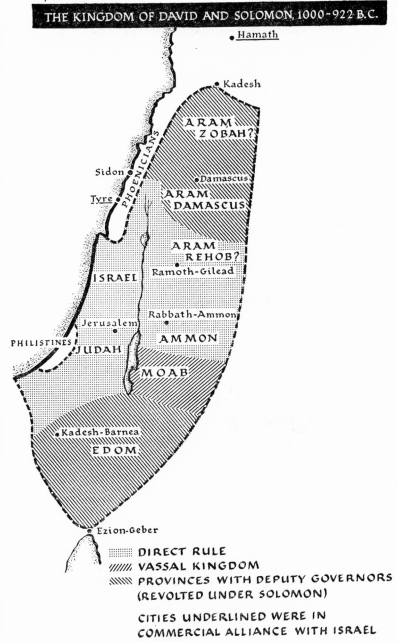

Map 15

THE KINGDOM OF DAVID AND SOLOMON, 1000~922 B.C.

• <u>Hamath</u>

• Kadesh

ARAM ZOBAH?

Sidon •

PHOENICIANS

• Damascus

<u>Tyre</u> •

ARAM DAMASCUS

ARAM REHOB?

ISRAEL

Ramoth-Gilead •

Rabbath-Ammon •

Jerusalem •

PHILISTINES

AMMON

JUDAH

MOAB

• Kadesh-Barnea

EDOM

• Ezion-Geber

DIRECT RULE
VASSAL KINGDOM
PROVINCES WITH DEPUTY GOVERNORS
(REVOLTED UNDER SOLOMON)

CITIES UNDERLINED WERE IN
COMMERCIAL ALLIANCE WITH ISRAEL

Map 16

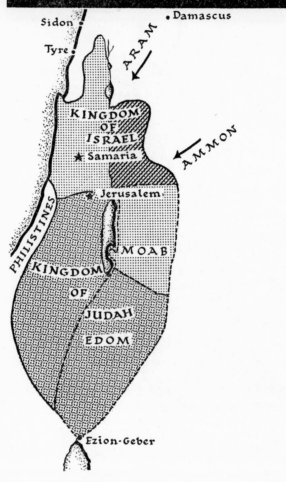

THE DIVIDED KINGDOMS, 922~800 B.C.

Sidon

• Damascus

Tyre •

ARAM

KINGDOM OF ISRAEL

★ Samaria

AMMON

PHILISTINES

★ Jerusalem

MOAB

KINGDOM OF JUDAH

EDOM

• Ezion-Geber

REVOLTED FROM JUDAH AFTER 850 B.C.

REVOLTED FROM ISRAEL AFTER 850 B.C.

TRANS-JORDAN TERRITORY LOST TO ARAM AND AMMON AFTER 838 B.C.

Map 17

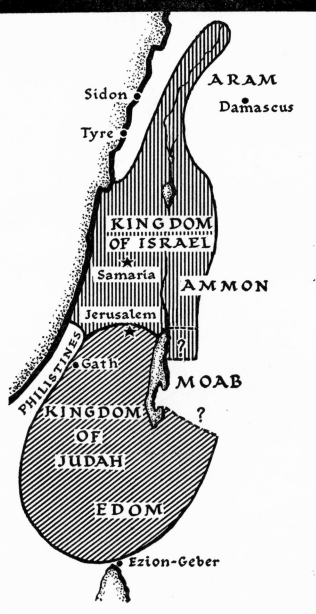

THE DIVIDED KINGDOMS, 750 B.C.

ARAM

Sidon

Damascus

Tyre

KINGDOM
OF ISRAEL

Samaria

AMMON

Jerusalem

PHILISTINES

?

Gath

MOAB

KINGDOM
OF
JUDAH

?

EDOM

Ezion-Geber

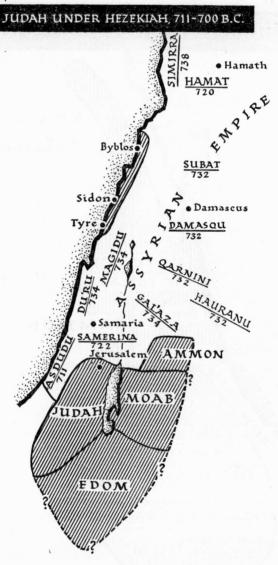

Map 18

JUDAH UNDER HEZEKIAH, 711~700 B.C.

SIMIRRA
738

● Hamath

HAMAT
720

E M P I R E

Byblos ●

SUBAT
732

Sidon ●

● Damascus

Tyre ●

DAMASQU
732

A S S Y R I A N

DURU
734

MAGIDU
734

734

QARNINI
732

● Samaria

GAL'AZA
734

HAURANU
732

ASDUDU
711

SAMERINA
722

Jerusalem ●

AMMON

JUDAH

MOAB

EDOM

?

?

?

?

UNDERLINED ASSYRIAN PROVINCES
WITH DATES OF INCORPORATION

TRIBUTARY BUT INDEPENDENT KINGDOMS
AND CITY-STATES

Map 19

JUDAH UNDER JOSIAH, 640-612 B.C.

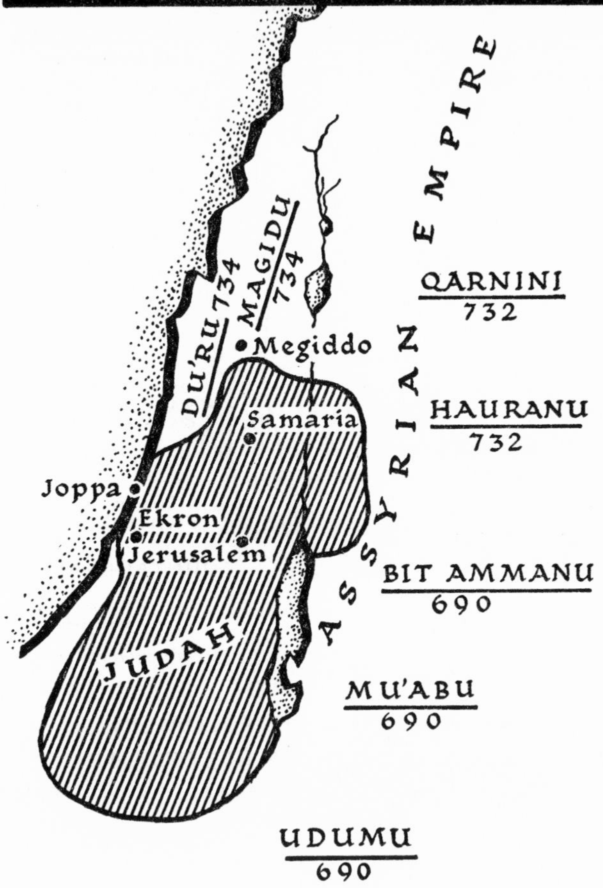

REVIVED KINGDOM OF JUDAH UNDER
JOSIAH, 640-609 B.C.
UNDERLINED ASSYRIAN PROVINCES
UNTIL 612 B.C.

Map 20

OLD TESTAMENT JERUSALEM

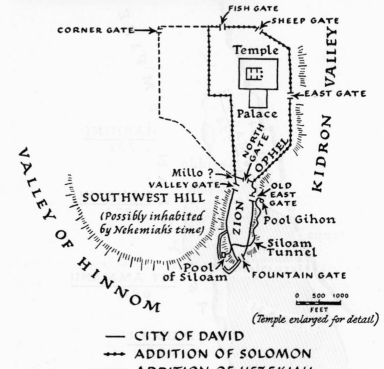

FISH GATE

SHEEP GATE

CORNER GATE

Temple

KIDRON VALLEY

EAST GATE

Palace

NORTH GATE

OPHEL

Millo ?

VALLEY GATE

SOUTHWEST HILL
(Possibly inhabited
by Nehemiah's time)

ZION

OLD EAST GATE

Pool Gihon

Siloam Tunnel

Pool of Siloam

FOUNTAIN GATE

VALLEY OF HINNOM

0   500   1000
FEET
(Temple enlarged for detail)

— CITY OF DAVID
••• ADDITION OF SOLOMON
═ ADDITION OF HEZEKIAH
--- ADDITION BY TIME OF NEHEMIAH

CHAPTER III

Israelite Prophecy and International
Relations in the Eighth Century

The latter half of the eighth century marked Israel's full initiation into international relations. In the ninth and early eighth centuries Assyria had occasionally penetrated into central and southern Syria (see Map 10), but from 745 onward she advanced repeatedly into southern Syria and Palestine (see Map 18). Year after year the campaigns of Tiglath-pileser, Shalmaneser, Sargon, and Sennacherib struck relentlessly against the western sections of the empire and reached deep into traditionally Hebrew territory. At last Israel was engulfed and Judah was reduced to vassalage.

In this chaotic milieu the prophetic paradox of total destruction and total rebirth (eschatology) was born. The single most momentous immediate historical factor was the introduction by Assyria of the systematic deportation of captive populations and their transplantation to distant parts of the empire. The grim prospect of a root-and-branch destruction of Hebrew culture stamped the threatening message of the prophets with dread realism. At the same time, by the curious alchemy of Israelite faith, the growing premonition that Israelite political life was to undergo drastic alteration—even outright annihilation—shaped the crucible for new forms of hope. It is not extravagant to claim Tiglath-pileser III, fashioner of the Assyrian deportation policy, as the father of Israelite eschatology. Only when total obliteration of Hebrew culture and political autonomy seemed assured was radical prophetic eschatology forged out of the elements of the older naïve nationalistic hope.

Amos

Amos deliberately places "the entire family which I [Yahweh] brought forth from the land of Egypt" among "all the families of the earth" (Amos 3:1–2). This notion of a broad international context is determinative for the prophet. Israel's fundamental similarity to all the other peoples of the ancient Near East is one of the two chief presuppositions of his thought. The other is the distinctive relation between Israel and her God, who "has known only you [Israelites]."[1] No view of Amos can be sustained which sacrifices one or the other of these fundamental articles of his belief. Yet their reconciliation is no small problem, particularly since on the surface they appear to be irreconcilable opposites. Either Israel is unique *or* she is like the other peoples. Either Yahweh treats her in a special way *or* he does not. Either the other nations exist solely as enemies or momentary means of punishment for Israel *or* they have intrinsic significance for Yahweh and thus for the prophet.

The Political Horizons of Amos' Thought

Preliminary to a serious analysis of the prophet's conception of Israel among the nations must be an accurate delineation of the horizons of his political knowledge. What is the extent of Amos' "earth" and who are "all the families" which populate it? *It is striking that the nations are not left as a nameless, formless back-*

[1] E. Sellin, *Geschichte Israels*, pp. 173–74, translates 3:2 "Have I known you of all peoples of the earth?" and thus eliminates the doctrine of Israel's election from Amos. But this is unjustified since in 2:5–19 Israel receives more attention than all the other nations combined. Thus "vs. 2a is entirely true but not the entire truth" (J. Rieger, *Die Bedeutung der Geschichte fuer die Verkuendigung des Amos und Hosea,* p. 39).

ground to Israel's election but are singled out and even given prominence. In the main these peoples are the immediate neighbors of Israel: the Aramean kingdom of Damascus (1:3–5); the Philistine city states of Gaza, Ashdod, Ashkelon, Ekron (1:6–8), and Gath (6:2); the Phoenician seaport and mercantile center of Tyre (1:9–10); the trans-Jordan kingdoms of Edom (1:6, 9, 11–12?; 2:1), Ammon (1:13–15), and Moab (2:1–3).

All these states had been in direct and largely hostile contact with Israel and Judah during the two centuries preceding Amos, dating from the victories of David (see Map 15), who had conquered all of them (II Sam. 8:1–14; 10; 12:26–31) with the exception of Tyre, with which he formed profitable trade agreements (II Sam. 5:11–12). The mere naming of these close neighbors of Israel hardly establishes the scope of Amos' international vision. Everything depends upon what is said about them. Indeed, according to one interpretation already appended to the close of the book (9:11–12), the prophet's interest in these peoples was an exclusively national one, for the writer expects a revived Davidic dynasty, perhaps incorporating both kingdoms, "to possess the remnant of Edom and all the nations on which my name [Yahweh's] has been called"; i.e., the former conquests of David in the name of Yahweh are to be reclaimed by Israel. If this passage, standing at the end of the book, is the key to the prophet's view of the nations, there can be little doubt of the subsidiary role of the nations. Before this interpretation is accepted, however, we must test it against the total interest of Amos in the nations.

In addition to kingdoms traditionally bordering on Israel or Judah (see Map 17), Amos names the Aramaic kingdom of Bit-Adini (1:5), located between the Habor River and the great bend of the Euphrates;[2] the apparently mixed Arameo-Hittite

---

[2] The identity of "the holder of the scepter in Beth Eden" in Amos 1:5 is not certain. He is possibly Ahuni, the Arameo-Hittite ruler of Bit-Adini who was captured by Shalmaneser III in 857–855 (W. W. Hallo, *BA* 23 [1960], pp. 38–39), or Shamshi-ilu, the Assyrian governor of Bit-Adini who during the reign of Shalmaneser IV in 783–773 exercised power as a virtual petty king (A. Malamat, *BASOR* 129 [1953], pp. 25–26). The sudden inclusion of this rather distant Aramean kingdom when Damascus alone has been the subject of the oracle is unexpected, and it is not surprising that

kingdom of Calneh (6:2),[3] approximately midway between
Carchemish on the Euphrates and the Mediterranean; and the
Aramean kingdom of Hamath (6:2),[4] the nearest state to the
north of Israel's boundaries as restored by Jeroboam II (II Kings
14:25). He knows of Egypt, not only as the traditional place
of Israel's origin (2:10; 3:1; 9:7), but also as a contemporary
power with interests in Palestine-Syria (3:9). The Greek version
of the Old Testament seems correct in finding Assyria explicitly
named as the Mesopotamian counterpart to Egypt (in 3:9, in
place of "Ashdod" which forms a very unequal political parallelism to the kingdom of the Nile), and, while the enemy of 3:11
may still conceivably allude to Egypt as well as to Assyria (although the singular "enemy" suggests that Amos had one particular power in mind), the "nation" of 6:14 which will oppress
Israel from its far northern to its far southern boundary (reading
"Brook of the Willows" in Moab instead of the vague "Brook of
the Arabah"—cf. Isa. 15:7)[5] will strike from the north. The

---

many commentators have preferred to locate Beth Eden northeast of Damascus at Jib Edin (G. Hoffmann, *ZAW* 3 [1881], p. 17). But the LXX of
Amos 1:5, ἐξ ἀνδρῶν χαρραν already connected Beth Eden with the area
around the upper Habor River. Perhaps the reason for the mention of Bit-
Adini was its alliance at the time with Damascus, possibly through marriage,
as may have been the case at an earlier period with Gozan on the Habor
River and Damascus (M. F. Unger, *Israel and the Arameans of Damascus,*
pp. 56, 141–42).

[3] The identification of Calneh with the north Syrian *Kullani* is in full
accord with the other cities mentioned here (Hamath and Gath) and in
Isaiah 10:9 (Carchemish, Hamath, Arpad, Samaria, Damascus); it is not
the Calneh of Genesis 10:10, associated with cities in Assyria (Nineveh,
Rehoboth-Ir, Resen).

[4] Although the form Hamath-Rabbah, "Great Hamath," is unique, there
can be no doubt that this is the well-known city on the Orontes River in
central Syria. It is perhaps designated as Rabbah to distinguish the capital
from the kingdom or from a smaller city of the same name or from its own
suburbs also called Hamath, in a manner somewhat analogous to although
not identical with the construction Rabbath Benei-Ammon, the chief city
of the Ammonites (II Sam. 12:26–27).

[5] The *naḥal haʿărābāh* is not otherwise attested and should probably be
changed to *naḥal hāʿărābîm,* a wadi on the northern boundary of Moab
(cf. Isa. 15:7) and apparently the point to which Jeroboam pushed the
frontier of Israel (II Kings 14:25). In fact, this threat by Amos is a scornful
reversal of the promise of Jonah ben Amittai that Jeroboam would "restore
the territory of Israel from the entrance of Hamath to the Sea of the
Arabah."

threat of an exile "beyond Damascus" (5:27) further localizes the enemy, even though the primary force of the designation is not precisely geographical but rather psychological: this time you will have to face an enemy more distant and dangerous than the customary Damascus! "Prepare to meet your God, O Israel!" (4:12c).

That the encounter with Yahweh is none other than the encounter with Assyria is clear from the ease with which Amos can speak on behalf of Yahweh in either of two ways: mediately, "I will raise up against you a nation" (6:14), or *immediately,* "I will rise against the house of Jeroboam with the sword" (7:9) or "I will take you into exile beyond Damascus" (5:27). So emphatically is the attack of the enemy asserted to be the work of Yahweh that the agent may fall from view and only the stark terror of Yahweh's judgment stands forth.[6] This focus may partially explain the failure to name Assyria more often as the means of judgment either on the nations at large or on Israel in particular.

As to the extent of Amos' knowledge of Assyria, much depends upon the date we assign him. Older chronologies found it possible to place Amos within the first years of the reign of the Assyrian king Tiglath-pileser III.[7] This reckoning meant that the prophet was aware of the sudden military and political renaissance which this king effected after a half-century of Assyrian weakness. Specifically it meant that Amos knew of his policy of transplanting large segments of conquered populations from one region of the Assyrian empire to another. Therefore the hammer-

---

[6] For numerous instances of the *direct action* of Yahweh in punishment of Israel, so that the historical agent drops from view, and for the implications for the Israelite view of God, see H. Fredriksson, *Jahwe als Krieger. Studien zum alttestamentlichen Gottesbild,* 1945, pp. 23–27; N. K. Gottwald, *Studies in the Book of Lamentations,* pp. 73–76; and esp. R. Volz, *Das Daemonische in Jahwe,* 1924.

[7] Amos' public appearance was dated in 745 or 744 B.C. and connected with the rise of Tiglath-pileser III by H. Zeydner (1886) and J. J. P. Valeton (1894). Recent scholars who placed his work after the rise of the great Assyrian conqueror are N. Snaith (745–744 B.C.; *Notes on the Hebrew Text of the Book of Amos,* 1946, II, 8–9), A Lods (probably 744–743; *Histoire de la littérature hébraïque et juive,* 1950, p. 231), and R. S. Cripps (742–741; *A Critical and Exegetical Commentary on the Book of Amos,* 2nd ed., 1955, pp. xxi–xxiii).

like stress of Amos on "exile" was often thought to follow directly from his knowledge of Tiglath-pileser III. More recent chronological studies, in spite of many differences among themselves, generally agree in denying any overlap in the reigns of Jeroboam II of Israel and Tiglath-pileser.[8] So firmly is Amos associated with the reign of Jeroboam, not only explicitly (1:1; 7:7–13) but also implicitly—since the political disintegration of subsequent Israelite reigns is nowhere apparent in the book—that it is impossible to shift the bulk of his prophecies to a later date. Nor is there any evidence that at some subsequent date Amos or another has "touched up" the threatening descriptions of exile.

In reality the descriptions of exile hover uncertainly between known practices and merely traditional threat formulas. Admittedly it is only with Amos that the threat of exile leaps suddenly to prominence in biblical writings. There is in fact no certain pre-Amosean usage of the root *glh* in the sense of a deportation of considerable elements of a population. Not that previous ages were ignorant of the forced dislocations of population brought about by war. The Ammonite captives who served in David's labor corps probably worked in various parts of the Israelite kingdom and thus were forcibly removed from their homeland (II Sam. 12:31). The use of *glh* in the sense of slave-trading appears in the oracles of Amos against the Philistine cities (Amos 1:6) and against Tyre (1:9), which are condemned for turning over "an entire captivity" or "a peaceful [i.e., non-combatant] captivity" to Edom (probably the population of particular border towns).[9] The apparent meaning of *galuth* in this case is forced removal of a person from his home.

[8] Among recent chronological computations, W. F. Albright dates Jeroboam II, 786–746; J. Begrich, 787–786 to 747–746; S. Mowinckel, 790–789 to 749–748; and E. Thiele, 793–753. On any of these reckonings Jeroboam was dead before the accession of Tiglath-pileser in 745.

[9] A. Neher, *Amos. Contribution à l'étude du prophétisme,* pp. 53, 61, offers a unified reconstruction of the interstate relations lying behind the oracles in chaps. 1–2. Aram (1:3) and Ammon (1:13) attacked Gilead from north and south and, taking advantage of the situation, Edom invaded Judah and Israel (1:11). Hebrew refugees fled to Phoenicia (1:11) and to Philistia (1:9) for asylum but were turned back into the hands of the Edomites. Aside from the nebulous charge against Edom which raises the question of its authenticity, it may be doubted that an Edomite attack was

The Philistine and Phoenician cities were strategically located to receive a steady flow of war captives from the Syro-Palestinian interior, not alone or even chiefly from their own conquests but from the spoils of other peoples. Among the chief buyers from Phoenicia and Philistia were the Edomites, whose land was a natural outlet to Africa and south Arabia by way of the Gulf of Aqaba and the overland routes (Amos 1:6, 9).[10] Edom was also the natural supply point for slaves to work in the mines of the Arabah, an operation which must have demanded constant replacements since the work was arduous and the heat intense.[11] The adjective "entire" or "whole" (or possibly "peaceful" or "non-resisting") underlines the large-scale operations involved, but there is nothing in the usage to suggest that the exile described is politically motivated. Rather, it is clearly a matter of economic gain. The persons captured in war are treated as lucrative booty. Doubtless such decimation of the population left the raided or conquered cities in a weaker condition and even permitted the victorious peoples to encroach on the sparsely settled territories. But this seems to have been a side effect and not of importance in comparison with the economic gain. It remained for the Assyrians to make political as well as economic capital of deportation policies which had hitherto been employed in a haphazard and shortsighted manner.

Tiglath-pileser III is indelibly connected with the inauguration of the deportation of conquered populations as a studied policy. Under his tutelage, deportation became actually a program of colonization. Previously the great empires had practiced deportation in the sense of carrying off rebellious leaders or interning their sons in the imperial court, in part as hostages and in part as loyal heir apparents to vassal thrones.[12] In a few instances, in

so overpowering that it forced Israelites to leave their own territory to find asylum in Philistia and Phoenicia.

[10] A. Kapelrud, *Central Ideas in Amos,* p. 23.

[11] I. Mendelsohn, *Slavery in the Ancient Near East,* pp. 92–99, notes that state slaves in Israel were employed to work the crown lands and to supply the mines of Arabah with unskilled and expendable labor.

[12] The Assyrians normally executed or deported rebellious vassal kings (A. T. Olmstead, *History of Assyria,* pp. 85, 88, 144, 161) although there are some outstanding exceptions (*ibid.,* pp. 377, 416). In the reigns of

particularly disturbed periods, the total population of a town or city was carried into exile.[13] Indeed, Assyrian kings before Tiglath-pileser had deported occasionally in this manner.[14] *The new element was the deliberate exchange of populations among various conquered regions with a view to the prevention of revolt and to permanent colonization.*

It is usual to emphasize the punitive character of the deporta-tions, and they surely were punitive. The results were often cruel to the deportees and at least temporarily destructive to the terri-tories suffering abrupt and extensive population changes. Espe-cially where semi-nomadic Arab and Aramean tribes were intro-duced into settled regions there was economic and cultural retrogression. Generally, however, such backward elements were mixed with other peoples possessing technical skills and sedentary experience. Inevitably, in some instances more advanced popula-tions had a salutary effect on less developed regions. It seems that the Assyrians were not oblivious to the talents which they skimmed from the leadership of their subjects. The Israelites Pekah and Nedabiah, who appear in the court of Sennacherib as the high officers *rab alani* and *mukil apate* respectively, and the Israelite officials Neriah and Pelatiah at Gozan on the Habor River were presumably not exceptions.[15] Deportees with

Esarhaddon and Ashurbanipal and during the Egyptian New Kingdom the sons and relatives of vassal kings from Syria and Palestine were regularly brought up in the Egyptian court—a process advantageous culturally for the vassals and politically for the pharaoh (G. Steindorff and K. C. Seele, *When Egypt Ruled the East,* p. 106).

[13] An example of the carrying off of a total urban population is reported in the fourteenth-century treaty of Suppiluliumas, the Hittite suzerain, and Mattiwaza, the Mitannian vassal (see discussion by E. F. Weidner, *Politische Dokumente aus Kleinasien,* pp. 6–15). The treaty shows, however, that the normal practice was to deport only the rebels, whether local kings or the *mariyannu,* i.e., the Mitannian nobility who incited the local leadership to revolt.

[14] For example, already in the mid-ninth century Ashurnasirpal settled Arameans in Nimrud (D. J. Wiseman, *Iraq* 14 [1952], 25–27); see also Olmstead, *op. cit.,* p. 164), and Shalmaneser carried off the restless popula-tion of Paqarahbuni in Syria.

[15] For Sennacherib's Hebrew officials see C. H. W. Johns, *Assyrian Deeds and Documents,* 2nd ed., 1924, vol. I, no. 234, 11. 8–9, and for Hebrew officials at Gozan see L. Waterman, *Royal Correspondence of the Assyrian Empire,* 1930, vol. I, no. 633. There are, of course, quite a number of

abilities were rewarded by the provincial administrations of their new homelands. Allowing for some rhetorical exaggeration, the Rabshakeh was able to present deportation to the defenders of Jerusalem in 701 as an economically desirable fate (Isa. 36:17). Certainly the economic and social condition of Assyrian-administered Israel was not worse and it was probably in many ways better than the Israel of the years from the death of Jeroboam to the fall of the state.

Amos shows no signs of knowing of deportation in this latter highly developed sense. He sees the exile as a radical one and thus probably on an even larger scale than the *galuth* described in the indictments of Philistia and Phoenicia. Apparently all survivors of the military attack upon Israel will be removed from the land, but this may not be a very large group since the majority of the populace will have fallen already in battle (Amos 5:3). The exile of the entire town of Gilgal is less an exact prediction than a word play on the name of the town (*haggilgāl gālōh yigleh*—5:5). *The advance beyond the usual depredations that Israel has suffered is reflected in the expected exile of king and high priest so that the basic institutions of the northern kingdom will cease to exist.* But as to whether this resulting void in Samaria will be filled by other peoples, much less those transferred there by the conquerors, there is no inkling. Non-Israelite peoples are not pictured as possessing the sadly devastated land.

The intense theological interest of Amos in the chosen people may well explain the gap in his thought with respect to events which are to follow the destruction of Israel. He may have held more precise views about the fate of the land after its conquest, but if, for example, he expected it to be made into an Assyrian province, he does not say so, since for him and for Israel—by that time utterly destroyed—it will not matter. In short, there is nothing in Amos' account of Israel's future fate which could not

---

probable and possible north Israelite names in the late eighth and seventh centuries which appear in upper Mesopotamia (see H. G. May, *BA* 6 [1943], 55–60; J. B. Segal, *Iraq* 19 [1957], 139–45; W. F. Albright, *BASOR* 149 [1958], 33–36; E. Loewenstam, "Gozan," *Biblical Encyclopedia*, I [1954], col. 454 [Hebrew]; A. Malamat, "Assyrian Exile," *Biblical Encyclopedia*, I [1954], col. 302 [Hebrew]). These names, however, cannot be certainly identified as members of Assyrian officialdom.

have been derived from his knowledge of current practices in Assyria during her ninth-century expansion into north and central Syria under Ashurbanipal and Shalmaneser III. *Nothing in his prophecies requires us to think that Tiglath-pileser was already on the Assyrian throne, yet this intuition of what was to come was startlingly accurate.*

Yet this clear coincidence of chronology and the content of the prophecies does have important consequences. It shows that Amos sounded his threats at an utterly improbable time. Assyria, under three weak monarchs in the first half of the eighth century, was by 750 so hard pressed by Urartu from the north and the Arameans from the south and west that the leaders of Israel could be forgiven for thinking that Assyria had ceased as a relevant factor in Syro-Palestinian politics. Egypt was suffering the death throes of the weak Libyan dynasty (XXII); in Amos' time there were rival dynasties and a number of petty kings with great freedom of action.[16] For the rest there was no prospect of a Syro-Palestinian state stronger than Israel and Judah; in their combined territories these had, with the exception of Damascus, restored the borders of the Davidic conquests (II Kings 14:25; II Chron. 26:6–15) (see Map 17). The outburst of Amos against the dynasty of Jeroboam and the leaders of Samaria must have seemed to them out of all relation to any possibility of fulfillment. The trenchancy of Amos' social criticism must have been vitiated by the sense of unreality which haunted his vituperative threats, and the totalitarian character of his assault must have placed him in a category altogether different from the one occupied by those prophets, like Elijah and Elisha, who had opposed rulers on particular issues but had not gone to the extreme of predicting the institutional obliteration of Israel. Amos understandably met with indignation and incredulity and even a touch of suspicion that so reckless an indictment and threat was motivated by the political animus of a Judean toward an Israelite—

[16] J. A. Breasted, *A History of Egypt from the Earliest Times to the Persian Conquest,* pp. 533–36, describes the disintegrating situation and notes that at least eighteen contending local dynasts are known to us during this time, when "the land again resolved itself into those small and local political units of which it had consisted in prehistoric days."

one who had perhaps been paid to spread doom in the north, a contemporary Balaam, so to speak, on whose lips Yahweh had *not* chosen to put blessings in place of the curses (Amos 7:12).

A retrospective analysis of the political forces in the first half of the eighth century appears to support the conviction of doom held by Amos, but in terms of political calculation it was no more than a faint possibility. Political calculation was certainly not the base of his attack but it served as an important ingredient. If one had been asked to select a future threat to Israel, there was hardly another to choose but Assyria for she had been a threat to Israel much more recently (under Shalmaneser III in 853) than had Egypt (Egypt had last troubled Israel and Judah in the time of Sheshonk, about 926–917). Thus having adopted a particular theopolitical point of view on the basis of his call as a prophet, Amos was perfectly consistent when he concluded that since Israel existed by virtue of Yahweh's will, and since her inner life had betrayed Yahweh's terms for her existence, she must fall. He was equally realistic when he pointed to Assyria as the most likely instrument of that judgment. *Yet all depended upon accepting the basic theopolitical presupposition.* Those who found Israel's inner life pleasing to Yahweh, as the political and religious leaders certainly did, could draw much more solace from the contemporary international situation than the prophet could draw warnings.

The Foreign Oracles (Chaps. 1, 2)

To underscore the foreign power as an agent of Yahweh's will against Israel is by no means to grasp the whole of Amos' viewpoint. The sweeping concatenation of prophetic oracles which follow one another with breath-taking incisiveness in chaps. 1–2 has drawn considerable comment by biblical interpreters. Perhaps the outstanding gain from recent study has been the recognition that those oracles have a previous history. The two chief arguments in support of the theory that Amos has used pre-existing material are literary and historical. The elaborate and even monotonous structure of the framework of the oracles, the order of the nations treated, and the climax of the series with a fuller and differently constructed oracle concerning Israel point to connections either with a New Year's Festival curse upon foreign nations analogous to the Egyptian execration texts from the Middle Kingdom (nineteenth–eighteenth centuries)[17] or with an ancient prophetic scroll which was apparently also employed in Joel 3:16–18.[18]

The historical allusions in the body of the oracles seem to refer to a period as much as fifty to seventy-five years before the prophet.[19] In general they imply a time when Israel's neighbors were strong enough to attack Israel and one another with impunity, which was hardly the case during the expansionist reigns of Jeroboam in Israel and Uzziah in Judah. Certain details in the oracles support this contention. The threats against Damascus and Ammon appear to refer to the attack of Hazael of Damascus (perhaps in collusion with Ammon) against trans-Jordan in the reigns of Jehu and Jehoahaz between 837 and 805, when the Assyrian kings failed to conduct campaigns in Syria and thus left Hazael free to lord it over weaker Israel (II Kings 8:7–15; 13:1–9, 22, 25). Tyre's disregard of "the covenant of brothers"[20] may reflect the rupture of relations between Israel and Tyre which followed Jehu's extirpation of Omri's dynasty and especially the murder of Jezebel, daughter of the king of Tyre. Yet

[17] Fragments of pottery bowls inscribed with names of enemies and then smashed were published by K. Sethe, *Die Aechtung feindlicher Fuersten, Voelker und Dinge auf Altaegyptischen Tongefässsscherben des Mittleren Reiches*, 1926, and some are translated in *ANET*, pp. 328–29. Inscribed figurines of bound captives were published by G. Posener, *Princes et pays d'Asie et de Nubie. Textes hiératiques sur des figurines d'envoûtement du Moyen Empire*, 1940. A. Bentzen, "The Ritual Background of Amos I. 2—II. 16," *OS* 8 (1950), 85–99, has expertly noted the relations between Amos and the texts while also cautioning against the assumption of direct borrowing or of identical meaning.

[18] Y. Kaufmann, *History of the Religion of Israel*, III. 1, pp. 61–62 (Hebrew).

[19] *Ibid.*

[20] B*e*rîth 'ahim, "covenant of brothers," although not exactly paralleled elsewhere, is a perfectly good description of a parity treaty. Neher's identification of the term as a reference to the Noachian covenant in Genesis 9:1–17 (*op. cit.*, p. 66), so that the "brothers" are all of the nations of the earth, the sons of Noah, is not quite convincing. If this were the thought we should have expected it to be elaborated or the phrase to have been repeated throughout the oracles. The fact that it is restricted to Tyre argues rather for a particular treaty that has been broken.

there is some doubt that this is the incident Amos has in mind, for the oracle condemns a breach of covenant by Tyre rather than by Israel, and the infamous deed is not assassination of a partner's royalty but sale of prisoners of war. Possibly it alludes to retaliatory actions by Tyre once Jehu had acted wantonly against Tyre. More probably the covenant referred to is one concluded between Tyre and one or more of the surrounding states whose extradition clauses were understood to preclude the selling into slavery of citizens from the respective states.[21] If Israel is one of these states it must have been a breach of covenant prior to Jehu's revolt in 842, for Tyre would scarcely have agreed to a treaty with Israel as long as Jehu's dynasty ruled. The oracle against Philistia is not datable, but the Philistine crimes took place before Uzziah's far-reaching conquest of the Philistine cities (unfortunately we cannot date this campaign except to conjecture that it was probably in the first half of his reign, c. 783–760 B.C.). The desecration of the body of a dead Edomite king condemned in the oracle against Moab is an incident unattested in any other source.

Such oracles, therefore, as can be approximately dated appear to be pre-Amosean but the historical argument is not decisive in itself for it is always possible that Amos selected well-known instances of national wrongdoing without respect to their modernity. The fact that they were committed years ago would not diminish his conviction that such wrong must be requited. It is when the historical argument is joined to the literary character of the oracles that the probability of a pre-Amosean prototype for the foreign oracles becomes very strong. We are probably to think

[21] To date there are no Near Eastern treaties in which slave-dealing is treated, doubtless because it was taken for granted that states in treaty did not war against one another and thus took no captives. Extradition clauses in Egyptian and Hittite treaties of the fifteenth to the thirteenth centuries (V. Korošec, *Hethitische Staatsvertraege;* for some examples cf. *ANET*, pp. 200, 203) and an Aramean treaty of the eighth century (J. A. Fitzmyer, *CBQ* 20 [1958], 444–76) prohibit asylum to refugees from a state with which one has a treaty and therefore states were unable to keep fugitives as slaves or to sell them to others. When Max Weber spoke of "presumably a sworn military agreement of international law concerning the treatment of prisoners of war," he went much beyond any evidence in hand (*Ancient Judaism,* 1952 [trans. of German ed., 1921], p. 302).

of Amos as making an extremely limited selection from a larger body of oracles against foreign nations. The formula "three . . . four rebellions" which prefaces each indictment demands a fuller catalog of wrongs for each nation (note that in the typical graduated-numbers formula the full list of items is given—cf. Prov. 6:16; 30:15, 18; Eccles. 11:2). There is really little logical point to speaking of a plenitude of national wrongs, as the "three . . . four" formula certainly does, only to mention a single wrong in each instance. Thus the discrepancy between the framework and the indictment is surely due to Amos' free use of the material. In the citation of only one crime for each nation, even in logical defiance of the traditional execration pattern, Amos gave just enough to show that the foreign nations are culpable while at the same time throwing the weight of his indictment upon Israel. From the very first oracle his listeners must have been struck by the extremely sketchy character of the charges brought against the neighboring nations.

It has been suggested that the movement in the sequence of the oracles from northeast (Damascus) to southwest (Philistia) to northwest (Phoenicia) to southeast (Ammon and Moab) probably reflects an original cultic cosmic orientation, i.e., the four quarters of the world.[22] If so, the original motif was treated with great freedom in Amos, as doubtless also in the Israelite cult. Other theories to explain the order of Amos' attack on the foreign nations are equally problematic.[23] There is an interesting chiastic order in the indictments too: Damascus charged with war atrocities, Philistia with slave-trading, Tyre with slave-

[22] Bentzen, *op. cit.*, p. 90. Such a pattern assumes the deletion of the Edom oracle, which must remain problematic.

[23] Shemaryahu Talmon has suggested the following associational explanation for the order of the oracles in Amos: The prophet begins with Damascus as the major rival power of Israel and turns next to Philistia, described in Isaiah 9:12 as an ally of Damascus in an attack on Israel. Tyre comes next because its indictment is similar to Philistia's, followed by Edom, to whom the slaves are sold, and finally Ammon and Moab by geographical proximity. Yet this does not explain why Ammon should precede Moab instead of follow it, as expected if the prophet is viewing trans-Jordan from south to north. It is likely that he wished to end with Moab for the reason given, *infra*, pp. 109–110.

trading, and Ammon with war atrocities (pattern of ab b'a').[24]
The oracle against Moab seems to be the immediate transition to
the oracles against Israel, for it contains, as we shall observe, a
surprising element only hinted at in the previous oracles. As it
stands, the oracle against Edom is so colorless that it is impossible
to claim any of it for Amos.

We may infer from the mention of Edom in other oracles that
originally Amos had a word of doom for that people also which
has since become corrupted, but it may be that Edom's complicity in the slave trade (1:6, 9) was assumed by the prophet
to draw Edom into the vortex of judgment without a special
oracle. Or, since the immediate purpose of the oracle sequence
was to focus judgment on the northern kingdom, Edom may
have been omitted by the prophet because it was a land normally
more closely related to Judah than to Israel.

The Judah oracle is also to be excluded as containing nothing
recognizably from Amos and in a sense misrepresenting the view
of the prophet as to the fundamental unity of the two kingdoms.
There may have been a Judah oracle which appeared alongside
the Israel oracle as a substitute for it when the prophet spoke in
the south; but it is far more likely that a later editor sensed a
lack of reference to specific conditions in Judah and supplied
them. It is impossible to resist the impression that at any rate in
2:6–16 and in 3:1–2 Israel is the whole people of God and not
merely the northern kingdom. The double allusion to Uzziah and
Jeroboam (1:1) argues that the editor so interpreted the term
"Israel" in the book, whereas "house of Israel," "Joseph," and
"Jacob" refer exclusively to Jeroboam's kingdom. The occurrence of "Zion" in 6:1 is debatable (especially in conflict with
"house of Israel" in the same verse) but there is no conclusive
reason for deleting it. The term "my people Israel" as applied to

[24] Kaufmann, *op. cit.,* p. 63, proposes the theory that the oracles are
arranged symmetrically so that enemies of Israel (Aram, Tyre, Ammon)
alternate with enemies of Judah (Philistia, Edom, Moab—as the enemy of
Edom at a time when she was an ally of Judah). Yet the proposal falls before the fact that Philistia was not solely the enemy of Judah nor Ammon of
Israel, and the supposition that Edom was an ally of Judah at the time of
the oracle against Moab is purely conjectural (see note 27).

the northern kingdom (7:8; 8:2) is probably not intended restrictively, and similarly Amos' identification of Israel as "the sinful kingdom" (9:8) should not be understood to imply that Judah was righteous.

One might conjecture that Amos spoke similar severe words against Judah which have since been deleted or were found in another document that has been lost or was deliberately destroyed by someone in Judah who found it too treasonous. One thing does seem conclusive: the prophet's omission of remarks pointed at Judah does not stem from a pro-Judean political or religious bias. His attack on Jeroboam, the upper classes, and the cult bears no sign of special pleading for the Davidic dynasty or for the Jerusalem sanctuary, for the Zion of 1:2 appears in a cultic formula introducing the oracle series and does not imply judgment on other cult sites merely because they happen to be outside of Jerusalem.[25] If anything, the occurrence of Zion to introduce the series poses the interesting possibility that the foreign-oracle tradition was brought by Amos from Judah to Israel. The Zion of 6:1 is a condemnatory reference, and the David of 6:5 is merely a musician who has contributed to the debilitating luxury of the rich.

Two of the prophetic indictments are reasonably to be connected with wrongs against Israel. Damascus and Ammon have committed atrocities against Israel in the course of expansionist campaigns in Gilead. Possibly Tyre is in the same category if the charge refers to her violation of a close relation with Israel from the time of David to the reign of Ahab by selling Israelite war captives into slavery; but we have seen the difficulty involved in connecting "the covenant of brothers" with an exclusively Israelite-Tyrian pact. Philistine slave-trading may allude to raids against Judah, such as were carried out in the reigns of Jehoram

---

[25] Arvid S. Kapelrud, *op. cit.*, p. 37, rightly observes that, although from Amos' rejection of the northern cult places without a similar repudiation of southern cult places "His audience must at least have got the impression that Yahweh had to be sought elsewhere, i.e., in Jerusalem" (cf. "seek Yahweh," 5:4, 6), the prophet's whole preaching should have quickly corrected the impression, for "he rejected all kinds of the usual cult, . . . and the corollary was necessarily that he was not willing to accept a similar cult in Jerusalem either."

(II Chron. 21:16–17) and Ahaz (II Chron. 28:18). Since Edom also revolted from Judah in the reign of Jehoram and he was unable to quell the revolt, it is possible that we should locate the Philistine-Edom slave-trading at that time; but not merely Judah was subject to such raids in the Palestinian southland for David in the service of Achish of Gath undertook similar razzias against the Amalekites (I Sam. 27:7–12).

The wrong of Moab against Edom stands sharply apart from the others in that it identifies the nation wronged. Attempts to connect the desecration of the Edomite royal dead[26] with an action of Moab against Edom when the latter was a vassal of Israel and Judah are not convincing.[27] Whether Amos has deleted mention of the nation wronged in all cases but this or has added the name of Edom in a series that otherwise did not name the victims, the result is the same: the silences and the one explicit mention seem to have a purpose. In the case of the silences the exact nation wronged is immaterial for it is the cruelty and barbarity of nation against nation which Yahweh condemns.[28]

[26] The Targum of 2:1b, "because he had burned the bones of the king of Edom and had made a coating of chalk for the walls of his house," has been followed by A. B. Ehrlich, *Randglossen zur hebräischen Bibel,* 1912, V, 230, and K. Cramer, *Amos,* 1930, to explain *lassîd* as "to calcinate." Neher, *op. cit.,* p. 53, believes that the reference is not to the bones of the king of Edom but to those of Israelite dead left on the battlefield by the king of Edom. Needless to say, this is a very strained interpretation. It does seem likely that the phrase "bones of the king of Edom" reflects the practice of calcinating human skeletons to acquire lime. The incident, however, is strictly between Moab and Edom and in no way involves Israel.

[27] Kaufmann, *op. cit.,* p. 62, emphasizes the nationalistic character of all the foreign prophecies including that of Moab against Edom. Decisive also for Kaufmann is his belief that the Moabite-Edomite incident must, like those behind the other oracles, come from the ninth century. Nevertheless, even if he is correct on the general date it cannot be supposed that the only time in the ninth century that Moab fought its close neighbor Edom was the war recounted in II Kings 3.

[28] Kapelrud, *op. cit.,* pp. 22–26, has argued with great cogency that Amos has formulated these oracles so as to call attention to *international* cruelty, which is heinous whoever the victim (cf. also M. A. Beek, "The Religious Background of Amos II. 6–8," *OS* 5 [1948], 132–33). Kaufmann himself reneges when he notes that even if Moab is condemned for a crime against Israel's ally Edom the nationalistic element should not be overplayed since at the same time, according to 1:11–12, hatred is rampant between Edom and Israel and "in spite of this hatred Moab will be punished for the evil she has done to Edom" (Kaufmann, *op. cit.,* p. 68, n. 20).

It is enough to know who has sinned. But in the instance of the one victim named there is also a purpose. Here the nation is named because it is *not* an Israelite state. The naming of Edom does not mean that none of the other wrongs were against non-Israelite states. Neither does it mean that the prophet thinks a wrong against a non-Israelite state is more serious than one against Israel or Judah. Rather, Edom is named precisely at the crucial point of emphasis, just prior to the oracle against Israel. It sets the pattern beyond any shadow of a doubt: *Yahweh is the indiscriminate judge of the earth. He who does not hesitate to judge Moab for its wrongs against Edom will surely not hesitate to judge Israel for her wrongs.*

That this interpretation is not a modern rationalization seems borne out by three other passages in Amos. In 3:9–11 Amos is able to represent Yahweh as assembling foreign nations "to look upon" the iniquity of Israel. Something more than a poetic account of the execution of judgment seems involved, for the nations are assembled as witnesses who will bring criticism to bear upon the northern kingdom. This would be possible only if Amos thought of some sort of consensus among the nations as to what it is "to do right." Assyria and Egypt are able to appreciate the social rottenness of Israel, just as Moab should be able to understand when it has done wrong to Edom.

A second confirmation of this "universalistic" understanding of the Moab oracle is in 6:1–3. The notoriously difficult reference to Calneh, Hamath, and Gath may be rendered to express the Israelite leaders' confidence that Samaria and Judah are stronger than any other Syro-Palestinian state:

"Woe to those lounging in Zion and to those at ease in Samaria,
To the distinguished officials—the first of the nations!—who are consulted by the House of Israel, who say:
'Pass over to Calneh and look and go from there to Hamath and down to Gath of Philistia.
Are there better kingdoms than these? And yet are their boundaries greater than yours?'
O those who postpone the day of evil and bring near the cessation of violence!"

In such a rendering the reference to the neighboring nations is the boastful reply of the leaders to the queries of their subjects:[29] "Fellow Israelites, can you think of stronger western states than Calneh, Hamath, or Gath? Yet none of them has the territory occupied by Israel and Judah. We have nothing to fear!" The expression "first of the nations," i.e., "the chief, the most important," is apparently drawn from the popular terminology connected with the Day of Yahweh (note its use in the oracle against Amalek attached to the Balaam oracle, Num. 24:20, where the meaning is, however, slightly different, "the earliest of the nations," i.e., among the first encountered by Israel). It expressed the sense of national superiority which at this period seemed objectively supported by the historical situation. Doubtless, the officials were correct in regarding Israel and Judah as the strongest powers between the Nile and the upper Tigris-Euphrates.

Amos' opinion of this line of reasoning is evident in the setting he gives to the words of the nobility. They are the complacent ones, "lounging" and "at ease," who insist that violent judgment is remote. The following oracle (6:4–7) is closely related in thought and emphasizes the luxury-oriented habits of the upper classes, who "are not sick at heart over the ruin of Joseph" (vs. 6c). The prophet insists that comparison of the respective power of states is not the criterion of national welfare; rather it is the internal social and economic conditions. On such an understanding the three states named (Calneh, Hamath, Gath) are not to be thought of as already destroyed and thus referred to as examples of coming destruction. It is instead their thriving independence in the period of Assyrian relapse which draws the prophet's attention to them and makes them appropriate examples of the nobility's satisfaction with Israel's status. Since at least two of the three had lost territory to the resurgent kingdoms of Israel and

---

[29] Several commentators have recognized in the reference to Calneh, Hamath, and Gath a seriously intended comparison of the relative strengths of Syro-Palestinian states (e.g., W. R. Smith, *The Prophets of Israel,* 2nd ed., 1895, p. 138; S. R. Driver, *Joel and Amos,* 2nd ed., 1915, pp. 195–97), but they have attributed the questions to the prophet when they are in fact better understood as the expression of the Israelite leaders' superficial optimism. Other examples of boastful or reckless words on the lips of speakers are found in 2:12; 4:1; 6:13.

Judah: Gath (II Chron. 26:6) and Hamath (II Kings 14:25), they were especially inviting examples for comparison.

The third instance is the most explicit. It is the verse which appears to be the climax of the book, that astounding verse in which Amos seems for the moment to take back all that he has said about the unique position of Israel in the plan of Yahweh (9:7). It is a verse which noticeably expands the horizons of the world of Amos for it reaches southward to Nubia on the Upper Nile between the first and fifth cataracts, and in tracing the origins of the Philistines and Arameans it reaches westward to Crete or Asia Minor and eastward to Kir, an as yet undetermined area in or near Mesopotamia (Ur? Elam?).[30] There can be no doubt of the importance of this verse. Yahweh not only regards all the nations as similar in his sight ("Are you not as the Nubians to me, O people of Israel?") but extends his concern to the whole history of peoples so as to include the migrations and present holdings of the Philistines and the Syrians. Thus the special knowledge of Yahweh toward Israel cannot be understood to mean that only Israel has been brought to birth and guided by Yahweh to her present position. The same can be said of the most hated of Israel's enemies, whose own barbarous conduct in war and war profiteering has earned for them judgment (1:3–5; 6–8). *In the endless surge and flux of nations in the international corridor Yahweh's watchful eye is at work, both protecting and judging the peoples he has brought into being.*

So it seems that we must assess the traditional material of Amos 1–2 in the light of the passages which appear to give the more original thought of the prophet. If we do so, the following appears: Amos has employed older oracles of execration upon foreign nations in which he has introduced a number of changes. He has shortened the indictment against each nation so that the listeners will not dote unduly upon the sins of other peoples. He has deleted or avoided mention of Israel as the wronged people, for this would incite the nationalistic feelings of his audiences, but has allowed the mention of Edom to stand in order to stress Yahweh's interest in nations apart from Israel.

[30] J. Simons, *The Geographical and Topographical Texts of the Old Testament,* p. 8.

Israel's Uniqueness Among the Nations

Probably the oracle against Israel is largely Amos' own, although the recital of Israel's salvation history in 2:9–12 may be drawn from a traditional source. The uniqueness of the oracle against Israel is partly in the fullness of its indictment, in contrast to the sketchy charges against the nations at large. Indeed, though the formal structure of the earlier oracles is abandoned after the opening formula *'al,* "because of . . . ," it is likely that Amos has intended to give all four of the rebellions of which Israel is guilty: wronging of the poor ("their selling of the righteous for silver and the poor for a pair of shoes, those who trample on the head of the poor and turn aside the cause of the oppressed"); sexual offense ("a man and his father patronize the same maiden in order to profane my holy name");[31] holding of garments taken in pledge ("on garments taken in pledge they recline by every altar"); drunkenness ("wine taken as a fine they drink in the house of their god"). The merging of religious and social sins is especially striking and typical of Amos, but having fulfilled the formal requirement of stating four sins, Amos followed up his brief survey of Israel's sacred history with a further indictment of her rejection of the voice of prophecy ("You gave the Nazirites wine to drink and you commanded the prophets, 'Do not prophesy!' "—2:12).

It is also likely that if the original prophecy sequence included an execration of Israel, it was restricted to particular sinners within Israel, in line with the Egyptian execration texts where first foreign nations and then Egyptian individuals are condemned,[32] and also in keeping with certain Israelite cult forms, such as the psalms directed against "the workers of evil."[33] *It*

[31] Beek, *op. cit.,* pp. 135–38, has argued soundly that the *na'ᵃrāh* "maiden" of 2:7 is not a hierodule but a common slave, and the prohibition is the corollary of the law of Leviticus 20:11 that a man shall not have intercourse with his father's wife. As such it was an example of the prophetic rigor in going beyond existing law. L. Duerr, "Altorientalisches Recht bei dem Propheten Amos und Hosea," *Biblische Zeitschrift* 23 (1935–36), 153, notes that a man and his son were permitted to have sexual intercourse with the same slave in general Near Eastern practice.

[32] Bentzen, *op. cit.,* p. 95.

[33] Whether "the workers of evil" are sorcerers (S. Mowinckel, *Psalmen-*

*comes as a wholly novel thing, as a devastating shock, to have the
entire nation condemned, or, properly speaking, to describe the
sins of individuals within Israel as so widespread and so deep-
seated that the entire state will suffer dissolution.* This consequence, uttered again and again throughout the book, with only
the slightest glimpse of an alternative (5:15), was apparently too
pessimistic to be left as the final word of the book and so several
hopeful prophecies were added. It is altogether possible that some
or all of these prophecies were contained in the traditional material Amos made use of in chaps. 1 and 2,[34] but as they stand
they bear no discernible connection with all that the prophet has
said heretofore. In fact they bridge the vast moral dilemma of
Amos by claiming that among the survivors, the sinners only will
be slain (9:9–10) and the rest will participate in the revived
state, which will conquer all of its enemies (9:11–13).

Would such a solution have been tenable for Amos? No doubt
he thought of the poor in Israel as relatively innocent of the social
rot which had infected the state, but nowhere does he offer the
slightest suggestion that they might form a purified remnant surviving the wreck of the state, a remnant which would in turn
create a new Yahwistic state. The one mention of "the remnant
of Joseph" (5:15) seems to refer not to a handful to survive the
catastrophe but to the present Israelites, who are a mere shadow
of their former selves but whose one chance of averting catastrophe is to establish justice in the land. That a seemingly powerful people could be designated "a remnant" is not impossible, for
Amos intercedes on behalf of the same people with the plaintive
appeal, "How can Jacob stand? He is so small!" (7:2, 4). Such

---

studien I Awān und die individuellen Klagepsalmen, 1922) or legal ac-
cusers (H. Schmidt, *Das Gebet der Angeklagten im Alten Testament,* 1928),
their attempts to harm innocent believers constitute not merely a personal
danger but a threat to the people of God and must be countered by confession and cultic expurgation of malicious or inadvertent evil. This is not
to deny that in some psalms it appears that "the workers of evil" are enemy
nations and "the humble one" is the Israelite king (H. Birkeland, *Die Feinde
des Individuums in der israelitischen Psalmenliteratur,* 1933), but rather
shows that the execration tradition had a twofold development in the cult:
execration of sinful foreign nations and execration of sinful Israelites.

[34] Kaufmann, *op. cit.,* pp. 62, 88–89.

terms are in part a case of pathetic diminution ("poor little thing!") but they have moral overtones as well. Israel has so attenuated her true strength by disobedience to Yahweh that she is "small," a hapless "remnant" of her former greatness. It remains true that for Amos rich and poor, evil and righteous are to perish together.

Furthermore, considering all that Amos says about the states in the ancient Near East it is impossible to believe that he could foresee a fulfillment of Yahweh's purpose in the armed subjection of neighboring states. Indeed this was to a large extent what he now witnessed. The popular Day of Yahweh which he derided was a day of celebration of victory over the foreign powers (5:18–20). It was just such chauvinistic fervor which he recognized as diverting the attention of Israel from the chronic neglect of a righteous internal order. Cult was irrelevant to this basic task and so was militarism. Neither could touch the essential Yahwistic charge to Israel, and both could delude Israel into thinking herself righteous. Amos did not attack warmaking per se, but by all of his assumptions and by his radical attack on the expansionist patriotism of court and citizenry (6:13) who rejoiced in the recent Israelite reconquest of Lo-Debar and Karnaim in Bashan from Damascus, he demonstrated how peripheral were such military exploits to the will of Yahweh. To be sure, according to the logic of the foreign oracles, Israel might administer deserved punishment to other nations. At the same time, however, such campaigns might only be a sealing of Israel's punishment through the deepening of her insensitivity to social abuses and by an exaggerated self-confidence. There is no way to turn in the net which Amos casts around the petty states of the ancient Near East, Israel included. In their entanglement of hatred and cruelty they shall go down together. The excesses of war committed by combatants and the profiteering in human life uprooted by war practiced by neutrals are alike condemned.

If heinous extraterritorial acts are not explicitly named in the case of Israel it is not because Amos knows of none or because he thinks Israel exempt from the judgment which Yahweh has laid upon the nations. It is doubtless rather because these international standards are assumed as the absolute minimum of Yahweh's requirement which Israel as one of "the families of the earth" must observe as a matter of course (civility in war, respect of captives, observance of treaties, honor for the dead) whereas the higher requirements of a righteous social order are the special demands laid upon Israel. This is what it means that Israel is especially "known" by Yahweh. He seeks to establish in her a peculiar social order in which men live in brotherhood. This unique sense of brotherhood which suffuses all social and economic relations cannot be expected of Damascus or the Philistines. They rise or fall on their observance or rejection of elemental decencies, but Israel rises or falls on the degree to which she fulfills her inner obligations before Yahweh. Perhaps Amos also feels that if men will have so little regard for their fellow countrymen they are hardly likely to show consideration to those of other countries.

The two sets of standards do not really meet in Amos' recorded words. We are never shown how Israel fares in her conduct toward other nations, except in an indirect way, and we are never shown how the foreign nations measure up in internal affairs. The latter omission is entirely understandable on the ground of the election faith, since the prophet has no commission to speak to these nations even about their foreign affairs, much less about their internal conduct. He only mentions these nations as a warning to Israel. The omission is not quite total since Israel's conduct toward foreign nations is apparently embraced in his attack upon the pseudo-patriotic Day of Yahweh concept, and his very choice of the indictments against the neighbor states assumes that such misconduct is forbidden for Israel. He is thus chiefly concerned with the extra demands of Yahweh upon his people.

Admittedly this leaves us with a far from well-proportioned view. Certain questions may be posed which are not readily answerable in such a framework. For example, if the Israelite social order is the peculiar province of the covenant faith of Israel, how is it possible for Amos to summon Assyria and Egypt to witness and to condemn Israel's inner decay? In some way Amos must have believed also in an inner core of "natural law" which was valid within all societies, but he has omitted all mention of this because it did not directly touch upon his urgent immediate warning to Israel.

The one pressing purpose of Amos is to show that in terms of her summons, as known to all Israelites in the familiar traditions, Israel has failed as the one specially chosen family; she has failed so totally that she shall pass away. How is she to be replaced? Surely it is no accident that Amos has brought his book to a close with a survey of the great scope of the ancient Near East embracing a vast region from the headwaters of the Nile to the isles of the Mediterranean and thence to far Mesopotamia (9:7). From this immense area, from peoples who mean as much to him as Israel, Yahweh is able to raise up a new people. When and if he does, righteousness and justice will again be his criteria for judging their continuation as the one special people.

At once questions occur which neither are formulated by Amos nor receive any explicit answer from his recorded words. Is not Judah the logical successor to Israel; in fact, as long as Judah exists does not the family called forth from Egypt still exist? We have seen that he may have spoken in similarly judgmental terms to Judah, but in this immediate context of threat against Israel even the future of Judah is not important. Perhaps Judah will be the sole bearer of the covenant faith when Israel has fallen or it may be one of the utterly distant peoples. It matters not. Yahweh and "the families of the earth" will continue when Israel, once known by Yahweh but failing to answer that knowledge with obedience, has ceased to exist. *Amos succeeds in establishing both Israel's importance as a unique people and her merely proximate importance to a God for whom all peoples count and who possesses many resources for bringing justice to earth.*

It follows that Amos was well informed on the affairs of the ancient Near Eastern states although his information was not such as was drawn from state archives or from written records except of a religio-political nature. What is astonishing about Amos is not the breadth of his knowledge, which was considerable and doubtless vaster than his brief surviving words indicate, but the scope of the intellectual framework into which he placed all the facts available to him. *The framework was simply that of*

*a single God Yahweh related as it were in two concentric circles
to all the peoples of the ancient Near East—at the center to Israel
and Judah and on all sides to the peoples of the known world.*

As to the conceptual influences contributing to such a belief,
it is likely that the process of Yahwistic-Elohistic syncretism—
illustrated in the Yahwehization of the patriarchal deity—was a
potent background factor.[35] A tendency toward an El monotheism in Syria-Palestine by 2000 B.C. is not to be disregarded.[36] It
should nevertheless be strongly stressed that this could only have
been an indirect influence on the prophet and an extremely dif-
fuse one at that. There is, for example, in Amos' development no
trace at all of a Yahweh pantheon with the several non-Israelite
national deities subordinated to Israel's God. The only allusion to
non-Israelite deities, Sakkuth and Kaiwan (5:26), does not support such an interpretation. And the nature doxologies, whether
inserted by the prophet or not, strongly underscore a single will
behind all created phenomena with no room for intermediary
deities.

Probably the more immediate impulse to such a bold assertion
of Yahweh's lordship over the nations came from elements of
"universalism" which had already taken root in ancient Yahwistic tradition, such notions as are expressed in the Yahwist's
use of Genesis 1–11 and the call of Abraham in Genesis 12:1–3.[37]

[35] Kapelrud, *op. cit.,* pp. 27–29, 33–47, after a careful weighing of the
evidence, concludes that Amos' lack of an anti-Baal polemic and the vitality
of Baal-El cults in Syria—not only in earlier times, as the Ras Shamra texts
show, but also in Amos' time, as the Azitawadda stele shows—argue for his
"taking over the universalism which was characteristic for the ancient
supreme god, El 'Elyon." When due emphasis is given to the counter trend
to "Yahwehize" El by a radical morality and a jealous loyalty, there is much
to be said for this as a working hypothesis.

[36] O. Eissfeldt, *El im ugaritischen Pantheon,* 1950.

[37] Neher, *op. cit.,* pp. 64–67, argues forcefully that the leading motifs of
the Noachic covenant of Genesis 9–10 are sounded by Amos: the guarantee
of cosmic stability (Gen. 9:8–18; Amos 4:13; 5:8; 9:5–6), the inclusion
of all peoples as offspring of the family of Noah (Gen. 9:1; 10; Amos 1:9,
11), and the content, consisting not of a creed but of articles of moral
practice (Gen. 9:1–7; Amos 1:3—2:5). In spite of the fact that exception
may be taken to his attribution of the cosmological passages to Amos (cf.
Kapelrud, *op. cit.,* pp. 38–39), thus seriously weakening support for the first
motif, the other two correctly interpret the purport of Amos' viewpoint.
Also, "the covenant of brothers" (1:9) does not clearly possess the wide

These insights, which the Yahwist had not obviously applied to contemporary events, were vigorously activated by Amos and given alarming freshness by the specification of particular peoples with whom Israel was then engaged.

In addition, the prophet's view of the natural world with its harsh reign of violence taught him of a God whose justice does not observe national and ethnic boundaries any more than do rain-filled clouds or marauding beasts. His was an outlook singularly devoid of hopes not based on evidence and of that ideological passion which blinds citizens to the faults of the social, economic, and political groups to which they belong.

Although he did not address himself to foreign nations nor even chiefly to Israel as a participant in foreign affairs, it is logical to see in Amos solid intellectual foundations for the development of natural law and a genuine religious universalism which forms the matrix of international law.

Hosea

Although Hosea's ministry followed shortly upon Amos' and may have overlapped it, the differences of content and emphasis in the two prophets are noteworthy. It has long been observed that, whereas Amos chiefly indicts Israelite social conditions, Hosea attacks the nation's political and religious blemishes. While Hosea's analysis of political weaknesses is definitely fuller than Amos', the references in the two prophets to foreign powers are roughly comparable in frequency although not in scope.

The Political Context of Hosea's Thought

The political interest of Hosea is stimulated by the sudden disintegration of kingship in Israel. Amos spoke chiefly of economic and social wrongs for they were the obvious grievances during the politically stable rule of Jeroboam. Hosea turned his attention to the political chaos which accompanied a series of kings who

---

meaning Neher gives to it, but he should have cited 9:7, which gives even stronger proof of Amos' belief in mankind as a group of families under one God.

failed to bring order to Israel, kings who were tragically lacking in the assertion of balanced leadership and who seem to have been motivated largely by personal ambition, court cliques, and nationalistic fervor. It is by no means certain that a strong and able leader such as Jeroboam would have been equal to the dramatic Assyrian penetration of Syria-Palestine in 743–738, again in 735–732, and finally in 725–722. Still, the external crisis was only aggravated and deepened by leaders who mainly sought personal advantage by throwing in their lot either with Aram-Damascus or with Egypt against the Assyrians or by capitulating to Assyria.

Treaties with or against Assyria could have expressed the valid intent of Israelite kings to secure quiet for a peaceful development of their kingdom. In fact, however, all that we gather from the historical records and from Hosea's prophecies points strongly in the opposite direction. The kings were not seeking to placate Assyria or to check its advance for the sake of Israel at large but chiefly for momentary personal gain. Under the circumstances it is not surprising that the dynasty of Jehu was the last real dynasty in Israel. All those who followed were leaders of factions that contended for the throne and occupied it for varying lengths of time without enlisting wide popular support. The irresponsibility of the supposed kings and the collapse of popular confidence in them are sharply etched in the words of the prophet.

At Jeroboam's death in 753,[38] his son Zechariah was unable to hold the throne beyond six months. Shallum assassinated Zechariah while he was away from the capital (read "Ibleam" with LXX in II Kings 15:10). Shallum was able to maintain his rule for only one month before he was assassinated by Menahem of Tirzah (II Kings 15:14). Menahem established himself only by brutal acts of repression such as the sack of Tappuah on the border between Ephraim and Manasseh (read with LXX rather

[38] The chronology of the last kings of Israel here adopted is that of Edwin R. Thiele, *The Mysterious Numbers of the Hebrew Kings,* and supplemented by "A Comparison of the Chronological Data of Israel and Judah," *VT* 4 (1954), 185–95; "New Evidences on the Chronology of the Last Kings of Judah," *BASOR* 143 (1956), 22–27; "The Question of Coregencies among the Hebrew Kings," *W. Irwin Anniversary Volume,* 1956, pp. 39–52.

than MT, "Tipsah") and atrocities committed against its women. Presumably the city was a center of resistance to the pretensions of the new king. By means of his forceful acts Menahem managed to reign for ten years but continued to have serious difficulties, as is apparent in the fact that the tribute he paid to Tiglath-pileser near the end of his reign was intended "to strengthen his grip on the kingdom" (II Kings 15:19). The heavy tribute of one thousand talents of silver collected by an impost of fifty shekels each on between forty and sixty thousand landowners liable for military service, and perhaps computed as a kind of ransom to allow Israel to stay independent,[39] must further have alienated the people from Menahem and prepared the way for his downfall. This extreme act of Menahem to secure the succession to the throne for his own house may have been directed against one or more rival claimants who ruled in parts of the kingdom. The theory that Pekah ruled in Gilead contemporaneously with Menahem in Samaria certainly helps to account for the chronological disarray in computing the reigns of Israel's last kings.[40] Pekahiah, Menahem's son, succeeded his father in 742 but was murdered by Pekah in 740–739 as part of an evident anti-Assyrian mood.

Pekah profited greatly from a three-year diversion of Tiglath-pileser's energies away from Syria and Palestine in the period 737–734. He joined Rezon (or Razon cf. *ANET,* p. 283; preferable to MT Rezin) of Damascus in an alliance against Assyria although he may well have been less than a free agent. Being a Gileadite he may already have drawn on Damascene assistance in wresting the throne from the house of Menahem. Other Palestinian states, Philistia and Edom, joined in the alliance, but

[39] D. J. Wiseman, *Iraq* 15 (1953), p. 135, observes that the 50-shekel-per-head impost is identical with the average Assyrian slave price at Kalah in the seventh century and may conceivably have been intended as a kind of "ransom" for the male citizens of Israel.

[40] The sixteen years attributed to the reign of Pekah in II Kings 15:33 includes apparently the reign of Menahem, whom he usurped, and this is best explained if Pekah did actually claim control over part of Israel during at least the last years of Menahem's reign. Otherwise there is no clear accounting for the later conflation, for which Thiele gives no reason (*Mysterious Numbers,* p. 114) and Hallo (op. cit., p. 46) accounts by saying "that some other rival king could have given rise to the late conflation."

not so Ahaz of Judah, who refused to participate although his co-regent Jotham was still living and probably sympathetic to the alliance. The attempt of Rezon and Pekah to replace Ahaz with a cooperative ruler, Tabeel, who was perhaps of the Davidic house (another son of Azariah or Jotham?),[41] issued in a fateful disturbance of the balance of power in southern Syria (see the section on Isaiah for fuller discussion). Ahaz suffered serious reversals in the opening warfare on the border between Judah and Israel and was besieged in Jerusalem. In desperation he sent a request for help to Tiglath-pileser, pledging himself as henceforth a willing vassal ("I am your servant and your son"—II Kings 16:7). Whether the request had been preceded by Assyrian approaches to Ahaz is unknown, but Tiglath-pileser shrewdly recognized an opportunity to split the unity of the Palestinian states and to secure a foothold in the far south of the corridor to Egypt. Since Israel was the weaker of the two chief rebels, he resolved to conquer her first, thereby isolating Damascus. Tiglath-pileser swept through Galilee, the plain of Esdraelon, the plain of Sharon, and Gilead as far as the border with Moab in a pincer movement, incorporating all but the mountainous heartland of Samaria into Assyrian provinces (see Map 18). Thousands of Israelites were deported to Assyria and were presumably replaced by colonists from other parts of the empire (II Kings 15:29; *ANET,* pp. 283–84).

No doubt Tiglath-pileser thought seriously of abolishing the northern kingdom altogether. As it was, he reinstated Pekah briefly but when he turned to the siege of Damascus a pro-Assyrian movement appeared in Samaria under the leadership of Hoshea, who may well have been encouraged in the first place by the Assyrian king. At any rate, it seemed a safe gamble to entrust Hoshea with the throne of the kingdom now so reduced territorially that it could offer little threat in the future. But, whereas Menahem had been consistently pro-Assyrian and Pekah consistently anti-Assyrian, Hoshea finally wavered in his allegiance. During the years when Tiglath-pileser was occupied with quell-

----

[41] W. F. Albright's suggestion (*BASOR* 140 [1955], 34 f.) that Tabeel was a son of Azariah or Jotham by a trans-Jordanian princess is plausible but conjectural.

ing a revolt in Babylon (731–728) the pressures on Hoshea to revolt must have been intense. He resisted them at first for he could not quickly forget the swiftness with which Tiglath-pileser had moved against the revolt of Pekah and Rezon.

The accession of Shalmaneser IV to the Assyrian throne in 727 signaled a general revolt by Phoenician and Palestinian states. The failure of the new king to take measures for more than a year encouraged even the cautious Hoshea to think that the time for Israel's independence had come. The note that "Against him [Hoshea] came up Shalmaneser king of Assyria; and Hoshea became his vassal, and paid him tribute" (II Kings 17:3) probably refers to Hoshea's protestations of non-participation in the revolt and his belated payment of tribute. Shalmaneser might have overlooked the arrears in tribute, but the fact that Hoshea had sent an emissary to Egypt in order to plan rebellion was more than he could tolerate. Hoshea was imprisoned and the ensuing siege of Samaria led to its capture in August-September 722. Before his death in December of the same year Shalmaneser may have begun to deport the inhabitants of Samaria, but it remained for Sargon in 720 to assimilate Israel into the Assyrian provincial system by establishing the province of Samerina with an Assyrian governor, deporting large numbers of Israelites (27,290 according to the Assyrian annals) to the Habor River region and to Media and perhaps to Assyria proper (II Kings 17:6; 18:11–12), replacing them by captives from Babylon and northern Syria (II Kings 17:24), and forming army units from some of its crack troops (*ANET*, pp. 284–85).[42]

Hosea the prophet did not hesitate to pass judgment upon these chaotic events in the last years of Israel's life. He saw them with an objectivity which was not matched by the succession of rulers who bought and fought their way to the throne.

That his ministry began before the assassination of Zechariah in 752 is clear in the name he gave to his first child as a sign of judgment on the house of Jehu—Jezreel (Hos. 1:4–5). Jezreel

---

[42] The extremely difficult problem of ascertaining the respective roles of Shalmaneser and Sargon in the capture and incorporation of Samaria is aired by H. Tadmor, *JCS* 12 (1958), esp. 33–38, and his allocation of the kings' accomplishments is accepted here.

was the second capital of Ahab and in its valley Jehu had taken decisive action to wipe out the dynasty of Omri, for there he killed the ruling king, Jehoram, and Ahaziah, the king of Judah, and the wily Jezebel (II Kings 9:14–37). This plot, which had been instigated and fully supported by Elisha, was condemned emphatically by Hosea "for yet a little time, and I will punish the house of Jehu for the blood of Jezreel, and I will bring an end to the kingdom of the house of Israel" (Hos. 1:4). As with Amos, the cessation of the reigning dynasty was thought of as the end of the kingdom and may well have been due to "prophetic foreshortening" of the future. Although technically inaccurate, the judgment contained a sober element of truth. There were other kings to follow, none of whom could be called strong rulers, and the forces of disintegration in Israel were manifested with terrifying speed once the stable rule of Jeroboam had passed. It is not clear how literally Hosea intended his threat, "On that day, I will snap the bow of Israel in the valley of Jezreel." It is less likely that he wished to emphasize *the exact place* of the military defeat of Israel (although it was a natural strategic location for battles) than that he intended to stress *the intention* of Yahweh to destroy the kingdom and *the means* to be used. It will be blood vengeance for the violence perpetrated by the founder of the dynasty and as such it will be accomplished by equally violent means. We not uncommonly find the principle of recapitulation applied in prophecy in the sense that the place of sin becomes the place of judgment (e.g., in Hosea: Shittim, 5:2; Gibeah, 10:9).[43]

The greater part of Hosea's ministry coincided with the rule of the weakling kings from Zechariah through Hoshea. The turmoil of that period forms the background of a majority of his oracles, and repeatedly explicit references to contemporary events show through the bitter indictments unfortunately so poorly preserved textually.

Two oracles reflect the reign of Menahem. In 10:3–8 the

---

[43] This mode of thought is the logical climax of the strong Hebraic sense of historical retribution. Although to an extent rhetorical, it seriously expresses the belief in poetic justice which Hosea elsewhere generalizes: "they sow the wind and they shall reap the whirlwind" (8:7).

heavy tribute of Menahem serves as the basis for the threat that the calf-idol of Bethel "shall be carried to Assyria, as tribute to the great king." Menahem paid his initial tribute in an enormous quantity of silver, but the prophet foresees even heavier demands by the Assyrian king, which can be met only by sending the golden calf to Assyria. A contrast is posed between Yahweh as Israel's king, whom the people voluntarily reject ("For we have no king, we fear not Yahweh and the king, what could he do for us?"—10:3, *hammelek*, the divine king as in Isa. 6:5), and the Assyrian *sharru rabu*[44] (10:6), whom they will forcibly serve. The neglect of the administration of justice fits the reign of Menahem, so largely consumed with harsh repression of internal opposition (10:4):

They mouth words, mere empty oaths and cut covenants;

but judgment springs up like poison in the furrows of the field.

The oracle of 13:15–16 singles out Ephraim for destruction from among the surrounding states: "From among his brothers he shall be scattered" (following XX, 13:15a), and in the threat of the emptying of the state treasury of its valuables Menahem's tribute may again be alluded to (". . . and it [the east wind?] will plunder the treasury of all its choice contents"—13:15fg; note also that foreign powers are likened to the east wind in 12:1). The threat of atrocities against pregnant women to be visited on Samaria, if it is not merely a conventional phrase for war brutality, alludes to recompense for Menahem's similar atrocities against Tappuah (II Kings 15:16).

The violence of Pekah's purge seems to have left traces in a broken and disordered oracle which originally referred to crimes committed by Pekah and his Gileadite henchman at the fords of the Jordan River at Adam (cf. Judg. 12:1–6 for an earlier account of civil strife at the fords of the Jordan between Ephraimites and Gileadites) and their plundering as they approached Shechem and Samaria (6:7–8, 9b):[45]

[44] The now generally preferred reading of 10:6 (also 5:13) as *malki rāb*, "great king"=*sharru rabu* instead of *melek yārēb*, "king Jareb," was first suggested by W. M. Mueller, *ZAW* 17 (1897), 334–36, and elaborated by G. R. Driver, *JTS* 36 (1935), 295–96.

[45] A. Alt, "Hosea 5:8—6:6," *KS*, II, 186, has rightly noted that the pas-

At Adam they broke the covenant and there treated me treacher-
ously.

Gilead is a city of evil doers, smeared with blood. . . .

Enroute to Shechem they have murdered, and behaved wickedly.

The aftermath of Pekah's and Rezon's unsuccessful attack on
Jerusalem in 735–734 is treated by the prophet in a highly dialec-
tical oracle, affording an interesting glimpse of the complexity of
his thought on the relation of states.[46] The prophet pictures the
counterattack launched by Ahaz once the Israelite and Syrian
forces had retreated at word of Tiglath-pileser's approach (5:9–
10). The nearby Benjaminite strongholds of Gibeah and Ramah
were secured as part of the northern defenses of Jerusalem but,
not content to halt at the former border between the two kingdoms, Ahaz will penetrate (or has already done so) into
Ephraimite territory from Bethel northward and his officers will
be like those who "remove the boundary mark" between the two
kingdoms. Vs. 11 seems to describe the far-reaching attack of
Tiglath-pileser in 734 for Israel is "oppressed, crushed in judgment, because he was determined to go after his enemy,"[47] i.e.,

---

sage 6:7—7:2 refers to the progress of a revolutionary attack originating in
Gilead, crossing the Jordan at Adam, and reaching to Shechem. Yet his
identification of Shallum and Menahem (why the two together?) as the
leaders of the revolution is baseless. The verses he cites (II Kings 15:10,
14, 16) do not substantiate his claim, for neither Gilead nor Adam nor
Shechem is mentioned! Pekah is much more likely since the core of his
revolutionary following was from Gilead (II Kings 15:25). The textual
rearrangement here follows J. Mauchline, *IB*, VI, 630, who transposes 9a
and 9b, thereby distinguishing two distinct units: vss. 7–8, 9b, which refers
to murderous Gileadites, and 9a, 10, which refers to evil priests.

[46] Alt, *op. cit.*, pp. 143–87, offers a historical exegesis which is eminently
satisfying and is followed here without modification. This is achieved with
only the slightest emendation (in 5:11 he follows B. Duhm, *ZAW* 31 [1911],
23, in preferring *tsārō*, "his enemy" to MT *tsāw*, "command"). The fact that
chronological gaps between verses and shifts in subject are required does
not in itself undermine his interpretation, for such breaks in poetic texts
are common even when they allude to history. It is also open to question
that one can specify whether the prophetic allusions are after or before the
events with the exactitude Alt claims (e.g., how far has the Judean counterattack against Israel really progressed in vss. 9–10?).

[47] Alt, *op. cit.*, p. 175, seems quite justified in retaining the passive participles of MT, *'āšûq and rātsûts,* thereby making Ephraim the one who is
oppressed rather than the oppressor and at the same time accounting for the

Israel's doom resulted from her alliance with her long-time enemy Aram-Damascus.

The oracle strikingly gathers together the anti-Assyrian policy of Pekah and the pro-Assyrian policy of Ahaz as equally fallacious because under the cloak of self-defense the kingdoms have been drawn into internecine strife in an effort to gain territory and superior status in Palestine at the expense of one another. Yahweh's judgment falls with equal force upon the two kingdoms. Israel has wronged Judah in its savage attack upon Jerusalem and, for this, Israel has suffered the double blow of a Judean counterthrust and an Assyrian invasion from the north. At the same time Judah exceeded her warrant of chastisement against Israel and sought self-aggrandizement by invading Ephraim, and she too will suffer the consequences. *Hosea sees, as it were, a complicated network of political sin and punishment, one nation's wrong giving rise to a counter-wrong. Yet neither nation can excuse its political sins by blaming them upon the enemy. Yahweh's wrath works through the swift-moving and rapidly shifting events to judge first one kingdom and then another.*

The sudden and devastating invasion of Israel by Tiglath-pileser is more explicitly reflected in a threat against the king and priests, whose religio-political sins have proved "a trap at Mizpah," "a snare stretched on Tabor," and "a pit at Shittim" (5:1–2). Mizpah ("watchtower," "lookout") is a common biblical place name. In addition to the well-known Mizpah of Benjamin, there are sites so named in the Judean Shephelah (Josh. 15:38), in the vicinity of Mount Hermon (Josh. 11:3), in Moab (I Sam. 22:3), and one or two in Gilead (Gen. 31:49; Judg. 10:17; 11:11, 34). Mount Tabor was in Galilee on the northern edge of the Esdraelon Valley. Shittim was located in the plains of Moab near the northwest corner of the Dead Sea where the Israelites had sinned by worship of Baal-Peor (Num. 25; Hos. 9:10; Mic. 6:5). In this instance Israelite immorality and idolatry are said to deepen the pit once dug at Shittim. Tabor

---

active participles in LXX by the influence of the active forms of the same two verbs in Amos 4:1.

and Mizpah do not possess similar clear-cut associations with Israelite apostasy in any of the preserved biblical traditions. The probable allusion is to the regions of Galilee (Tabor) and Gilead (Mizpah and Shittim) which were overrun by Tiglath-pileser and made into Assyrian provinces (II Kings 15:29; *ANET*, p. 283).[48] The sins of Israel's kings and priests have thus "snared" and "netted" Israel in the Assyrian trap. The "pit of Shittim," the gross immorality and idolatry of Israel, will soon be too deep for any to escape, and all who have dug it will fall into it. The prophet insists that the campaign of Tiglath-pileser in 734 is not the last of the humiliations to be suffered by Israel.

The Assyrian king's attack on Israel was apparently also accompanied by attacks on trans-Jordan by Israel's long-time enemy, Moab. The Shalman who destroyed Beth-arbel mentioned by Hosea (10:14) is probably the Moabite King Salamanu described in Tiglath-pileser's annals as one of several Syrian and Palestinian rulers, including Jehoahaz of Judah, who paid him tribute in 733–732 (*ANET*, p. 282).[49] Beth-arbel has been plausibly located at Tell-Irbid in Gilead.[50] It was not un-

---

[48] Rieger, *op. cit.*, p. 82, believes that the outcome of Tiglath-pileser's attack on Israel, with the loss of Galilee and Gilead, is presupposed in 5:1–2, but his location to the east of the Jordan of all three of the place names in the prophetic oracle offers no identification of Tabor, which is obviously the mountain on the southern frontier of Galilee (note that Hosea says *"on* Tabor," not *"at* Tabor," or *"near* Tabor").

[49] The Shalman here mentioned is scarcely the Assyrian Shalmaneser III (859–827), whose western campaigns did not carry him into Israelite territory, nor Shalmaneser IV (783–773), who was occupied defending Assyria against Urartu, nor Shalmaneser V (726–722—his name appears in full form in II Kings 17:3; 18:9), who captured Samaria in 722 B.C., for his attack moved directly against Ephraim and did not need to concern itself with the regions of Galilee or Gilead, which since 733 had been Assyrian provinces. Furthermore, reference to Arbela on the Euphrates River seems out of the question for the great distance from Israel and lack of reference to a severe attack on that city during the reign of any of the Shalmanesers militate against it. The Moabite king Salamanu was first proposed by E. Schrader, *Keilinschriften und das Alte Testament,* 1st ed., 1872, p. 441 (but rejected by him in the 3rd ed.). So, also, Mauchline, *op. cit.,* pp. 679–80, and A. H. Van Zyl, *The Moabites,* pp. 23–24, 149, who notes a similar Moabite raid in Elisha's time (II Kings 13:20), but it is a dubious parallel since the raids are described as annual incursions by small bands of insufficient size to take cities.

[50] The location at Irbid was first hinted at by Eusebius, who described

common for Assyria to reward a loyal vassal with territory and spoil; apparently in return for Salamanu's submission he was allowed to harass the weakened Israelites. The terrible carnage, in which women and children were killed, was typical of trans-Jordan warfare. Sometimes it was more savage than that waged by the Assyrians who, apart from rebellious leaders, did not normally slaughter civilians. It was for the prophet a symbol of the worst that was to befall Israel.

We have noted the politically complex oracle on the Israelite-Judean War of 735–734 in 5:8–12, which refers to the reign of Pekah. The following strophe (5:13–14), which appears to be connected with it (note similarity of vss. 12 and 14), may allude to events in chronological succession.[51] If so they may refer to the submission of Hoshea to Assyria at the beginning of his reign as Ahaz of Judah had submitted to Assyria two years earlier. This interpretation is facilitated by the restoration of "Judah" in 13d (cf. parallelism in vss. 13 and 14) but does not depend upon it:

> When Ephraim saw his sickness,
>   and Judah his wound,
> then Ephraim went to Assyria,
>   and (Judah) sent to the great king.
>   (5:13)

Even if the verse does not allude to a specific event but to the general alliance policy of the northern and southern kingdoms,[52] it could have been written only after Ahaz' submission to Tiglath-

---

Arbela as "beyond the Jordan in the region of Pella, a town of Palestine" (*Onomasticon* 48, 50), and has been widely accepted (W. F. Albright, *BASOR* 35 [1929], 10; A. Jirku, *ZDPV* 53 [1930], 150; F. M. Abel, *Géographie de la Palestine*, II, 267).

[51] So argues Alt, *op. cit.*, pp. 177–82, but he divides the literary units so that vss. 12–14 are a whole; thus the images of Yahweh as moth and rot in vs. 12 and lion in vs. 14 create an "envelope" form.

[52] Such is the tentative view of Mauchline, *op. cit.*, p. 622, who insists that "we seek in vain for a crisis caused by a foreign invader when both Judah and Ephraim appealed to Assyria for help" and therefore tends to regard Menahem as the king who "went to Assyria." While it is strictly true that Hoshea did not seek Assyria, for he was hand-picked by Assyria or at least pro-Assyrian from the start, the prophet could certainly say that in the support given Hoshea's revolt "Ephraim went to Assyria," i.e., became pro-Assyrian, by whatever means.

pileser in 734 and probably only before Hoshea's approach to Egypt in 729 since the kingdom of the Nile is not mentioned at all where one would naturally expect it. Another oracle to be dated early in the reign of Hoshea is 8:7–10. Israel is already in exile, "swallowed up . . . among the nations as a worthless vessel" (vs. 8), following Tiglath-pileser's drastic reduction of the kingdom and large-scale deportations. Yet with all that, Hoshea courts Assyria's favor, but this time "the wild ass" Israel "wanders alone," without her Damascene ally (vs. 9).

The negotiations of Hoshea with Egypt in 727–726 after the death of Tiglath-pileser are reflected in two passages in which Egypt suddenly appears beside Assyria as a much-sought-after political partner. The prophet warns that Egypt will be as futile a source of help as Assyria (7:11–16). The last lines of the passage are textually difficult but at the most they do not imply the exile of Israel to Egypt but only the failure of help so that Israel suffers "mockery in the land of Egypt" (vs. 16). The association of "tongue" (*lāshôn*) with "mockery" (*laʿag*) suggests that the original text, now corrupted beyond hope of restoration, coupled the terms as in Isaiah 28:11 and referred to "stammering or strange speech," and thus constituted a rebuke to trust in foreign power. The warning of 12:1 is against the consequence of foreign alliances with Assyria and Egypt, which like the east wind will only reward those who pursue them with scorching destruction. Of particular interest is the identification of the price of Egyptian alliance as the delivery of olive oil,[53] one of the chief Palestinian products, and is indicative of the drain of the economy caused by the repeated consignment of Palestinian agricultural produce and precious metals to the courts of Egypt and Assyria. To drought must be added the depletion caused by exports without corresponding imports (8:7):

> The standing grain has no heads,
>> it shall yield no meal;
> if it were to yield,
>> foreigners would consume it.

[53] For oil as a covenant gift see E. Sellin, *Zwoelfprophetenbuch*, 1921, pp. 94–95, and J. Pedersen, *Der Eid bei den Semiten*, 1914, pp. 25, 49.

The threat of 9:10–14 may date from the final year or two of the northern kingdom, for although vs. 13 is textually corrupt, the Masoretic text includes the city of Tyre, which figured in the final rebellion of the northern kingdom. The verse may be read:

> When I looked, Ephraim's sons were transplanted to Tyre;
> Ephraim sent forth his sons to slaughter.

If so, Hosea anticipates the sale of Israelite captives as slaves to Tyre (cf. Amos 1:9). Or possibly it should be reconstructed:

> When I looked, Ephraim like Tyre was bereaved of her sons;
> Ephraim sent forth his sons to slaughter.

This gives a somewhat closer parallelism but is historically less convincing for after Tyre settled with Assyria, following a five-year siege, the island city was not touched, and the seaport soon regained her control over Citium on Cyprus.[54] Thus it is not clear that a prophetic threat that Samaria would be like Tyre would hold much terror. The former meaning is more likely but the uncertain text forbids dogmatism.

In many passages the disintegration of law and order through default of leadership is vividly portrayed. Organized banditry thrives under the protection of the kings (7:1–4), and the court circles hatch plots of murder against the kings (7:5–7). The burning ambition of the robber and the lust for power of the princes make them like heated ovens. *We are afforded a picture of the erosion of central authority in Samaria* so that the presumed "kings" could not enforce law and order throughout the realm and therefore had to depend upon the cooperation of local strongmen (such as Menahem of Tirzah in the days of Zechariah and Shallum, and Pekah of Gilead during the rule of Menahem), who were given free reign to plunder the countryside as they saw fit. By turns these regional leaders aspired to the throne in Samaria and succeeded in seizing it. *Intrigues and assassinations are the subject of several of the prophet's messages* (7:5–7; 8:4–5; 9:15; 13:9–11), and always he voices a feeling of horror and contempt that is widely shared, in contrast to Amos' con-

---

[54] Olmstead, *op. cit.*, pp. 204–5.

tempt of Jeroboam, which stood alone in its inexplicable negativism.

Against this breakup of the social and political norms, the confidence in arms and fortifications is strangely incongruous and pitiable. Israel has "forgotten his Maker" and regarded the laws of Yahweh "as a strange thing"; instead he has preferred sacrifice (8:13) and has trusted in palaces (8:14a) and in the latest military equipment (14:3a; Hebrew 14:4a).[55] But this is all to no avail for "they shall return to Egypt" (8:13b) and upon Judah's fortified cities Yahweh will "send a fire . . . and it shall devour his strongholds" (8:14b; the echo of the foreign-oracle framework in Amos 1–2 is probably drawn from the same execration traditions that were used by Amos and Joel).

"The Return to Egypt"

The threat of a return to Egypt (8:13b; 9:3, 6a) has sometimes been understood as evidence of Hosea's uncertainty about the source of Israel's ultimate downfall. It may even appear that early in his ministry, before Assyrian power became pronounced, he regarded Egypt as the real danger. The difficulties in such an interpretation are, however, formidable.

In the first place, Egypt was not a factor in Palestinian politics until precisely at the time when Assyria had reasserted her strength and established provinces deep in Palestine and had largely obliterated the northern kingdom in 734. In fact, the So (often but probably erroneously connected with the *Sib'e* mentioned by Sargon) with whom Hoshea intrigued (II Kings 17:4) in 727–726 was not a pharaoh but at most a vizier of the pharaoh or probably a local dynast, of whom there were many at this period, and possibly merely a commander-in-chief of one such dynast.[56] Of any earlier genuine threat from a badly divided and weakened Egypt we know nothing.

---

[55] Y. Kaufmann, *The Religion of Israel,* 1960, p. 375, goes so far as to say, "The first biblical author, indeed the first man in history, to condemn militarism as a religious-moral sin was Hosea . . . it may be only exaggerated militarism and the cult of power that he was denouncing. Even so, such a reproof in the days of Tiglath-pileser and Shalmaneser must be regarded

In the second place, when Egypt did appear in 727 it was as an ally of Israel *against* Assyria, and Hosea gives not the least hint that he expected Egypt to defeat Assyria and then to turn on Israel. If anything, a passage such as 9:1-6 suggests that he thinks of the flight of Israelite refugees to Egypt in the face of an Assyrian attack.[57] That he expects a last-minute desertion of Israel by Egypt, so that both powers would feast on the spoils of Israel, is questionable inasmuch as, with the exception of the last years of Assyrian power, Egypt was never prone to join with Assyria—especially against nearby states. Such a prospect might be understandable only if the So with whom Hoshea was negotiating was aiming at establishing himself as pharaoh by means of Assyria's help. But if that is the case he chose an improbable way of securing Assyrian help and our sources are silent.

Thirdly, the prophecies of Hosea concerning Egypt as the place of Israel's return and punishment are in strongly cultic condemnations upon Israel for failing to keep her special vows to Yahweh. Israel was to have been a special people obedient to Yahweh and set apart from the worship typical of the other peoples ("Exult not like the peoples!" 9:1, and possibly "Ephraim mixes himself with the peoples," 7:8) but has preferred the harlot's life by turning to religious idolatry and political intrigue internally and pointless alliances externally. For this she has forfeited her special status with Yahweh and her right to the land.

---

as a climax of religious-moral idealism" (cf. the fuller remarks in *History of the Religion of Israel,* III, pp. 138–39 [Hebrew]).

56 It is now widely agreed that So = Sib'e cannot be the later Pharaoh Shabaka. A. Alt, *Israel und Aegypten. Die Politischen Beziehungen der Koenige von Israel und Juda zu den Pharaonen,* pp. 56–58, believes that he was a provincial prince. S. Yeivin, "Who Was So' the King of Egypt?" *VT* 2 (1952), 164–68, suggests that So is a title for vizier and not a proper name at all and that I Kings 17:4 refers to the vizier of Lower Egypt responsible for Asiatic affairs. R. Borger, "Das Ende des aegyptischen Feldherrn Sib'e = So'," *JNES* 19 (1960), 49–53, argues that the ideogram SIPA of Sargon's annal should be read as the Egyptian equivalent of the Akkadian *re'u,* and thus as a folk etymology, not a proper name, by which the Egyptian commander is called "the Shepherd." This would remove all connection between the general in Sargon's annals and the So of II Kings 17:4 or the Pharaoh Shabaka.

57 T. H. Robinson, *Die Zwoelf Kleinen Propheten, Hosea bis Micha, HZAT,* 1938, pp. 35–36.

The return to Egypt is, therefore, a typological concept tantamount to "an annulling of all the redemptive work which had
been done for and in Israel."[58] It possesses certain similarities to
the recapitulation motif of sin and judgment in Hosea: the deepening of the idolatrous pit of Shittim (5:2), the requiting of the
immorality of the days of Gibeah in Gibeah (10:9), and the
visiting of the blood of Jezreel upon the house of Jehu in Jezreel
(1:4–5). There is the difference, however, that the Egyptian
bondage and wilderness motifs emphasize a forthcoming action
of God similar to earlier decisive actions of judgment and redemption, whereas the references to Shittim, Gibeah, and Jezreel
emphasize that particular political and religious crimes of the past
will be judged shortly in a manner commensurate with their hei-
nousness. The Egyptian motif is thus genuine typology, whereas
the others are declarations of moral cause and effect.[59] Accordingly, the allusions to return to Egypt should not be taken
literally, if only because they cannot be reconciled with an
equally literal return to the wilderness, for the prophet could
hardly have threatened Israel with both fates at the same time
unless he had provided for a second exodus from Egypt, which
he did not.

In the beautiful oracle telling of Yahweh's love for his son
whom he called from Egypt the prophet in fact corrected a literal
understanding of his return-to-Egypt motif. If we read 11:5 with
the MT rather than treating the opening negative particle as the
last word of vs. 4, we have the following plain sense:

> They [Israelites] shall not return to Egypt,[60]
> but Assyria shall be their king,
> for they have refused to return to me.

[58] Mauchline, *op. cit.*, p. 653.

[59] The motifs of a return to Egyptian bondage and of a return to the
wilderness, stressing as they do the recurrence of phrases in God's relation
to his people, are perhaps to be described as *Endzeit ist Urzeit*, but that
they depend upon a particular pre-Hebraic eschatology is doubtful in the
extreme (against H. Gunkel, *Schoepfung und Chaos in Urzeit und Endzeit*,
1922).

[60] The verse is also understood as a negative assertion by S. M. Lehrman,
"Hosea," in A. Cohen, ed., *The Twelve Prophets*, p. 43, but he does not
relate the verse to others in which the prophet uses Egyptian exile figuratively.

Hosea interprets the typological concept by underscoring its present historical actualization. *In the present situation what is meant by the return to Egypt is exile to Assyria.* This bold identification of Assyria as the instrument of punishment is echoed in 8:1–3, where the enemy is pictured "as a vulture over the house of Yahweh," hovering, waiting for the inner collapse which results from breaking Yahweh's covenant and transgressing his law. Although the term *nesher* is used for various powers—Assyria (Deut. 28:49), Neo-Babylonia (Jer. 4:13; 48:40; 49:22) and their kings: Nebuchadnezzar (Ezek. 17:3) and Necho (Ezek. 17:7)—in this case only Assyria could be seriously described as "over" or "upon" the house of Yahweh.

We conclude then that Hosea's references to Egypt are typologically determined when he speaks of exile to Egypt (with the possible exception of 9:1–6, where the flight of refugees to Egypt or a coalition of Assyria and Egypt against Israel may be envisioned) *but historically determined when he speaks of negotiations for alliance.* There is no evidence for a development in his thought from an early identification of Egypt as the actual threat to Israel to a later identification of Assyria; nor did he ever regard Egypt as a more serious threat than Assyria.

As to the form of the national punishment, there is virtual unanimity between Hosea and Amos, although they use quite different language to describe it. *There is to be a devastating military assault upon the country (10:9–10) of which the Judean counterattack of 734–733 (5:8–9) and the Assyrian and Moabite attacks on Galilee and trans-Jordan (5:1–2; 5:10; 10:13–15) are a foretaste.* Although the root *glh* is never used by Hosea in the sense of exile, the fate is clearly enough prophesied. Yahweh will "gather up" (8:10) and "carry off" (5:14) the Israelites and they shall be "wanderers among the nations" (9:17).

Political Hope in Hosea

It is customary and proper to recognize a strong note of hope in the thought of Hosea. But what was the nature of this hope and, in particular, did it have a discernibly political character?

Of the several promises for the future expressed by the book only some may be reasonably attributed to the prophet. Others cannot be reconciled with the oracles of indictment and threat, not merely because they express hope but because of basic inconsistencies in outlook.

The sharp distinction of 1:7 between Israel, on whom Yahweh will not have pity, and Judah, on whom he will have pity, is utterly inexplicable alongside the several passages in which Judah and Israel stand side by side under the judgment of God (5:8–15; 6:4; 12:2; and possibly 10:11, although the mention of Judah may be secondary since it tends to disrupt the poetic parallelism). The altogether unqualified promise of 1:7 finds no point of connection with these other passages, for it takes no account of Judah's conversion. It possesses rather a blunt pro-Judean bias typical of another passage, namely, 11:12, in which Judah's continued faithfulness to Yahweh is baldly stated in contrast to Israel's "lies" and "deceit." The most that can be said for 1:7 is that it is a passage deriving from someone other than the prophet, certainly after 722 and probably after 701.

The expectation that a reunited people of God will "return and seek Yahweh their God, and David their king" (3:5) is equally difficult to locate in the thought of Hosea, who speaks so negatively of the contemporary kingship and whose norm for the past is not the righteous king but the desert $t\bar{o}r\bar{a}h$-teacher Moses (4:1–3; 12–13). That Hosea may have expected a restoration of kingship is possible but that he should place the seeking of the southerner David on a level with the seeking of Yahweh is not very likely.[61] The verse is apparently a later Judean commentary on the preceding verse.

We must turn elsewhere for the genuine outlook of Hosea upon the future. The key is in the allegory of the faithless wife who is brought back to the husband's home, at which time he says to her: "You must remain as mine for many days; you shall

[61] N. Snaith, *Mercy and Sacrifice*, p. 50, argues compellingly that the idea of a reunion of north and south under a Davidic head must be a southern idea and thus later than Hosea. He applies the argument to 3:5 and to 1:10—2:1 (but see 64).

not be a harlot, or give yourself to another man; and I will be (faithful) to you" (2:3). To this the prophet adds the interpretation: "For the children of Israel shall remain many days without king or prince, without sacrifice or pillar, without ephod or idol" (2:4). The prophet proclaims the punishment of Israel's institutional collapse; all of her wedding rights with Yahweh have been canceled by her faithlessness and she is to live in a kind of probation. The apparent intent is to determine whether or not she can be rid of her previously incurable waywardness. Presumably the prophet is as uncertain of Israel's future constancy as he is uncertain of Gomer's. In the period of probation he pledges his refusal to seek another wife or concubine. *By implication, this is also Yahweh's promise that he will not turn to another people in the interim of Israel's exile.* Already we see a departure from the thought of Amos, who was quite prepared to see Yahweh raise up a new people. Hosea is not so prepared. The period of probation, "the many days," is not determinable but is not inconsistent with the temporal reference of a similar prophecy in 8:10:

> Though they seek allies among the nations,
> I will now gather them up.
> They shall cease for a time
> from raising up king and princes.

The former period of time is seen from the standpoint of the quarantined wife Gomer and of the exiled wife Israel. For them, whatever the actual time, it will seem like "many days." The latter reference is from the standpoint of the frenzied alliance-seeking activity of the Samarian court. Soon the northerners will have to take a breathing spell "for a time," which emphasizes their impatience and the unalterability of Yahweh's decision.

Furthermore, it appears that this period of the suspension of Israel's political and religious institutions is equated in the prophet's mind with the return to the wilderness, succinctly expressed in 12:9:

> I will once more cause you to live in tents,
> as in the days of the festival.

He seems to think of the simple nomadic life prior to the occupation of Canaan when festivals were observed in tents without the
deep corruption of the priesthood and sacrifice which has en-
trapped Israel in Canaan (chap. 4; 6:6). The fullest development of this concept appears in the long allegorical interpretation
of chap. 2. In this instance the future wilderness sojourn is pictured as a time of retrysting when Yahweh will renew his relation
with Israel. The stress is not upon the probationary punishment
but upon the glorious renewal of Israel, and the passage has very
possibly been recast by later hands. Nevertheless, the element of
Israel's moral renewal, so conspicuously lacking in the promissory
passage of Amos, is present here.[62] Israel "shall answer as in the
days of her youth, as at the time when she came out of Egypt,"
i.e., obediently to her divine husband. The Baal cult will be
rooted out so that Yahweh will no longer be called Baal, for his
nature will be sharply distinguished from that of Baal. Israel will
no longer need to rely upon implements of war; Yahweh will be
her security. Finally, the terms of the new marriage vows will be
righteousness, justice, steadfast love, mercy, and faithfulness. The
reappropriation of the symbolic names, so that Jezreel now refers
to God's sowing agricultural bounty in the land, Not Pitied becomes Pitied, and Not My People is reversed to My People, may
or may not be directly from the prophet. Elsewhere, however, in
his authentic words he underscores the curse upon nature owing
to Israel's sin so that the emphasis in this passage upon the blessing accorded to nature in the time of Israel's repentance and
conversion is not improbable, even to the point of a covenant
with the animal world (2:18a).[63]

[62] P. Humbert, "La logique de la perspective nomade chez Osée et l'unité
d'Osée, 2:4–22," *Festschrift Karl Marti,* 1925, pp. 158–66, finds 2:4–22
entirely Hoseanic, with the exception of vs. 20. He shows that its leading
themes are part and parcel of oracles in chaps. 4–14. His analysis, however,
takes too literally the nomadic conditions of the future renewal and does not
sufficiently grasp the typological character of the prophet's thought.

[63] It is true that the motifs of amity with wild beasts (2:18a), peace
among men (2:18b), and the conversation among the elements of nature
(2:21–22) are all fully developed in apocalyptic writings at a much later
date. Nevertheless a very interesting passage from the fourteenth-century
Canaanite Baal and Anath text associates the theme of peace with the theme

A further elaboration of the symbolic names in 1:10–11 = Hebrew 2:1–2 may also contain genuine Hoseanic recollections —for example, the reunion of the two kingdoms and their coming up from exile as "one company" (so reading instead of "one head")—but the conception of the vastness of the renewed Israel and its restoration are not related to moral regeneration (although conceivably such was implied).[64] The strongest contention against the passage, however, is the awkward expression "in the place [passage? geographical location?] where it was said to them, 'You are Not My People,' " which is an allusion either to the already written account of the symbolic names or to the place Jezreel where Hosea is thought to be at the time of the naming. In either case Hosea did not write such an expression, for the one usage shows too much literary self-consciousness and the other is a plain misunderstanding of the term "Jezreel" in vss. 4–5.

For Hosea, then, the expected exile from the land and return to the wilderness are identical occurrences seen from two points of view—the standpoint of contemporary history (punishment and hoped-for purgation by deportation) *and the standpoint of tradition history* (punishment and hoped-for purgation by wandering in the wilderness). This equation is clearest in 9:1–6 and in 12:9. In the latter verse Yahweh threatens,

> "I will once more cause you to live in tents,
>   as in the days of the festival."

---

of conversation among natural elements, and the amity with beasts may be implied in the annunciation of peace:

> Take war [*away*] from the earth,
>   Banish (all) *strife* from the soil;
> Pour peace into earth's very bowels,
>   *Much* amity into earth's bosom. . . .
> For
> I've a word I fain would tell thee,
>   A speech I would utter to thee:
> Speech of tree and whisper of stone,
>   Converse of heaven with earth
>   E'en of the deeps with the stars.
>   (V C 12–15, 18–22 [*ANET*, 136])

[64] H. H. Wolff, "Der grosse Jesreeltag (Hosea 2:1–3)," *Evangelische Theologie* 12 (1952–53), 78–104, as the result of a careful comparative linguistic and ideological analysis, concludes that the passage is basically authentic.

In the former the prophet, having threatened Israel with exile in
Assyria and Egypt, asks,

> "What will you do on the appointed day,
>   and on the occasion of the feast of Yahweh?"

The point is that Israel, about to return to the wilderness of exile,
will be forced to worship without the elaborate cult of Canaan
(cf. 3:4). Her festivals will be simple as they once were in the
wilderness after the escape from Egypt. She will find it difficult
to adjust to this simple religious order but it will be necessary, if
only because the foodstuffs once given in sacrifice will now be
needed to keep the captives alive. Thus in the Hoseanic view
of the future there is an irreducible blend of punishment and
purgation which belongs to his fundamental outlook, and these
polarities he is able to represent in the images of Gomer's probation and of Israel's return to bondage or to the wilderness.[65]

The Futility of Foreign Alliances

The religious and political sins of God's people ("their twofold iniquity," 10:10) are closely joined in the imagery of the
husband Yahweh and the wife Israel. Israel has come to think
of Baal as the giver of the essentials of life, which were ample in
the era of Jeroboam but have since become increasingly scarce
owing to famine, civil strife and consequent plundering of fields
and neglect of agriculture, and heavy tribute to Assyria and
Egypt. There is a tragic causal relation between dependence upon
Baal for food and clothing and the loss of these goods to foreign
powers. These boons, which Israel regarded as her wage for con-
sorting with Baal, are now surrendered to Assyria and Egypt.
Once pursued by Baal, she now pursues him and "her lovers" in
a frenzied effort to secure minimal sustenance. The figure of the
"lovers" is drawn from the Baal cult and refers in chap. 2 partly
to the Baal worshipers who have corrupted Israel. It has, how-

[65] E. Sellin, *Mose und seine Bedeutung fuer die israelitisch-juedische
Religionsgeschichte,* 1922, illuminates the reconciliation of the idea of
judgment in Hosea, especially the servitude in Egypt, with the ultimate
salvation hopes of Yahweh.

ever, a second meaning in that it refers also to foreign powers with whom Israel consorts for her protection. Ezekiel has more fully developed the imagery in a political manner ("You played the harlot with the Assyrians," 16:28; "you gave gifts to all your lovers," 16:33), but the concept is already present in Hosea. Consequently the political complexion of the allegory of Hosea and Gomer is as strong as the religious complexion, as is already hinted in the symbolic name of Jezreel (1:4–5).

Foreign alliances are as much the blandishments of strangers as are the cult practices which Baalism has introduced into Yahwism. Hosea opposes the alliances in a measure because Israel enters them "foolishly and unthinkingly" (7:11). Her leaders grasp desperately for assistance in shoring up their collapsing thrones. Further, the pursuit of alliances with the great powers is as vain as "herding the east wind," for they cannot be caught and held; indeed, at any moment they are likely to turn and destroy those who have put their trust in them. The fickleness both of Israel's rulers and of the Egyptian and Assyrian masters makes such alliances risky in the extreme. The Assyrian vassal treaties in the west involved the invoking of the Assyrian gods and the vassal's gods as a sanction against oath-breaking.[66] Hosea does not openly criticize the invoking of Assyrian gods, unless "you (should) know no God but me" (13:4) alludes to treaty oaths, but it is probably a reference to Baal (cf. 13:1).

This is not to imply that Hosea found swearing by Assyrian gods acceptable. We suggest rather that he was much more shocked by the hollow and misplaced oath in the name of Yahweh. It was an invocation of Yahweh in an effort to change Yahweh's nature and to forestall his plans of judgment. But, although Assyria as Yahweh's instrument can destroy Israel, it is

---

[66] Such western Assyrian vassal treaties as we possess, e.g., Esarhaddon with Baal of Tyre, Ashurnirari with Mati'ilu of Bit-Agusi (E. F. Weidner, *Archiv fuer Orientforschung* 8 [1932], 17–34), and Mati'ilu with Barga'yah of KTK (H. Bauer, *Archiv fuer Orientforschung* 8 [1932], 1–16) invariably invoke the gods of both suzerain and vassal. In this matter the Assyrians seem simply to have become willing heirs of the Hittite practice. On the contrary, no Assyrian vassal treaty from Mesopotamia is known to contain an oath witnessed by the vassal gods. For a brief survey of the evidence see M. Tsevat, *JBL* 78 (1959), 199–200.

"unable to cure you," for Yahweh as a lion will rend Israel and Judah (5:13–14). Israel has turned to brazen boasts in arms and wealth (10:13; 12:8) and "their heart has been lifted up" (13:6); thus "Israel has forgotten his Creator" (8:14). *Hosea, like Amos, was more concerned with the covert paganism which called itself Yahwism than he was with outright and clearly identifiable rejection of religion.* The vassal treaties were, therefore, sheer deceptions which Yahweh could not bless. The armaments of Assyria and Egypt which these treaties summoned would only turn against Israel and Judah and bring their downfall, "for they sow the wind, and they shall reap the whirlwind" (8:7).

Had any of the terms in the historical situation been different, would Hosea have felt differently about alliances or was he opposed to them unalterably? Let us suppose, for instance, that a faithful Yahwistic king had sought an alliance in order to keep Israel independent and to develop a covenant-based community with social justice and economic prosperity. From the extant book of Hosea no certain answer can be derived, for it would presuppose so different a historical context that we should have to imagine an entirely different call for the prophet Hosea and a whole new message in which his basic convictions would be quite otherwise expressed.

Hosea does not seem to reject all treaties with foreign powers on dogmatic grounds because they necessarily represent a breach of the marriage compact between Yahweh and Israel. His polemic against the alliances is rather historically based and must be seen against the chaos of the last years of the Israelite kingship with its social and economic ruin. To be sure, Hosea emphasizes Israel's uniqueness among the nations, for she is like the first fruit on a fig tree (9:10); and she is not to rejoice in the nature cults which delight other nations (9:1), for when she does become like these nations Israel "fades away," loses her strength, and becomes senile (7:8–10). The uniqueness of Israel is not defined, however, as a self-contained religious and social community which is unable to intermarry or to establish ties of an economic and political nature with other states. *Israel is not warned against foreign alliances because they are undertaken with non-Yahwistic states. She is warned against them because, under the present cir-*

cumstances, such alliances are symptoms of her desertion of Yahweh, for they reflect a basic inner want of faith and stability.

Amos and Hosea Compared

The most striking differences between Hosea's and Amos' references to the foreign nations are Hosea's almost total disregard of the neighboring Syro-Palestinian states and the absence of an assertion of the equality of all peoples in the manner of Amos 9:7. Although Hosea apparently knew the cult traditions against foreign nations which Amos employed in chaps. 1–2 (cf. Hos. 8:14b), he preferred a quite different starting point, namely, the husband-wife image and the symbolic names of his children. It is possible that he already knew the book of Amos, or at least the spoken oracles of the prophet, and felt that the judgment on the nations had been sufficiently established. There is also the change that had come over the Syro-Palestinian corridor with the vigorous militarism of Tiglath-pileser. There was now less doubt that Assyria could overthrow these little western states. Israel had seen it happen again and again. By 732 most of the states threatened by Amos either had been incorporated as Assyrian provinces (Damascus; the greater part of Israel) or were tributary vassals of Assyria (Tyre; Edom; Ammon; Moab; Judah). Only Philistia was still independent and even she had suffered an Assyrian attack in 734. Thus, to a very large extent the threats of Amos against the neighboring peoples had been fulfilled, although not with the total destruction which his oracles had envisioned. This may help to account for Hosea's omissions.

Another factor is the strong personal character of the husband-wife imagery, which threw into sharp relief the intimate relation between God and his people. Since Yahweh has no other wives, the other nations of the Near East are largely disregarded. They do not figure in Hosea's prophecies except as possible sources of corruption for Israel ("lovers") or as instruments of Yahweh's chastisement of his faithless wife ("the enemy"; cf. also 8:7b–8; 10:10). The two probable allusions to neighboring states, Moab (10:13–15) and Tyre (9:13), speak apparently of actions taken by these states against Israel. Moab has attacked Beth-arbel in trans-Jordan, and Tyre will take Israelite captives as slaves in spite of their agreement as rebels against Assyria. Neither action, however, is condemned; both are simply noted as warnings of further attacks on Israel. Nowhere in the book is there a specific indictment against a foreign nation.

Yet it would be a mistake to conclude that the silence of Hosea on this point demonstrates conscious disagreement with Amos. The fact that Israel was the bride of Yahweh need hardly require that the other peoples of the earth are worthless or unaccountable to Yahweh.[67] Facing as he did the immediate and rapidly worsening conditions in Israel following the death of Jeroboam, Hosea's attention, not surprisingly, turned decisively to internal matters. While he calls Yahweh Israel's "Creator," it does not necessarily follow that Hosea regarded all other peoples as beyond the pale of Yahweh. In fact, the contrary is indicated by Yahweh's raising up of Assyria to chastise Israel (10:10):

> I will come against the apostate people to punish them;
> and peoples shall be gathered against them.

Moreover, the prophet's indictment of Israel does not suggest that he had a merely nationalistic outlook upon the other states of the ancient world. He indicts the sins of Israel as strongly as Amos did, and he is equally unyielding in his insistence upon a total judgment in the sense that all Israelites will be affected by the radical alteration of national life. This radical transformation of Israel by judgment is hopeful only in the sense that Yahweh

---

[67] It is obvious that Hosea stresses Israel's distinctiveness and especially so in cultic terms: by her recourse to idolatry "Israel is defiled" (5:3; 6:10; 9:4), but it is extreme to say that 9:1, "Do not rejoice, O Israel, as one of the peoples," is the strongest formulation of Israel's exclusiveness until the prophet's time or that "peoples" here are in effect "heathens" (against A. Bertholet, *Die Stellung der Israeliten und der Juden zu den Fremden,* pp. 82–84; cf. also Rieger, *op. cit.,* pp. 87–88; B. Duhm, *Die Theologie der Propheten,* 1875, p. 130). Nor is this supposed separation of Israel from the heathen any adequate explanation of the prophet's absence of reference to foreign nations in a positive sense, for nothing is said by Hosea that represents a basic departure from Amos. That Israel is not to have anything to do with foreign cults does not for a moment mean that Yahweh has no connection with the other peoples or that Israel is barred from various kinds of economic, social, and political contacts with them.

will continue to seek a response of obedient love from his people. Yet toward that end all of his people will suffer severe judgments.

Hosea also makes use of the traditions of Israel in an extremely free and non-chauvinistic manner. The "Yahwistic" revolution of Jehu was a horrible and entirely unjustified bloodbath (1:4). Jacob is pictured as an ancestor whose grasping attitude toward Esau had to be repented of (12:2–6).[68] Ephraim's wealth under Jeroboam has spurred her on to reckless self-confidence (12:8), but the weight of Israel's guilt is too great to be overlooked. *Thus Israel is like the nations in that she seeks power and wealth without corresponding social and moral obligations. She is unlike the nations in that she should know better and will be held accountable to the revelation she has had,* a process of judgment described with characteristic Hebraic directness (6:5):

> Therefore I have hewn them by the prophets;
> I have slain them by the words of my mouth.

We must conclude, therefore, that in spite of his pronounced cultic definition of Israel as a peculiar people and in spite of his omission of comment on Yahweh's relation to foreign nations in a positive sense, Hosea's outlook on Israel's and Judah's relations with foreign states is only relatively different from Amos' outlook.

On several chief points Amos and Hosea are at one. The ground of their outlook on the foreign nations is religious. All that they say presupposes the peculiar faith of Israel in Yahweh, who rules history and has raised up one particular people for an especially close relation to him. But granted this faith, each prophet is well informed about international affairs and generally shows a realistic understanding of the balance of power in the

---

[68] Rieger, *op. cit.*, pp. 46–64, argues that chap. 12 is based on oral traditions which are differently arranged and different in content and orientation from the traditions in Genesis 27. The intent of Hosea in employing this material was to reproach the sinful society of his time with the corruption which had actually characterized the highly regarded fathers of the people. H. L. Ginsberg, "Hosea's Ephraim; More Fool than Knave," *JBL* 80 (1961), 339–47, regards Hosea 12:1–14 as an unfavorable legend of the El-beth-el cult whereas Genesis 35:1–7 is a favorable legend of the same cult. He is inclined to believe that the prophet wholly fabricated his own version in order to denigrate the non-Yahwistic fetishistic tendency of the cult.

ancient world. Each thinks of Assyria as the means of Yahweh's punishment of Israel. Hosea is especially sensitive to the machinations of Israel's foreign policy, swept first one way and then the other.

The differences between the two prophets are also noteworthy. Amos shows a broad international outlook which he expresses not only by indicting foreign powers but by a sweeping formulation of God's concern for other nations. Hosea possesses no such open interest, and we may only infer that he was aware of Amos' view but did not choose to deny or to endorse it. *In general, Hosea's silence favors agreement with Amos rather than dissent and the silence may best be accounted for by the peculiar character of his imagery for God and by his intense preoccupation with the disintegration of the northern kingdom. Hosea, on the other hand, is more exact about the political sins he witnesses: internal intrigue and assassination,* the horrible legacy of the Jehu revolution which was not ended with the obliteration of Jehu's dynasty but had become chronic methods of internal politics; *and foreign alliances,* which express on the level of international life the basic insecurity of the kingdom, its lack of trust in God, and its failure to chart a stable course in the world.

Both of these interests of the prophet accord with the historical situation from 752 to 722, for they were precisely the matters of public moment in those distressing years. Hosea insisted that political violence and opportunism could not be atoned for by increased cultic activity, for in fact all of Israel's sins were of one piece, whether religious or political, inasmuch as they stemmed from a breach of relationship with Yahweh and were sins against the knowledge of the God who had chosen to know Israel in a special way. A vassal covenant with Assyria that takes its rise in breach of Israel's covenant with Yahweh cannot be a constructive factor in Israel's life. Hosea's religious convictions and his knowledge of the impermanence of revolutionary dynasties and of hastily conceived vassal treaties combined to assure him that Israel as a state was not long to survive. *That there was the possibility of a new beginning in a renewal of Israel's youth, even in the midst of her exile, is the one decisive point at which Hosea advanced beyond Amos' outlook upon Yahwism.*

Isaiah of Jerusalem

On international affairs in the ancient Near East Isaiah offers a wealth of comment commensurate with his long career, which coincided with the peak of Assyrian imperialism as prosecuted by the able rulers Tiglath-pileser III, Shalmaneser V, Sargon, and Sennacherib. The narrative episodes of the prophetic book, in part drawn from the book of Kings, supplemented by the oracles of Isaiah, illuminate several crises in Syro-Palestinian affairs in the last half of the eighth century. Especially are we afforded insight into the feelings of leaders and of people whom Isaiah generally opposed but whose views he nevertheless recorded with striking empathy if not genuine sympathy.

Isaiah's world vision shows his kinship to Amos, but his internationalism is even more explicit for he raises the motif of Yahweh as the judge of all national prides, including that of Assyria, to the level of a controlling principle which he applies to the flux of historic events. Isaiah sets the stage for the great prophets who were to follow him more than a century later, Jeremiah, Ezekiel, and Deutero-Isaiah, by providing them with the rudiments of a philosophy of history. In particular he shows with great effectiveness that one and the same nation, whether it be Judah or Assyria, may be both the instrument of Yahweh and a rebel against Yahweh and that the divine plan for history must reckon with both of these realities—and so also must the plans of men. Toward the end of his life he conceived of a confederation of nations which solves its disputes by prophetic arbitration.

The outlook of Isaiah on foreign affairs, while discernible in its main lines, is complicated by thorny problems of interpretation. The book of Isaiah has undergone expansion by later hands, even in chaps. 1–39, and it is not always possible to delineate the original prophetic units. Sometimes the materials do not lend themselves easily to a clear historical reconstruction, because of discontinuities within the narratives (e.g., in chaps. 6–8 and 36–39). Above all, the rather subtle dialectic of Isaiah's thought impelled him to encompass polarities which seem on the surface to be mutually contradictory. It will be our task to grapple with these literary, historical, and ideological issues. By noting in historical succession the prophet's response to contemporary international relations, we must attempt to grasp the basic structure of his thought. Although the way is treacherous, fraught as it is with constant temptations to simplify problems, certain illuminating conclusions can be reached about the religio-political thought of Isaiah.

Isaiah's Early Career: The Dialectic of Faith (742–740 to 721)

Isaiah's call to be a prophet came c. 742–740, the year of Uzziah's death and of Pekah's anti-Assyrian revolt in Israel. It was thus the consummate moment of the passing of Israelite-Judean hegemony over Syria-Palestine and simultaneously the moment of rapid Assyrian penetration of the West. The cosmic scope of Isaiah's interest is manifest in his call vision of the transcendent Yahweh, king of the world, who is associated with but not confined to the temple in Jerusalem. He is the Holy One, beyond all comparison with his creation, but nonetheless present to his creation inasmuch as "his glory fills the entire earth." Although neither Assyria nor any other foreign nation is mentioned in Isaiah 6, the orientation of the charge to Isaiah is such that all the peoples in the world, which belongs to Yahweh, are drawn at least potentially into the orbit of his concern. The grouping of the materials in chaps. 6–8 so that the reports and oracles of the international crisis of 735–733 in chaps. 7–8 follow immediately upon the call vision further expresses the unity of Isaiah's view of God and his view of the international scene. In this call vision and audition, as elsewhere in the book of Isaiah, the prophet is dependent upon the royal cult traditions in which the kingship of Yahweh was celebrated in the coronation of the Israelite king and in subsequent state ceremonies.[69] Isaiah naturally turns these

---

[69] Although the royal cult in Israel received its first significant treatment by S. Mowinckel, *Psalmenstudien II. Des Thronbesteigungsfest Yahwaes und der Ursprung der Eschatologie,* 1922, the most penetrating and judicious study has been made by A. R. Johnson, *Sacral Kingship in Ancient Israel* (cf. also his essay, "Hebrew Conceptions of Kingship," in S. H. Hooke, ed., *Myth, Ritual, and Kingship,* pp. 204–35). With respect to Isaiah's call

traditions to his own ends and, particularly in his announcement of the devastation of Israel (presumably he has both Israelite kingdoms in mind), he departs altogether from the cult traditions which spoke of the political upbuilding of Israel interrupted at most only by minor setbacks.

Soon after his call a son born to Isaiah was named Shear-jashub ("[only] a remnant shall return," 7:3) in order to stress the radical character of the destruction which he envisioned. This living sign was a warning both to Israel and to Judah. But shortly the paths of the two states diverged sharply and they pursued diametrically opposed foreign policies. The revolt of Pekah and the subsequent three-year withdrawal of Tiglath-pileser from the west led to a thriving anti-Assyrian coalition headed by Rezon of Damascus and submitted to with reluctance by Pekah of Israel. The coalition began to negotiate with other south Syrian states in the hope of enlarging participation. Philistia and Edom acceded, but Judah was divided in sympathy. Jotham, who may actually have represented Uzziah at the head of the Judean-led Syrian coalition of 742,[70] apparently continued the anti-Assyrian policy of his father.

At first Rezon and Pekah may have taken for granted that Judah would participate in the revolt. Since Jotham had strengthened Judean fortifications and campaigned successfully in Ammon (II Chron. 27:3–5), they had reason to regard Judah as an effective ally. There was, however, a strong pro-Assyrian party in Judah which was led by Ahaz, son and co-

---

vision proper, I. Engnell, *The Call of Isaiah*, 1949, establishes the influence of royal ideology in its form, although many of the author's proposals are wide of the mark and must be treated with caution.

[70] H. Winckler's theory of a north Syrian Ja-u-di (Judah), whose chief city was Samal, and who by coincidence had a king Izrijau (Azariah = Uzziah) at the same time as Azariah ruled in Jerusalem, was given wide currency by most historians, e.g., Olmstead, *op. cit.*, pp. 186–88, and Oesterley and Robinson, *A History of Israel*, 1932, I, 374. Of late the consensus has shifted to the opinion that the Azariah of the Assyrian records was, in fact, king of the biblical Judah; see, e.g., M. Noth, *The History of Israel*, 1958, p. 257, and J. Bright, *A History of Israel*, pp. 252–53. This hypothesis was convincingly set forth by H. M. Haydn, "Azariah of Judah and Tiglath-Pileser III," *JBL* 28 (1909), 182–99, and has been thoroughly reassessed and reconfirmed by H. Tadmor, "Azriyahu of Yaudi," *Scripta Hierosolymitana* 8 (1961), 232–71.

regent of Jotham. The struggle was so intense that the conspirators sent aid to Jotham (note that II Kings 15:37 reports, before
the death of Jotham: "In those days Yahweh started to send
Rezon king of Aram and Pekah son of Remaliah against Judah,"
which apparently means against Ahaz and the pro-Assyrian
party). Jotham died after only five to seven years of independent
rule.

Whatever the circumstances of his coming to power, it is at
least clear that Ahaz had a very different attitude toward Assyria
from that of his father. He was firmly pro-Assyrian and resolved
to resist pressure from neighboring states who favored revolt
against Assyria. His precise motives are not clear but his willingness to scrap Yahwism as the state cult and to introduce Assyrian
cult practices and revive indigenous cult practices suggests that
he held no strong religious convictions. Apparently he merely
assessed the international situation since the rise of Tiglath-pileser
with cool detachment and concluded that submission to Assyria
as a loyal vassal would bring him more advantages than resistance to Assyria. Whether he was moved by behind-the-scene
negotiations with the Assyrians cannot be judged. Perhaps it was
an open promise of Tiglath-pileser which gave him the courage
to oppose Rezon and Pekah when he might have equivocated.

Ahaz' pro-Assyrian policy left him isolated. He was speedily
attacked on all sides by the conspirators, Pekah and Rezon from
the north and east, Edom from the south, and the Philistines
from the west. Kings reports his appeal to Tiglath-pileser as a
desperate measure to relieve the siege of Jerusalem (II Kings
16:5-9). It is much more likely, however, that the appeal had
been made earlier and that the attacks by Judah's neighbors
came as punitive action against a traitorous fellow state which
threatened to jeopardize the alliance. The reported intent of
Pekah and Rezon, "Let us ascend against Judah and put the
pressure on it, and let us break it open for ourselves, and set up
the son of Tob'el[71] as king in its midst" (Isa. 7:6), suggests that

---

[71] The case for regarding the original form as *tōb'ēl* in place of MT tāb' al
has been argued by H. Torczyner, ed., *The Lachish Letters*, p. 9 (Hebrew),
and accepted by B. Mazar, "The Tobiads," *IEJ* 7 (1957), 236. The change
was a pejorative substitute which rendered the meaning of the name from

the rebels planned to replace Ahaz by another son of Uzziah or of Jotham, borne by a princess from Tob'el, who would have his father's anti-Assyrian leanings and who even now was a land-holder in Gilead, a prototype or actual ancestor of the later Tobiads of Persian and Hellenistic times.[72] Rezon and Pekah doubtless counted on assistance from Judeans who were still loyal to Uzziah and Jotham and to their anti-Assyrian policy. Particularly if Ahaz had gained the throne under suspicion of patricide, his hold would have been insecure, and the purpose of terrifying Judah was to encourage defection from Ahaz' already wavering ranks.

The initial campaign of Damascus and Ephraim was highly successful. Jericho and the northern approaches to Jerusalem were seized with heavy losses for Ahaz in dead and captured (II Chron. 28:5–15). With the loss to Edom of the seaport of Elath (II Kings 16:6) and the capture of several border towns by the Philistines (II Chron. 28:18), Ahaz was in serious difficulty. His one hope was the timely intervention of Tiglath-pileser, but would the Assyrian act with sufficient speed? Although the water supply of Jerusalem was adequate for a long siege,[73] the loyalty

"El is Good" to "No good." The change from *Tob* to *Tab* is a result of the Aramaizing of the name.

[72] The royal connection of Tob'el is argued by W. F. Albright (*BASOR* 140 [1955], 34–35) and W. Vogt (*Biblica* 37 [1956], 263–64) on the basis of a letter from Kalah published by H. W. F. Saggs (*Iraq* 17 [1953], pp. 131–33) in which Tab-el occurs as a geographical name. (Others, however, prefer to understand it as *'eretz tôbh* [Judg. 11:3, 5], the Egyptain Tūby [so Koehler, *LVTL,* p. 350; Van Zyl, *The Moabites,* p. 37]). Mazar seems correct, however, in objecting that Albright places the kingdom too far to the north and that it actually bordered on Moab. Ben Tab'al will have presumably been a general term for an officeholder, i.e., " 'son' of X," who was possibly replaced in southern Gilead by Aianûr, an Assyrian administrator named in the Kalah letter. At any rate, there is nothing irreconcilable between the Albright-Vogt proposal that Tab'al was a son of Uzziah or Jotham and the Mazar hypothesis that he was the descendant of an important Jewish family, perhaps of the Tobiads, who probably received trans-Jordan estates as a pledge for his loyalty to Pekah of Israel (see Mazar, *op. cit.,* pp. 236–38).

[73] Exploration of the waterworks of ancient Jerusalem shows that the pre-Hebraic inhabitants of Ophel had devised channels and an underground stairway and shaft to bring water from the Spring Gihon outside the wall to a catch basin within the city. It was this system which Ahaz was inspecting when Isaiah confronted him (7:3). See J. Simons, *Jerusalem in the*

of his own people was in doubt and even Ahaz' stoutest partisans must have had second thoughts. Consequently, "his heart [Ahaz'] and the heart of his people shook as the trees of the forest shake before the wind" (Isa. 7:2).

After a siege of unknown length, Tiglath-pileser appeared in southern Syria with startling suddenness. As he swept into northern Israel the forces of Rezon and Pekah were forced to hurry home lest they be cut off from Damascus and Samaria. It was too late to mount an effective coalition force. Virtually unopposed, Tiglath-pileser had no trouble in occupying the greater part of Israel (excepting only the mountainous region around Samaria) and in separating the Philistines from the Damascenes. After a brief strike against Philistia the Assyrians turned to a long but determined siege of Damascus which was to end with its capture in 732. Ahaz seized the opportunity to counterattack, recouping his losses to the north of Jerusalem and invading Ephraim. The Assyrians were probably pleased to have their vassal take as much territory from the southern boundary of Ephraim as he could manage.

We have already seen Hosea's opinion of this crisis—his condemnation of the initial attack by Damascus and Israel against Judah, his equal condemnation of the counterattack by Judah, and his insistence that both the alliance of Israel *against* Assyria and the alliance of Judah *with* Assyria were misplaced attempts to evade Yahweh's judgment. Isaiah's reactions are similar to Hosea's but more explicit and are recorded in conjunction with historical episodes in chaps. 7 and 8 whose value and meaning have been much debated.

The Isaianic narratives of 7:1–14, 16–17, and of 8:1–4 must be interpreted against the above historical backdrop and in connection with prophetic oracles from the same period, namely, 7:18–25; 8:6–8a, 11–15; 9:8—10:4 + 5:25–29; 10:27b–32; and 17:1–3. That Isaiah had followed the course of events in Israel even before Pekah began to threaten Judah is evident in the echoes of Menahem's arrogant boast that he could rebuild

---

Old Testament, pp. 164–78; also M. Hecker, "Water Supply of Jerusalem in Ancient Times," in M. Avi-Yonah, ed., *Sepher Yerushalayim*, I, 191–95 (Hebrew).

Israel even after the heavy tribute he had to pay to Tiglath-pileser (9:10):

The bricks have collapsed, but we will build with dressed stones;
the sycamores have been felled, but we will rear cedars in their place.

And the attack on Israel by "Syrians from the east" and "Philistines from the west" (9:12) refers to an otherwise unattested attempt of these states to force Menahem into an anti-Assyrian stance or actually to replace him with a cooperating king such as Pekah. Thus the attack appears as a close parallel to the later invasion of Judah by Syria and Israel. The same oracle sequence continues with extreme pictures of the chaos of civil war in Israel during the reigns of Menahem and Pekah (9:19–21a):

By the anger of Yahweh of hosts
the land is consumed,
and the people are like fuel for burning;
no one shows mercy to his brother,
they grab on the right, but are still hungry,
devour on the left, but are not satisfied;
each consumes his neighbor's flesh,
Manasseh Ephraim, Ephraim Manasseh
and together they are against Judah.

In this case the designations Manasseh and Ephraim have probably lost their original denotation of tribes and refer rather to regions, Manasseh being trans-Jordan and Ephraim Samaria. The struggle between Menahem of Samaria and Pekah of Gilead in trans-Jordan was at least in part a regional rivalry and, even in Samaria, Menahem was unable to hold his own without imposing his rule forcibly on at least one recalcitrant city. Fratricide and cannibalism racked the northern kingdom until it seemed that destruction by an outside power would be unnecessary. Yet one thing the warring northerners could agree upon finally and that was to join in war on Judah.

Even before they made an overt move against Judah, however, Isaiah was aware of the close collaboration between Pekah and Rezon. The naming of a second son of the prophet Maher-shalal-hash-baz seems to have preceded the attack on Judah and thus is misplaced in the present order of the narratives. The argument for a rearrangement is largely in the silences of the account in 8:1–4, which, unlike chap. 7, does not mention Ahaz and does not conclude with a threat against Judah. Rather "the wealth of Damascus and the booty of Samaria will be taken away before the king of Assyria" (8:4) within a very short time, two or two and one-half years at the most (counting the time of pregnancy and the infancy until the child begins to say "Mommy" and "Daddy"). The anti-Assyrian character of the relation between Damascus and Samaria was clear to Isaiah and he was certain that Tiglath-pileser would not long tolerate such machinations. The purpose of the tablet inscribed with the child's ominous name and of the witnesses was to impress publicly upon Judah the futility of participation in such an alliance. The naming of the child and his conception will thus have fallen about 737–736 when Jotham was still alive and when there were real prospects of Judean participation in the alliance. Judah is not threatened by the prophet precisely because the king has made no decision about the proposed coalition. To this same initial period in the formation of the alliance belongs the oracle of 17:1–3, in which the doom of Damascus and Ephraim is announced but Judah is not involved.

It is otherwise, however, with the sign of Immanuel in chap. 7, for the third son of Isaiah[74] is firmly anchored to the reign of Ahaz and the episode culminates in a threat incorporating the doom of the two hostile kingdoms as a preliminary step in the doom of Judah: "the land before whose two kings you are terrified will be abandoned. Yahweh will bring upon you and upon your people and upon your dynasty days such as have not come

---

[74] The case for regarding Immanuel as the prophet's son is based chiefly on the contextual argument that the symbolically named child, since not otherwise identified, is naturally to be understood as a brother of Shear-jashub and Maher-shalal-hash-baz. It is also suggested as a logical alternative to the nebulous and forced identifications with a messianic figure. Full discussion will be found in J.-J. Stamm, "La Prophétie d'Emmanuel," *Revue de Théologie et de Philosophie* 32 (1944), 97–123; "Die Immanuel-Weissagung Ein Gespräch mit E. Hammershaimb," *VT* 4 (1954), 20–33; and N. K. Gottwald, "Immanuel as the Prophet's Son," *VT* 8 (1958), 36–47.

since the day of Ephraim's departure from Judah." This too will transpire soon, perhaps sooner even than the previous sign-prophecy had indicated, within one and one-half years (counting the pregnancy and the infancy until the child asserts his own preference for what is "good" [tasty] and what is "bad" [not tasty].[75] The editorial introduction of 7:1-2, drawn in part from II Kings 16:5, accurately connects the incident with the threat of Pekah and Rezon to Jerusalem but gives the misleading impression that the prophet's meeting with the king occurred during the siege. In actuality it preceded the siege, as is clear from the fact that Ahaz is examining his water supply outside the city wall when Isaiah confronts him. This prophetic sign should accordingly be dated 735 when Maher-shalal-hash-baz was still too young to walk and so did not accompany his father and four-year-old brother Shear-jashub when they went to meet Ahaz.

Isaiah speaks to Ahaz in full knowledge of the design of Pekah and Rezon. He is also aware that the direct attack of the confederates was precipitated by Ahaz' previous submission to Assyria. We are to think of Isaiah's tone throughout as ironic and of his words as possessing overtones of contempt and dismay at Ahaz' appeal to Assyria. Ahaz' immediate fear is for Rezon and Pekah but they are merely "two sparking stumps of firewood" about to be extinguished by Assyria, and their plan to replace Ahaz by an anti-Assyrian brother or uncle is a futile one. *So the apparent danger is not the real danger. The actual threat is in Ahaz' failure "to believe," to trust in Yahweh.* He has appealed to outside help but in vain does he seek "to be established." He has already turned his back upon the one source of dynastic well-being: trust in Yahweh.

To be sure, Isaiah knew very well that Assyria would divert and overrun the besieging forces and thus would appear to "save" Ahaz, but his deliverance from the hostile neighbors will not affect the deeper crisis in Judah, namely, its lack of faith, which exposes it to the same fate as has moved inexorably against Israel and Damascus. Assyrian arms, invoked once by Judah, will

[75] G. B. Gray, *A Critical and Exegetical Commentary on the Book of Isaiah I–XXXIX, ICC,* p. 131. Gray rightly calls attention to the same notion in Deuteronomy 1:39 and II Maccabees 7:27.

advance steadily onward into Palestine. Not content to capture Damascus and Samaria, Assyria, like the Euphrates at flood tide, will "rise over all its channels and go over all its banks, and it will sweep on into Judah . . . extending even to the neck and its outstretched flood will fill the expanse of your land" (8:7–8). Or, in another apt figure, the razor which Ahaz hired to shave his enemies will be turned against him so that not a hair will be left on his scalp, his chin, or the soles of his feet (7:20). Ahaz has signaled for Tiglath-pileser to aid him, but when Yahweh "will raise a signal for a nation far away, and will whistle for it from the ends of the earth," there will be no reprieve for Judah (5:26–30). Assyria is an essentially unpredictable and humanly uncontrollable power which Ahaz invokes to his own detriment.

The oracle which comes closest to providing the key to Isaiah's attitude toward the Syro-Ephraimite crisis is 8:11–15. Yahweh "will become a sanctuary[76] [for those few who believe] and a stone of stubbing and a rock of stumbling [for the majority who do not believe] to both houses of Israel, a trap and a snare to the citizenry of Jerusalem, and many shall stumble thereon" (vss. 14–15a). The "conspiracy" of Rezon and Pekah against Judah (or possibly of Isaiah against Judah[77]) is not the central issue at all. The central matter is whether Yahweh is accepted "as holy,"

---

[76] When R. B. Y. Scott (*IB*, V, 227) objects that *miqdāš*, "place of worship," has not the secondary meaning, " 'place of refuge' which it has in English" and thus prefers *môqēš*, "snare" (with Targum), his judgment is not conclusive. There appears to be at least one other Old Testament reference to *miqdāš* as a place of refuge (Ezek. 11:16) and this secondary meaning can be easily explained by the fact that the temple was customarily a place of asylum for criminals.

[77] Interpretation of the "conspiracy" is complicated by the plural form of address throughout the oracle when from the introduction we are led to expect a divine word to the prophet. Apparently vs. 11 is an introductory "private oracle" which explains the spirit in which Isaiah is to deliver the following oracle (vss. 12–15), but the persons addressed are distinguished from "this people" so that either the disciples or the king and his advisers are here addressed. It is possible that the "conspiracy" is a charge brought against the prophet for his attacks on the king and state, but no hint of such a charge appears elsewhere in the book, and the fact that Isaiah announced the immediate failure of the Syro-Ephraimite attack will have tended to undercut the force of a treason charge against him. The "conspiracy" is better referred to the plan of Pekah and Rezon to overthrow Ahaz and to place an anti-Assyrian on the throne.

and as the "fear" and "dread" of Judah so that in obedience to him Judah will "not fear what they fear," i.e., will not fear for the Assyrian which has so frightened Pekah and Rezon. Thus Yahweh is a rock of refuge when the waters sweep through the land but only for those who fully regard him as "holy," i.e., as absolutely worthy to be trusted in. Such a rock is one to be built upon, a solid foundation (cf. 28:16). But to the others, Yahweh is a rock of stumbling, lying awkwardly in the easy path of power politics, a mere annoyance to those who count power by chariots and horsemen, but nonetheless a stone so strategically placed that his people cannot avoid it. If Ahaz will not find his rest upon this stone then he will trip over it to his humiliation.

Isaiah knows that Ahaz has already made up his mind. Thus the prophet is resolved to give one further sign that the king will not fail to understand. Isaiah mockingly asks Ahaz to request a sign and Ahaz piously refuses. In an outburst of impatience the prophet scolds the king for exhausting the patience of men and of God himself. The sign will be one entirely beyond Ahaz' control. It will be in the form of another son, who will be named Immanuel, "God with us," as a solemn token of God's judging presence. The threat is expanded so that Judah will suffer the devastation of Assyrian invasion as well as Israel and Damascus. Thus the entirety of Isaiah's audience with Ahaz bears out the call vision. The heart of the people is insensitive, its ears are blocked and its eyes blinded, and Isaiah's preaching has only seemed to deepen their determination to disregard Yahweh's judgment through continued social evil and through alliances intended either to defeat Assyria or to placate it.

Most of Isaiah's pronouncements on the Syro-Ephraimite crisis preceded the actual invasion of Rezon and Pekah. There is, however, one oracle describing the invasion (10:27b-32) and another commenting on the invasion's aftermath (8:19—9:1). The former has often been interpreted as a description of the rapid advance of the Assyrian army against Jerusalem either as a general threat or particularly in 701. Yet the main north-south highway along the central ridge from Samaria to Judah was not the route by which Sennacherib's troops approached Jerusalem. The prophecy could be understood as a schematic vision of "the foe from the north," but the full list of place names and the parallel in Hosea 5:8–12 favors the passage's original association with the attack of Rezon and Pekah against Jerusalem. It is doubtful if vss. 33–34, introducing an imagery associated with 2:12–13, belong to the preceding unit. Nevertheless, evoking as they do the judgment of God upon a proud enemy, they do make explicit the underlying mood of vss. 27b–30. The arrogant foe, having swept all opposition before him, now brandishes his fist defiantly at Jerusalem. He expects that it will fall to him as effortlessly as did the villages to the north. The lack of a threatening conclusion, which the editor intended to fill by vss. 33–34, against either Judah or Israel, is somewhat strange.[78] This is best explained by treating the oracle as a fragment of "journalistic" history in poetic form written before the outcome of the siege was known and dependent upon chaps. 7 and 8 to supply the necessary backdrop. The stratagem of the enemy to overthrow Jerusalem "shall not stand, and it shall not be consummated" (7:7b).

The second oracle belongs to a time after 734–733 when Samaria had suffered from the punitive strike of Tiglath-pileser and her territories had been drastically reduced. The unit 8:19—9:1[79] concluded Isaiah's Book of Waiting or Book of Signs (cf. 8:16–18), which he drew up about 732 after the first stage of his predictions had been fulfilled: the terrifying Israelite-Aramean alliance had utterly collapsed at one sudden stroke of the Assyrians. The oracle is extremely difficult to interpret in detail and

---

[78] Gray, *op. cit.*, p. 207, concludes that, because the poem ends without any promise that Jerusalem will be spared, it cannot be reconciled with Isaiah's attitude at the time of the Syro-Ephraimite War. This overlooks the fact that Isaiah's "promise" to Ahaz was one based solely on the plan of God and that it would be accomplished in the face of Ahaz' unbelief. Therefore, a dramatic poem describing the attack on Jerusalem by its enemies would throw into prominence the rapacity of Pekah and Rezon and the helplessness of Ahaz. What Yahweh will do will be *in spite of* Ahaz.

[79] It is better to regard 9:1 (Hebrew 8:23) as the conclusion of the unit 8:19–22 (with H. L. Ginsberg, "An Unrecognized Allusion to Kings Pekah and Hoshea of Israel [Isa. 8:23]," *Eretz-Israel* 5 [1958], 61–65) than to treat it as the beginning of the poetic messianic oracle in 9:2–7 (contra A. Alt, "Jesaja 8:23—9:6. Befreiungsnacht und Kroenungstag," *KS*, II, 206–14). Alt restores a 2:2 meter to 9:1 so that it accords with the following messianic poem but it is not convincing, for the linguistic ties are all between 9:1 and the preceding verses and not between 9:1 and the following verses.

has been given up often in whole or in part as a garbled editorial addition. It does contain, however, some clearly datable allusions although the precise intent of the prophet is obscured by the poor state of the text. The prophet speaks of the desperate attempt of the citizens of the northern kingdom to restore the fortunes of the state after the disaster of 734–733. This is evident in his allusion to the rejection of king and God in favor of necromancy and especially in the conclusion of the oracle, which by the regions it names shows that it could not have been added after 722.[80]

The oracle should be translated approximately as follows:

> Will there not be gloom for her [the land] who has suffered,
> As he first brought contempt upon Zebulun and Naphtali
> And later made heavy the way of the Sea, the region beyond
>   the Jordan, the entire Galilee ["circle"] of the nations?

This rendering depends upon reading the opening declarative statement as a rhetorical question, following the Targum, and upon interpreting the verb *hikhbîd* as "to make heavy, to oppress" instead of "to honor." It is possible that Tiglath-pileser annexed the Israelite territories in two stages in 734 and in 733 although the exact regions involved in the two phases are unknown.[81] Or it may be that a single campaign is referred to, its first successes occurring in Galilee, whence the Assyrian army spread into Gilead on the southeast and into the plain of Sharon on the southwest. The final "Galilee of the nations" seems simply to repeat the allusion in the foregoing "Zebulun and Naphtali." But it may be rather in the nature of a summary, the entire area to the west, north, and east of Ephraim being known as "the

[80] It is certainly significant that Ginsberg, *op. cit.,* p. 61, Alt, "Jesaja 8:23—9:6," pp. 209–11, and Y. Kaufmann, *The History of the Religion of Israel,* III, p. 165 (Hebrew)—who disagree in so much else in the interpretation of 9:1—are of one mind in believing that the verse refers to Tiglath-pileser's campaign(s) in northern Israel in 734–733.

[81] Kaufmann, *loc. cit.,* suggests that the first phase of the conquest embraced Naphtali and Zebulun and the second, the coastal area west of Manasseh ("the way of the Sea"), Gilead ("beyond Jordan"), and Issachar ("Galilee of the Nations"). S. Mowinckel, *Acta Orientalia* 10 (1932), 186–93, argues that the annexation of territory in 734 included Galilee, Sharon, and perhaps northern trans-Jordan, while that of 733 incorporated the remainder of trans-Jordan. The evidence for two actions is, however, extremely tenuous.

circle of the nations." Be that as it may, the incorporation of the three Assyrian provinces of Magidu ("Zebulun and Naphtali"), Duru ("the way of the sea," i.e., the Sharon Valley south of Mount Carmel), and Gal'aza ("the region beyond Jordan," i.e., Gilead) is referred to (see Map 18). A reconstruction of the text by supplying additional geographical terms which have presumably fallen out is too subjective to provide more than sheer conjecture.[82] At any rate, Isaiah sees further setbacks for Israel because she has learned nothing from her severe losses but only flees blindly to necromancy in an effort to descry the future (the hunger referred to is apparently figurative, i.e., the gnawing desire for an auspicious sign; cf. Amos 8:11–12).

Sometime before the fall of Samaria in 722 Isaiah announced further woe upon the beautifully built city crowned with its circumvallation, yet filled with drunkards, indeed "a withering blossom (formerly) of resplendent beauty," or "like a ripe fig" about to be eaten by the hungry passerby Assyria (28:1–4). Hoshea's court, although less elegant and lavish than that of his predecessors, apparently continued to revel with customary unconcern for future reckoning with Assyria. The oracle then shifts to the Judean religious leadership, likewise too confused and helpless to supply a clear direction for state policy (28:7–8). Drunkenness is intended not only literally but in the figurative sense of inability to control oneself and to see one's environment objectively. Having given up prospects of converting Ahaz, Isaiah indicts the prophets and priests, who instead of criticizing the king have urged him on in his policies by scoffing at the imminent dangers to which Isaiah points. To them the message of the prophet is reiterative nonsense. They will not be lectured to like children being taught the alphabet or a silly ditty (28:9–10). Because the leaders have not listened to the demands of Yahweh for social justice, he will teach them by the harsher methods of

[82] Alt, "Jesaja 8:23—9:6," p. 211, reconstructs 9:1 to read:
> As in the former time / Yahweh dishonored
> The Plain of Sharon / and Mt. Gilead
> The land of Zebulun / and the Land of Naphtali
> Later He has honored / the Way of the Sea
> The region beyond Jordan / Galilee of the Nations.

men who do not speak Hebrew at all, but their lesson will be clear enough in the end (28:11–22).

Derisively the prophet formulates the brazen confidence of the rulers of Jerusalem, whose attitude testified in effect that "we have cut a covenant with death and with Sheol have established cordial relations, so that when the devastating flood sweeps through the land it will not affect us, for we have made deceit our refuge and in what is false we have taken cover" (28:15). Religious and political considerations are mixed together in this image. The covenant with *maweth* is probably an allusion to the Canaanite god of death *Mot,* whom Judeans have appeased by renewed worship. Mot will therefore not betray his worshipers; they have already offered a supreme sacrifice in the form of Ahaz' son, immolated "according to the hideous ways of the nations whom Yahweh drove out before the people of Israel" (II Kings 16:3). At the same time the covenant with death and the entente with Sheol refer to the vassal treaty by which Ahaz had purchased his reign. This treaty, the cornerstone of his foreign and domestic policies, had stood Judah well and allowed her to thrive while Israel suffered from the severe reprisals of Tiglath-pileser. The Judean leaders had reason to boast and take confidence from this bond with Assyria. Surely in terms of the recent decade, Isaiah's proclamation of judgment on Judah deserved the incredulity and scoffing of these pro-Assyrian officials and their religious subordinates.

The reply of the prophet to this pragmatic self-confidence is emphatic. *The test of the structure in which Judah has sought refuge is not its apparent weatherproof condition but rather its correspondence to the measuring instruments of divine justice and righteousness.* By such a test the foundations are shown to be altogether faulty for they are based only upon the oaths of men, easily professed and easily broken. Yahweh's judgment will be like that on Mount Perazim against the Philistines (Baal-perazim; II Sam. 5:20) or in Gibeon against the Philistines (LXX, II Sam. 5:25; I Chron. 14:16), or earlier against the Canaanites (Josh. 10:10–13), but this new judgment of Yahweh will be altogether inexplicable, "strange" and "uncanny" to the chauvinistic rulers of Judah, for he will judge his own people. The passage implies that the "sweeping flood" with its hail and rain is Assyria (cf. a somewhat similar figure in Isa. 8:7–8a) and that the vassal treaty will not avail but will be broken.

The prophet may well have in mind Ahaz' perfidy since in his view the king will not hesitate to seek additional alliances to his own advantage. If the oracle postdates the negotiations of Hoshea with Egypt's So, Isaiah may suspect or actually know of similar conversations with Ahaz. However, the only "rest" possible for Judah is a security won by "giving rest to the weary" (i.e., the wronged poor of Judah)—in other words by an internal social revolution in which the covenant terms are honored by faithful administration of justice.[83] The king who will do this has no need for a covenant with death for he will build upon the one sure foundation stone of faith in Yahweh[84] and he will not be agitated by each sudden shift in the tide of international affairs. Isaiah, however, sees no hope of his word's being heeded and so, for such a state, he foresees nothing but "a decree of destruction upon the entire land [or even earth?]," in which the scoffers will only be further implicated by tightening their own fetters.

Isaiah's Middle Years: Warning Against Revolt (720–706)

It was not long thereafter, in 720, that a revolt led by Iaubidi of Hamath and abetted by Egypt swept through Syria and Palestine, drawing into its vortex Arpad, Simirra, Gaza, and even Damascus and Samaria. Hanno of Gaza was lured into an agreement with Sib'e of Egypt who agreed to supply forces to oppose Assyria in Palestine. In this period should be dated the oracle of Isaiah against an Egyptian (Ethiopian = Nubian) delegation that had come to Jerusalem to enlist Ahaz' participation (chap.

[83] S. H. Blank, *Prophetic Faith in Isaiah,* p. 24, correctly emphasizes that the phrase "give the weary rest" in Isaiah 28:12 "is really the historical Isaiah's epitome of his teaching."

[84] J. Lindblom, "Der Eckstein in Jes. 28:16," *Festschrift S. Mowinckel,* 1955, pp. 123–32, shows that "the cornerstone" is the metaphorical counterpart of "the covenant with death." As the latter represents all self-erected defenses against catastrophe such as, for example, blind adherence to the cult (cf. 1:10–17), so the former represents the true relation to Yahweh founded on faith, justice, and righteousness—and this reality is already established in the persons of Isaiah's disciples.

18). Only in 720, apparently, did Egypt actively lobby for revolt, whereas in the later uprisings under Sargon and Sennacherib it was the Syro-Palestinian states that implored Egypt for help. This was probably the same delegation that arranged the treaty between Egypt and Gaza. Isaiah's word to the messengers, who came by ship to the Philistine coast and thence inland to Jerusalem, was a supplement to the official reply of Ahaz, which declined participation in the revolt. The prophet employs the flattering language of diplomacy, lauding the swiftness of the embassy and praising the physical appearance and the military prowess of the Ethiopians. The reply is intentionally cryptic, similar to the Delphic oracle's claim that if Croesus crossed the Halys he would destroy a mighty empire.[85] Isaiah alludes to the defeat of Egypt and her allies without actually stating it. The rather prolix image of the pruning of vine tendrils seems to refer to the Egyptian aspirations in Asia, which are to be cut short (vss. 5–6).

It is a clear instance of the prophet's dialectic that he who opposed Ahaz' pro-Assyrian policy should at the same time warn an anti-Assyrian power that it would soon suffer a shattering setback. Isaiah was aware of the internal weakness of Egypt and in another oracle (19:1–15) paints a severe picture of the civil wars that racked the land of the Nile for several decades before the Ethiopian dynasty finally secured control and all Egypt was given "into the hand of a hard master and harsh king" (19:4, probably Pianki or Shabaka). The outcome of the western revolt was that Sargon speedily crushed it by dividing the forces, first defeating Hamath and her neighbors on the ancient battlefield of Qarqar and then scattering the forces of Gath and Egypt in southern Palestine.

In this same period, or shortly before, originated the oracle in 14:28–32 against the Philistines. The superscription, which dates it in the year of Ahaz' death, creates a chronological difficulty if one accepts 716–714[86] as the time of the death of the king, since the first verse makes sense only if one Assyrian king[87] has recently

---

[85] H. M. Wiener, *The Prophets of Israel in History and Criticism*, 1923, pp. 35–36.

[86] The death of Ahaz is dated by Albright in 715, by Mowinckel in 715–714, and by Thiele in 715.

[87] The proposal to see in the "rod" a reference to Ahaz and in the

died and his successor has not yet asserted his authority, a situation not obtaining in 715 but well suited to 727[88] or possibly even to 722–720:

> Rejoice not, O Philistia, all of you
>> that the rod which smote you is shattered,
> for from the serpent's root will come forth an adder,
>> and its fruit will be a flying serpent.

The prophet warns against thinking that Tiglath-pileser's death ("that the rod which smote you is shattered"), and the subsequent quiescence of Shalmaneser toward the Philistine cities, means the end of Assyrian power in southern Palestine. The new king Sargon will prove to be "a flying serpent," swift and deadly in his punishment of revolt. This oracle and chronological note regarding the termination of Ahaz' reign ought of course to be taken seriously, but the exact connection of the oracle and the note cannot be ascertained. It is quite possible that the oracle, written either in Shalmaneser's reign or shortly after his death, was used again by the prophet during the revolt of 715 and supplied with the note about Ahaz' death at that time, or subsequently by a disciple who first remembered hearing the oracle in that year.

Perhaps as early as 715[89] Ashdod began to scheme against Assyria. Sargon reports that its king Azuri "schemed not to deliver tribute any more and sent messages (full) of hostilities against Assyria, to the kings (living) in his neighborhood" (*ANET*, p. 286). Apparently it is a delegation from Azuri to Ahaz or Hezekiah (we do not know whether Ahaz' death occurred before or after the initial preparations for the revolt)

"adder" allusion to Hezekiah does not suit the evidence; rather than harassing the Philistines Ahaz was attacked by them (II Chron. 28:18). Furthermore, the expected invasion will come from the north, whereas Judah would have attacked from the east. See Gray, *op. cit.*, pp. 266–67.

[88] The death of Ahaz is dated by Begrich and H. Tadmor in 727 (cf. the latter's article on "Biblical Chronology" in *Encyclopedia Mikraith*, vol. IV [Hebrew], 1963).

[89] The complex question of the dating of the Ashdod revolts and campaigns has been discussed in the light of the newest but still inconclusive evidence by H. Tadmor, "The Campaigns of Sargon II of Assur," *JCS* 12 (1958), 79–80.

which is referred to as "the messengers of the nation" (14:32). To them the Judean king is advised to answer, "Yahweh has established Zion, and in her the afflicted of his people will find safety." An alliance is unnecessary to Yahweh's people. Of course the king refuses to speak in this manner and even shows an interest in the proposed rebellion (a strong indication that it is indeed Hezekiah with whom the delegation negotiated). Sargon's treatment of the Ashdod uprising was not so peremptory, probably because he was greatly occupied elsewhere in his empire during these years. Apparently in 713 the Assyrians captured Ashdod and replaced Azuri with his brother Ahimetu, who was overthrown by Iamani (often but doubtfully identified as a Greek, i.e., "the Ionian").[90] The second reprisal of the Assyrians fell either in 712 or 711.

The accession of Hezekiah to the throne was both hopeful and discouraging from Isaiah's standpoint. The new monarch was to all appearances a pious Yahwist greatly disturbed by the non-Yahwistic religious revival in Judah which his father had encouraged. Since the alien cults were part and parcel with Assyrian suzerainty, it is natural that Hezekiah should have resented Judah's vassalage to Assyria. The flat assertion of II Kings 18:7 that "he revolted against the king of Assyria and would not serve him" seems to attribute the open break of Hezekiah with Sennacherib to a time early in the Judean king's reign. Doubtless Hezekiah entertained the idea during the revolt of Ashdod and Gath in 715 and following, but he is generally thought to have stopped short of withholding tribute and contributing troops to the insurrectionists. Sargon's report distinguishes between the Philistine states, which spearheaded the revolt, and Judah, Ammon, and Moab, which were enticed to participate. The extent of Hezekiah's action may have been to take advantage of Sargon's absence from the west to purge the many indigenous and Assyrian cult practices from Judah (II Kings 18:3–6 and

---

[90] Tadmor (*ibid.*, p. 80), finds the Akkadian name Iamani incomprehensible as "the Ionian" (the same with the variant Iaadna as "the Cypriot"). The bibical parallels (Yamîn, I Chron 2:27; Yimnā, Gen. 46:17; and Yimna‘, I Chron. 7:35) suggest that he was "of local Palestinian origin."

II Chron. 29–31, which is an extremely tendentious report but nevertheless preserves some accurate memories of the reform and of the attempt to enforce it also in the north). While such acts might be interpreted as treasonous, they might also be overlooked if tribute were not withheld.

On the other hand, a cuneiform fragment probably referring to this campaign seems to name Azekah of Judah as a city that surrendered to Assyrian attack before the invaders turned to Ashdod a second time (in 712 or 711). Hezekiah's participation in the revolt may have been overt after all but, with the capture of Azekah, he may have at once been induced to pay the outstanding tribute.[91] In his religious reform Hezekiah was influenced by north Israelite traditions which eventually were published in the book of Deuteronomy.[92] These traditions received attention in Jerusalem after the fall of Samaria, especially since they purported to give the Mosaic basis for the continuation of a Yahwistic state. The nominal Yahwistic state in the north had disregarded them and perished. Was there not something for Judah to learn from her sister state's tragic experience?

That Isaiah looked with some satisfaction upon the resurgence of Yahwism under Hezekiah is probable. The messianic poem of Isaiah 9:2–7 may well have been a composition for the coronation of Hezekiah formulated by the prophet from traditional sources and repeated in the ceremony to remind the new king of his solemn duties as Yahweh's adopted son.[93] It is easy to understand that Isaiah, who had finally despaired of influencing Ahaz, now saw a fresh opportunity with his more tractable son. Hezekiah, co-regent with his father for some years, had already given attention to Isaiah's preaching, and the recitation of 9:2–7 may have been the part assigned to the prophet by the king, who

[91] The text, although transcribed by Winckler more than fifty years ago, has only recently been included in a historical discussion of the period (cf. Tadmor, "The Campaigns of Sargon II . . . ," pp. 80–83).

[92] The ancient north Israelite character of most of the laws in Deuteronomy has been underscored by T. Oestreicher, *Das deuteronomische Grundgesetz,* 1923, and A. C. Welch, *The Code of Deuteronomy,* 1924, and *Deuteronomy: the Framework to the Code,* 1932. They correctly emphasize that the cult centralization motif in Deuteronomy is quite secondary to the demand for cult purification.

[93] Scott, *op. cit.,* pp. 231–32.

wished to rule as a devoted Yahwist. Some feel that Isaiah was too disaffected with Judean kings to take so active and positive a part in the official liturgy, but there are certainly signs that the prophet was much indebted to royal cult ideology and language. The messianic hymn breathes a traditional sentiment and could have been given various meanings by those who heard it. It certainly need not imply that the prophet looked unconditionally upon Hezekiah as the perfect Yahwistic leader. To the contrary, he did not hesitate soon thereafter to influence the policies of the new king so that they would more nearly correspond to the exalted titles of the enthronement ritual: "a wonder of a counsellor, a mighty warrior, an abiding father, and a prince of peace" (9:6). *The rule of Hezekiah represents a renewed attempt of Isaiah to gain a hearing with the king and especially to influence the domestic and foreign policies of Judah.*

From the start Isaiah was conscious that Hezekiah's Yahwism was limited by comparison with prophetic standards. *The most disturbing aspect of the king's policy was his inclination to accept the logic of his anti-Assyrian tendencies and to join in open revolt against his overlord.* With Sargon occupied elsewhere and Ashdod confidently promising Egyptian assistance, Hezekiah had the opportunity he sought to carry through his program of neo-Yahwism. Whatever connotation the prophet may have given to the title *'ēl gibbôr,* "mighty warrior," as applied to the Judean king, he made it clear to Hezekiah that dependence upon Egyptian arms was not his idea of the fulfillment of the terms of Hebrew kingship. In fact, so intense was the temptation to the king that Isaiah decided to perform a bold symbolic action in order to dramatize his certainty that the rebellion against Assyria would prove ineffectual (chap. 20). He doffed his long prophet's robe and sandals and walked through the streets of Jerusalem in the loincloth of a prisoner of war. To the crowds who gathered to see this indecorous behavior he cried out: "(this) is a sign and warning against Egypt and Ethiopia, so shall the king of Assyria lead away the Egyptians as captives and the Ethiopians as exiles, both young and old, naked and barefoot, with rear ends exposed, to the shame of Egypt. Then they [the rebels] shall be disappointed and confused because of Ethiopia their hope and of

Egypt their confidence." The dismayed and about-to-be-defeated Philistines will then cry out, "Behold, this is what happened to those in whom we trusted and to whom we scurried for help to be rescued from the king of Assyria. And how shall we now escape?" To this general interpretation has been prefixed a phrase that could only have been spoken in 712 or 711 as the punitive strike of Sargon was about to occur: "As my servant Isaiah has gone naked and barefoot for three years. . . ." This sort of self-conscious reference is not likely from the prophet and is one of several signs that this introduction is editorial.

While the Assyrian records indicate that the revolt was spread over a considerable period of time, three full calendar years were not necessarily involved, and we cannot know, furthermore, at exactly which point in the revolt Isaiah began his action. The public sign enacted by the prophet may not have coincided with the period of open revolt but may have begun beforehand while the "secret" negotiations were in process and may have ended before Sargon's second attack on Ashdod was completed. Strictly interpreted, the exordium of 20:1–2 is logically contradictory since it says that in the year that Sargon's *turtanu* fought against Ashdod Isaiah was commanded to perform the symbolic deed as though for the first time although in fact he had been performing it for three years. It looks as though the "at that time" of vs. 2 originally had nothing to do with vs. 1, but there is no clue in the passage as to the original reference. There is certainly no difficulty in assigning the symbolic act to the prophet since it did not require him to spend all or even most of his time parading through the streets. It will have been enough to appear at given intervals and especially when fresh political developments, such as a visit by delegations from Ashdod, raised the danger of the king's capitulation to the rebels' appeals.

The above-quoted oracle places so much emphasis upon Egypt that the reader is likely to think Egypt fomented the revolt of 712, as it had previously in 720, but Sargon's accounts of the revolt do not support such an interpretation. If the Pir'u of Musru in Sargon's annals is indeed pharaoh of Egypt, which seems almost certain, then the secondary role of Egypt becomes clear. It was Iamani who, having seized the throne of Ashdod, "sent bribes to Pir'u, king of Musru—a potentate incapable to save them—and asked him to be an ally" (*ANET*, p. 287). Even if this debatable allusion is not connected with Egypt, Sargon makes no mention of an Egyptian force and notes that the fugitive rebel from Ashdod was extradited by Egypt to Assyria. This is hardly what we should expect if Egypt had initiated the revolt or even if she had firmly promised help to Ashdod. As a matter of fact, the point of Isaiah's warning in 713–711 was the falsity of the rebel's trust in Egypt. His quite fulsome account of Egypt's military defeat was of course not fulfilled.

The aloofness of Egypt in this uprising suggests a definite tactic of Shabaka not to intervene as ineptly in Palestine as had So in 726 and Sib'e in 720. He wished to have full guarantee before his intervention, and a league of two Philistine cities with the uncertain participation of two or three other south Palestinian states did not seem like a very promising coalition. In fact, on the basis of a seal impression of Shabaka found at Nineveh, it may be reasonably conjectured that the pharaoh concluded peace with Assyria, a move which helped to confirm his Ethiopian dynasty as the dominant one.[94] An Assyrian-Egyptian entente at this time would also explain the political stability in Palestine from 711 to 705, since the smaller states received no encouragement to revolt. The upshot of the second revolt in Ashdod was that Sargon, who was detailed on the northern frontier, in 712 (or 711) sent his *turtanu* (the *tartan*, "commander in chief" of Isa. 20:1) with 420 picked troops, and the small force was sufficient to quell the uprising.[95]

The prophet's opposition to the revolt seems not to have been confined to public protest. In the same period probably occurred the perplexing threat against Shebna, the steward, which has elicited grave doubts as to its authenticity (22:15–25). The most telling objection to the present form of the oracle is the difficulty of believing that Isaiah would announce a successor to Shebna and praise him fulsomely, only to conclude with a declaration of

[94] Tadmor, "The Campaigns of Sargon II . . . ," p. 84.
[95] Olmstead, *op. cit.*, p. 219.

the successor's unworthiness and dismissal from office.[96] Even if we assume that the rejection of Eliakim (vs. 25) was added later —whether by the prophet or another does not matter—we still must explain Isaiah's serious misjudgment of the character and policies of Eliakim. Not that Isaiah was incapable of a mistake, but he is not easily thought of as giving himself to such unrestrained praise of a man with potentiality for failure. Probably the soundest solution is to regard the name of Eliakim in vs. 20 as an addition supplied by someone who noticed that Shebna was indeed no longer the steward in 701 but had been replaced by a certain Eliakim son of Hilkiah (36:3), and further to treat vs. 25 as an addition after this Eliakim subsequently proved as disappointing to the prophet or his followers as had Shebna. The extraordinary praise of vss. 20–24 has the character of a messianic counter-prophecy announcing a future ruler of faithfulness in the house of David whom Yahweh will fasten in his office "like a peg in a sure place" (vs. 23).[97] This type of messianic expectation is even more easily assigned to Isaiah than that expressed in 9:2–7 with its stress on militarism. The notion of a revival of righteous leadership is already adumbrated in 1:26.

And I will bring back your judges as formerly and your advisors as in the beginning,
And then you will be called city of righteousness, faithful city.

Unfortunately the basis for the indictment of Shebna is not expressly given,[98] unless his preparation of a rock-cut tomb was

---

[96] Cf. Scott, *op. cit.*, p. 292; Gray, *op. cit.*, p. 375; E. Jenni, *Die politischen Voraussagen der Propheten*, 1956, pp. 42–47.

[97] O. Procksch, *Jesaia I, Kommentar zum Alten Testament*, 1930, pp. 291–92.

[98] The attack by the prophet cannot be explained on the theory that Shebna was an upstart who had no lineal right to high office. S. Yeivin, "Families and Parties in the Kingdom of Judah," *Studies in the History of Israel and Its Land*, pp. 256–60 (Hebrew), has convincingly argued on the basis of seal impressions that Shebna belonged to a family of officials that extended over several generations. The Shebna of Isaiah 22 was apparently earlier a high official of Uzziah, but not necessarily steward. He named his son Azariah in honor of the king he had served (a typical Egyptian practice), and a grandson was named Shebna and possibly a great-grandson Menahem. A probable daughter of Shebna the second is also known. This chain of evidence seems to favor the view that the Shebna of Isaiah 22 is also the

in itself the sin for which the prophet condemned him. This, however, is very unlikely, for officials provided such tombs for themselves without criticism. It is, as a matter of fact, possible that a tomb found on the hill east of Ophel is the very tomb of Shebna.[99] Whether Isaiah's warning that he would not be buried there was fulfilled cannot, of course, be judged since the tomb, like others in the vicinity, was looted long ago. On the contrary, the tomb is condemned as a symbol of Shebna's belief in the permanence of his office; but in this he is entirely mistaken for he will be hurled away violently "into a broad place," which need only imply expulsion from office and not necessarily exile to a foreign land.

We may conjecture that the actual sin of Shebna which in-

Shebna of Isaiah 36; i.e., he and his sons continued in high office. Yeivin's suggestion that the Shebna of Isaiah 22 is the Shebna, son of Ahab, mentioned on another seal and therefore a northerner (his father was named after the Israelite king) and that this would explain the spelling of his name with a final *aleph* (as in the Samarian ostraca) is attractive though necessarily conjectural. His further suggestion, however, that Shebna's northern origin was objected to by the court prophet Isaiah is without point, for we have no evidence that the prophet was a Judean purist; in fact, his concern with other nations makes it inherently unlikely. His opposition to Shebna was not based on the official's origins but rather on his policies.

[99] N. Avigad, "The Epitaph of a Royal Steward from Siloam Village," *IEJ* 3 (1953), 137–52, reads a rock-cut tomb inscription found by Clermont-Ganneau in 1870 as follows:

> This is [the sepulchre of . . .] yahu who is over the house.
> There is no silver and no gold here
> but [his bones] and the bones of his slave-wife with him.
> Cursed be the man who will open this!

He suggests that, of the seven Old Testament figures who bear the title *ʾasher ʿal hab-bayith,* Shebna (full form Shebnayahu) is most probably the owner of the tomb and notes that paleographical evidence dates the inscription c. 700 B.C. The prominent position of the rock-cut tomb exposed to view some distance up the hillside opposite Jerusalem and the Phoenician-like style of the inscription (he notes that the term *skn,* used only for Shebna in the Old Testament, is a common Phoenician title) tend to support the identification. He admits, however, that there may have been other stewards, unknown to us, whose names ended with -yahu. Another suggestion is that the occupant of the tomb was Hilkiyahu, father of Eliakim who was later steward (H. J. Katzenstein, "The Royal Steward (asher ʿal ha-Bayith)," *IEJ* 10 [1960], 153). In that case Shebna might be something of a usurper who broke the succession of the stewardship in Hilkiah's family and sought to imitate the latter's tomb.

curred Isaiah's wrath was his vigorous leadership of the insurrectionist faction in Hezekiah's court. This is perhaps hinted at in the prophet's designation of Shebna as *sōkēn*, not otherwise used for a high official in the Old Testament. The term is followed by the officer's name and another title in a manner so awkward as to raise the suspicion of a gloss: "Go to this *sōkēn*, to Shebna who is over the house." The latter term is a familiar Hebrew office of royal steward.[100] The Akkadian equivalent of *sōkēn*, namely, *shakin*, appears in political documents from Syro-Palestine during at least eight centuries before Isaiah. As employed in Canaan it seems to have referred to an officer in the foreign service of a great power who represented it as resident governor or commissioner in an actual or nominal vassal state.[101] Isaiah does not, however, employ the title because Shebna was an appointee of Egypt or because he actually bore the title. It is rather a term of derision, intended to stigmatize Shebna as a foreign agent: "Go to this quisling, this collaborator, to Shebna, the royal steward." This explains the double titulars in the prophecy without recourse to an editor and it also shows Isaiah as an extremely outspoken critic of political leaders and policies with which he did not agree. One who would speak thus would certainly not hesitate to press Hezekiah for the official's dismissal or transfer. By 701 Shebna was no longer steward but was apparently demoted to *sōphēr* or "state scribe" (36:3). It is possible

---

[100] Katzenstein, *op. cit.*, 152–53, believes that, since Eliakim is named first among the high officials who represent Hezekiah to Rabshakeh (II Kings 18:18 = Isa. 36:3) and to Isaiah (II Kings 19:2 = Isa. 37:2), the royal steward in Hezekiah's time must have been the chief minister of state. He finds that Isaiah's "vivid description of his [the steward's] position, dignity and task" in 22:20–24 "seems to indicate an established tradition."

[101] A. Alt, "Hohe Beamte in Ugarit," *KS*, III, 186–97, divides the usages of *shakin* in the ancient Near East into roughly two categories: In the Assyrian and Hittite empires the *shakin* was apparently a high officer with particular administrative responsibilities in the homeland, which may have included foreign affairs at a high level. In Egyptian practice the *shakin* was a governor or high commissioner appointed by the pharaoh to look after his interests in Palestine and Syria. Alt concludes that "it appears as though the word *skn* in Canaanite speech was applied only as a title for high officers in the foreign service of great powers." He suggests, however, that Shebna, the *skn* of Isaiah 22:15, may be an exception since he seemed rather to be one of the highest officials in the Davidic court.

that after a peroid of banishment from public life he was returned to a key office which handled foreign correspondence precisely as a part of Hezekiah's plan to join Egypt in the revolt
following Sargon's death. As a long-time Egyptophile, Shebna
would have been a logical choice.

That portion of the oracle against Moab in chaps. 15–16
which is evidently the original work of Isaiah (16:1–5) seems
also to belong to the reign of Hezekiah. It is generally recognized
that the bulk of the long oracle was an ancient taunt song against
Moab employed not only by Isaiah, or an editor, but also by the
author of Jeremiah 48. It is likely that the prototype was a non-
Israelite composition (or compositions) celebrating in fact an
Amorite defeat of Moab.[102] Such an interpretation is strengthened by the explicitly non-Israelite context given to the taunt
against Heshbon in Numbers 21:21–30, portions of which appear also in the longer taunt used in Isaiah and Jeremiah. It is
also apparent that the profusion of place names in the oracle,
many of which were no longer identifiable in the time of the
monarchy, has been rather imperfectly preserved as an archaic
survival. Moreover, the discrepancy between the anti-Moabite
and pro-Moabite sentiments in chaps. 15–16 suggests that 16:1–
5 has been inserted in its present position by someone who wished
to subordinate its sympathetic attitude toward Moab to a mood
of general condemnation. If Isaiah was responsible for this arrangement and also for the note in 16:13–14, it must have been
made at some time subsequent to the delivery of 16:1–5. Probably the final arrangement and the concluding notation belong
to the years just after the fall of Jerusalem in 587 and just before
the attack of Nebuchadnezzar on Moab.

In 16:1–5 the prophet pictures Moab as severely devastated

---

[102] M. Diman (= Haran), "An Archaic Survival in Prophetic Literature,"
Yedi'oth 13 (1947), 7–15 (Hebrew), believes that the prophets independ-
ently used fragments of a pre-Israelite elegy over Moab (Jer. 48:1–6, 16–25,
29–38, and Isa. 15; 16:6–12) and a triumphal song over Moab (Jer. 48:
45–46) which originally dealt with a defeat of Moab by Sihon, the Amorite.
Diman has certainly called attention to the archaic geographical and ethnic
references in the Moab oracles which are difficult to explain as late as the
eighth or seventh centuries. See also Kaufmann, *The History of the Religion
of Israel,* VI, 43, 47–48, 225 (Hebrew).

and its fugitives as scattered, some having taken refuge in Sela, the Edomite stronghold. By way of the desert, i.e., south of the Dead Sea, they have sent a delegation with gifts of lambs to Judah, imploring aid from its ruler, Hezekiah. Judah and Moab were on close terms during the plans for the revolt of 713–711 although neither committed herself irretrievably. At the death of Sargon in 705 they joined in a revolt, although Moab pulled back after Sennacherib's conquest of Sidon and paid tribute. Consequently it is not feasible to attribute the destruction referred to in the oracle to an Assyrian attack since not only in 701 but also in 711 Moab refrained from flagrant revolt. There were, however, other disturbances in trans-Jordan in the period 740–705, as evidenced by a letter from a high Assyrian official in the west to the king which reports an invasion of Moab by the Gidiriya (Kedar tribes? Gederoth in Judah? Gader in trans-Jordan?).[103] In this attack the population of at least one Moabite city has been killed. Naturally we cannot simply equate this attack with the one presupposed in Isaiah's oracle, but the letter does indicate the instability along the desert frontier and the difficulty even Assyria had in coping with the disorders.

Of greater importance is the prophet's demand for Judah to receive the Moabite refugees warmly. He does not present his case on the ground of an existing treaty by which Judah is legally bound to assist Moab. He argues rather from the concept of Hebrew kingship by throwing the standards of the enthronement hymns before Hezekiah's conscience and reminding him that it is precisely in such acts of mercy, in the offering of asylum to political refugees, that the Davidic dynasty will show its mettle and will thus outlast all oppressors. The messianic allusion, which has jarred many commentators, is in fact a quotation from an enthronement hymn (cf. 14:32):

[103] In his commentary on the Kalah letter, H. W. F. Saggs, *op. cit.*, pp. 131–33, proposes that *mat gi-di-ra-aia* is the Arab tribe of Kedar but he also notes that it may be the south Palestinian Gederoth of II Chronicles 28:18. Albright, *BASOR* 140 (1955), 34–35, preferred the latter identification. Mazar, *op. cit.*, p. 238, favors Gadora, located to the north of the land of Tabiel, a city which Josephus named as the capital of Perea in his days.

When the tyrant is no more, and violence has ceased
    and the trampler has vanished from the earth,
(Then) a throne will be established in covenant love
    and one will sit on it in truth
who judges and seeks justice
    and is swift in righteousness.

Isaiah here evidences the broad compassion of Amos and goes beyond it, for *he urges that even a nation which has committed wrongs and is a traditional enemy must be shown consideration in its time of need.* The willingness to extend such help without prejudice of the past is an important test of a nation's claim to bear Yahweh's blessing.

Isaiah's Later Activity: Woe to Assyria (705–701)

With the death of Sargon in 705 a new element began to appear in the preaching of Isaiah—in fact, a new element in Hebrew prophecy. Hitherto prophecy had been concerned almost exclusively with the punishment of Israel and Judah at the hands of foreign powers. *Now for the first time a foreign nation actually engaged in the chastisement of Judah is itself castigated for its pretensions and excesses as a world conqueror* (14:4b–21). Yahweh has set a limit to the wrongs of Assyria and has, with the death of Sargon, at last broken the rod and staff which "has struck the peoples in rage with unending blows and lorded it over the nations in wrath with unceasing oppression." The taunt song, in the form of a dirge, artfully pictures a welcoming committee of former world rulers in Sheol who receive the latest arrival with sarcastic glee: "You have become also as powerless as we! You have become merely like us!"

Of particular interest is the prophet's use of Canaanite material to describe Sargon's arrogant aspiration and his catastrophic fall. The Assyrian, like the mythological Helel ben Shahar (Morning Star, son of Dawn), tried to ascend to the zenith of the heavens but has been cast down to the nadir. Previous to the prophet's use of the image, the Canaanites appear to have drawn it from an old nature myth of a struggle between a star and the sun. They applied it to the attempt of one of the lesser deities (Helel ben Shahar is mentioned in Canaanite texts) to overthrow the head of the pantheon.[104] Sargon, says Isaiah, tried similarly to share dominion with God or actually to replace him; but the world ruler will not abdicate to a power-intoxicated man and thus has cut him off so that his tormentors in Sheol will cry out incredulously:

Is this the man who terrorized the earth, who shook kingdoms,
> who turned the earth into a wilderness,
>> overthrew its cities, and did not permit his captives to return home?

Although the taunt song is presently referred to the king of Babylon in the introduction and in the conclusion (14:4a; 22–23), this identification is purely editorial and represents a re-appropriation of Isaiah's original poem by an exilic writer. That the poem describes the death of an Assyrian monarch is supported by the poetic parallelism of "rod" and "staff" (used for Assyria by the prophet in 10:5) and by reference to forcible deportation of captives ("and did not permit his captives to return home," 14:17c). That it is specifically Sargon's death which is celebrated rests heavily on the claim that the dead king will not be given proper burial with his ancestors, for this was precisely the fate of Sargon, who fell in Elam and whose body was not returned to Assyria for interment; a cuneiform text says that "he was not buried in his house."[105]

With the attribution of the "lament" over Sargon to Isaiah one might think that the prophet had undergone a change of heart, that he now favored open revolt against Assyria. With

---

[104] Gunkel, *op. cit.*, pp. 133–34.

[105] The text was translated into French and commented upon by P. Dhorme, *RB* 7 (1910), p. 389. A. Parrot, *Nineveh and the Old Testament*, pp. 49–51, also favors the identification of Sargon as the fallen monarch in Isaiah 14. Kaufmann, *The History of the Religion of Israel*, VI, 175–81, and partly translated in his *The Religion of Israel*, pp. 382–83, assigns chaps. 13 and 14 to an imaginative composite portrait of an Assyrian king. He regards 14:24–27 as Isaiah's deliberate insertion in order to elucidate the otherwise cryptic nature of the chapters.

Sargon removed, the way would be free for a general uprising throughout the empire, and the combined peoples would visit Yahweh's vengeance upon the oppressing empire. Yet the lament does not contain the slightest mention of the end of the empire— only the end of the particular emperor. Nevertheless it was not long before Isaiah had to face again the prospect of such a revolt and it was problematic how much longer he would be able to restrain Hezekiah. The death of an Assyrian king always raised the hopes of the rebelliously inclined. Perhaps his successor would be weaker, and the more quickly the revolt could be instigated the better its chances to succeed before the new king could establish himself.

In such circumstances, probably in the year 704, the Chaldean prince Marduk-apal-iddina (the biblical Merodach-baladan) sent an embassy to Hezekiah and doubtless to other western vassals of Assyria in the hope of enticing them into an uprising against the new monarch Sennacherib (chap. 39). His hope of fomenting rebellion simultaneously in the east and the west was an ambitious but tactically sound plan. Marduk-apal-iddina was in fact a notable political and military tactician who knew how to retreat and live to harass the Assyrians another day.[106] He had defeated or at least stalemated the Assyrians with the help of Elam at Der in 721 and had occupied the throne in Babylon for some years before being driven out by Sargon. Hezekiah welcomed Marduk-apal-iddina's delegation warmly. He shared the general Near Eastern feeling of relief at the death of Sargon and believed that participation in a large-scale revolt was desirable. He opened his arsenal and storehouses to the delegation, which was apparently impressed with the supplies of gold, silver, and spices, the provisions of oil, and the weapons of war. For the ruler of a small kingdom Hezekiah had no reason to be ashamed of his wealth and strength. It is clear that Hezekiah's cordiality in sharing state secrets with the foreign embassy was tantamount to joining in the conspiracy and it is doubtless at this time that Judah committed herself formally to a rebel coalition.

[106] See Olmstead, *op. cit.,* pp. 250–57, 284–96, for the full account of Marduk-apal-iddina's remarkable career.

Isaiah had no difficulty in seeing through the import of the visit by Marduk-apal-iddina's messengers, and his boldness in rebuking Hezekiah, as well as the king's very willingness to share his plans with the prophet (although after he had made up his mind!), shows that the two must have been on close terms. The prophet's threat of Babylonian exile is authentic although it has been expanded and slanted by the Deuteronomic historian in order to point up the events of 587 as related in II Kings 24:10–25:17. The threat as given by Isaiah had the force of punishment by poetic justice: you, Hezekiah, have flirted with Babylon and you will be punished in Babylon—if not actually by Babylon. Isaiah was aware that deportees from Syria and Palestine had been resettled by the Assyrians in Babylon, and his prophecy to Hezekiah need not have meant more than that the failure of Marduk-apal-iddina's rebellion would lead to the carrying away of Judah's goods and nobility ("your sons") to Mesopotamia.

Shortly thereafter Sennacherib moved swiftly to drive Marduk-apal-iddina out of Babylon. He fled into the swampland of Mesopotamia. The master plan for empire-wide revolt was never executed, but this did not end the stirrings of revolt on a regional basis. Many of the western states again began to look to Egypt for assistance against Assyria. Hezekiah, undeterred by Isaiah's continued opposition to revolt, took a position at the forefront of the rebels and was joined by Luli of Sidon. The Philistine cities were divided; Ashdod and Gaza remained loyal—they had learned their lesson seven years before!—whereas insurrectionist parties in Ashkelon and Ekron deposed the vassal kings and introduced their own leaders. Padi, the vassal king of Ekron, was delivered to Hezekiah for safekeeping. A key factor in the revolt was dependence upon Egyptian aid. Judging by the oracles of Isaiah (30:1–7,[107] 31:1–3), help was promised only after the rebels made considerable payments to Egypt, which may very well have been in the form of tribute to support vassal oaths to the pharaoh. The prophet pictures the camel and ass trains of

[107] Following Scott, *op. cit.*, p. 330, who with the suggestion of the Targum reads *yiss'ū baḥammat negeb*, "they carry through the heat of the Negeb" instead of *massā' baḥamōth negeb* of MT, 'oracle on the beasts of the Negeb." Thus 30:1–7 reads continuously as a single oracle.

Judah and Philistia laboring toward Egypt through the hot and treacherous Negeb. Apparently the pharaoh has sent officials to Zoan (Avaris) in the eastern delta in order to spare the tribute-bearers the trouble of traveling the entire distance to the capital of the Ethiopian dynasty at Napata far up the Nile almost to the fourth cataract (see Map 11).[108]

Isaiah remained unyielding in his assessment of the futility of overtures to Egypt and condemned the plan of the rebels "to make a covenant" (*linsōk massēkhāh*, 30:1c, "to pour out a libation" or "to weave a web") since "they decided to go down to Egypt without asking my opinion." In an oracle which sets forth the prophet's faith with particular pointedness, he declares (31:1–3):

Woe to those who descend to Egypt for help and rely on horses,
> Who put their confidence in chariots because they are plentiful
>> and in horsemen because they are very strong,
But do not pay attention to the Holy One of Israel
> nor seek Yahweh.
Yet precisely he is wise and brings evil
> and does not turn back his words,
And he will arise against the house of the wicked
> and against the help of the doers of evil.
The Egyptians are human and not divine
> and their horses flesh and not spirit,
For Yahweh will stretch forth his hand and the helper will stumble
> and the helped will fall
>> And they will be destroyed together.

The war potential of Egypt is indeed plentiful and strong but it

---

[108] A. Kuschke, "Mitteilungen zu Jes. 30:1–5," *ZAW* 64 (1952), 194–95, has offered the interesting suggestion that Isaiah 30:4 refers to the couriers of Shabaka who go as far as Hanes on the border between Upper and Lower Egypt, i.e., within the area ruled directly by the Ethiopian dynasty, while Shabaka's vassal princes in Zoan rule Lower Egypt. However, it is not clear that the *sārîm* assembled at Zoan are vassals, for such meetings of several vassal princes were not encouraged by suzerains who wished to deter intrigue. More likely they are a special delegation of high officials charged to receive the Judean emissaries and they receive directions from pharaoh via Hanes in Middle Egypt (apparently Herakleopolis [cf. Simons, *op. cit.*, p. 440, #1294]).

is not divine nor is it of the nature of spirit. *Those who elevate armed force to the level of final arbiter will therefore fall when Yahweh stretches forth his hand to prove that his is the decisive word in history.* Consequently, the tide of battle will roll to the very walls and gates of Jerusalem, siegeworks will be raised, and Jerusalem will become a veritable altar for human sacrifice. In her extremity Judah, prostrate and virtually dead, will whisper to Yahweh "from the dust" (29:1–4). Thus whatever salvation Yahweh has in mind for Judah, it will come only through great travail.

Side by side with the prophet's conviction that Judah was to be brought low, indeed lower than during the Syro-Ephraimite crisis, grew another conviction, namely, that Assyria had exceeded her function as a rod of God's anger against his people (10:5–15). Sargon's death had not removed the arrogance and violence of Assyrian ways. Sennacherib was pursuing the identical policies. Much had happened since Amos first sounded the improbable threat of Assyrian invasion in Palestine. The northern kingdom had been obliterated and Judah had been humbled as a vassal state and was shortly to be driven to near extinction. Yet in all this Assyria merely boasted and strutted through the ancient Near East, thinking not of divine justice but rather of self-aggrandizement. In a masterful oracle, rife with colorful and telling imagery, Isaiah pictures Assyria as "the rod of Yahweh's anger." It is, however, not a passive instrument but one which has its own malignant designs "to cut off many nations," and which brags unrestrainedly, "my hand has discovered like a nest the goods of the peoples and as a man gathers abandoned eggs so I have gathered all the earth." Without effective opposition the Assyrian tide has rolled through Syria and Palestine. The prophet names six cities in pairs, each doublet representing a successively deeper penetration of the west:

> Is not Calneh like Carchemish?
> Is not Hamath like Arpad?
> Is not Samaria like Damascus?

The Assyrian logically concludes that all gods are alike in their impotence to defend their lands—and shall not Jerusalem fare as Samaria? The deportation of peoples and the assimilation of former kingdoms as provinces ("I have taken away the boundaries of peoples") and the seizure of booty and imposition of tribute ("I have looted their treasures") are among the cardinal boasts of the conqueror (10:13).

The proud tone of the Assyrian, the revelry in conquest and plunder, the scoffing at the enemy and his gods are altogether typical of the Assyrian records—but with one notable exception. The Assyrian kings always attribute their victories to the state god Ashur, in whose name they go to war, before whom they express servility and humility, but who is a terrible scourge of enemy or rebel peoples.[109] The total absence of this theme in Isaiah's prophecy about Assyria calls for explanation. It can hardly have been due to ignorance on Isaiah's part. With all the contacts among embassies and the presence of Assyrian officials in Jerusalem to collect tribute and to examine Judah's loyalty, the religious basis of Assyrian kingship could not have been unknown to him. Therefore the exclusion was deliberate and is explicable on two grounds: First, there is the holiness of the one universal God, who overrules even Assyria. Ashur, however real he may be to Assyrian minds, is not the effective power that moves the world conquerors. To Sennacherib the prophet says (37:26–27),[110]

[109] E. A. Speiser, "Ancient Mesopotamia," in R. C. Dentan, ed., *The Idea of History in the Ancient Near East,* pp. 60–67, argues persuasively that the Assyrian annals were actual condensations of letters addressed to the gods in which the kings reported their achievements. The bombast and arrogance of the annals arise from the excessive formal piety of the kings, who visualize their wars as the wars of the gods. This strenuous assertion of Ashur's lordship through Assyrian power was not merely an Old Assyrian or Middle Assyrian phenomenon but actually grew stronger toward the end of the neo-Assyrian empire and is especially well attested in the vassal treaties of Esarhaddon and in the seal of Sennacherib with which Esarhaddon stamped the treaty tablets (D. J. Wiseman, *Iraq* 20 [1958], 1–91, and esp. pp. 15, 22–28).

[110] This passage seems to express the incredulity of Isaiah that Sennacherib should overlook Yahweh and fix rather upon another deity, Ashur, as his protector and sponsor. The sense of the unalterable decrees of national gods which was abroad at this time and which Isaiah expressed with particular power is well communicated in the seal of Sennacherib impressed on Esarhaddon's vassal treaty of 672 from Kalah (Wiseman, *Iraq* 20 [1958], 15):

Seal of Destinies
by which Ashur, king of the gods,

Haven't you heard that I arranged it [your success] long ago?
 I planned from ancient times that which now I execute—
that fortresses should be brought to ruins
  while their inhabitants, without strength, are dismayed and be-
   wildered,
  and have become like wild plants, and like young grass,
  like grass on the rooftops, scorched before it grows up.

The prophet sweeps aside all the claims of Assyrian monarchs to possess "a trust-inspiring oracle given by my lord Ashur" and to have defeated their enemies with the signal help of "the terror-inspiring glamor of Ashur, my lord." *Insofar as any god has been involved in the deeds of the Assyrians, it has been Yahweh.*

In the second place, the Assyrians have themselves had strong wills to conquer the earth, and they need not lay their arrogance and rapacity to their national god. What they have done they have done in the name of the national collectivity Ashur, which is, to be sure, objectified as a god, but it is *they* who have devised wrong against the peoples of the earth. Yahweh's use of this instrument is thus insufficient to account for what it has done to spoil the earth. Assyria's aggressions have been conceived in self-will and carried out in self-will. *From the point of view of Assyrian responsibility, Yahweh's use of their aggressions to punish his people has been incidental.* Without the benefit of national-religious propaganda to glorify the militarism of the Assyrian

---

   seals the Destinies of
   the gods of the Upper and Lower worlds,
   of heaven, earth and Lower worlds,
   of heaven, earth and man[kind]
   Whatever he seals
   is not to be changed. As for him
   who changes (it),
   may Ashur, king of the gods (and) Ninlil
   together with their children slay him
   with their mighty weapons
   I (am) Sennacherib
   King of [Assyria], the prince who reveres thee,
   He who erases (my) written name
   or alters this, your seal of Destinies
   Erase his name
   and his seed from the land.

kings, Isaiah sets them forth in all their naked ugliness as essentially selfish and cruel men.

However one-sided this estimate, it is at any rate made by the prophet on the basis of a wide familiarity with Assyrian policies and methods and *it is a case so presented that neither Judah, the victim, nor Assyria, the aggressor, can take any special pride but must rather each face up to its own wrongdoings.* The internationalism of Amos and the sense of mutual guilt among the nations apparent in Amos and Hosea are here carried to their logical consummation: in the tangle of international relations Yahweh brings down to judgment the small and the great, the covenant people, their neighbors in the Fertile Crescent, and the world conquerors, for all have sinned and none may claim innocence or exemption. Foreign affairs, and especially the interminable wars of the reigns of Sargon and Sennacherib, are the threshing floor of Yahweh's judgment and none is able to escape his coming.

The exact extent of the original oracle in 10:5 ff. is difficult to determine, for the conclusion is composed of three units (10:16–19, 20–23, 24–27), none of which is certainly from the prophet, and the one most integrally bound to the preceding oracle possesses a banal and confusing mixture of judgment (by sickness or starvation, by a field fire, by the felling of trees) which is hardly worthy of the foregoing vivid characterization of Assyrian pride. It is likely that 14:24–27 formed the original conclusion to 10:5–15;[111] even if not, it certainly stands in the same line of thought and belongs to the same period of the prophet's work. The prophecy affirms in bold and certain terms that there is "a design designed for the entire earth" and there is "a hand extended over all nations" to execute that design. Accordingly Yahweh has decided: "I will break the Assyrian in my land, and upon my mountains trample him under foot, and his yoke shall vanish from them, and his burden from their shoulder." Parallel imagery in 9:4 and 10:27 (although in both instances the imagery may be wholly traditional and not original with the

---

[111] T. K. Cheyne argued thus on the basis of style and rhythm in *Introduction to the Book of Isaiah*, 1897, pp. 79–80.

prophet) seems to argue that the reference is to relief for Yahweh's people Judah, who will no longer need to suffer from the Assyrian oppression. But on the basis of 10:5–15 a larger interpretation is not only possible but probable, for "the peoples" who have been wronged by Assyria will all be relieved by the breaking of Assyrian power and not Judah alone. *Thus the "design" and the "hand" of Yahweh, while especially active in the life of the covenant people, also extend to the activities of the nations.* The *hybris* of Assyria has vaunted itself against all nations of the Near East, and its wrongs have not been exclusively against Judah. Those wrongs can be requited only if the military defeat of Assyria in Judah will bring relief to all those who have been wronged (cf. also 14:5–7).[112]

While the preparations for the revolt against Assyria were under way, among them Hezekiah's securing of his water supply, Isaiah continued to preach two motifs untiringly. First, he asserted the uselessness of reliance upon Egypt for help against Assyria since both Egypt and Judah will suffer crushing defeat. Second, the Assyrian has become too boastful and rapacious and will himself suffer a crushing setback in Judah but without human assistance—at least without the assistance of Hezekiah. Once again, and supremely so now that he bore down so heavily upon the punishment of Assyria, the dialectic in Isaiah's thought must have been a source of amazement and bewilderment to Hezekiah and to the Judeans. It would not be surprising at all if Hezekiah simply gave up trying to understand Isaiah and turned to the apparently logical political course of action: rebellion against an empire that seemed to be relaxing its grip on the west since the death of Sargon.

It is of particular importance to disabuse ourselves of the frequently held notion that the polarity in Isaiah's political thought can be simply stated as a contrast between the legendary Isaiah of chaps. 36–39 and the historical Isaiah of the genuine oracles.[113]

[112] The view that 14:26 refers to world-wide freedom from Assyrian oppression has been well stated by O. Procksch, *op. cit.*, p. 180, and J. Fichtner, "Jahwes Plan in der Botschaft des Jesaia," *ZAW* 63 (1951), 23–25.

[113] This erroneous simplification of the prophet's thought is advanced vigorously by S. Blank, *op. cit.*, pp. 11–13, 28–29, and by R. H. Pfeiffer, *Introduction to the Old Testament*, 1941, pp. 399–401, 427–29.

Quite apart from chaps. 36–39, the thought of Isaiah displays a curiously thoroughgoing dialectic, for he discerns the judgment of God as a racing fire striking hither and yon among the nations, in one and the same cluster of events consuming both sides, and acting with utter disregard of the arrogant and inflated self-conceptions of nations and kings. Those who strive to hold that judgment at arm's length, those who seek to twist it to personal gain and who glory in another people's misfortune, those who fail to read in the punishment of another their own call to repentance —all such will stumble and fall to their own destruction.

It must be frankly admitted that the culminating event in the religio-political experience of Isaiah is one but imperfectly known. This circumstance is particularly frustrating since we have the good fortune to possess biblical and Assyrian accounts of this event—the campaign of Sennacherib in Palestine in 701—and doubly frustrating because, as ancient documents go, the story is told with a fair amount of detail. Unfortunately the two sets of records contain so many differences that it is impossible to reconstruct events in detail without resorting to questionable synchronization of the accounts or to selection of the details of one account at the expense of the other.[114]

That being said, some theories are more probable than others, and there is a clear common core to the two versions, which runs as follows: Sennacherib advanced down the coastal plain after quelling the revolt in Sidon and turned to the punishment of the rebellious Philistine cities. An Egyptian relief force was defeated by Sennacherib at Eltekeh, not far from the Philistine cities. Sennacherib devastated the Judean countryside, received a heavy tribute from Hezekiah, but did not actually enter Jerusalem or turn it into an Assyrian province. *Two articles of Isaiah's expectations were borne out: First, Judah suffered severe devastation.* Many of its cities (46 walled cities, says Sennacherib) were destroyed and their citizens deported (the 200,150 of Sennacherib's

[114] It is the merit of L. L. Honor, *Sennacherib's Invasion of Palestine. A Critical Source Study,* that he relentlessly exposes the uncertainties in all proposed historical reconstructions of the campaign. Although serving as a useful analysis of the possibilities and as a caution against hasty conclusions, the work is ultimately unsatisfying, however, for the historian must hazard probabilities, and Honor has not been willing to do so.

report is incredible; 2,150 is more likely).[115] *Second, the Assyrians did not capture Jerusalem or turn it into a provincial capital,* although Hezekiah remained at least the nominal vassal of Sennacherib. In any case, the large-scale destruction of Assyria which Isaiah had foreseen did not materialize.

The chief historical question is whether Sennacherib left Palestine voluntarily or under duress. On one reading of the events, the enormous tribute of Hezekiah and his surrender of the detained king of Ekron were sufficient amends. Furthermore, the devastation of the Judean countryside and the handing over of large sections of the Judean territory to loyal administrations in the Philistine cities of Ekron, Ashdod, and Gaza[116] would sufficiently insure against Hezekiah's rebellion in the future. On another reading of the same events, it is noted that the Assyrians very rarely displayed clemency toward active leaders of revolts. Unless something had interfered with his plans, Sennacherib would normally have removed Hezekiah and replaced him either with another vassal or with an Assyrian governor in a newly organized province. All the more is this to be expected since Sidqia of Ashdod was deported and replaced by a loyal vassal, and the rebel Ekronite officials and nobles were executed and Padi was

[115] A. Ungnad, "Die Zahl der von Sanherib deportierten Judaer," *ZAW* 59 (1942–43), 199–202, notes that the figure of 200,150 Judean deportees is paralleled by other abnormally large figures in Sennacherib's annals, e.g., 100,225 sheep from Armenia and 800,100 sheep from Mesopotamia. On the basis of the Assyrian decimal system he seeks to show how an error arose from an original 2,150 deportees.

[116] Sennacherib's annals are imprecise: "His [Hezekiah's] towns which I had plundered, I took away from his country and gave them (over) to Mitinti, king of Ashdod, Padi, king of Ekron, and Sillibel, king of Gaza. Thus I reduced his country" (*ANET*, p. 288). A. Alt, "Die territorialgeschichtliche Bedeutung von Sanheribs Eingriff in Palaestina," *KS, II* (1930), 242–49, believes that all of Judah apart from Jerusalem was divided among the three Philistine cities, and probably Ashkelon also was in on the spoils. The evidence, however, is open to other interpretations, e.g., that the area taken from Judah was restricted to the Shephelah (W. F. Albright, "The Biblical Period," in L. Finkelstein, ed., *The Jews, Their History, Culture and Religion*, 1950, p. 43), that it lay in southern Judah south of a line running approximately from Moresheth-gath to Tekoa (so K. Elliger, *ZDPV* 57 [1934], 81–152), or that the southeastern section of Judah fell into the hands of Edom rather than Philistia (H. L. Ginsberg, "Judah and the Transjordan States from 734 to 582," *Alexander Marx Jubilee Volume*, 1950, pp. 349–51).

restored as king. Only if Sennacherib had reason to think of Hezekiah as an unwilling hostage to an insurrectionist party in Judah would he normally have left him on the throne, but exactly the opposite was the case.

Thus there is some support for the view that Sennacherib was forced to leave Palestine before his disposition of Judean affairs was completed. The biblical account, which speaks of a severe epidemic in the Assyrian ranks, is patently legendary in its form but may contain a truth (II Kings 19:35–37 = Isa. 37:36–38), and another, which speaks of a rumor of dissension at home so that Sennacherib will have to return home hastily only to fall an assassin's victim, although perhaps touched up *ex eventu,* may reflect exactly what did happen (II Kings 19:5–7 = Isa. 37:5–7). Serious plagues[117] and court turmoil[118] were among the repeated obstacles to Assyria's imperial efforts in the eighth century, and if Isaiah had wished to announce a defeat of Sennacherib's army without the help of Egyptian or Judean forces he would logically have thought of just such interferences with Sennacherib's plans. Of course, the fact that either a plague or a court plot or both were prophesied by Isaiah would not in itself prove that either occurred fortuitously so as to spare Hezekiah. As the biblical record stands, Isaiah prophesied a court uprising but a plague actually relieved Jerusalem (the assassination of Sennacherib by his sons twenty years later is incorrectly conflated with the events of 701; 38:36–38). If such a brief reprieve from Sennacherib's retributive hand did take place, it was not suffi-

---

[117] During the eighth century there are reports of plagues striking the Assyrian homeland repeatedly, e.g., in 768, 764, 757, and 756 (Hallo, *op. cit.,* p. 44). A. T. Olmstead's claim that Adad-nirari's conquest of Damascus (805) and Ashurdan's attacks on Hazrek = Hattarika (772, 765) were blighted or even interrupted by virulent plagues (*op. cit.,* pp. 164, 169) is now generally dismissed as a mistaken reading of the annals (according to a conversation with H. Tadmor). It is likely, however, that armies would be as exposed to epidemic diseases as civilians and probably even more so.

[118] From late in the reign of Shalmaneser III, beginning in 827, until the rise of Tiglath-pileser III in 745 Assyria suffered seriously from dynastic troubles. Particularly devastating to Assyrian power were the revolts against Shalmaneser III (827–822) and against Ashurdan III (763–759), and even the transfers of power from Tiglath-pileser to Shalmaneser V and thence to Sargon were not without internal tensions (Olmstead, *op. cit.,* pp. 153–57, 172, 206–7; Hallo, *op. cit.,* p. 44).

cient to free Judah from vassalage. So it appears, on any reading of the events of 701, that neither Isaiah nor Hezekiah found the outcome wholly up to his expectations.

As Sennacherib advanced on Phoenicia, Isaiah raised a mock lament over Tyre and Sidon, the latter at this period being the dominant city politically and commercially, "the trader of the nations" (23:1–12). The retention of Tyre in the superscription and its prominent place in the body of the oracle reflects the historical fact that Israel's previous contacts with Phoenicia had been largely with Tyre, and therefore by tradition Tyre came to be a virtual equivalent for Phoenicia. This accounts for the vacillation in the references between Tyre and Sidon, making gratuitous the assumption of a Tyre recension and of a Sidon recension which were later conflated.[119] The section devoted exclusively to Tyre (vss. 13–18) is a series of reapplications of Isaiah's lament to later events. It transfers the execution of Isaiah's threat against Tyre from Assyria to Chaldea.[120] The body of the lament, however, is characterized by Isaiah's style and theological conceptions. For their wanton pride the Phoenician cities are about to be humbled. The closing mock appeal, "Arise, cross over to Cyprus, even there you will find no rest," is perhaps an allusion to Luli, king of Sidon, who, according to Sennacherib, "fled far overseas and perished" (*ANET*, p. 288).

One of Isaiah's oracles dates from the campaign of Sennacherib against Judah and portrays in biting imagery the extreme plight of the country (1:4–9). Like a desperately sick man the land is full of bruises, sores, and wounds which have gone unattended. The land has been desolated and its cities have been put to the torch, while the invaders live off the crops. Jerusalem

---

[119] Scott, *op. cit.*, p. 294, correctly concludes: "Actually the general tenor of the oracle is clear enough if it is recognized that it is concerned with the Phoenician people under various designations." B. Duhm, *Das Buch Jesaja, HZAT*, pp. 147–48, saw it as an original taunting elegy over Sidon when it fell to Artaxerxes III in 348. Later the author of vss. 15–18 applied it to Tyre (23:1), added vs. 5, and changed "Sidon" to "Tyre" in 23:8. O. Procksch, *op. cit.*, p. 305, understood that a poem on Sidon by Isaiah (vss. 1–4, 12–14) was combined with a much later one on Tyre (vss. 5–11).

[120] It is possible, however, that vss. 14 and 16 formed the conclusion to the lament in vss. 1–12 and the original sequence has been interrupted by the intrusion of vss. 13, 15, 17–18.

itself "remains like a booth in a vineyard, as a watchtower in a vegetable patch." This glimpse of the isolated city is reminiscent of a simile applied to Hezekiah in Sennacherib's annals: "himself I made a prisoner in Jerusalem, his royal residence, like a bird in a cage" (*ANET*, p. 288). The fact that Judah has not been altogether overwhelmed is solely because of Yahweh's mercy; otherwise it would have been as utterly ruined as the traditional wicked cities of Sodom and Gomorrah.

The inclusion of an oracle from 701 at the beginning of the book seems at first doubtful, and some have connected it rather with the Syro-Ephraimite attack of 735–734.[121] It is true that most of the details can be associated with that attack as well as with Sennacherib's invasion, but the extreme situation of Jerusalem seems suitable only to 701, when not merely the cities north of Jerusalem and on the Philistine border were conquered but scores of key cities throughout Judah. There is also some doubt that Isaiah would have used the term *zārîm*, "foreigners," to denote the enemy in 735–734 since it included not only Damascenes but also fellow Yahwists from the northern kingdom. The purpose in placing the prophecy at the beginning of the collected oracles of the prophet was to emphasize that the threats of his earlier prophecies were not idle but did indeed eventually bear the bitter fruit of invasion and destruction. The opening chords of the oracle show that as the ring of Assyrian arms tightened around Jerusalem Isaiah did not relent in his call for repentance.

Woe, O sinful nation, a people burdened with guilt,
    . . . why will you still be chastened, that you continue to rebel?

Especially noteworthy is the speech of the high Assyrian officer, the Rabshakeh, who sought to secure Hezekiah's surrender or, failing that, to encourage defection among his troops (36:4–20, in which Sennacherib is quoted verbatim by the officer, and 37:8–13, delivered to Hezekiah by messengers but adding no new arguments to the previous speech). The speech is of an un-

---

[121] Cf., e.g., Wiener, *op. cit.*, pp. 27–28, who argues that vss. 29 ff. come from a time before Hezekiah's reformation. Aside from the fact that the extent of Hezekiah's reform is debatable, there is no valid reason for dating all of the oracles in chap. 1 in the same year or period.

usual fullness and forcefulness. The Assyrian chides the Judeans for reliance on Egypt, "that broken reed." As for trust in the national god Yahweh, "Has any of the gods of the nations delivered his land out of the hand of the king of Assyria?" For that matter, how interested is Yahweh in saving Judah inasmuch as Hezekiah has closed down so many of Yahweh's high places and altars? Furthermore, hasn't Yahweh directed me—Sennacherib—to come against Judah so that in resisting Assyria you resist Yahweh? As to the war-making potential of Judah, it is distinctly inferior in that it does not include chariots. In an aside in which Rabshakeh departs from his prepared speech, he claims that even if Sennacherib should offer Hezekiah 2,000 horses to fill this lack, the Judean couldn't find men who know how to ride them! Inducements to surrender are offered in the form of idyllic descriptions of life in exile where the agricultural opportunities are every bit the equal of Judah's. All in all, concludes the Rabshakeh, Hezekiah has entered a revolt without sufficient backing: "Just what is this security plan of yours worth? Just how are glib words a plan and strength for war?"

For the most part there is no difficulty in thinking of the substance of this speech as having been delivered to Hezekiah by Assyrian negotiators. The verisimilitude of historical conditions is impressive, so that it cannot easily have originated much later than Isaiah's time. Nevertheless the form and content of the speech testify against its having been delivered as now written. It is shot through with a Yahwistic tendentiousness which we can hardly attribute to an Assyrian mind. In fact it appears that the basic arguments of the Assyrian attackers have been modified by the incorporation of prophetic warnings against Hezekiah, as well as some of the popular feelings against the king's policies. It is rather surprising to find the open allusion to Hezekiah's closure of sanctuaries outside of Jerusalem, for we should not have expected Assyria to be aware of such internal religious reforms, but the non-Judean source of the argument is supported by the misunderstanding of the argument, which totally fails to take into account that Hezekiah closed the outlying sanctuaries *as a pious Yahwist* and not in opposition to Yahweh. An Assyrian could only regard the abandoning of shrines and the destruction of altars as an anti-religious measure displeasing to the god formerly worshiped there. The information about the reform probably came to Sennacherib's attention in the course of his investigation of Hezekiah's revolutionary tendencies which had begun when he freed himself from Assyrian cult practices, but the Assyrian could understand the reform only as an impious act. Doubtless the majority of Hezekiah's subjects also opposed the closing of the local sanctuaries or at least held grave misgivings about so reckless a course. The serious plight of Jerusalem in 701 may have been explained by many Judeans as angry punishment from Yahweh for upsetting his cult. So it seems that Hezekiah was buffeted not only from the prophet's side but also from the side of his subjects.

Not attributable to Sennacherib, however, is the form of the contention that Yahweh has sent him against Jerusalem to destroy it. To be sure, the western vassal treaties of the Assyrians apparently invoked the gods of both parties so that an infraction of the treaty would bring the judgment of two sets of deities upon the rebels.[122] Undoubtedly one of the points of Rabshakeh's case was the displeasure of Judah's god in a broken treaty, and Sennacherib could well have said that Yahweh was permitting him to punish his sinful people. It is not likely, however, that he would represent himself as receiving a direct command from Yahweh since in Assyrian records the commands for retribution upon rebellious states are always given by Ashur. This is in fact another instance of the naïve attribution of Yahwism to a foreign ruler of which the Old Testament offers other examples (to Darius in Dan. 6:25–27 and to Cyrus in Ezra 1:2–4). In fact, the chief reason for believing the Assyrian speech to have undergone Yahwistic revision is the complete absence of reference to Assyrian gods, either directly or indirectly. In negotiations in which the respective power of Assyria and Judah and its religious foundations were central, such an omission on the part of Sennacherib or his high officials is inconceivable. Original Assyrian diplomatic arguments, generally well preserved, are presented in Yahwistic dress so that Sennacherib appears as a

[122] See Tsevat, *op. cit.*, pp. 199–200, and Weidner, *op. cit.*, pp. 17–34.

monotheist who urges against Judah's revolt objections which accord largely with Isaiah's views: Egypt cannot be trusted to produce aid; chariotry will be of no assistance to Judah; Yahweh himself has decreed its defeat.

Unlike Isaiah, however, the speech presents no moral basis for Judah's chastisement, her conquest being simply one more example of Assyrian power. Sennacherib in no way reckons with limits upon his own behavior or aspirations. *The speech reveals how power-political views and the prophet's views could coincide in certain details and yet spring from entirely different sources and lead to conclusions that, while superficially similar, were actually remote in meaning.* It gives us some idea of the confusion which Hezekiah faced as the responsible leader of Judah, for he was subject to pressure from Assyria, from Isaiah, from his subjects, and from court factions favoring and opposing revolt. That Assyria and Isaiah seemed to be saying the same thing, especially in their denigration of Egyptian aid, must have disturbed the king deeply and confirmed the charges of those who regarded the prophet as dangerous to national security if not actually treasonous. That Hezekiah did not fully accept their interpretation and, like Ahaz, reject the prophet altogether speaks for his sincerity as a Yahwist. The king knew that there was another dimension to Isaiah's thought though he grasped it but dimly and failed to see how he could obey its dictates. Isaiah for his part saw Yahweh's plan as powerful over history, bringing defeat to Ashur and a new opportunity to his people to obey him, but not without severe punishment. Zion may take heart, therefore, not because of her righteousness but because Sennacherib "has mocked and reviled the Holy One of Israel" and, as unwillingly as a war captive, he will be led back to Assyria on the way by which he came to Palestine. Here is a second expression of the expectation that Sennacherib will be recalled to Assyria (cf. also 36:7).

The forthright oracle of Isaiah 37:33–35, which claims that Judah will not even be subjected to siege, is difficult to reconcile with Isaiah's other threats to the contrary and can only be understood as a later misunderstanding of the prophet's actual belief. Its promise that "I will defend this city to save it, for my own sake, and for the sake of my servant David" is not a recognizable formulation of Isaiah's, but it correctly recalls that, as the Assyrians drew near to Jerusalem, Isaiah advised Hezekiah that Assyria would be frustrated in her plan to take the city—not because there had been any great change in Judah's attitude or conduct but because of the overriding plan of Yahweh, in effect, "for my own sake."

It is apparent that the prophet did not surrender his dialectic and suddenly revert to an unconditional nationalism.[123] We see this most clearly in his oracle on "the valley of vision" (22:1–14, *ḥizzāyôn* being presumably a word play on Hinnom, a valley south of the city noted for its pagan worship). The prophet upbraids the citizens of Jerusalem for their boisterous celebration at the city's deliverance. The losses have been too great for any light-hearted festivity. Although no open battle occurred, there were many who died of plague and famine so typical of ancient sieges ("your fallen are not fallen by the sword nor dead in battle"). Certain leaders fled and were captured, which may well refer to a defection from Hezekiah described more concretely by Sennacherib: "irregular and elite troops which he had brought into Jerusalem, his royal residence, in order to strengthen (it), had deserted him" (*ANET*, p. 288). Isaiah employs the term *qetsînîm*, which, though normally meaning "officials" or "leaders," in some contexts means "military commanders" (Josh. 10:24; Judg. 11:6, 11; Dan. 11:18). In vss. 5–8 the siege is recalled onomatopoetically as "a day of uproar [*mehûmāh*], of subjugation [*mebûsāh*], and of confusion [*mebûkāh*]." The reference to Elam, which has frequently prompted interpreters to date the passage during the exile, is apparently no more than a refer-

---

[123] H. Schmoekel, *Jahwe und die Fremdvoelker,* pp. 41–43, sees Isaiah coming to the support of Hezekiah and the people in 701 in contrast to his earlier condemnations of their policies and threats against them. Later, he returned to a condemnatory attitude. "The struggle of the prophets with the popular view was great as in Jeremiah and is it impossible that in a time of great national distress he took the side of his people?" (p. 41). This view rightly perceives a change in Isaiah's attitude in the crisis of 701 but it fails to discern its basis and character. It was based on Yahweh's plan for the nations and meant judgment for Assyria's *hybris* and not merely because of her enmity toward Judah. It is wrong to speak of "sides"—for or against the people. The only "side" Isaiah ever knew was that of Yahweh's will for the nations.

ence to the chariots and bowmen from national military units incorporated in the Assyrian army, in this case from Elam, Kir, and possibly Syria. Such units may well have served in the campaign against Palestine in 701 although we possess no information from Assyrian sources.[124]

The prophet castigates Hezekiah for responding to Judah's precarious position only in terms of military defense (22:8b–11). The king checked his arsenal, he broke down a number of houses along the city wall and added their stones to the city walls, and he secured his water supply by making a reservoir between the two walls to receive water from the old pool, an apparent reference to the tunnel which was hewed through the solid rock of Ophel for almost a third of a mile in order to bring water from Gihon, outside the wall, to Siloam within the city (see Map 20). The project is known to us from an inscription left by his workmen near the Siloam end of the tunnel (*ANET,* p. 321). The tunnel testifies to the astuteness of Hezekiah, who was not prepared to revolt without assuring himself that Jerusalem could withstand a prolonged siege. Isaiah objects, however, that Judah's preparation ended there, for "you did not look to him who did it, nor consider him who planned it afar off." Yahweh was not taken seriously into account even though his name was invoked to justify the uprising against Assyria. This indictment, in almost the same terms as the one leveled against Sennacherib (37:26), shows that *in Isaiah's view of history the two opposing kings were equally agnostic in their disregard of a higher will that orders events. They have each acted as though his strategic preparations and tactical decisions were the determinative factors in the struggle's outcome.*

In their defense, the Jerusalemites could point to their piety as Yahwists even though they may have had some doubts about all the measures carried through by Hezekiah—particularly the closing of many if not all of the places of worship outside Jerusalem.

---

[124] One of the Assyrian military innovations of the last half of the eighth century was to incorporate military contingents of conquered regions into the imperial army; e.g., from Samaria Sargon drew a force of 50 (or 200) chariots and from Hamath he recruited 200 chariots and 600 horsemen (*ANET,* pp. 284–85; Tadmor, "The Campaigns of Sargon II . . . ," p. 34). Similar recruitment is reported from many parts of the empire.

Yet the frenzy of their religious activity did not impress Isaiah. Yahweh was still seeking repentance and change of conduct, for he "summoned to wailing and mourning, to baldness and dressing in sackcloth," but the people rejoiced in an orgy of sacrifice and feasting with the last of their provisions in an effort to avert Yahweh's wrath and with an air of nihilism shouted, *"Eat and drink, for we die tomorrow."* But never the cry which Yahweh sought: *"Repent, for we die tomorrow!"* The social and religious rottenness which Isaiah, like Amos, had castigated through the years went on unchanged in spite of the official cult and government protestations to the contrary. *Yahweh had spared the city in order to prove something to Assyria, to expose its* hybris *and inherent weakness, and simultaneously to prove something to Judah, to reveal Yahweh's power and to evoke repentance and humility. Yet in both respects the outcome of 701 was disappointing.* Assyria had learned nothing, except perhaps to plan its campaigns more carefully, to keep court turmoil at a minimum, and to improve sanitation so that epidemics would not break out among the troops. There is no sign that Sennacherib or any of his officials were impressed with Yahweh's power or thought of themselves as any less entitled to rule the ancient Near East. Likewise, Judah had learned only to revel in its good fortune and to profess Yahweh as the national deity without being moved to honor him as the judge of Judah. Here and there individual Judeans accepted the prophet's interpretation of the events, but it seems that they had learned this point of view first from him and only incidentally from the events.

So the climactic crisis of Isaiah's career left him with only a partial victory. He had still the people of Judah with whom to reason for they had not been carried into exile and the Assyrian provincial system had not been imposed upon them. But this was merely a buying of time, significant only as it might give new opportunities for repentance. The outcome must have been a deep disappointment. He learned afresh the bitter taste of hardness of heart and the ineffectuality of terror and violence to convince those who will not be convinced. His belief in the vast plan of Yahweh for the nations of the earth was not diminished; in fact it grew, but it took on a new character. To think of Yahweh

merely as the scourge of the earth was an inadequate and ultimately futile view of God. Unless Yahweh could establish his
authority in some other way, the surging nations and peoples
would continue to flail one another in arrogance and fear, without material profit and without learning anything.

Prophetic Arbitration Among the Nations

We cannot know for how long a period after 701 Isaiah continued to prophesy. No later date or historical allusion can be
identified with certainty. We have only the late tradition that he
was put to death by Manasseh, thus at some time after 687 (the
Ascension of Isaiah). It does appear, however, that the famous
prophecy of Zion as the center of the nations belongs to this
period of the prophet's life (2:1–4). A good case can be made
for the originality of the oracle in Isaiah and its subsequent inclusion in the book of Micah (Mic. 4:1–3), but the version in
Micah seems to have preserved a conclusion since lost in Isaiah
(Mic. 4:4).[125] The present position of the oracle in Isaiah is
without clear explanation, but it may have been intended to
stand at the beginning of the subcollection of oracles in chaps.
2–5, thus giving them a universal orientation. The superscription,
which duplicated 1:1 in part, may therefore indicate that chap.
1 was prefixed subsequent to the collection of chaps. 2–5 and
that, in any case, the identification in 2:1 was left in the finished
book of Isaiah in order to claim the prophecy for Isaiah since it
was by then already attributed to Micah as well.

This brilliant oracle can be fully understood within the bounds
of Isaiah's thought. Its form is indebted to the "enthronement
songs," but the prophet has put his distinctive stamp upon the
content. Aside from the spacious thought of the oracle it has no
marked affinities with exilic and post-exilic prophecies. To appre-

[125] The originality of Isaiah 2:1–4 and Micah 4:4 has been supported with
convincing argument by H. Wildberger, "Die Voelkerwallfahrt zum Zion,
Jes. II. 1–5," *VT* 7 (1957), 62–81. But earlier even so radical a critic as
B. Duhm, *op. cit.*, pp. 36–39, found no valid reason to deny the authenticity
of 2:2–4, and placed it in the prophet's old age. Although Scott, *op. cit.*,
p. 180, denies the poem to the prophet, he thinks the literary context is
original in the book of Isaiah rather than in Micah.

ciate the position of this oracle in the thought of Isaiah it is necessary, however, to recall certain features of his oracles and of the
enthronement traditions.

The enthronment songs which appear in the prophecies of
Isaiah are of two types: those in which the king figures as the
bearer or executor of Yahweh's salvation (9:2–7; 11: 1–9) and
those in which he does not appear but rather Yahweh alone, without human agency—or at least without Israelite help—works
his salvation (12:4–6; 14:25; 17:12–14; 29:5–8). It is apparent that much the same distinction exists in the psalms which
concern Yahweh's victory at Jerusalem: some are truly royal
psalms in that the Israelite king by force of arms will impose
justice in the earth (Ps. 2; 18; 20; 21; 45; 72; 110; 132; 144),
while others speak only of Yahweh's direct protection of Zion
by miraculous intervention (46; 48; 76; 83). There are, of
course, important differences of opinion as to how these psalms
are to be dated and as to their original settings. There is, in addition, a series of enthronement songs which declare Yahweh's dominion over all the earth (47; 93; 95–100); these are thought by
some to have been used in the pre-exilic royal cult (Mowinckel)
but are regarded by others as post-exilic affirmations of Yahweh's
lordship without reference to an earthly ruler (Gunkel). Nevertheless, allowing for disputed issues, an impressive consensus suggests that both lines of Zion tradition existed in Isaiah's time and
that he therefore had ample opportunity to know of their viewpoints and to use them for his purposes.

It is clear that the tradition of Zion as the place of Yahweh's
revelation in which all nations would be involved, chiefly in their
defeat and submission to Israel, was an ancient one. It apparently
derived from a twofold source: (1) the belief of the old tribal
league that Yahweh was the defender of his people against the
enemy,[126] a belief which David succeeded in transferring to the

---

[126] For the political and military character of pre-monarchic Yahwism, and
especially the tension between waging war charismatically and waging it
professionally, see Weber, *op. cit.,* pp. 90–138. F. Schwally, *Semitische
Kriegsaltertuemer I. Der Heilige Krieg im Alten Israel,* 1901, fruitfully com-
pares early Israelite war practices with general primitive and nomadic
practices.

monarchy,[127] although here and there it appears in the later cult in more or less unadulterated form, e.g., Psalm 60, and (2) the native Jerusalem religious traditions, which were once associated with Canaanite worship of gods of peace (*shālēm*) and righteousness (*tsedek*) and in which priest-kings seem to have played a part (cf., e.g., Gen. 14:18–20).[128] David and his priesthood also succeeded in accommodating this tradition to Yahwism. Yet the victory of David was only partial, for time and again the prophets could arise to seize upon one or the other of these traditions as a tool of criticism against current dynastic conduct and ideology. Such was the role of Isaiah.

The prophet's dependence upon and interest in these amphictyonic and Jerusalemite traditions—especially the latter—is striking. Contrary to previous and later prophets, Isaiah has virtually nothing to say about Moses, either as deliverer or as lawgiver of his people. The *tōrāh* which he knows is the *tōrāh* rooted in Zion as the place of Yahweh's revelation.[129] Yet this *tōrāh* retains the dynamism and the cultural transcendence of the Mosaic traditions; it is not linked automatically to the Davidic dynasty in the sense that the *tōrāh* forms the natural matrix of the dynasty and is, therefore, by definition that which the king declares. The relation is more nearly that of constitution and executive action. Isaiah could make use of enthronement liturgies which were patently monarchic in character in order to impress upon the king his high duties, but he felt free to criticize the same king in a way that was normally considered out of bounds for those who acknowledged the dynasty's divine right.

[127] David's transfer of the ark and the ephod (priestly oracle) to Jerusalem at the beginning of his reign is to be understood as an attempt to rally the old tribal Yahwistic allegiances to his throne. The preservation of his dynasty for more than two hundred years shows that he succeeded in part but only with his own tribe Judah and with portions of Benjamin, while the other Yahweh tribes created their own state.

[128] Cf. especially the careful examination of the evidence by Johnson, *op. cit.*, pp. 27–46. For the likelihood that the Zadokite priesthood was originally Jebusite cf. H. H. Rowley, "Zadok and Nehushtan," *JBL* 58 (1939), 113–41, and "Melchizidek and Zadok," *Festschrift A. Bertholet*, 1950, pp. 461–72.

[129] G. von Rad, *Theologie des Alten Testament*, 1957, I, 46–48, 55, and Johnson, *op. cit.*, pp. 27–46.

When it came to his own distinctive oracles, Isaiah preferred precisely those oracles in which Yahweh secured his own victory, and he succeeded in applying this theme to the expected defeat of Assyria, in a sense "historicizing" the rather nebulous notion.[130] The tribal memories of great victories for Israel in which her own arms played but a minor part in comparison to stratagems and natural catastrophes contributed to the formulation of the tradition: the hail against the Amorites (Josh. 10:11; Isa. 28:21), the flooding Kishon against the Canaanites (Judg. 5:21; Ps. 83:9), and the torches, trumpets, and battle shouts of Gideon's men against Midian (Judg. 7:16–25; Ps. 83:9–11; Isa. 9:4). Yet, as we have noted, the radical transformation of this motif appears in Isaiah's steadfast association of severe punishment for Israel with her salvation and *an especially dramatic shift from the earlier idea that the enemy was to be punished chiefly because he was Israel's opponent to the notion that Assyria must be punished for her intolerable pride and her crimes against all peoples.*

In this perspective, Isaiah 2:2–4 draws upon existing motifs in the enthronement tradition but it brings the prophet's thought to a culmination and represents the point of Isaiah's maximum tension with the naïve nationalism which informs most of the enthronement traditions. He envisions a confederation of the peoples of the ancient Near East in which they shall employ the religious traditions and personnel of Zion to adjudicate in their contending claims for justice so that force will no longer be necessary between nations. Beneath the lapidary poetic form, the oracle combines a sturdy realism about the conditions necessary for world order with a daring egocentricity as to the means for fulfilling these conditions. Simply put, the needs are (1) *a common frame of reference for settling differences among nations* and (2) *a machinery of adjudication which will make war unnecessary.* The impelling force in this climactic vision was the prophet's bitter experience with foreign affairs through some forty years and his discovery that selfish regional and national interests seem always to prevail over the larger interest and that nations fall repeatedly into the same errors. Furthermore, Isaiah felt with

---

[130] Wildberger, *op. cit.,* pp. 69–71, 81.

particular cogency the futility of violence to settle anything, since the deep repentance and change of policy demanded of nations could not be secured even by the most cataclysmic defeat because it merely awakened in the victor self-confidence and complacency and in the victim resentment and hatred.

But how are the nations to break out of the downward spiral of sin and death in which they now pursue one another to destruction? Isaiah foresees that Zion will become a kind of amphictyonic center for a confederation of nations who remain independent of Israelite political power. The prophet resists the usurpative tendencies of the Davidic dynasty and its implication that Yahwism will be spread by Judean imperialism. This chariness toward the Yahwistic state is perhaps partly the result of his realistic assessment of the Near East in which he saw no prospect of a neo-Davidic empire. Fundamentally, however, the central place of *tōrāh* within the world plan of Yahweh forbade Isaiah to accept a simple nationalistic interpretation of faith, and particularly did he find the notion of imposing Yahwism upon other peoples to be fallacious and repugnant.

Nonetheless there was an important sense in which Yahwism had a role to play among the nations. Yahweh was to serve as the supranational God to whom all nations were to pay allegiance in certain spheres of their life. The terms of the oracle do not require that the confederated nations totally embrace Yahwism, i.e., that they extirpate all other deities and replace national cults and traditions by Yahwism. The confession on the lips of the suppliant nations is a modest one, not necessarily evidencing total conversion to Yahwism in the manner expected by the later Isaiah of the exile. When the nations declare, "that he may teach us his ways and that we may walk in his paths," they speak specifically of those matters which concern the nations in their mutual relations, particularly their impulses to self-defense and to self-aggrandizement. These impulses will be submitted to Yahweh's judgment while internal matters are presumably to be left to the special traditions and institutions of the several nations.

The great oracle of Isaiah 2:1-4, supplemented by the original ending now preserved in Micah 4:4, reads as follows:

The word which Isaiah ben Amoz saw concerning Judah and
    Jerusalem:
"And it shall occur at the end of the days
    that the mountain of Yahweh shall be secure
On the summit of the mountains,
    and it shall be exalted on the heights;
And all the nations shall flow to it
    and many peoples shall go up to it.
And they shall say:
'Come and let us ascend to the mountain of Yahweh,
    to the house of the God of Jacob;
that he may teach us his ways
    and that we may walk in his paths.'
For from Zion shall go forth instruction,
    and the word of Yahweh from Jerusalem.
And he shall judge between the nations,
    and he shall reprove many peoples;
And they shall hammer their swords into plowshares
    and their spears into pruning hooks;
Nation shall not lift sword against nation
    nor shall they continue to learn war.
But they shall sit, each under its own vine
    and under its own fig tree, and none shall disturb another."
For the mouth of Yahweh of hosts has spoken.

In effect then Judah, politically speaking, is reduced to the rank
of one of the nations which must seek its place among the other
peoples of the ancient Near East. Her distinction is nevertheless
a very great one in that she is to supply the institutions for ad-
judicating among the nations. This role, as we shall shortly note,
creates its own special problems.

    The crucial question is surely that of the machinery for ad-
judication. Who in Zion are to be the interpreters of the Yahwistic
tradition? The passage does not anticipate such harmony among
the nations that they will automatically agree in all matters.
*Isaiah does not say that because they are Yahwistic the nations
will cease to have disagreements. He says, rather, that because*

they are Yahwistic the nations will submit their disputes to a jointly accepted arbitration. The arbitration is to be reached by *tōrāh* and *dᵉbar Yahweh*, which means precisely the deliberations of prophets.[131] Isaiah had thought of himself as instructor of Judah and of the nations as well, at least since the Syro-Ephraimite crisis of 735–732, and he regarded his own written words and public signs as serving the purposes of instruction (8:16–18; 30:8). Isaiah's previous career had included messages to or about foreign embassies in Jerusalem, although admittedly they had not come to receive word from him (to Philistia, 14:28–32; to Egypt, 18:1–6; concerning Merodach-baladan, 39). *Now the prophets are to be the regular and trusted spokesmen to the nations.*

Just how this confederation is to be established we are not told, since Isaiah does not give an account of its formation but only a glimpse of its import. Whether it must await the downfall of the Assyrian empire when the nations again have freedom of consent is not clear. The limiting phrase "in the latter days" (*bᵉ'aḥᵃrîth hay-yamîm*) does not mean the end of history but rather an important turning point in history. *Surely the new and distinctive role of Judah will not be fulfilled until Judeans listen to their own teachers, the prophets* (30:19–21, reading "your teachers" with a majority of manuscripts in place of "Teacher" as in six MSS and RSV). Only when Judah's blinded eyes and stopped ears are opened and "you [Judeans] will hear a word behind you, saying, 'This is the way, go in it' "—only then are the nations likely to say, "Come and let us ascend to the mountain of Yahweh . . . and learn of his ways and walk in his paths."

Not of least interest in the oracle is the conception of Isaiah that war is "learned." *War is not an unalterable institution in human life but rather one that has developed from a body of habits which can be replaced by another set of habits better serving the interests of nations.* The expectation of the prophet in this regard does not seem to be particularly idealistic. He does not hold that the eradication of war will bring about an eradication of evil in human nature or, vice versa, that the elimination

[131] *Ibid.*, p. 79.

of armed conflict requires first the complete removal of evil from the human heart. Apparently the confederated nations will continue to suffer the tensions of conflicting claims but they will at last see that the settlement of these claims by judicial means is preferable to bloodshed.

Yet one pivotal question remains to which the prophet gives no answer: How is the political objectivity of the adjudicators to be preserved? Or, at any rate, how are the confederated nations to be assured that the Yahwistic prophets can be trusted for a fair deliberation? Will they not incline toward favoritism in behalf of Judah or other states which have especially close ties with Judah? Can the prophets be sufficiently free from the political rulers of Judah to maintain an independent role? What will induce the nations, in the first place, to forgo appeal to their own gods and the force of arms in favor of the Yahweh confederacy? This is doubtless the least carefully thought through feature of the oracle. It seems to stumble on the simple but all-important condition of mutual trust.

This novel situation of a mutual trust is precisely the feature which marks the confederacy as an institution "in the latter days." It is not a stage to be reached by long evolution; like the defeat and humiliation of Assyria, it will be a work of Yahweh. But this work of Yahweh, unlike the former work of judgment, will be one of salvation for the nations. It cannot be accomplished by a dramatic miracle for it must spring from within nations and issue in a change of mind which leads them in all soberness and trust to see in Yahweh a God worthy and able to adjudicate among them. In so learning of his ways they may not be taught by the distinctive means which Yahweh has used with his people Israel, but the lash of history may still teach even the cruelest and blindest of peoples that the way of lawlessness and violence among the nations is a way of mutual death. And even Yahweh's people may learn that their future greatness is not to conquer the world in the name of Yahweh or even merely to hold their own as one nation among many, but rather to introduce an order among the nations derived from obedience to the minimal "natural law" which applies to the several nations of the then-known world.

The Pride of Nations and the Purpose of God

Isaiah's attitude toward international relations in the latter half of the eighth century B.C., as in the case of Amos and Hosea, was very largely determined by his conception of God vis-à-vis Israel and the nations. It was, however, a spacious view which owed more to the positive universalism of Amos than to the more limited punitive view of the nations that predominated in Hosea. The extent and variety of the contacts between Israel and Judah and foreign powers were vastly greater in the lifetime of Isaiah than they had been in the ministries of either of his predecessors. Above all, *Isaiah attempted for the first time on a broad basis to do justice to foreign nations as realities in their own right. He tried to discern their inner motivations, their guilt and deserved retribution, and their right to mutual consideration in a community of nations.* As in Amos there again emerged a broad perspective upon the nations and a sense of their common lot in history. Toward the close of his life, Isaiah even began to think about a confederation of Near Eastern nations united in their external relations by common obedience to Yahweh as interpreted by prophetic oracles.

Yahweh, the Holy One of Israel, who has a special connection with his people at Zion, has also a plan for the nations. *There is a purpose in the midst of the flux of history toward which the chaotic events of half a century have been moving in spite of appearances to the contrary.* All other gods disappear as effective forces in international life, although they may continue to exert influence in private and domestic matters. Yahweh's holy transcendence stands against all human creatureliness, and especially against political and national creatureliness. The chief sin of man, his restless and excessive pride, is nowhere more blatantly expressed than in the nation as epitomized in vain monarchs who take insufficient account of their own limits and who rationalize their crimes by committing them in the name of their people. Yet all this pride, symbolized in the most advanced military technology, in horses and chariots, is merely "flesh." It has no permanence and against Yahweh, who is "spirit," it avails nothing.

If he decides upon the defeat of an army it will fall to a weaker force or to a natural catastrophe. The pride of nations must be humbled—the pride of Israel and of Judah as well as that of her neighbors Philistia and Tyre, and of the imperial powers Egypt and Assyria. They are all alike in claiming too much for themselves; in varying ways, they shall all suffer the dire consequences of their *hybris*.

International crimes are in a sense the arch-theological sins for they are committed by men in positions of leadership who forget their limits and are inclined to throw all restraints to the wind in their quest for power. Fellow Yahwists in Israel and Judah have thus been driven to fight one another in bloody strife, and rival parties within each state have struggled for power, not hesitating to resort to murder and civil conflict. Stronger nations have plundered the property and goods and dislocated the populations of weaker nations. One and all rely upon power above morality and honor. The strong jealously guard and multiply their strength. The weak seek company in other powers and plan for the day of reprisal against the strong. They play the game of international power politics, succumbing to vassal treaties, which they break with impunity. *Each nation seeks to turn the precariousness of history into stability for itself, to avert disaster by "a covenant with death." Each tries to rise above history or at least to secure a permanent place within history. Yet all of them— including the Yahweh-worshiping states of Palestine—will be impaled by the weapons in which they trust.* Ahaz will be shaved by the razor, Assyria, which he cunningly hired. Hezekiah's hand will be pierced by the reed staff, Egypt, on which he eagerly leaned. Egypt, glorying in chariots and horses, will stumble to her destruction when Yahweh raises his hand. Assyria, whose loud boasts echoed through the Middle East and whose predatory deeds struck fear in all hearts, will be as a broken ax or club deserted on the battlefield.

So sweeping is his condemnation and so uniform his judgment upon the political and military pretensions of nations that the prophet appears to stand on the verge of renouncing politics altogether and of surrendering all hope of redeeming the utter relativity and rapacity of international life. Surprisingly, the opposite seems to have been the case. If anything his political activism increased throughout his lifetime as he saw new possibilities of response in Hezekiah's somewhat naïve Yahwism which were not present in Ahaz' calculating eclecticism. Isaiah named his own sons with slogans filled with political warning; he walked the streets as a war captive to admonish against revolt; he rebuked a high official to his face for his pro-Egyptian policy and agitated for his removal from office; he urged the Judean court to give asylum to political refugees from Moab; he predicted the collapse of Egyptian-Judean revolt and simultaneously the humiliation of Assyria in Palestine.

The quality in political leadership which Isaiah prized above all others was calmness of spirit and possession of mind, rooted in a deep trust in Yahweh's control of history. All that smacks of haste and fear is stamped by impermanence and only evokes its own forces of disintegration. Through his writings run several slogans which were not intended chiefly for private devotion but rather for public policy: "If you will not trust, you will not be established" (7:9b), "He who trusts will not be in a hurry" (28:16), "In repentance and rest you shall find salvation, in quietness and in confidence you shall find strength" (30:15). Yet the specific recommendations of Isaiah to Judean rulers bore a negative character and smacked also of strange inconsistencies which must have alienated Ahaz altogether and baffled Hezekiah. When Assyria was so endlessly active how could other states desist from action if they were not to perish? And even if doomed to perish must they not defend themselves to the end? *The prophet's "answers" to these eminently practical considerations were always grounded in the total scope of his message. Seen in the light of the natural world, there was no gainsaying the logic of rulers, but it was a logic that did not take account of Yahweh.* The Lord of history was at work on all fronts, not merely in his defense of his covenant people but also in raising up powers elsewhere in the world.

Isaiah thoroughly concurred with the leaders of the smaller nations that Assyria was no innocent agency of God's work. She was a cruel and selfish power and Yahweh had his time of reckoning with her. The dialectic of the prophet's thought never ceased to operate as he focused simultaneously upon points that seemed politically contradictory. In 735–732 *both* Israel *and* Judah would suffer. In 701 *both* Judah in alliance with Egypt *and* Assyria would be confounded. The chain of sin and death in international life binds victors and victims, and those who seem momentarily to prosper are in reality preparing their eventual humiliation. *Thus the plan of Yahweh possesses a unity beyond human comprehension, for the parts visible to any one man at any one time are often strangely and bafflingly inconsistent.* Like a farmer who engages in several seemingly unconnected actions— in plowing, harrowing, sowing, and threshing, and each in accordance with the crops desired—so Yahweh knows what he is doing, although as yet man does not see the final harvest and therefore questions the wisdom of the Divine Sower (28:23– 29).[132]

Another apparent consequence of such a lofty view of God and such sensitivity to the inexplicability of his movements was, however, avoided by the prophet. He did not turn to determinism or fatalism. The waiting he urged upon man was a trustful obedience. Man possessed Yahweh's instructions and he knew the divine will sufficiently to obey it in many particulars of social and political life. The fact that a person or nation did not understand everything did not excuse it from obedience to that which it did understand. Yet the horrible whiplash of events in the eighth century which opened gaping lacerations in the bodies and spirits of men and nations was totally incapable of awakening faith. *History could only discipline those who already acknowledged the reality and standards of faith.* There is a foundation stone of quiet faith in Yahweh to be built upon by those who really care to ascertain what is fundamental and, therefore, permanent in this world. History with all its grandeur and horror pivots around personal choices; incessantly it calls man to personal and national repentance, to humility and a true sense of proportion, to self-knowledge and self-acceptance as one of many persons and

[132] That 28:23–29 is not unrelated to the foregoing passage but is in fact an extended agricultural metaphor intended to illustrate the mystery but irrevocability of Yahweh's plan is now widely recognized (Scott, *op. cit.,* p. 321, and Y. A. Liebrich, "The Agricultural *Mashal* in Isa. 28:23–29," *Tarbiz* 24 [1955], 126–28 [Hebrew]).

peoples who have a place in God's plan. On such a foundation even the nations of the Near East will one day build, for Yahweh wills not merely to punish them but also to save them. When they, at Judah's leading, will turn to Yahweh as arbiter of the nations, the crippling fear and insecurity of nations will be sufficiently relaxed so that there will be no more need for the peoples of the Near East to crush one another in the terrible threshing floor of war. Those who take up the sword shall perish by the sword, and those who venture trust shall live by trust.

Micah

The book of Micah contains surprisingly little material to throw light on international relations at the time of its composition. Micah is placed as a contemporary of Isaiah according to the book's superscription, which locates his work in the reigns of Jotham, Ahaz, and Hezekiah. The oracle of 1:2–9 presupposes the independence of Samaria and thus comes from a time prior to 722. There are no references, other than 4:9–10, which compel—though some may suggest—a date later than the reign of Hezekiah, and it is of note that contemporaries of Jeremiah, who lived about a century later, recalled Micah as a prophet who preached to Hezekiah (Jer. 26:18–19).

In Micah 1:10–16 a vivid warning against invasion is sounded to cities in the coastal plain and in the Shephelah of Judah. The text is cryptic and corrupt at points. Several of the place names are otherwise unknown and cannot be located with any degree of certainty: Beth-le-aphrah,[133] Shaphir,[134] Beth-ezel,[135] Maroth.[136]

---

[133] Beth-le-aphrah has been located at Khirbeth Beit Farah, five miles northwest of Beth-shemesh (Y. Peres, *Eretz Yisrael Encyclopedia Geographith-historith,* 1951, I, 89 [Hebrew]).

[134] Shaphir has been located at es-Suwafir, three and one-half miles southeast of Ashdod, and also at Khirbeth el-Kom, overlooking Wadi es-Saffar, about halfway between Lachish and Hebron (*IDB,* IV, 308).

[135] Beth-ezel is perhaps Dir el-Asal, two miles east of Debir (*IDB,* I, 393).

[136] Maroth may be the Maarath of Joshua 15:59, sometimes identified as Khirbeth Qufin, two miles north of Beth-zur, but this seems somewhat remote from Micah's locale (*IDB,* III, 196).

The fact that some of the names are employed as puns suggests that the prophet either concocted them or else chose small village names at random to suit his purpose. Of the three otherwise attested cities, Gath,[137] Lachish, and Zaanan,[138] only the identification of Lachish has been accomplished with some certainty.[139] A much better-preserved example of a herald's warning of invasion is found in Isaiah 10:27-32,[140] and from it we can perhaps judge that Micah's agitated cries were in anticipation of an imminent invasion. Probably one of the Assyrian invasions of Philistia is expected, but whether it was that of Sargon in 720[141] or one of his two attacks in 714-711,[142] or the campaign of Sennacherib in 701,[143] we cannot finally say. It is true that only Sennacherib's campaign apparently carried to the very gates of Jerusalem as the prophet envisions (vs. 12), but it now appears that one of the campaigns of Sargon in 714-711 affected at least the Judean town of Azekah and perhaps others.[144] Micah describes the invader as one brought by Yahweh against Israel, who, hard pressed as David in the cave at Adullam (I Sam. 22:1-2), will go bald into exile. The similarity to Amos and the early Isaiah are evident in this conception of exile and, if one assumes that

[137] Gath's location remains a mystery. To the previously suggested sites of Tell Araq el-Menshiyeh, four and one-half miles northwest of Lachish; Tell Sheikh Ahmed el-Areini, just across the road from the former tell; and Tell es-Safi, nine and one-half miles north of Lachish, should be added the recent proposal of Tell Nagila, seven miles southwest of Lachish (S. Bülow and R. A. Mitchell, *IEJ* 11 [1961], 101-10). B. Mazar's claim that there was a northern Gath (or Gittaim) in the vicinity of modern Ramleh has added some precision to the search for the Philistine Gath (*IEJ* 4 [1954], 227-35).

[138] Zaanan may be the Zenan of Joshua 15:37, perhaps to be connected with 'Araq el-Kharab, three and three-quarters miles northeast of Lachish, or with Khirbeth Dahina, five miles east of Lachish (M. Naor, *Hammiqra weha-aretz*, 1954, II, 49-50 [Hebrew]).

[139] Tell ed Duweir in the Shephelah about midway between Jerusalem and Gaza was excavated 1932-1938 by the Wellcome-Marston Expedition; cf. report volumes: H. Torczyner and O. Tufnell, eds., *Lachish* I-IV, 1938-57.

[140] See *supra*, pp. 156-57.

[141] See *supra*, pp. 162-63.

[142] See *supra*, pp. 164-66.

[143] See *supra*, pp 185-96.

[144] See *supra*, p. 166.

Sargon in 711 put an end to the independence of Gath, the opening line of the oracle ("Tell it not in Gath!") may date Micah's
words before that year.

The older literary critical attitude which denied chaps. 4–7 to
the eighth-century prophet has been vigorously challenged in
recent study.[145] It seems likely that the original severe words
against Samaria and Jerusalem in chaps. 1–3 have been supplemented in two stages by a collection of prophecies about Israel
and the nations in chaps. 4–5 and finally a collection of threats
and promises in chaps. 6–7. This arrangement has produced a
repetition of the threat-promise pattern: threat (chaps. 1–3),
promise (4–5), threat (6—7:7), promise (7:8–20). There seems
no sound reason for denying that some of the oracles in the appendix are by Micah, e.g., 5:10–15; 6:9–16; 7:1–7.[146] In fact,
if one assumes that he shared with Isaiah some use of the Davidic
enthronement traditions, 5:2–6 may be attributed to Micah.[147]
At any rate the question is open.

*It is more germane to our purposes to recognize in chaps. 4–5
a collection of oracles which at any rate belong in the main to the
Assyrian period.*[148] Apart from 4:9–10 (and possibly 7:11–13,
16–17), decisive exilic or post-exilic characteristics are lacking.
How many of the oracles can be carried back to Micah is problematic. From a tradition-historical perspective it is noteworthy
that two pieces have been included in the appendixes to Micah
which are markedly Isaianic in character. One of these appears
in a slightly different recension in Isaiah 2:1–4 where it is
probably original.[149] The other, 7:16–17, is stylistically close to

---

[145] E. Nielsen, *Oral Tradition,* pp. 79–93; W. Beyerlin, *Die Kulttraditionen
Israels in der Verkuendigung des Propheten Micha;* A. S. Kapelrud, "Eschatology in the Book of Micah," *VT* 11 (1961), 392–405.

[146] N. K. Gottwald, *A Light to the Nations,* 1959, p. 307 (correct 7:1–8
to 7:1–7); R. E. Wolfe, *IB,* VI, 899, 936, regards 6:1—7:4 as "the misplaced ending of the book, split away from chapters 1–3 by the later insertion of chapters 4–5."

[147] See *supra,* pp. 196–99.

[148] Bentzen, *Introduction to the Old Testament,* II, 148–49, contends that
most of chaps. 4–7 is pre-exilic, from either the age of Micah or the reign
of Manasseh, stemming from "an *anti-Assyrian,* nationalistic milieu." He
finds only 4:6–7 and 5:6–7 to be exilic.

[149] Wildberger, *op. cit.,* pp. 75–76, and see *supra,* pp. 196–201.

Deutero-Isaiah.[150] *This suggests that Micah and Isaiah, as Judean contemporaries who prophesied about Assyria, have become prototypical prophets against the foreign invader, and their own oracles have been supplemented by many others which speak of a happy resolution of Israel's relations with the nations.*

We should, then, be prepared to find Micah's words in any particular oracle in the appendix or, on the contrary, to have to conclude that a particular oracle is not his own or, perhaps even more frequently, that the issue must be left unresolved. It is certainly striking that the attitude toward the nations is extremely inconsistent in chaps. 4–5, the pieces alternating in their conceptions about the ultimate fate of the enemies, whether for conversion or for destruction.

It does not help much to claim to see two written sources to account for this difference.[151] It is enough to recognize diverse oracles gathered around the theme of Israel vis-à-vis the nations.[152] Assyria in the oracle of 5:5–6 need not be understood as an archaism for some later power such as Babylon, Persia, or Seleucid Syria.[153] At first sight the promise of "seven shepherds and eight princes of men" may suggest the cryptic style of apocalyptic writing. It is more likely, however, that it is the wisdom feature of graduated numbers which is employed to express indefinite increase (cf. Amos 1:3, 6, 9, etc.; Prov. 30:15, 18, 21, 29; and especially Eccles. 11:2).[154] The expression may then simply mean that Israel will be well supplied with military rulers to throw off the Assyrian yoke. Whether this multiplicity of rulers

---

[150] Wolfe, *op. cit.*, p. 945.

[151] *Ibid.*, pp. 921–22, isolates a late exilic document in 4:1–4, 6–8; 5:7, 10–14, which exhibits a magnanimous attitude toward the nations, and a post-exilic document in 4:5, 9–13; 5:1–5a, 8–9, 15, with an expectation of military conquest of the nations.

[152] As also in Isaiah 19:18–25; see *infra*, pp. 224–25.

[153] Nielsen, *op. cit.*, pp. 85–91, offers the plausible hypothesis that the oracles of chaps. 4–5 are arranged chiastically around the central Bethlehem prophecy (5:2–6). His further claims that 5:3 should be understood to refer to a return of the northern kingdom to the Davidic dynasty depends upon extremely vague syntax. Kapelrud, *VT* 11 (1961), 398, 401–2, also contends that most, if not all, of the oracles in chaps. 4–5 should be connected with the fall of Samaria rather than the fall of Jerusalem.

[154] J. M. P. Smith, *ICC*, pp. 108–9; H. M. Wiener, *The Prophets in History and Criticism*, 1923, p. 46.

is consistent with the one ruler in 5:2–4 and whether such a
hopeful outlook for Judah is conceivable on the part of the man
who wrote chaps. 1–3 is another question. The probability is that
someone in the late seventh century partaking in the revival of the
Judean monarchy against the waning Assyrian power is responsible for this passage.[155]

In sum, the book of Micah throws almost no light on the
historical situation of the late eighth century that is not already
illuminated by Isaiah. Oracles in the appendix to the main body
of threats do reflect attitudes toward the nations either by the
prophet or, in most instances, by prophets in the seventh century.

Zechariah 9:1–8

With good reason, Zechariah chaps. 9–14 have been dissociated
from the first eight chapters of the book. They form two separate
collections of oracles headed by the formula *massā'* ("burden" or
"oracle") : chaps. 9–11; 12–14. Many of the oracles in these appendixes show marks of a period later than 520–516, when the
earlier section was written by Zechariah.[156] It is, however, inaccurate to characterize these oracles as apocalyptic in any consistent and full-blown manner.[157] At most, some of the oracles
stand on the boundary between prophecy and apocalyptic and
show how prophecy was straining toward portrayals of cosmic
catastrophe and redemption in order to describe God's universal
work. At the same time, it cannot be ruled out that there are
materials in chaps. 9–14 which come from the time of Zechariah.
In fact, it may be confidently asserted that an oracle *earlier* than

155 Bentzen, *Introduction to the Old Testament,* II, 148–49.

156 The classic analysis is by B. Stade, "Deuterosacharja," *ZAW* 1 (1881),
1–96; 2 (1882), 151–72, 275–309. Useful summaries of the main evidence
for a late Persian or Greek date for chaps. 9–14 will be found in A. Weiser,
The Old Testament: Its Formation and Development, 1961 (English trans.
of 4th German ed., 1957), pp. 272–75, and O. Eissfeldt, *Einleitung in das
Alte Testament,* 2nd rev. ed., 1956, pp. 534–43.

157 J. Lindblom, *Die Jesaja Apokalypse Jes. 24–27,* 1938, has shown that
more of the typical features of apocalyptic are absent from this so-called
"Little Apocalypse of Isaiah" than are present. A similar analysis of Deutero-
Zechariah would probably produce the same conclusions.

Zechariah by two centuries has actually been incorporated in 9:1–8.[158]

The oracle which opens the appendix to Zechariah describes the punitive word of Yahweh against Aramean cities (Hadrach, Hamath, Damascus), Phoenician cities (Tyre, Sidon), and Philistine cities (Ashkelon, Gaza, Ekron, Ashdod). These cities, as the object of military campaigns, fall most naturally in the late eighth century B.C. A great deal has been made of the fact that Alexander the Great alone in antiquity succeeded in conquering mainland Tyre and island Tyre by force,[159] but there is no circumstance referred to in vss. 3–4 which would not as well fit the attacks of Assyrian kings who did manage to capture mainland Tyre and to induce island Tyre to surrender voluntarily.[160] The city of Hadrach, to the north of Hamath in interior Syria, is frequently cited in early Aramean and Assyrian documents but disappears entirely thereafter.[161] While some of the other cities men-

---

[158] The main lines of argument are accepted from E. G. Kraeling, "The Historical Situation in Zech. 9:1–10," *AJSL* 41 (1924), 24–33, and A. Malamat, "The Historical Setting of Two Biblical Prophecies on the Nations," *IEJ* 1 (1950–51), 149–54. Their positions are not identical, however. Kraeling provided evidence chiefly on the Philistine cities, and Malamat brings new evidence on the Syrian cities. While Kraeling believes that the prophecy alludes to events from 739 to 720 B.C., Malamat finds that all references are to the western campaign of Sargon in 720. Kraeling treats vss. 1–10 as the literary unit, whereas Malamat restricts it to vss. 1–6. Those who treat vss. 1–8 as a unit have by far the better case (cf. H. G. Mitchell, *ICC,* pp. 260–72, K. Elliger, "Ein Zeugnis aus der juedischen Gemeinde im Alexanderjahr 322 vor Chr.," *ZAW* 62 [1949–50], 63–64, and M. Delcor, "Les allusions à Alexandre le Grand dans Zach. 9:1–8," *VT* 1 [1951], 110, whose literary instincts are sounder than their historical judgments).

[159] Elliger, *op. cit.,* p. 63, and Delcor, *op. cit.,* pp. 110–24; and R. C. Dentan, *IB,* VI, pp. 1093–94.

[160] Kraeling, *op. cit.,* p. 27, locates the capture of Tyre at the climax of the siege by Shalmaneser V reported by Menander in Josephus (*Ant.* IX. xiv. 2), but Malamat, *IEJ* 1 (1950–51), 151, believes that the city's destruction should be associated with the capture of the city by Sargon after a five-year siege. A naval victory over Tyre may have occurred then for Sargon boasts of the defeat of the Greek (Cypriote) fleet, which was possibly in league with Tyre (see Cylinder Inscription, line 21 in D. D. Luckenbill, *Ancient Records of Assyria and Babylonia,* vol. II, no. 118).

[161] A. Malamat, "Hadrach," *Encyclopedia Mikraith,* vol. III, cols. 33–35 (Hebrew), 1958.

tioned are known to have continued to be inhabited in post-exilic times, they were all caught up in the Persian empire, and a special oracle threatening them with attack seems ill-fitting, especially since there is no trace in the oracle that the cities named have revolted against Persia. The assumption that the passage refers to the invasion of Alexander, as he advanced from Asia Minor to Egypt, is without any detailed support.

At most, it can be said that 9:1–8 *might* come from the Persian or Greek periods. If so, it is an archaizing oracle which deliberately imitates the old pre-exilic oracular form and envisions the political circumstances of a later period under the names and institutions of an earlier period. On the other hand, it can be shown that the verses *probably* come from the late eighth century by the fact that all the cities named were independent at that time and, with the possible exception of Ashkelon, they may be related coherently to the vassal revolts and Assyrian invasions in Syria-Palestine, on which the book of Isaiah and the Assyrian annals and inscriptions give us considerable information. There are, in addition, two specific allusions in the oracle strongly corroborating the general correspondence of names and relationships.

When it is said that "The king shall perish from Gaza" (vs. 5), we are at once reminded of the campaign of Sargon against Gaza in 720, which culminated in the exile of its king Hanno to Assyria.[162] While there were doubtless kings before and after Hanno in Gaza, it is not likely that local kings were allowed to retain their titles under the more centralized Persian government or that the eunuch Batis, who opposed Alexander at Gaza in 332, was designated king.[163] Even more decisive is the statement that "a bastard [*mamzēr*] shall dwell in Ashdod" (vs. 6). The only other biblical use of this term refers it to a person (Deut. 23:2) rather than a whole people and syntactically there is no reason to believe that it means "a bastard or mongrel people" on the model of

[162] See *supra,* pp. 163–63.

[163] A. T. Olmstead, *History of the Persian Empire,* pp. 507–8. Dentan, *op. cit.,* p. 1094, notes the objection to a post-exilic context for the allusion but concludes that the reference to a king in Gaza is "conventional."

[164] Contra Mitchell, *op. cit.,* pp. 267–68, and Dentan, *op. cit.,* p. 1094.

Nehemiah 13:23–24,[164] as the RSV understands it. In fact the parallelism requires that the *mamzēr* of Ashdod be analogous to the *melek* ("king") of Gaza. Rather, this doubtless refers to Iamani, who seized the throne in Ashdod and fomented a revolt against Assyria which was suppressed in 711.[165] Whether or not Iamani was a Greek, the Assyrian record says emphatically that he was "without claim to the throne," and it is apparently in this sense of political illegitimacy that he is called "bastard."[166] Such a figurative political use of the term is far less forced than that which applies it to culturally or religiously mixed populations.

As to Ekron, it was one of the Philistine cities to rebel at the death of Sargon in 705.[167] Its officials, aristocrats, and commoners rose against the king and committed him to Hezekiah's keeping in Jerusalem. Ashkelon was also involved in this revolt and its king Sidqia deported. It seems, however, that Ekron had earlier been the object of attack by the Assyrians during Sargon's reign, for a city called in the Assyrian Amqaruna is pictured under siege on a relief at Sargon's unfinished capital of Dur-Sharruken.[168] Amqaruna is felt to be the Akkadian equivalent of Ekron.

The association of Israel (the northern kingdom) with the Aramean states of Hadrach, Damascus, and Hamath may point to the reign of Tiglath-pileser when he incorporated the Aramean states and most of Israelite territory into the Assyrian empire (see Map 18). The leading northern rebel in 720 was Iaubidi of Hamath, and it is possible that such a date is suitable for all of the Aramean references in Zechariah 9:1–8. A stele erected by Sargon on the Orontes River, possibly in connection with the revolt of 720, mentions Hamath and Hadrach in an obscure section.[169] The siege of Tyre was carried on for five years, Menander reports, and it appears that after Shalmaneser captured

---

[165] See *supra*, pp. 164–66.
[166] Kraeling, *op. cit.*, p. 28; Malamat, *op. cit.*, pp. 150–51.
[167] See *supra*, p. 178.
[168] M. el-Amin, "Die Reliefs mit Beischriften von Sargon II in Dur-Sharrukin," *Sumer* 9 (1953), 35–59, 214–28; 10 (1954), 23–42. The scene is reproduced in B. Mazar, ed., *Views of the Biblical World*, III, 277.
[169] F. Thureau-Dangin, "La Stèle d'Asharné," *Revue d'Assyriologie* 30 (1933), 53–56, and remarked by Malamat, *IEJ* 1 (1950–51), 153.

mainland Tyre Sargon received the surrender of island Tyre on lenient terms.[170]

The particular order in which the Philistine cities are listed here does not throw any certain light on the historical situation. In fact, an analysis of the various lists of the Philistine cities in the Old Testament shows that no single invariable sequence was employed. In a very general way the citations seem to be geographical, the more southerly cities being cited first and the northerly ones last.[171] Thus, for example, Gaza, the southernmost city, is never cited in the third or fourth position and Ekron, the northernmost city, is never cited in the first or second position. The "purest" form of such a geographically oriented list is Zephaniah 2:4, where the sequence is Gaza, Ashkelon, Ashdod, and Ekron. Joshua 13:3 and Amos 1:7–8 follow the order Gaza, Ashdod, Ashkelon, Ekron, while Jeremiah 25:20 and Zechariah 9:5–6 agree on Ashkelon, Gaza, Ekron, Ashdod.

Particularly striking in this oracle is its climactic assertion that some or all of the surviving Philistines will be incorporated as a semi-autonomous unit within Israel. Once Philistia has been humbled and its abominable practices have been removed, "it shall be left over to our God; it shall be like a clan in Judah; and Ekron shall be like the Jebusites" (vs. 7). The conception is not a purely visionary one, for the writer offers the historical analogy of the Jebusites, the original occupants of Jerusalem, who were absorbed into Israel when David captured the city (II Sam. 5:6–9). Other possible analogies suggest themselves, such as the Gibeonites (Josh. 9; II Sam. 21:1–9) and Nethinim (Ezra 2:36, 40–43; Neh. 10:28) or the Kenites, Kenizzites, Calebites, Othnielites, and Jerahmeelites, who seem to have merged into a

---

[170] See note 160.

[171] The absence of Gath from the lists of the Philistine cities in prophetic writings supports the conclusion that either the city was never rebuilt after Sargon destroyed it in 711 B.C. or it was incorporated as a Judean city. R. A. S. Macalister, *The Philistines, Their History and Civilization,* pp. 71–75, discusses the biblical and archaeological data concerning the five cities, but it is now badly out of date and should be supplemented and corrected by the articles on the Philistines and on the five cities in the *IDB;* cf. also T. Dothan, "Archaeological Reflections on the Philistine Problem," *Antiquity and Survival,* 1957, II, 151–64, and G. A. Wainwright, *VT* 9 (1959), 73–84.

Yahweh amphictyony which eventually constituted the larger
tribe of Judah, so that "Judah became Great Judah" (Josh.
14:6, 14; 15:13–19; Judg. 1:11-20; I Sam. 25:1–3; 27:10;
30:14, 29; I Chron. 2:9, 18, 25, 42, 55).[172] At any rate the
conclusion of the destructive oracles against Philistia seems deliberate in its assertion that Philistines will become Yahweh worshipers as a separate unit within Israel. Why Ekron is specifically
cited cannot be judged with certainty. It may be because it was
the largest of the Philistine cities,[173] or because it was the closest
to Israel of the four surviving Philistine cities (Gath may have
been nearer but was partially demolished in 760 by Uzziah of
Judah; II Chron. 26:6), or because there was some reason to
believe that its inhabitants would be more susceptible to conversion.

Another unanswered question in the oracle is the nature of the
authority by which the conversion and incorporation will occur.
All that is sure is that "no oppressor shall again overwhelm them
[Yahweh's people]," but we cannot say whether the oracle has a
neo-Davidic empire in mind so that the Philistines will be forced
to join Israel or whether they will come voluntarily. Likewise,
it cannot be asserted conclusively that the prophecy of an unwar-
like messiah who will "command peace to the nations" which
follows immediately in vss. 9–10 belongs to the milieu of vss.
1–8.[174] It is possible but not certain. While not a passage with any
specific information on pre-exilic international relations, it is a
prophecy that builds on the pre-exilic experience and is not inconsistent with it. *Strictly speaking, it is probably not a pacifist-
king here referred to but rather one whose rule is so firmly established that war as an instrument of foreign policy will no longer
be necessary.* The peaceful beneficent rule of the prince seems
then to presuppose the prior act of God in sweeping away the
enemies of Israel, and it is just this which is spoken of in vss. 1–8.

---

[172] M. Noth, *The History of Israel,* pp. 55–58; K. Elliger, *IDB,* II, pp.
1003–4.

[173] J. Naveh, "Khirbat Al-Muqanna'—Ekron," *IEJ* 3 (1958), 166–70.

[174] Mitchell, *op. cit.,* pp. 275–76.

CHAPTER IV

Israelite Prophecy and
International Relations in the
Seventh and Sixth Centuries

Prophecy from Zephaniah to Isaiah of the exile was united in its preoccupation with the question of whether or not Mesopotamian imperialism would obliterate the cultural and political independence of Judah. The collapse of Israel in the eighth century and its incorporation into Assyria served as a somber reminder of what Judah could expect. Yet by a combination of servility (under Manasseh) and assertiveness (under Josiah), Judah outlived Assyrian imperialism. While neo-Babylonia in many ways proved to be the heir of Assyrian imperialism, her methods of assimilating conquered peoples were less stringent than Assyria's had been. The deportation of Israelites in 720 was a permanent resettlement of peoples; the deportation of Judeans in 597, 587, and 582 was a temporary detention of rebels.

Prophets of this period fall into approximately three groups: those chiefly fascinated by the renascence of Judean culture and statehood under Josiah and the simultaneous decline of Assyria (Isaiah 19:18–25, while Assyria was still a world power; Zephaniah; Nahum), those foreseeing the annihilation of the state of Judah by the neo-Babylonians (Habakkuk; Jeremiah; the early Ezekiel), and those looking to the restoration of Judeans either by the neo-Babylonians or by the Persians (the later Ezekiel; Isaiah of the exile). In this climate, prophetic eschatology was encouraged by the general decline of Judean fortunes—notwithstanding Josiah's successes—and enriched by the persisting certainty of God's purposes for his people. The wide vision of Amos and Isaiah of Jerusalem came to dramatic fruition in Isaiah of the exile, in whom prophecy and international relations were most intimately and profoundly wedded.

Zephaniah

The prophet Zephaniah is located, according to the heading of the book, in the reign of Josiah. His severe indictment of pagan practices in Judah (Assyrian astral worship, the Ammonite Milcom cult, and Philistine threshold-leaping) indicates a time before the reform of Josiah in 621 B.C. It has been proposed that the attackers to whom he refers were the Scythians, who, according to Herodotus (*History* I. 104–5), swept over the Near East in the years 630–624 and became "masters of Asia," stopping only at the entrance to Egypt. Herodotus' account is suspiciously exaggerated, for the twenty-eight-year Scythian domination of Asia of which he speaks is not otherwise attested in ancient sources. It has been suggested that 1:18 ("neither their silver nor their gold shall be able to deliver them") echoes the Egyptian bribery of the Scythians to avert an invasion of the Nile Valley, but buying exemption from attack was a common happening.[1]

Zephaniah's oracles are apparently the only Old Testament materials, apart from historical literature, stemming from the early reign of Josiah. The sense of impending world catastrophe which suffuses the book does not require us to date most of its oracles in the exilic or post-exilic periods. This mood apparently spread in the ancient Near East as the Assyrians began to lose their grip on their empire.[2] Certainly by the death of Ashurban-

[1] J. M. P. Smith, *ICC*, p. 207.
[2] The spirit of archaism in politics and culture during the seventh and sixth centuries in the ancient Near East is illustrated and commented on

ipal the rapid dissolution of the empire was sensed by many. In recent years it has been supposed that this last strong Assyrian monarch died in 639 and it has been proposed that the statement in II Chronicles 34:3 concerning the initiation of Josiah's religious reforms in 632 and in 628 refers to attempts to assert political independence in precisely the years when Ashurbanipal and Assur-etil-ilani, his successor, died.[3] Yet the recently published Harran inscriptions clearly state that Ashurbanipal ruled until 627–626 and it now appears difficult to find any room at all for Assur-etil-ilani's reign.[4] The chronology of the last Assyrian kings and the timing and phasing of Josiah's reforms and revolts in relation to them remain as problematic as ever. Zephaniah does not offer any visible help with the difficulty.

The awakening prophetic urge for drastic reform in the face of colossal historical upheaval must have had more than a little to do with preparing a climate of opinion in which the Deuteronomic Reform could find popular support. It is, therefore, of note that *the international perspective of Zephaniah is considerable, paralleled only by Isaiah among the earlier prophets.* He speaks of "nations" (3:6, 8), "kingdoms" (3:8), "lands of the nations" (2:11), "peoples" (3:9), "peoples of the earth" (3:20), and "inhabitants of the earth" (1:18). There is no reason to believe that these admittedly world-wide conceptions look to the end of history or are explicitly tied up with apocalyptic notions of world periods, of doom and rebirth.[5] Here and there marks of the exile are apparent and there is reason to believe that oracles have been added or modified (2:8–11; 3:19–20).[6]

---

by W. F. Albright, *From the Stone Age to Christianity,* 2nd ed., 1957, pp. 315–21.

[3] F. M. Cross and D. N. Freedman, "Josiah's Revolt Against Assyria," *JNES* 12 (1953), 56–58.

[4] C. J. Gadd, "The Harran Inscriptions of Nabonidus," *Anatolian Studies* 8 (1958), 69–72.

[5] The terminological problems connected with "eschatology," "myth," and "apocalyptic" are helpfully treated by S. F. Frost, "Eschatology and Myth," *VT* 2 (1952), 70–80, and T. H. Vriezen, "Prophecy and Eschatology," *Supplement to VT,* I, 199–229. No amount of careful definition, however, can remove the difficulty of deciding in any given text when "the end" is understood as a crux *in* history and when it is "the End" *of* history.

[6] It is characteristic to deny 2:8–11 and 3:19–20 to the prophet but recent

But the reference to the restoration of the fortunes of Judah in
2:7 need only indicate the reacquiring of territory in the Shephelah which had been awarded to Philistine cities by Sennacherib in 701.[7]

The sequence of foreign oracles in chap. 2 begins with the
near neighbors of Judah to the *west* (Philistia) and to the *east*
(Moab, Ammon) and then extends the horizon to the *south*
(Ethiopia) and to the *north* (Assyria).[8] If 2:1-3 refer to Judah,
it appears that vs. 4 has been dislodged from its place within the
following oracle or from an oracle which never got into the book.
It is more likely, however, that vs. 3, addressed to "you humble
of the land," has been intruded into an oracle against Philistia in
2:1-2, 4-7.[9] The language of these oracles is too general and
the period not sufficiently well known to say much about the
foreign relations reflected in them.

Particularly striking are three oracles in the third chapter
(3:6-7; 8, 9-10; 11-13), which may or may not have been
originally associated but in the present version of the book have
an impressive continuity. The first is a lament over the failure
of historical catastrophe to teach Judah repentance. "I have cut
off nations . . . ," the passage begins, and ends with Judah all
the more firmly entrenched in her wickedness (cf. Amos 4:6-11).
Since this series of historical judgments of God has failed, the
second element announces the special "day when I arise as a
witness, for my decree is to gather nations" in order to judge
them. This leads to a proclamation of the purification of the
peoples, symbolized in "clean speech," and to the world-wide

---

studies have done so with far less dogmatism and often with outright reser-
vations: cf. E. A. Leslie, *IDB,* IV, 952; Bentzen, *Introduction to the Old
Testament,* II, 154; O. Eissfeldt, *Einleitung,* 2nd rev. ed., 1956, pp. 521-
22. A. H. Van Zyl, *The Moabites,* p. 24, finds no reason to doubt that
2:8-11 is pre-exilic (note resemblance to Isa. 16:6), for he observes that
disdain of Moab was shown on many occasions before 587 (e.g., Judg.
3:12-30; 11:4-36; 12:1-3; I Sam. 11; 14:47; II Sam. 8:1, 2, 12; II
Kings 3:1 ff.; 13:20; 24:2; II Chron. 20:1 ff.; 26:8; 27:5).

[7] See *supra,* p. 186, and *infra,* p. 303. The reference to Ashkelon means,
of course, that no strict restoration of territory is intended since Judah never
extended to the coast.

[8] For the cosmic significance of the oracles toward the four directions of
the compass, see *supra,* pp. 104-106.

[9] C. L. Taylor, *IB,* VI, 1019-21; Smith, *op. cit.,* pp. 214-15.

service of Yahweh, particularly the bringing of offerings to him by Ethiopia. The closing oracle consoles Judah and promises that in the sadly decimated land "a people lowly and humble" will survive unmolested and purified. *The association of these oracles has produced a most impressive cycle of divine chastisement and renewal,* involving (1) *previous historical judgments* on nations which have failed to lead to repentance and (2) *an impending decisive judgment* that will lead to purification of the nations and also to the purification of Judah, which will continue historically in the form of a cleansed minority. There is no firm basis for affirming or denying that Zephaniah was the one who arranged the sequence.

The announcement of the worship of Yahweh by the peoples of the earth is a vivid one. They shall all have a "pure speech," i.e., they shall speak what is pure and right, and they shall worship Yahweh "with one shoulder," i.e., in the joint consent and harmony represented by a yoke of oxen at work. The second line of vs. 10 is suspicious, for it reads literally "my suppliants, the daughter of my scattered ones." Conjectural emendations produce either the reading "to the sides (or limits) of the north,"[10] or "the princes [lit. he-goats] of the daughter of Put."[11] Perhaps the best proposal is to read "the suppliants of the daughter of my scattered ones," which involves no consonantal change but only different vowels for the first word; the meaning would then be that the Egyptians will implore the Jews living among them to receive their worship of Yahweh.[12]

It is apparent that this oracle moves in the sphere of those assembled in Isaiah 19:18–25 and Zechariah 14:16–19. The latter passage has been grouped within an account of the last assault upon Jerusalem by the nations which describes earthquakes and plagues as the agents of God and already shows certain of the lurid marks of apocalyptic. Nevertheless, there are ancient features incorporated, and such is the description of "the families of the earth," Egyptians in particular, coming up to observe Tabernacles at Jerusalem.

---

[10] Read *'ad-yarkᵉtê tsāphôn,* as in BH⁷, and cf. Isaiah 14:13.

[11] Read *'attudhê bath pût;* Smith, *op. cit.,* pp. 249, 253.

[12] G. A. Smith, *The Book of the Twelve Prophets,* II, 1929, 69.

The prominence of Egypt in several of these oracles looking to the worship of Yahweh by the nations is a peculiar feature which has not been sufficiently noted. Even in Deutero-Isaiah it often seems that the Egyptians and Ethiopians, much more than the Babylonians, are the ones to be converted (e.g., Isa. 45:14–17).[13] This peculiarity can perhaps best be explained if we attribute the strong pre-exilic emergence of the idea of the conversion of the nations to a time when Jewish colonies in Egypt were in touch with the Judean community.[14] When poets and prophets sought to give expression to the universal worship of Yahweh, they saw Egypt as the prototypical foreign power and from that point they drew in the other nations either by general reference (for example, "peoples" in Zeph. 3:9 and "nations" in Zech. 14:16) or by directly naming them (for example, Assyria in Isa. 19:19–22). *Thus one of the earliest ways of giving content and color to the motif of the conversion of the nations was to cite Egypt typologically, and this pattern held even when the Judean community came to have much more interest in Babylon than in Egypt.* Therefore, even Deutero-Isaiah felt tied to the older way of expressing the conversion of mankind, and so for him Ethiopians and Sabeans are certainly to be understood as standing figuratively for Babylonians and Persians and all the peoples of the known world.

If the above conclusion is at all correct, it shows that *the hope in the universal salvation of mankind was not a creation of Deutero-Isaiah nor did it have to await the exile. It seems to have sprung up in the late Assyrian period,* perhaps first in Isaiah of Jerusalem, and then to have struck its roots in the last of the seventh century so that by the time of the exile it was an established motif. That it had still more ancient connections in the cult traditions of Yahweh's victory over the nations is not to be denied,[15] but the characteristic of this prophetic motif in the Assyrian period, except perhaps for Micah 5:5–6, is that it did not depend primarily or even at all upon the belief that Yahweh would overwhelm the nations with the force of Hebrew arms, as

[13] See *infra,* p. 339.
[14] See *infra,* pp. 225–26.
[15] See *supra,* pp. 104–106, 112, 196–98.

the monarchic cult seemed to insist. Something rather like the amphictyony of pre-monarchic times would be extended to the peoples of the earth, who would voluntarily come together. To be sure, in all this Israel had an honored religious position, but her political status was not that of world conqueror.

Isaiah 19:16–25

These verses comprise five clearly distinguished prophecies concerning Egypt (the last two involving Assyria also), all of which begin with the formula "in that day." The first anticipates only the destruction of Egypt, whereas the remaining four envision the salvation of Egypt in one form or another. It is possible that one or more of the pieces stem from Isaiah of Jerusalem, for 2:2–4 shows that even he expected a general turning of the nations toward Yahweh.[16] Nevertheless, the style and cultic conceptions are not noticeably Isaianic. As a matter of fact, there is such a unique stamp in the outlook and style of each of the five oracles that it would be easy to imagine them as having been written by five entirely separate authors. The second and third are similar in their cultic interests but by no means alike, and the fourth and fifth express a dimension of universalism which is perhaps the most astonishing in the Old Testament.

If it is somewhat difficult to believe that Isaiah of Jerusalem was the author of these oracles, it is also very difficult to imagine them written later than the Assyrian era.[17] At least, such a line of reasoning seems to hold good for the last four units. After the promulgation of the Deuteronomic Reform, which proscribed all sacrifice outside of Jerusalem, it is difficult to conceive any Palestinian Jewish writer's heralding the erection of an altar (*mizbēaḥ*) to Yahweh in the center of Egypt and a sacred pillar (*matstsēbāh*) on its border. True, the pillar might be construed

---

[16] G. A. Smith, *The Book of Isaiah*, rev. ed., n.d., I, 281–82; T. K. Cheyne, *Prophecies of Isaiah*, 1880, I, 150 ff., but abandoned in *Introduction to the Books of Isaiah*, 1895, pp. 99–110.

[17] H. Schmoekel, *Jahwe und die Fremdvoelker*, pp. 97–98, dates vss. 19–25 in the period after Psamtik threw off the Assyrian yoke (670) but before the death of Ashurbanipal (626), preferably in the reign of Manasseh.

as a memorial stele to commemorate an act or decree of God[18] or to seal an alliance between Egypt and Israel.[19] To such memorial pillars the Deuteronomist perhaps did not object (cf. Deut. 16:22), although it is doubtful that our distinction between symbol and idol would have impressed him as valid. But such an interpretation can hardly be given to the altar on which Egyptians will offer their sacrifices to Yahweh. Furthermore, the names Egypt and Assyria ought to be taken in their literal reference since there are no suggestions whatsoever in the passage that they are apocalyptic code words for some other powers.[20] In that event the last two pieces at least were written before 609. Also, the prophecy that Egyptian cities would speak "the language of Canaan" is somewhat anachronistic if written after the exile, when the Jews spoke Aramaic instead of Hebrew.

Attempts to identify the five cities referred to as destined to worship Yahweh have been unsuccessful. One is called "the City of the Sun," possibly indicating Heliopolis, but the latter is normally called On or Beth-Shemesh in the Old Testament (Gen. 41:45, 50; 46:20; Jer. 43:13). It is doubtful that the writer has any specific city in mind for the central altar referred to in vs. 19. Finally, the five cities are not clearly distinguished as populated by Egyptians and possibly the verse really speaks of Jewish colonies in Egypt.[21] Some evidence points to the fact that Judeans were already living in Egypt before the Babylonian exile, serving

---

[18] G. B. Gray, *ICC*, p. 338.

[19] H. M. Wiener, *The Prophets in History and Criticism,* 1923, p. 173, finds that the association of altar and pillar in vs. 19, as in Exodus 24:4, shows knowledge of "the technical language of the transactions by which the special relationship of Israel to God had been created" and that such technical terms were not understood in post-exilic times. His dogmatic conclusion is unacceptable but he does rightly see that there is nothing against, and much in favor of, a pre-exilic milieu for these verses. Also E. J. Kissane, *The Book of Isaiah,* rev. ed., 1960, p. 212.

[20] Those who favor the typological application of these old political designations to later empires offer singularly little evidence, apart from the assumption that apocalyptic habits have been at work; cf. Gray, *op. cit.,* p. 341, and G. W. Wade, *The Book of the Prophet Isaiah,* 2nd rev. ed., 1929, p. 132. Yet, in contexts where apocalyptic notions are not otherwise visible, this is a gratuitous line of reasoning.

[21] Wade, *op. cit.,* pp. 129–30.

as mercenaries in pharaoh's army, apparently by the time of Psamtik I (663–609)[22] and possibly soon after the fall of the northern kingdom. The change of City of the Sun (*heres*) to City of Destruction (*heres*) in a majority of Hebrew manuscripts was probably made at a time after this city was equated with the temple of Onias in Leontopolis.[23] The reading "City of Righteousness," in the LXX has much to commend it as the original reading.[24] All in all, the proposal that vs. 18 describes the conversion of Egypt by analogy with the conquest of Canaan in Joshua 10 is the most satisfying. The five cities are merely figurative of the five Canaanite cities (Josh. 10:3), and "the city of righteousness" is the Egyptian Jerusalem (cf. Isa. 1:26). If this interpretation is followed, the case for a post-exilic origin disappears.[25]

Josephus tells us of the refugee Judean priest Onias who erected a temple at Leontopolis in Egypt c. 169–168 B.C. which he justified by these words in vs. 19: "There shall be an altar in Egypt to the Lord God" (*Ant.* xiii. 3[1]; cf. *Bell.* i.1[1]; vii. 10[2-4]). Josephus is probably to be taken at face value. If Isaiah 19: 19–22 were a propaganda piece composed to justify the Jewish temple at Leontopolis, not only does it fail to use the word "temple" but, more fundamentally, it speaks of a place of worship *for Egyptians* and not for Jews in Egypt, which was the whole point of Onias' temple. Finally, by way of corroboration of this view, it should be noted that the St. Mark manuscript of Isaiah from Qumran (IQIsa.[a]), dating from 150–100 B.C., contains this passage and, in the view of most scholars, precludes the addition of passages in the prophecy much after 200 B.C.[26]

The unit vss. 19–22 seems to divide into two phases, the first referring to Jewish worship of Yahweh in Egypt and Yahweh's

[22] E. Meyer, *Geschichte des Altertums*, III[2], p. 146, and *Kleine Schriften*, 1910, I, 77; F. K. Kienitz, *Die politische Geschichte Aegyptens vom 7 bis zum 4 Jahrhundert vor der Zeitwende*, pp. 39–40; cf. also W. Staerk, *Die Anfänge der Judischen Diaspora in Aegypten*, 1908.

[23] R. B. Y. Scott, *IB*, V, 282; Gray, *op. cit.*, pp. 335–36.

[24] Gray, *loc cit.;* Kissane, *op. cit.*, pp. 211–12.

[25] Kissane, *op. cit.*, pp. 203, 210–11.

[26] F. M. Cross, *The Ancient Library of Qumran and Modern Biblical Studies*, 1958, p. 121.

deliverance of his hard-pressed people (vss. 19–20) and the second speaking of a manifestation of Yahweh to the Egyptians, who will sacrifice to him and, after punishment, will know the healing of Israel's God (vss. 21–22). The suggestion that the place of worship is the temple of Elephantine in Upper Egypt built by a colony of Jewish mercenaries in 525—and perhaps as much as a century earlier—is intriguing[27] but seems ruled out by the fact that the altar of vs. 19 is said to be "in the midst of the land of Egypt" and Elephantine was at the far south.[28] Nevertheless, it was to just some such Jewish settlement in Egypt in the latter part of the seventh century or beginning of the sixth that this pericope refers.

The two closing oracles form a fitting climax to the series. *They envision a tripartite confederation of Egypt, Assyria, and Israel accompanied by free movement among the member states,* regarded as a conscious fulfillment of the promise to Abraham in Genesis 12:3.[29] Egyptians and Assyrians, normally enemies, will worship together, and the three powers will be partners in the blessing of God.[30] The prophecies bear full citation:

In that day there shall be a highway from Egypt to Assyria and Assyria shall come to Egypt and Egypt to Assyria and Egypt shall worship with Assyria.

In that day Israel shall be a blessing, one-third in the midst of the earth, along with Egypt and Assyria, whom Yahweh of Hosts has blessed saying: "Blessed are my people Egypt, and the work of my hands Assyria, and my inheritance Israel!"

[27] Schmoekel, *op. cit.,* p. 97, and C. Steuernagel in *Theologische Studien und Kritiken,* 1909, pp. 8–12. E. Sellin, *Einleitung,* 8th ed., 1950, pp. 102–3, traced the Elephantine temple back into the seventh century (see also note 22).

[28] Gray, *op. cit.,* p. 339.

[29] R. Feuillet, "Un sommet religieux de l'Ancien Testament. L'oracle d'Isaïe, XIX (vv. 16–25) sur la conversion de l'Égypte," *Recherches de Science Religieuse* 39 (1951), 65–87; H. Gross, *Weltherrschaft als religioese Idee im Alten Testament,* p. 61.

[30] Israel is conceived in vss. 24–25 as the *berākhāh* in the midst of the earth, which in turn receives blessing, i.e., Egypt and Assyria receive the blessing through association with Israel. This clearly reflects "all the families of the earth shall be blessed [or bless themselves] in you" (Gen. 12:3); cf. Gross, *loc. cit.,* and Feuillet, *op. cit.,* p. 87.

This is, of course, not a bland syncretistic universalism, for it is Israel's God who says these things of the nations. There is, however, no trace of prejudice of any sort against Assyria or Egypt, no implication that they are to have inferior positions in the entente. If we are to conjecture about the concept of alliance lying behind the prophecy we should probably regard it as the concept of parity alliance among sovereign states, if viewed politically, or as an international Yahweh amphictyony, if viewed religiously.[31] *Here the early model of ancient Israel's covenant union of the tribes is projected upon the international scene, and politically independent states associate themselves in the common worship of Yahweh without compromising their sovereignty.* In the amphictyony certain leaders, possibly even clans and tribes (such as the Levites), served as the spokesmen and guardians of the Yahweh traditions.[32] In that sense, Israel is probably so conceived in these oracles. She is the interpreter of Yahweh but thus holds a privilege of religious service to the members of the international Yahweh league and not a position to be taken advantage of to impose the interpreter's own will upon the members in matters which do not have to do directly with the amphictyonic pledge of loyalty to the common deity.

This conception is remarkably like that of Isaiah 2:1-4 in its essential features,[33] although in that passage the stress is upon the focusing of all the nations at the amphictyonic center in Jerusalem, while in this one the stress is upon the catholicity of status and the partnership of the amphictyony's members. It is a conception which seems to know nothing of the Davidic or Israelite conquest of the nations but sees the nations voluntarily attaching themselves to a God whose significance for them they have come to appreciate. The strong and vivid form in which the notion is presented in Isaiah 19 may be judged by the fact that this is *the only place in the Old Testament where a non-Israelite nation is called "my people."*

[31] See note 19.
[32] M. Noth, *Das System der zwoelf Staemme Israels,* 1930, pp. 151 ff., and in condensed form in his *The History of Israel,* pp. 98–99.
[33] See *supra,* pp. 196, 199–203.

Nahum

The book of Nahum is an imaginative description of the downfall of Nineveh, capital of Assyria, in 612 B.C. (see Map 11). This assertion is borne out not only by the superscription but also by the allusions to Nineveh in 2:8 and 3:7 and to the king of Assyria in 3:18. It is a work of poetic excellence, although commentators have been too extravagant in their praise of its literary merit. Vivid imagery is mixed with banal and insipid clichés, but the former outweigh the latter in the total effect.

Perhaps the most striking single feature of the book is the difference between 1:2–15; 2:2 (Hebrew 1:2–2:1, 3), on the one hand, and 2:1, 3–13; 3:1–19 (Hebrew 2:2, 4–14; 3:1–19), on the other. The former declares Yahweh's victory over his foes in language that is either vague or archaic or both. From this portion it would be impossible to know that Assyria was in view. The latter segment is, however, the pointed account of a military destruction of Nineveh, "the bloody city" and tireless sacker of nations.

The exegetically troublesome first part of the book is further divisible into a hymn describing a judgment-theophany of Yahweh (1:2–8; cf. Judg. 5; Hab. 3) and consolatory remarks to Judah (1:12–13, 15; 2:2). The remaining verses in the first chapter (vss. 9–11, 14) appear to be addressed to Assyria but there are two obstacles to satisfactory exegesis of 1:9–2:1: one is the serious textual corruption of vss. 9–10, and the other is the difficulty in determining the unspecified antecedents of the profusion of pronouns, which must, by turns, refer to Judah and Assyria and perhaps to others.[34]

Whether there was an original unity to the first part of the book is problematic. The confident claim of the great majority

[34] W. C. Graham, "The Interpretation of Nah. 1:9—2:3," *AJSL* 44 (1927), 345–46, offers an identification of the pronoun antecedents and a paraphrase of the sense of the passage, but his tentative proposal to see Jeremiah in the "one scheming against Yahweh" in 1:11 is completely unfounded, and his otherwise appealing suggestion that "the shatterer" of 2:1 is Pharaoh Necho seems invalidated by the fact that Necho's first entry into Palestine was in 609, three years after Nineveh's fall.

of commentators to find an acrostic in vss. 2–8 (or 10), employing the alphabet as far as *kaph* or *samekh*,[35] depends upon trans-
position of verses and emendations of the text which have no
justification.[36] Failing the discovery of a more reliable form of
the text, it will remain impossible to determine the exact relation
of chap. 1 to chaps. 2 and 3. It is not unreasonable to imagine a
movement in the chapters from general to specific, from the almost totally "de-historicized" introduction (1:1–8), through specific encouragements to Judah and denunciations of an unnamed
enemy (1:9–15; 2:2), to the unmistakable excoriations of
Nineveh (2:1, 3–13; 3:1–19). Considering that other prophetic
books have combined liturgical generalities with specific historical
judgments (e.g., Amos, Isaiah, Habakkuk), only unwarranted
bias can insist that the poet of Nahum chaps. 2 and 3 had nothing to do with chap. 1.

Unity of authorship does not, however, imply chronological
unity. Knowledge of Ashurbanipal's sack of Thebes in 663 is apparent in 3:8 (see Map 11), and, at the other extreme, the
exuberance over the fall of Nineveh could hardly be imagined
long after the city's fall in 612 B.C. A great majority of the verses
seems to anticipate the destruction of Nineveh. There is some
cogency to the argument that the period between 663 and 640,
the accession of Josiah, afforded the most natural setting for
Nahum.[37] The sack of Thebes would have been fresh in memory,
and Judah would still have been suffering under the oppression
of the Assyrians. Furthermore, the noticeable absence of any
reference to the conquerors of Nineveh by name may suggest a
period before the Medes and neo-Babylonians had actually begun
to pose a threat to Assyria, i.e., before 616 or even 626. Of course,

[35] See the reconstruction of the acrostic and commentary in J. M. P.
Smith, *A Critical and Exegetical Commentary on Nahum,* 1911, pp. 287–302.
[36] W. A. Maier, *The Book of Nahum. A Commentary,* 1959, pp. 52–62.
[37] *Ibid.,* pp. 34–37. Maier's general case for a pre-Josianic date is obscured
when he argues for an origin before 654 when Psamtik I retook Thebes
from the Assyrians. Actually, Mentuemhat, the governor of the city, returned
soon after the sack of the city to make repairs on temples, and the decline
of Thebes seems to have been less due to the Assyrian attack than to the loss
of stature by the Theban priesthood of Amon (cf. W. S. Smith, *Ancient
Egypt,* pp. 137–38).

if most of chaps. 2 and 3 predate the reign of Josiah we should have to emphasize that they could not have been employed in the official cult since, under Manasseh and Amon, Judah was entirely subject to Assyria and her cult was heavily indebted to Assyrian religious ideas and practices.

The solution may be to recognize that the "ode" on Nineveh was a composition circulated in the anti-Assyrian "underground" in the reign of Manasseh. It appears, however, that 1:15 (Hebrew 2:1) and 3:18–19 are already aware of the fall of the city. Consequently, we may imagine that 1:2–15; 2:2; and 3:18–19 were supplied as introduction and conclusion for public recital after Assyria's downfall. Such a distinction would perhaps best explain the double superscription; "oracle [*massā'*] about Nineveh" will have been the title of the older poem in chaps. 2 and 3, whereas "book of the vision [*hᵃzôn*] of Nahum" refers to the revised and expanded version very near to or soon after the fall of Nineveh.[38]

To incline toward acknowledging a liturgical function for or at least a liturgical influence on the book of Nahum is not, however, to lead us any closer to knowing exactly when or how it was used. It can be no more than a guess to assert that it was written for the fall New Year's Festival of 612.[39] Conceivably the book is an imitation of a liturgy in which terms drawn from Yahweh's fight with the forces of chaos at creation have been applied to Assyria.[40] Nonetheless, the descriptions are at points so pictorial and the emotion is so virulent that it would be hard to resist the impulse to read this document aloud, even if the reading occurred outside of the framework of some established festival or ceremony. If Josiah knew of the book, is it not likely

[38] A. Weiser, *The Old Testament: Its Formation and Development,* 1961, p. 257.

[39] P. Humbert, "Essai d'analyse de Nahoum 1:2—2:3," *ZAW* 3 (1926), 266–80; "La vision de Nahoum II. 4–11," *Archiv fuer Orientforschung* 5 (1928), 14–19; "Le problème de livre de Nahoum," *RHPR* 12 (1932), 1–15; A. Lods, "Trois études sur la littérature prophétique," *RHPR* 11 (1931), 211–19.

[40] A. Haldar, *Studies in the Book of Nahum,* places the composition in 614 before the fall of the city and is explicit in describing the book as a prophetic borrowing from cult forms for political propagandistic purposes.

that he would have encouraged its official use fittingly to celebrate the demise of that power which he had opposed for sixteen years or more?

Sustaining the bitter denunciation and vengeful glee of Nahum is an unrelenting belief in the moral cohesiveness of history. Assyria, for so long the plunderer of the civilized world, was now to be plundered and, with one stroke, removed from any further imperial activity. The closing lines reflect sharply the sense of relief felt everywhere in the Fertile Crescent at word of the sudden decline of Assyria:

> All who hear of your fate clap their hands over you,
> For upon whom has not come your endless evil-doing?

Judah had ample reason for speaking in this way, for she had been directly confronted by neo-Assyrian power for more than a century and had, in fact, been an Assyrian vassal from 735 to 632 or 628.[41] But in this context there can be no doubt that the "all" and the "whom" refer to the nations of the Near East and not to Judah alone. This international perspective is also clear in 3:4, where it is said that Assyria is a harlot "who sells nations with her harlotries," i.e., either selling captives into slavery or in the sense of the Arabic root, "to betray."

Nahum expresses a pointed belief in God's righteous judgment of a morally offensive and inhuman empire. Judah had been one, but far from the only, victim of its conquest, plunder, and maltreatment. Beyond this, it is very difficult to judge, for example, how Nahum's outlook agreed with or diverged from those of his predecessor Isaiah and his contemporaries Habakkuk and Jeremiah, all of whom felt obliged to come to terms with Assyrian or Babylonian imperialism. Nahum demonstrates a limited theological range, and we are not necessarily correct in assuming that anything he does not mention he opposed, (e.g., salvation for non-Israelite peoples) or disregarded (e.g., the sins of Judah). We cannot without more ado conclude that Nahum was one of the false prophets condemned by Jeremiah. It may be that the promise "now I will shatter his yoke from off you" (1:13) is a

[41] See *supra,* pp. 149–52, 155–56, 220.

conscious counterreference to Isaiah 10:5, 15, but this would not necessarily imply an ideological breach with Isaiah for he himself had already foreseen a time of catastrophe for Assyria (cf. 14:24–27). On the other hand, it would not be sound exegesis to read notions into Nahum's mind which are not clearly contained in his writings. He had a single, unsophisticated message; for the rest, his views are unknown and unknowable.

Habakkuk

The book of Habakkuk carries no reference to the date of the prophet's activity or to the king who was his contemporary. Only the reference to the Chaldeans (neo-Babylonians) in 1:6 assists the interpreter in identifying the period. *If we take this reference at face value the book evidently is a theological inquiry into the injustice of neo-Babylonian imperialism.* The prophet insists on knowing why this callous imperial power prevails over the relatively more righteous nations, and especially over Judah. His struggle with international theodicy parallels Job's agony over individual theodicy. Nevertheless, there are many exegetical barriers to any such "natural" reading of the book.

It is possible that Chaldea is not the power spoken of in all sections of the book. We may safely dismiss the substitution of the Greeks under Alexander for the Chaldeans in 1:6 (reading *kittîm*, i.e., Cyprus, for *kasdîm*).[42] Not only is there no textual support for the emendation, but there is no evidence that Cyprus was used in the Bible for a political or ethnic reference rather than a geographical one.[43] Furthermore, no feature in the description of the marauding nation better fits the empire of Alexander than that of Nabopolassar and Nebuchadnezzar.[44] Some-

[42] B. Duhm, *Das Buch Habakuk,* 1906, pp. 4–5, 19–23; C. C. Torrey, "Alexander the Great in Old Testament Prophecies," *BZAW* 41 (1925), 281–86.

[43] W. W. Cannon, "The Integrity of Habakkuk, ch. 1, 2," *ZAW* 43 (1925), 78–79, shows that *kittîm* is overwhelmingly a geographical term in the Old Testament rather than an ethnic or political one (Num. 24:24; Isa. 23:1, 12; Jer. 2:10; Ezek. 27:6; Dan. 11:30). Only Genesis 10:7 may be ethnic, but under the guise of a genealogy, the table of nations in Genesis 10 lumps together names of places and of peoples somewhat indiscriminately.

[44] *Ibid.,* pp. 79–83.

what more plausibly, however, it has been proposed that at least in 1:1-4, 12-17, and in 2:6-19, the cruel and avaricious nation described is in fact Assyria, since it seems to have been a harsher conqueror and oppressor than neo-Babylonia.[45] On such a line of interpretation, 1:5-11 describes the Chaldeans as the chastisers of the Assyrians and perhaps should even be transferred to a point following 2:4.[46]

Doubtless such a rearrangement of sequence would aid the interpreter, but there is not the slightest hint that two nations were actually involved. Furthermore, now that we have a somewhat clearer view of neo-Babylonian history, with the help of the Babylonian Chronicles, it is evident that Nebuchadnezzar was a militarist who waged many more campaigns in the western part of his empire than was previously suspected, even though his main interests lay in building projects.[47] For that matter, the woe directed against "him who builds a town with blood and establishes a city on iniquity" (2:12) would be apter for the builder and beautifier of Babylon than for the weak Assyrian kings after Ashurbanipal. Yet it is difficult to argue with much confidence from the imagery of Habakkuk, who relies primarily on conventional terminology for describing a power-sotted conqueror, an imagery doubtless heavily influenced by two hundred years of firsthand experience with Assyrian imperialism.

Certain passages in the book give the impression that they speak of individual or domestic evil rather than international evil. This is especially the case with the first complaint of the prophet in 1:1-4 and, to a lesser extent, also with 1:12-13 and 2:6-19. It has, therefore, been argued that the real object of attack in the book is the Judean king and the syncretizing, socially oppressive elements in his realm.[48] It has been characterized as a

---

[45] K. Budde, "Habakkuk," *Encyclopedia Biblica,* 1901, vol. II, cols. 1921–28, and "Habakuk," *ZDMG* 84 (1930), 139–47; Weiser, *op. cit.,* pp. 262–63.

[46] Budde, *Encyclopedia Biblica,* cols. 1923–24; Eissfeldt, *op. cit.,* p. 512.

[47] See *infra,* pp. 252–58.

[48] J. W. Rothstein, "Ueber Habakuk, Kap. 1 und 2," *Theologische Studien und Kritiken* 67 (1894), 51–85; P. Humbert, *Problèmes du livre d'Habacuc;* E. Nielsen, "The Righteous and the Wicked in Habaqquq," *Studia Theologica* 6 (1952), 54–78.

prophetic liturgy composed for a state festival in 602–601 B.C. to attack Jehoiakim's religious and social policies.[49] Besides the fact that it is difficult to see how a work with that avowed purpose would be accepted in the state cult,[50] it is further apparent that the context shows most of the supposed "individual" references to be collective in meaning, i.e., to refer to the oppressing king who obviously accomplished his misdeeds through his subjects and who readily personifies the kingdom. The "wicked" who devours "the man more righteous than he" (1:13) appears to be identical with the one who "goes on slaying nations without mercy" (1:17).[51] The "arrogant" and "greedy" man, who is contrasted with "the righteous," is also the person who "collects for himself all the nations and gathers for himself all the peoples" (2:4–5). The hardhearted creditor of 2:6–7, who might at first reading be taken as a harsh landowner or merchant foreclosing mortgages, turns out to be the one who has "plundered many nations" (2:8).

Only 1:1–4 constitutes a serious problem to the sustained international scope of the theodicy. The casting of the problem of justice and injustice in individual terms is not insuperable. It is recognized that the impact of the decline and fall of Judah accelerated the transfer of individual lament imagery to the suffering nation, as exemplified in Lamentations and Deutero-Isaiah.[52] The havoc (*šōd*), violence (*ḥāmās*), controversy

---

[49] Humbert, *Problèmes du livre d'Habacuc,* and summarized by him in *Die Religion in Geschichte und Gegenwart,* 1959, vol. III, cols. 3–4.

[50] Bentzen, *op cit.,* p. 153.

[51] The imagery of the fisherman's net is singularly appropriate because Near Eastern monarchs were often represented as holding captives in a net, e.g., Eannatum in the Stele of the Vultures (*ANEP,* p. 94) and possibly Sargon of Akkad in a broken stele from Susa (B. Mazar, ed., *Views of the Biblical World,* III, 272).

[52] N. K. Gottwald, *Studies in the Book of Lamentations,* chap. 2. Therefore, while H. Schmidt, "Ein Psalm im Buche Habakuk," *ZAW* 62 (1950), 52–63, helpfully analyzes the individual lament imagery of 1:2–4, 12–13, and 3:18–19, he completely fails to see that the mixing of types is not a late, editorial operation but an occurrence in the mind of the writer, who appropriates individualizing features because he himself speaks for the community (1:1–4) or about a whole people as though it were a single person (1:12–13). In the case of 3:18–19, it is not quite clear in which of these two senses the "I" is used.

(*ribh*), and strife (*mādôn*) referred to in 1:3 are not exclusively used to describe domestic wrongdoing (Judg. 12:2; II Sam. 22: 44; Ps. 18:44 [LXX]; Jer. 51:35, 46; Hos. 7:13, 12:1; Joel 3:19; Obad. 10; Hab. 1:9; Ps. 80:6).

More difficult is the expression "the law is slacked [or numbed]" (*tāphûq tōrāh*). All other uses of *tōrāh* in the Old Testament appear to be either (1) references to the law of Israel, understood broadly as the norm of God's requirement for his people or more specifically as the teaching of the priests,[53] or even applied to particular stipulations; or (2) in a few instances the teaching and arbitration of God that will extend to the nations from Israel (Isa. 2:3; 42:4). If Habakkuk 1:1–4 is descriptive of Chaldean evil under individualizing imagery, law here must apparently be understood as "the law of nations," i.e., the norm of right conduct applicable to non-Israelites. While such a notion is strongly implied by several prophetic assertions (Amos 1:1—2:3; 9:7; Isa. 10:5–15; 14:24–27), it is nowhere made explicit in the Old Testament and, if that is the intention here, one would expect the point to have been made more precisely. All in all, 1:1–4 is probably a lament over domestic evil which evokes Yahweh's demand for Habakkuk to "look among the nations" in expectation of the chastising action of Yahweh against Jehoiakim. This in turn arouses in the prophet horror and aversion at the far-ranging evil of Babylon.

Understood in this way, Habakkuk is not so far removed from Jeremiah as some interpretations have portrayed him. He shares with Jeremiah a loathing for the social and religious lapses of Jehoiakim, in contrast to the relatively faithful policies and conduct of Josiah. He also recognizes the work of the neo-Babylonians as the agents of God against Judah. *Possessed of a mind that demanded consistency, he pressed the question of theodicy to the point of applying it immediately to neo-Babylonia's conduct.* Jeremiah was content to recognize definite limits to Nebuchadnezzar's power and virtue and to foresee the time when he too would have to reckon with the judgments of history.[54] Ha-

---

[53] So understood by Cannon, *op. cit.*, p. 65.
[54] See *infra*, pp. 265–69.

bakkuk looked for more immediate rectification but the answer of Yahweh which the prophet received was very much like the reply Jeremiah received concerning his plaints. The wicked man or nation will waste away; the righteous will endure.

It has often been felt that the "vision" promised to the prophet, coming as it does after two laments and preceded by dramatic suspense, is a distinct anticlimax. The extent of the vision cannot be easily delimited but not much more than 2:4–5 can be so specified:

> Behold, the person who is not upright is inflated[55]
>> but the righteous shall thrive in his faithfulness.
> Also, the presumptuous one[56] is treacherous,
>> the arrogant man shall not endure.
> The one whose greed is as vast as Sheol and as death
>> he is unsatisfied,
> So that he collects to himself all nations
>> and gathers as his own all peoples.

Vs. 5, with its "also" or "moreover" marks the transition from reference to the wicked Judean to the wicked neo-Babylonian oppressor. Admittedly, 2:4–5 is a pregnant statement capable of much consolation and extended application. Nevertheless, it does not seem to bear sufficient literary weight in its context.

The puzzling "psalm of Habakkuk" in chap. 3 is probably to be understood as an enlargement upon 2:4 which gives to that promise of God a solidity and to the brief assurance an amplitude and a majestic splendor.[57] The psalm is conceivably one

[55] MT *'upplāh*, although problematic, may be retained in the sense of inflated with a false self-confidence.

[56] Reading the consonantal text of the Qumran Habakkuk Commentary as *hawwān*, "presumptuous," as long ago suggested by M. T. Houtsma, "Habakuk 2:4 en 5," *Theol. Tijdschrift* (1885), pp. 180–83. W. F. Albright favors reading *Hayyan*, "the crafty," the Ugaritic Hermes, with whom the subject of Habakkuk 2:5 is compared (*BASOR*, 91 [1943], 40). For an excellent review of the options, cf. W. H. Brownlee, *The Text of Habakkuk in the Ancient Commentary from Qumran*, pp. 45–49.

[57] W. F. Albright, "The Psalm of Habakkuk," *Studies in Old Testament Prophecy Presented to T. H. Robinson*, 1950, pp. 1–18; and esp. S. Mowinckel, "Zum Psalm des Habakuk," *TZ* 9 (1953), 1–23, who sees a much clearer organic unity to the cult poem than does Albright. W. Irwin, "The

familiar to the prophet and placed here for its effect, but just as conceivably he composed it in the cultic manner to which he was accustomed. At any rate, the brilliant description of a Yahweh theophany, heavily indebted to old amphictyonic notions of God,[58] culminates in the crushing of the wicked and the vindication of the righteous. This is attended by the prophet's deep emotion and bodily trembling and by a confession of trust which shows perfect understanding of the motto that "the righteous shall live by his faith." It is even possible that the psalm originally stood after 2:4 but was transferred to its present position to give a fitting lyrical conclusion to the book.[59]

It is likely, then, that the book does contain a double reference to evildoers: the dominant reference to neo-Babylonia and the secondary reference to Jehoiakim and the wicked in Judah (1: 1–4 and also "the wicked" of 2:4).[60] Accordingly, the prophet was sensitive, as earlier prophets had been, to the mixture of evils on both sides in international conflicts. Jehoiakim in large measure deserved the Babylonian attacks, but Babylon was itself an oppressor and a defrauder of the nations. *God's righteousness would be established only when wrong within Judah and within Babylon had been requited.* A good case can be made for Habakkuk as a cult prophet,[61] although certainly not a conclusive one. We can well imagine him delivering such a liturgy, with its outright references to Babylonian evil and its more veiled references to Jehoiakim and Judean wickedness. Habakkuk and his followers, encouraged by the open denunciations of Jeremiah, could read their own meanings into the composition. One might listen to it with smug self-satisfaction, telling as it does of the doom of Babylon. But one might also listen more attentively and with

---

Psalm of Habakkuk," *JNES* 1 (1942), 10–40, regards the work as very probably pre-exilic but thinks that it was added to chaps. 1–2 by a post-exilic editor.

[58] M. Delcor, "La geste de Yahve au temps de l'Exode et l'espérance du psalmiste en Habacuc III," *Miscellanea Biblica B. Ubach*, pp. 287–302.

[59] Weiser, *op. cit.*, pp. 261–62.

[60] Cannon, *op. cit.*, p. 75.

[61] W. F. Albright, *Archaeology and the Religion of Israel*, 1946, pp. 125–29, 210, n. 100; Mowinckel, *op. cit.*, pp. 3–4; and especially Humbert, *Problèmes du livre d'Habacuc.*

trembling, as the prophet himself does (3:16), at the prospect of God, the Righteous One, who comes to judge the earth.

Jeremiah

Jeremiah's attitudes toward international relations bear many similarities to those of his prophetic precursors. In a sense he may be described as one who combined salient motifs of Amos, Hosea, and Isaiah, such as the foreign conqueror as the instrument of Yahweh and opposition to foreign alliances, particularly those with Egypt. Sometimes the dependence in phraseology is evident, but the general scantiness of "new ideas" in Jeremiah does not imply that he merely imitated his predecessors. He does in fact so join older elements as to present a new reality. In certain respects he entered even more passionately and boldly into the political process than had Isaiah, and his prophecies took on a precision previously unparalleled. His passionate subjectivity and "individualistic" insight allowed him to take the measure of the political manifestations of Yahwism and to prepare his people for a time shortly to come when its existence as a state would cease. He interpreted the critical era in trans-political terms, for he saw that within the matrix of the turbulent international political scene the most important realities were personal and social and that, under existing conditions, it was essential to Yahweh's purpose for Israel that the state of Judah come to an end. That the community might one day be reconstituted politically was quite secondary to the nature of the personal and social life which was demanded to fulfill Israel's purpose.

The Prophet's "Silent Period" (626–616 ? to 610)

Three issues in the early career of the prophet are complexly connected with one another, and the resolution decided upon will strongly affect the interpreter's view of the prophet's political thought. The issues are (1) the date of the prophet's call, (2) his attitude toward the Deuteronomic Reform of Josiah, and (3) the identity of the foe from the north described in oracles scat-

tered through chaps. 4–6. The evidence permits of several reconstructions, although each necessarily requires the filling of
gaps in our knowledge by means of hypotheses. The date of
Jeremiah's call supplied in the superscription of the book (1:1–3
and repeated or originated in 25:3) is 626 B.C.—the year of
Ashurbanipal's death, which heralded the breakup of the Assyrian empire. Unfortunately, the collected oracles and memoirs
contain no oracles which can be identified as belonging exclusively to Josiah's reign, from the prophet's call in 626 until
the monarch's death in 609.

The assumption that the agitated oracles about an enemy from
the north refer specifically to a Scythian invasion of Syria and
Palestine to the border of Egypt (reported by Herodotus, *History*
I. 105) is entirely gratuitous.[62] Herodotus' account has not been
borne out or clarified by other historical data. In fact the details
of the descriptions of the enemy manifest a war technology much
too advanced for the Scythians: massed infantry, chariotry, and
siege equipment. It has been suggested that Jeremiah's silence
after 626 resulted from professional discredit at the failure of the
Scythians to decimate Judah, but Jeremiah was not one to remain quiet merely because of opposition, hostile or condescend-
ing. Further, it has been frequently assumed that the young
prophet wholeheartedly embraced the reform of Josiah and therefore found little to preach against until the collapse of the reform.
He has even been regarded as a peripatetic propagandist for the
reform (11:1–4; note especially "Proclaim all these words in the
cities of Judah, and in the streets of Jerusalem: Hear the words
of this covenant and do them"—vs. 6).[63]

[62] For a succinct statement of the objections to the Scythian theory, see
J. P. Hyatt, *IB*, V, 799. J. Lewy, *Forschungen zur alten Geschichte Vorderasiens* (*Mitteilungen der vorderasiatisch-aegyptischen Gesellschaft* 29.2,
[1925]), 191 stresses the unreliability of Herodotus' information on the Scythians and sees in "the foe from the north" a general motif of prophetic
preaching without reference to particular political events (see also note 70).
[63] W. Erbt, *Jeremia und seine Zeit*, 1905, pp. 48–49, deleted vss. 4–5
of chap. 11 and also vss. 7–8 (with LXX). The result was a passage in
which appear (1) Jeremiah's excitement at the first public proclamation
of the Deuteronomic Reform, vss. 1–3, and (2) Jeremiah as an itinerating
advocate of the reform, vs. 6. Erbt is followed by J. Skinner, *Prophecy and
Religion*, 1938, pp. 100–102.

The strongest case for regarding Jeremiah as an advocate of the reform is the generous praise he heaped on Josiah (22: 13–15a, 17–19). The prophet admired Josiah's concept of the king as defender of the rights of the poor, as one who "executed justice and righteousness." On the other hand, the prophet has nothing to say about the centralization of the cult at Jerusalem, which was the chief institutional pillar of the reform. There are sufficient instances of the prophet's opposition to the cult: to circumcision (9:25–26), to the ark (3:16), and to sacrifice (6:20; 7:21–23) to cast grave doubts upon his supposed early enthusiasm for the reform, which later turned to disillusion when he saw its superficial consequences. Other arguments marshaled to prove Jeremiah's support for the reform actually prove little: his intimate association with the prominent officials from the "Deuteronomic" family of Shaphan and the marked Deuteronomic form of many of the prophet's words. As for the former, Jeremiah was quite willing to accept help from any source and to gain a hearing with officials. That he and they should be in total agreement was no precondition of his friendship and cooperation. As for the latter, the Deuteronomists made use of all the prophets known to them, and their extensive editing of Jeremiah was probably a result of the fact that, with Jeremiah and Baruch in Egypt (43:4–6), there were no appointed "guardians" of the Jeremiah prophecies in the Babylonian exile. To this task Deuteronomists turned eagerly and, in the course of preserving the prophet's words, they manipulated them frequently to accord with their own thoughts.[64]

All in all, the silent period of Jeremiah's life is not well accounted for either by the Scythian hypothesis or by the supposition that he propagated the Deuteronomic Reform, for both present the prophet as a rather inept and naïve person who took eighteen years to find himself but suddenly did so with startling self-assurance after Josiah's death. A more consistent and faithful

[64] See esp. S. Mowinckel, *Zur Komposition des Buches Jeremia,* 1914; the main arguments in modified form appear in the same scholar's *Prophecy and Tradition,* 1946, pp. 61–65, which also contains a helpful discussion of the way in which original prophetic words were transmitted, modified, and expanded. See also J. P. Hyatt, "The Deuteronomic Edition of Jeremiah," *Vanderbilt Studies in the Humanities,* 1951, I, 71–95.

picture of the prophet is obtained by placing his call later than 626, preferably in 616 (reading "twenty-third year of Josiah" instead of "thirteenth year" in 1:2, which, considering its fuller form, was perhaps copied from 25:3).[65] This would put his call after the commitment of the state to the Deuteronomic Reform. While the problem of "a silent period" is not wholly removed by this correction, it is not so acute for in the years 616–609 it is possible to locate oracles warning of Judah's sins and threatening punishment by means of a foe from the north.

It is difficult to say exactly which of the oracles in chaps. 2–6 were delivered before 609 since in the issuance of his scroll in 605–604 (chap. 36) *Jeremiah seems to have updated all his previous oracles in the light of the fateful realities which came fully into view during Jehoiakim's rule: namely, the transfer of power in the ancient Near East from Assyria to neo-Babylonia and the reckless decision of Judah to prefer Egyptian alignment to neo-Babylonian vassalage.* Domestically it was a time of reversion to many of the idolatrous practices, social evils, and royal excesses which had preceded Josiah's reign. Consequently the oracles of Josiah's reign have been revised by the prophet in the light of Jehoiakim's reign. Doubtless much of the revision had already occurred in the course of the years as Jeremiah repeated the threats in ever-changing circumstances. In the indictments of Israel's sins there are traces of situations which appear to postdate 609. Necho's subjection of Judah, his murder of Josiah, and his appointment of Jehoiakim as vassal are alluded to in painful terms (2:16–18). The ingrained pro-Egyptian tendencies of Jehoiakim's reign are roundly condemned (2:23–25, 36–37). Conditions such as the recurrence of open idolatry (2:26–28; 3:23), the lapse into immorality, especially adultery and perjury (5:1–5, 7–9), and failure in the administration of justice (5:4–5, 26–29) seem most readily explicable as reactions to the collapse of the reform.

[65] So argued persuasively by T. C. Gordon, "A New Date for Jeremiah," *ET* 44 (1932–33), 562–65, and accepted by H. Bardtke, "Jeremiah der Fremdvoelkerprophet," *ZAW* 53 (1935), 218–19, who emphasizes that 616–614 was a period of decisive disturbance of the balance of power for at that time the Chaldeans and Medes first openly attacked Assyria. Bardtke agrees with J. Lewy, *op. cit.,* p. 57, that Jeremiah 25:3 was the basis of 1:2.

Nevertheless, "the temple sermon" of Jeremiah (7:1–15 and a summary in 26:1–6), which occurred "at the start of the reign of Jehoiakim" (26:1), perhaps at the coronation ceremony, is shot through with bitter attacks upon personal immorality and social injustice which cannot be accounted for on the assumption that they had developed only in the few months since Josiah's death. To be sure, the evils were accentuated by a backwash of nihilism, but the revulsion will probably have been felt earlier than 609 when, as the reforming zeal of 621 began to fade, there were many reversions to religious and social practices which had been officially banned. A retrograde development will have been all the more likely since Josiah was much occupied in military campaigning in order to restore David's kingdom in northern Israel and in trans-Jordan (II Chron. 34:6–7: see Map 19). Although personally pious and socially honest, Josiah never had the means to enforce the spirit of the Deuteronomic law and increasingly even the letter was breached. Jeremiah expresses sentiments of dissatisfaction with the self-confidence (4:10) and circumscribed cult-mindedness (6:19–20) which the reform had not eradicated and may actually have deepened. Likewise, "the lying pen of the scribes has made it [the instruction of Yahweh] into a lie" seems to refer to the official custodians of the Yahweh traditions, who have neglected and perverted their calling (8:8; more customary terms "prophet" and "priest" appear in 8:10, and the very fact that they can be collectively described as falsifying their trust shows that *sōphĕrîm* in this context are not mere secretaries but interpreters of written traditions, specifically the Deuteronomic law; cf. also 2:8).

At the same time the oracles warning of the rapacious enemy from the north declare that its coming is to be punishment for Judah's wantonness of heart (4:14, 18, 22). There seems no valid reason for denying credence to the prophet's original summons: "I [Yahweh] have appointed you a prophet to the nations. . . . Behold, I have placed you this day over nations and over kingdoms to uproot and to demolish, to rebuild and to plant" (omit "to destroy and to cast down" as a disturbance of the splendid poetic chiasm: [a] to uproot plants; [b] to demolish buildings; [b'] to rebuild buildings; [a'] to plant plants; cf. 24:6;

42:10; 45:4, where the redundancy is lacking). The almond staff or *šāqēd* reminds the prophet that Yahweh is *šōqēd,* "watching over" his declared word to perform it (1:11–12). The boiling pot declares that "evil shall burst forth on all the inhabitants of the land" (1:13–14, 17–19). Both of these "visions" contain an ominous and mysterious quality, for the staff often possesses mantic power[66] and the north, from which the evil will come, is a mythological source of unnamed ills.[67] This demonic quality runs through the descriptions of the enemy, who is "a destroyer of nations" already stirring in the world (4:7), "a distant . . . durable . . . and ancient nation, whose tongue you do not know" (5:15), "a great nation rising up from the distant regions of the earth" (6:22), equipped with terrible weapons (4:13, 29; 6:23), arrayed in close ranks (6:23), advancing with unrelenting cruelty (6:23). Mystery and danger are underscored by the emphasis upon the invader's remoteness, bizarreness, formidability, and cruelty.

If 616 is the correct year of the prophet's call, the ominous warnings of a northern enemy were paralleled by the rise of forces inside and outside of Mesopotamia which were to join in the liquidation of Assyria (see Map 11).[68] The Chaldeans or neo-Babylonians of lower Mesopotamia wrested the city of Babylon from Assyria in 626 and Nabopolassar occupied the throne. In 616 he was strong enough to campaign up the Euphrates as far as the Balikh region. Already at this date the Egyptians had troops in upper Mesopotamia assisting the rapidly failing Assyrians. In the following year the neo-Babylonians laid siege to

[66] A staff (*maqqēl*) was used by Jacob to induce the abundant breeding of his flocks (Gen. 30:37) and in Israel in the eighth century it was used as a divining rod (Hosea 4:12). For the ominous character of this sign, see P. S. Wood, "Jeremiah's Figure of the Almond Rod," *JBL* 61 (1942), 99–103.

[67] A. Kapelrud, *Joel Studies,* 1948, pp. 100–104.

[68] This historical reconstruction depends largely on the neo-Babylonian Chronicles, which for the period 626–556 (with a short gap 622–617 and a long one 593–558) were published by D. J. Wiseman, *Chronicles of the Chaldean Kings (626–556 B.C.) in the British Museum.* Wiseman's edition reissued with revisions the earlier text of that portion of the Chronicles from 616 to 609 B.C. previously published by C. J. Gadd, ed., *The Fall of Nineveh.* Gadd's historical discussion is not reproduced by Wiseman and is still of merit on many points.

Ashur but were compelled to withdraw while the Indo-European Medes raided Arappha beyond the Tigris. In 614 the Medes captured Ashur and reduced it with cruel measures of massacre and enslavement, and by 612 the Medes and neo-Babylonians together had plundered and destroyed Nineveh with fire and rams. An Assyrian rump state formed at Haran in northwest Mesopotamia but was obliterated in 610 by another joint attack of Medes and neo-Babylonians, and the Egyptian allies of Assyria were put to flight. It is noticeable that in all these campaigns the Medes played the leading role; Ashur, Nineveh, and Haran were captured only at their initiative. The one city which the neo-Babylonians attacked alone repelled them, and Nabopolassar thereafter refused to face the Assyrians in a major contest until his Median allies had arrived. Thus in the latter years of Josiah's reign the Medes were recognized as a new factor in Near Eastern affairs. To Jeremiah's eye they might well have seemed to be the eventual heirs of the Assyrian empire. The oracles' reference to the horses in such a way as to imply their great number and high quality (4:13, 29; 6:23)[69] suggests an Indo-European attacker since the best horses came from the regions of Asia Minor and Iran. When neo-Babylonia came eventually to supersede Assyria in Palestine, Jeremiah had no trouble in clarifying the subject of the warnings, now passing over the Medes in favor of the new conquerors. In doing so he felt no loss of prestige in the transfer, which marked simply a postponement of some years in the execution of his prophecy. As a matter of fact, probably no conscious shift in identity was involved, since Palestinians in this period tended to think of the Medes and the neo-Babylonians, the allies who brought down Assyria, as a single historical force.[70]

[69] Median horses were much sought after by the Assyrians as booty or tribute and they even sent special delegations to obtain them (A. T. Olmstead, *History of Assyria*, pp. 231, 245, 248, 362). This detail should not be pressed, however, since the descriptions of the unnamed foe possess a schematic character and are duplicated to an extent in Isaiah and Habakkuk (cf. B Childs, "The Enemy from the North and the Chaos Tradition," *JBL* 78 [1959], 189–93).

[70] The view that Jeremiah at first conceived of the foe in general and inexact terms, later identifying it with the Chaldeans, has much to commend it (cf. A. Lauha, *Zaphon. Der Norden und die Nordvoelker im Alten*

Assyria's Successor: Egypt or Babylon? (609–606)

As he had in previous years, in 609 Pharaoh Necho moved toward the Euphrates to assist the surviving Assyrian forces at Haran. Josiah, who had gladly thrown off Assyrian domination years before, was not now interested in seeing an Egypto-Assyrian alliance, which would impose vassalage upon the small states of Palestine. The Judean king attempted to block Necho's advance through the pass at Megiddo, but Josiah was killed and the Judean forces were routed (II Kings 23:29 says vaguely, if not deceptively: "In his [Josiah's] days Pharaoh Neco king of Egypt went forth to the king of Assyria to the river Euphrates. King Josiah went to meet him; and Pharaoh Necho slew him at Megiddo, when he saw him," whereas II Chron. 35:20–24 speaks more explicitly and accurately of a battle pressed by Josiah from which Necho was unable to dissuade him). A son of Josiah, Shallum = Jehoahaz, was set on the throne for three months by the people but Necho replaced him with a hand-picked vassal, yet another son of Josiah, Eliakim = Jehoiakim, who impressed him as pro-Egyptian and more inclined to rule Judah with a strong hand than was his younger brother. The change of name from an El compound to a Yah compound suggests that pharaoh desired to work with the prevailing Yahwistic religious forces rather than to impose Egyptian forms of worship—as long as the vassal did not attempt to implement Josiah's political and military expansionism!

If the temple sermon of Jeremiah is representative of his preaching in the years between 609 and the Battle of Carchemish in 605, he concentrated on Judah's moral and religious defection from Yahweh, attacked cult as a substitute for change of heart, and preached "about the nations" (36:2) insofar as they represented a false temptation to rebellion or security or insofar as they served as the means of Judah's punishment. As yet, the larger view of the nations which appeared with Nebuchadnezzar's

---

Testament, pp. 62–75, and W. Rudolph, *Jeremia, HZAT,* 1947, pp. 41–43). This, however, need not exclude the fact that knowledge of the Medes and neo-Babylonians contributed details to the prophet's descriptions, such as the excellent horsemanship of the Medes.

reign had not emerged in the prophet's thought. Throughout these years the prophet remained convinced that the fulcrum of power in the ancient Near East would continue to be Mesopotamia and not Egypt. Although this was his message he had yet to savor its vindication before he announced the full plan of Yahweh for the nations.

It is doubtful whether the oracle against Philistia in chap. 47 belongs, as the superscription suggests, to a time "before Pharaoh smote Gaza," i.e., c. 609–608 b.c., following Herodotus' note that Necho overran Kadytis (Gaza?) after the Battle of Megiddo.[71] The introductory biblical notation is lacking in the LXX. However, the oracle looks for a destruction from the north, not from Egypt and, finally, there is no sufficient reason for transferring the Scythian attack on Ashkelon which Herodotus dated in 626 to the same year as the supposed Egyptian attack on Gaza (609). The threat which the prophet directed against Philistia is perhaps more appropriate to the early years of Nebuchadnezzar's reign. In the years before undisputed neo-Babylonian mastery of Palestine the prophet did not hesitate to criticize Jehoiakim's dependence on Egypt in terms similar to Hosea's condemnation of Hoshea and Isaiah's condemnation of Hezekiah. In this case, however, it is all the more shocking that Judah should rely upon "the men of Memphis and Tahpanhes (who) have broken the crown of your head" (2:16), i.e., have killed Josiah, for what can possibly be gained? The prophet appears to overlook that Jehoiakim had little choice in the matter since he was an Egyptian vassal appointee, but it may well have been that he cooperated so cheerfully with Necho that he came to depend upon Egypt far more than the strict terms of the treaty required. During this period the foe-from-the-north passages were evidently repeated so as to leave no doubt in the minds of his listeners that

[71] This position is argued by A. Malamat, "The Historical Setting of Two Biblical Prophecies on the Nations," *IEJ* 1 (1950), 154–59. In a later discussion of the relevance of the new chronicle for biblical history he notes that the account of the destruction of Ashkelon strikes "a note reminiscent of the biblical prophecies of wrath directed at this city (Jer. 47:5–7; Zeph. 2:4–7)," but he does not indicate any modification of his view of the date of Jeremiah 47 ("A New Record of Nebuchadnezzar's Palestinian Campaigns," *IEJ* 6 [1956], 251–52).

a great power other than Egypt was on the verge of conquest in Palestine.

The battle at Carchemish (see Map 11) in which the neo-Babylonians under Nebuchadnezzar, the crown prince, decisively defeated the Egyptians is prophesied by Jeremiah (46:1–12, probably omitting vs. 10, which is more vengeful and abstract than usual in this prophet). For several years there had been military operations in the upper Euphrates area in which Egypt had been vitally involved, first to bolster the Assyrian regime at Haran, in 610–609, and later to maintain Egyptian suzerainty at least as far as the Euphrates and to extend it beyond to the Balikh or Habor rivers, in 607–606, as opportunity allowed.[72] In 607 Nabopolassar had succeeded in establishing a hold on the western bank of the Euphrates some distance south of Carchemish, which was held by the Egyptians, but the latter retaliated and drove the neo-Babylonian garrison from the fortress. After ineffectual reprisals by Nabopolassar, the Egyptians crossed the Euphrates and moved southward defeating the Babylonians at Quramati in January-February 605.

The major conflict occurred apparently in May-June of the same year, but Jeremiah's forewarning, composed in the form of a dirge after battle, must have been scoffed at by Jehoiakim—and disbelieved even by the prophet's friends. With minor exceptions the Egyptians seemed always to get the better of the neo-Babylonians when the latter had not the help of the Medes, and since 610–609 the Medes had been occupied in extending their empire beyond the Fertile Crescent. News of Egypt's successes in two consecutive years would not dispose Judeans to take the prophet's prediction of Egyptian defeat too seriously. Although the mock dirge by the prophet is largely imaginary, it incorporates sound knowledge of Egyptian operations in northern Mesopotamia. He was generally familiar with the component elements and equipment of the Egyptian army (vss. 3–4) and he knew that Greek mercenaries from Lydia were serving with the pharaoh's forces (vs. 9). He surmised correctly from earlier engagements that the key battle would take place near the Eu-

---

[72] Wiseman, *op. cit.*, pp. 18–23.

phrates during the struggle to control the crossings and the key fortress of Carchemish (vs. 6). The victory achieved by the neo-Babylonians was presumably due to the superb generalship of the crown prince and to the factor of surprise since, after the defeat at Quramati, the Egyptians did not expect another major foray by the enemy within a few months. Most of the Egyptians were annihilated and the fugitives were pursued to Hamath and captured.

Nebuchadnezzar as Yahweh's "Servant" (605–590)

News of the victory over Egypt was a turning point in Jeremiah's work. It was now indisputably proved to the prophet that his earlier expectations were accurate and some of his misgivings as to the validity of his call were relieved. The balance of power in the Fertile Crescent once again settled in Mesopotamia. Egypt was a nuisance and delusion which could be of no real help to Judah. Shortly after Nebuchadnezzar had extended his sway over Syria and Palestine to the very frontier of Egypt at Pelusium, his father died in Babylon and the crown prince hastened home to accept the throne. Possibly the rapid advance of Nebuchadnezzar's forces toward Egypt occasioned the prophetic threat that he would invade and devastate Egypt (46:13–24). It is insufficient objection to the authenticity of the oracle that Nebuchadnezzar did not in fact conquer Egypt. If the wordplay of vs. 17, however, refers, as seems likely, to Pharaoh Hophra,[73] the passage should be placed somewhat later, although still within the lifetime of Jeremiah.

The dramatic collapse of Egyptian power in Asia and the accession of Nebuchadnezzar to the Babylonian throne, all within a few months time in 605, prompted a renewal of the prophet's energy. He was determined to bring the critical situation of Judah to the attention of the rulers and people in so clear a fashion that they could not escape it. The occasion offered itself in the early winter of 605 when a large crowd had gathered in Jerusalem for a public fast. Yet the prophet was not permitted

[73] B. Duhm, *Das Buch Jeremia*, 1901, p. 340; C. H. Cornill, *Das Buch Jeremia*, 1905, pp. 450–52.

entrance to the temple precincts, apparently as a result of his savage criticisms of the temple cult. Undeterred, Jeremiah dictated his oracles to Baruch, who copied them on a scroll which is said to have contained "all the words that I [Yahweh] have spoken to you concerning Jerusalem [reading LXX instead of MT 'Israel'] and Judah and all the nations from the time I spoke to you in the days of Josiah until the present" (36:2). Baruch was instructed to read the scroll to the assembled celebrants. Three times that day the scroll was read aloud: first to the people, then to the court officials, and finally to Jehoiakim. The words in their grim poetic dress must have had a sobering and even frightening effect. Certainly most of the people had previously heard the gist of Jeremiah's message and many had heard at least one of his oracles delivered in person; but to hear the mounting crescendo of condemnation and threat in a single reading must have heightened the impression of doom. The officers who listened to the scroll were tactfully non-committal although generally apprehensive. Jehoiakim was unmoved by the prophetic thunder. In an air of cool contempt, he cut off several columns of the scroll at a time and cast the sections into the brazier before which he sat. The king had little choice unless he planned to reverse his policies, for the scroll contained strong words against him climaxed by the prediction that his body would not be buried, as horrible a fate as a Semite could contemplate (22:13–19). Jeremiah was not discouraged but immediately dictated a new and expanded edition to Baruch, doubtless adding fresh words of judgment upon the arrogant king and his wayward subjects (36:32).

The exact contents of the scroll dictated in 605 are unknown, although several plausible reconstructions have been offered.[74]

---

[74] Typical of the reconstructions of the content of Baruch's scroll are those of Rudolph, *op. cit.* (1:4–3:13; 3:19—5:17; 5:21—6:30; 8:4–9, 13–17; 13:1–11, 20–22, 25–27; 14:1—15:3; 23:9–12; 25:15–38; 46:1—49:33 [largely]; perhaps also 9:9–10, 16–21, 24–25; 11:15–16; 13:23–24; 17:1–4; 18:13–17), and Y. Kaufmann, *The History of the Religion of Israel*, VII, 426 (Hebrew) (4—6; 25:3–11a, 13; 46:3–26; 47; and possibly 3; 48:1—49:27). Hyatt, *IB*, V, 787, however, restricts the scroll to portions of chaps. 1–6 (1:4–14, 17; 2:1–37; 3:1–5, 9–25; 4:1–8, 11–22, 27–31; 5:1–17, 20–31; 6:1–30) and possibly 8:4—9:1.

It seems at the minimum to have contained the political, social, and religious indictments of Judah and the threats of a northern invader (most of chaps. 2–6, 8–9), the temple sermon (7:1–15), condemnations of Jehoahaz and Jehoiakim (22:10–19), some of the attacks on the prophets (23:9–40), the vivid account of the Battle of Carchemish (46:2–12 and possibly 46:13–28), and the announcement that Judah was to be given over to Nebuchadnezzar for a time of punishment (the essence but not the exact wording of 25:1–14).

The last-cited passage, which is dated in the same year as the composition of the scroll, has been heavily edited. Its verbose phraseology, punctuated by Deuteronomic expressions, is different in many respects from the simpler text in LXX. It is regrettably useless to attempt a restoration of the original words underlying 25:1–14,[75] for even the Septuagint text cannot be taken without question. Its omission of references to Nebuchadnezzar and Babylon in favor simply of "a family from the north" is not above question, as often assumed,[76] for Jehoiakim's reaction to a reading of the scroll was this amazed question: "Why have you written in it that the king of Babylon will certainly come and destroy this land, and will annihilate from it man and beast?" (36:29). If the prophet had not somewhere in his scroll openly identified Babylon as the invader, the sharp retort of the king is difficult to explain. The suggestion that the original form of 25:1–14 actually concluded the scroll is an attractive one.[77]

On the other hand, the MT references to "all these nations round about" and "these nations shall serve the king of Babylon" appear to reflect an editorial preparation for the foreign oracles which at one time stood in the text at this point (now chaps. 46–51) and are found in the LXX after 13a (13b is omitted entirely). Such a general threat to the nations roundabout seems first to have arisen in Jeremiah's thought some years later when

[75] John Skinner, *op. cit.*, pp. 240–41, makes a valiant effort to find the original of 25:1–14 with the help of the simpler LXX text, but the result is no more than a possibility.

[76] E.g., Skinner, *loc. cit.*; Rudolph, *op. cit.*, p. 136; Hyatt, *IB*, V, 999.

[77] Skinner, *loc. cit.*; Hyatt, *loc. cit.*, suggests that 25:1–14 in its original form was written by D "as a conclusion to what he believed was the scroll of Baruch written at Jeremiah's dictation. . . ."

widespread revolt against Babylon was brewing in the western regions of the empire. Even if such a sentiment is to be admitted in 605, the survey of nations upon whom Nebuchadnezzar will come (25:15–29) and the foreign oracles themselves (46–51) can only in the most limited manner be associated with 605 since the great majority of the countries mentioned received Jeremiah's attention only as neo-Babylonian campaigns and vassal rebellions drew more and more nations into the circle of his interest. *Thus the information that Baruch's scroll contained prophecies "concerning the nations" must have meant principally Babylon and Egypt or, at most, the nations in the sense of a body of witnesses to the sin of Judah* (6:16; 8:13; cf. Amos 3:9).

Jeremiah's counsel had little to do with Jehoiakim's transfer of loyalty from Necho to at least nominal acknowledgment of Nebuchadnezzar as his suzerain. In 604 the Babylonian king spent six months in the west receiving the submission of "all the kings of Hatti" (a term in the Babylonian Chronicles which means all of Syria from the Euphrates to the border of Egypt).[78] This was the occasion for Jehoiakim's submission (II Kings 24:1) and he will have been in the company of the majority of Syro-Palestinian rulers. Yet not all was mild, for Nebuchadnezzar tells of a fierce battle to capture Ashkelon and, in the next year, he had to take extraordinary measures to raise "a powerful army" whose field of action is unfortunately lost in the text. Since, however, Nebuchadnezzar was in Syria the year before and the year after this event, the broken text probably also referred to a Syrian campaign. The events of 603 and 602 taken together may offer the proper context for the threat against Philistia and Phoenicia in chap. 47. The occasion appears to be a revolt of Palestinian cities; Tyre and Sidon, Gaza and Ashkelon are named. It is difficult to conclude whether there is any significance to the forms of the verbs, as though Gaza and Ashkelon are already destroyed while Tyre and Sidon are yet to be destroyed. If so, the two Philistine cities may have been attacked in 603 (we know that Ashkelon was), while the Phoenician cities are the chief target of attack in a campaign in progress in 602 although helped by

[78] Wiseman, *op. cit.*, p. 28.

Philistia. The heading to the oracle is difficult, since except for the brief "concerning the Philistines" it is lacking in LXX; Phoenicia is altogether ignored in it; and the destruction of Gaza is described as in the future when the oracle was given, while in the body of the oracle it seems already to be destroyed. The secondary heading may allude, however, to the major battle which occurred on the Egyptian frontier in 601, possibly at or near Gaza. Admittedly the oracle is as yet not entirely explicable in any historical context, but the events of the Babylonian Chronicles for 603–601 seem to come nearer to providing such an explanation than those of any other period.

In extremely frank words the Chronicles reports that the encounter between Nebuchadnezzar and the Egyptian force resulted in severe losses for both sides. "In open battle they smote the breast (of) each other and inflicted great havoc on each other."[79] Nebuchadnezzar was forced to withdraw to Babylon. This event, reported for the first time in the Babylonian account, puts a new light on Jehoiakim's decision to withhold tribute from Nebuchadnezzar. He was in fact taking a calculated risk which seemed to have a better than even chance of success.[80] If we count three full years of Judean loyalty to Nebuchadnezzar (II Kings 24:1), from the summer of 605 to the summer of 602, the revolt must have fallen in the latter half of 602 or in 601, the latter being the more likely since the biblical notation probably means that he paid tribute for three years (604–602). The surprising strength of the Egyptian army in December of 601 when it stalemated or actually defeated the Babylonians suggests that the pharaoh had been actively seeking to stir up Judean insurrection and that he was able to point with persuasion to the strength of his forces. Apparently only a part of Egypt's army had been annihilated at Carchemish. Nebuchadnezzar was so taken aback that he retired to Babylon where for a year he worked to re-equip his army, especially with chariotry. Presum-

[79] *Ibid.*, pp. 29–30.
[80] J. P. Hyatt, "New Light on Nebuchadnezzar and Judean History," *JBL* 75 (1956), 277–84, and A. Malamat, "A New Record of Nebuchadnezzar's Palestinian Campaigns," *IEJ* 6 (1956), 246–56, both emphasize that at this period Babylon was somewhat weaker and Egypt somewhat stronger than heretofore thought.

ably when Jehoiakim refused payment of tribute in 601 he suffered no immediate reprisals, for Nebuchadnezzar was more concerned to strike at the root of rebellion and chose to face Egypt rather than the rebellious vassal kingdom.

When action was taken against Judah it was of a peculiar kind, for "Yahweh sent against him [Jehoiakim] Chaldean raiders, Aramean raiders, Moabite raiders, and Ammonite raiders" (II Kings 24:2). In pre-exilic usage the $g^e d\bar{u}d\hat{\imath}m$ are marauding bands who strike and run, rather than regular troops who wage sustained campaigns. Nebuchadnezzar, short on troops and in haste to regroup his reeling army in Babylon, arranged for a small detachment of his forces to lead vassal units from nations round about Judah. Of course the vassals were under some duress but some of them at least welcomed the opportunity to recoup territory in trans-Jordan which Josiah had recovered and which had remained in whole or in part within the rule of Jehoiakim.[81] Instead of a concerted military action, these separate bands probably struck periodically in order to harass Egyptian-Judean communications and in general to keep Jehoiakim sufficiently on the defensive so that he could not think too seriously of further insurrection.

The castigation of Ammon in 49:1–6 seems to belong to this period. Territory recovered by Josiah and retained by Jehoiakim has been transferred to Ammon (it is referred to under the name of the Hebrew tribe Gad, which had first settled in the area of trans-Jordan roughly between the northern end of the Dead Sea and the Wadi Jabbok). While garbed in the nationalistic language of the old foreign oracles, the real point of the passage is the prophet's condemnation of an attempt by one nation to take advantage of its neighbor. To be sure, Babylon was administering punishment in the name of Yahweh against Jerusalem, but the motives of the assisting vassals were unworthy ones in that they

[81] Although we do not know whether Necho was able to hold or interested in holding the trans-Jordan regions within the vassal kingdom of Judah, H. L. Ginsberg is right in stressing that a strong Jehoiakim would threaten the trans-Jordanian states and so they aligned with Babylon against Judah ("Judah and the Transjordan States from 734 to 582," *Alexander Marx Jubilee Volume*, 1950, pp. 363–65).

sought to gain territory as a result of their compliance with Nebuchadnezzar.

His forces greatly strengthened, Nebuchadnezzar returned to Syria late in 599 and from headquarters at or near Hamath decided to pacify the Arab tribes which had been harassing the flank of Syria and Palestine. Detachments of Babylonian troops went forth and "scouring the desert they took much plunder from the Arabs, their possessions, animals and gods." The oracle "concerning Kedar and the unwalled kingdoms[82] which Nebuchadnezzar king of Babylon smote" (49:28–33) suits this campaign perfectly for it speaks of enormous booty and, although Nebuchadnezzar does not name the tribe he attacked, it was precisely Kedar which Ashurbanipal had also struck at because of its support for his brother in 641–638. This same tribe would have reason for continued agitation against Babylon since it was to the advantage of the nomads to undermine strong central authority in the Crescent and thus open up fruitful areas for occupation or periodic razzias.

When it seemed that Nebuchadnezzar had all but forgotten about Jehoiakim's insubordination, he suddenly struck against Jerusalem. The king and his army left Babylon in December of 598 and completed the capture of Jerusalem by mid-March of 597, which suggests that Judah was the first, if not the sole, target of the campaign.[83] The capture and deportation of the Jewish king and his replacement by a king of the Babylonian's choice is reported but no names are given. Apparently the Babylonian Chronicles confirm the biblical report that Jehoiakim died before the enemy reached the city and that his son served only three months before his capture (II Kings 24:8–12). Josephus reports Jehoiakim's death at the hands of the Chaldeans in a campaign in the year previous (*Ant.* X. vi. 3) and this view is foreshadowed in II Chronicles 36:6. Yet it is likely that Josephus

[82] The view that *ḥātsôr* in this passage is not a place name but a collective for *hᵃtsērîm,* the unwalled tent villages of the nomads, is borne out by the connection of Kedar and *hᵃtsērîm* in Isaiah 42:11 (Rudolph, *op. cit.,* pp. 253–54, and Hyatt, *IB,* V, 1122).

[83] Wiseman, *op. cit.,* p. 33.

is here merely fabricating his account on the basis of Jeremiah's prophecy that Jehoiakim would not be given decent burial. Although Jeremiah may have been wrong in this detail of his prediction, the general sense of his warning was entirely correct: Jehoiakim's pro-Egyptian policy came to a disastrous end. In fact, it is not beyond possibility that the king's life was taken in a court uprising and that Jeremiah's prophecy of the dishonorable treatment of his corpse did come true.[84] The "heavy tribute" received included many of the valuable temple vessels and was doubtless an imposition greatly in excess of the normal amount of tribute which Jehoiakim had presumably withheld for four years (601–598).

The Bible reports the deportation of approximately ten thousand captives, including the deposed king, his family and courtiers, officials, craftsmen, soldiers, and priests (II Kings 24:12, 14–16; Jer. 52:28).[85] The absence of comment on the deportation in the Babylonian Chronicles is easily explained by the chiefly military interest of the record. As successor to Assyrian realms, Nebuchadnezzar used their policies as occasion arose, although seldom with the thoroughness typical of the greatest Assyrian kings. In this instance he appears to have regarded Judah as the key to Egypt. He wished so to sap Judean leadership that it would not be able to respond to Egyptian overtures. Secondarily, he benefited by the influx of military, political, and technological skills to Babylon, many of which found ready use in his government. The new king, Mattaniah=Zedekiah, was faced with a demoralized court peopled largely by leaders who were of dis-

---

[84] *Ibid.*, p. 35, holds open the possibility, on the basis of Josephus and II Chronicles 36:6, that "his [Jehoiakim's] fate might be linked with some initial Babylonian approach to the city" (also Jer. 22:24–30; cf. II Kings 24:6–7), and in that case Jehoiakim may after all have died an unnatural death.

[85] The discrepancy in II Kings 24 between 10,000 captives in vs. 14 and 8,000 in vs. 16 may be explained by the theory that the former number includes the court officials and priests while the latter includes only the army and craftsmen. The 3,023 captives of Jeremiah 52:28 probably represent only males, whereas the round figures of II Kings 24 include the total number of persons. Although coming to no startling new conclusions about the number of deportees, a thorough review of the evidence and various solutions is given by E. Janssen, *Juda in der Exilszeit*, pp. 25–39.

tinctly inferior gifts and who tended to think of themselves as superior to the Judeans carried away to Babylon. A notable exception was the family of Shaphan, or at least some of its members, which was spared deportation for some special purpose, perhaps because the Babylonian king wished them to serve as a balancing and restraining influence against the agitators for revolt.

Once again, as at the time of the Battle of Carchemish, to the complete consternation of the pro-Egyptian Judeans the Babylonians had shown surprising strength at the critical moment following apparent weakness and, on the contrary, the seemingly powerful Egyptians had not delivered their promised help, whether through design or default. Just such unexpected vindications of Babylonian power must have deepened in Jeremiah the conviction that Nebuchadnezzar was the special agent of Yahweh, for when the prophet next spoke to rulers he presented the world dominion of Babylon as the absolute and unyielding will of God for the present generation.

In 596–595 Nebuchadnezzar was occupied in warfare along the Tigris River, apparently with the king of Elam.[86] The strongly worded prophecy against Elam in Jeremiah 49:34–39 may belong to this period and will have been particularly relevant if some of the exiles of 597 were known to be banking on Elamite aid in overthrowing Babylon. In the following year of Nebuchadnezzar's reign (595–594) a serious army uprising in Babylon had to be crushed with heavy loss of life among the rebels, and at least one high officer was executed. This did not interfere, however, with the monarch's collection of tribute in Syria. In 596 and 594 respectively Nebuchadnezzar appears to have been able to collect the tribute through local authorities in Syria without taking a large army with him. For 594–593, however, the Babylonian Chronicles concludes, "the king of Akkad [mustered his] troops [. . . .] and marched [to the] Hatti-land."

Between the Babylonian army revolt and the last-mentioned campaign something occurred to jeopardize Nebuchadnezzar's position in the west or at least to justify the show of force which

---

[86] Wiseman, *op. cit.*, p. 36.

he called up to accompany him. From Jeremiah's book we know that between the army revolt and the last campaign a confederation of Palestinian states seriously plotted a revolt against Nebuchadnezzar (chap. 27). The representatives of the Phoenician cities Tyre and Sidon and of the trans-Jordan states of Edom, Moab, and Ammon gathered at Jerusalem, probably not because Judah led the revolt but either because of the city's convenient location or because Judah was not fully committed and the other coalition members wished to apply extra pressure on Zedekiah. As Isaiah had addressed himself to similar embassies from Egypt, Jeremiah seized the opportunity to oppose the plan and to strengthen Zedekiah's uncertain hand.

From Judean and Babylonian sources we conclude that Jehoiachin was regarded by both parties as the legitimate king of Judah,[87] *whereas Zedekiah was a temporary appointee looking after the king's affairs in his absence.* Some Judeans may have planned it otherwise, but both in character and by virtue of his ambiguous position Zedekiah was ill fitted to win any large allegiance, even among those who wished to rebel against Babylon. The new "king's" position was certainly an awkward one for if he succeeded in pacifying Judah altogether he stood to be dismissed in order to make way for Jehoiachin's restoration, whereas if he headed or even permitted revolt he might soon follow in his predecessor's train. This dilemma helps to account for the vacillating appearance which Zedekiah gives.[88] It also reflects on the administrative judgment of the neo-Babylonians. The Assyrians

---

[87] W. F. Albright, "The Seal of Eliakim and the Last Pre-exilic History of Judah," *JBL* 51 (1932), 77–106, showed convincingly that according to the majority of Judeans and in the view of the Babylonian authorities Jehoiachin, even in exile, was the legitimate king of Judah and Zedekiah was merely his regent or representative. Even after 597 crown land in Judah continued to be administered in the name of Jehoiachin. Tablets listing rations for "Jehoiachin king of Judah" and his five sons have been found in Babylon (*ANET*, p. 308). Nevertheless, Zedekiah had a following and sought to establish his own claims to the throne (cf. A. Malamat, "Jeremiah and the Last Two Kings of Judah," *PEQ* 83 [1951], 81–87).

[88] Malamat, "Jeremiah and the Last Two Kings of Judah," p. 87, briefly notes that the supposed fickleness and cowardliness of Zedekiah may be a mistaken interpretation, his caution being explicable since he had to pacify his powerful opponents in Judah who favored Jehoiachin and who apparently stood on solid legal ground.

would probably not have left a man in a poorly defined role to watch over a kingdom that had recently revolted and had had its stable leadership uprooted.[89] In the Babylonian defense, however, Zedekiah may have been the only available choice within the Davidic dynasty, which the neo-Babylonians decided to retain on the throne. To interrupt the ancient Davidic succession would only have earned them still further difficulties.

The revolutionary party in Judah was strong, in spite of the large deportations of 597. A new pharaoh, Psamtik II, had just taken the throne in Egypt and immediately continued Necho's Asiatic interests.[90] The Babylonian army was an uncertain factor and the rebels hoped that it would prove an unreliable one. Since it had not appeared in force in Syria since 597, the revolt of a year before raised doubts about its effectiveness. Zedekiah himself had nothing to gain from a revolt, but the assembled embassies were putting him in a difficult position and, with the recent disorders in Babylon, the imperial representative for Judah may not have been on hand to remind Zedekiah of his vassal responsibilities. Jeremiah filled the breach with a powerful symbolic action, similar to Isaiah's enactment of the lot of a war captive. On a public occasion the prophet appeared wearing the wooden yoke bars used for draft animals. He intoned to the embassies: "I [Yahweh] made the earth and man and the animals on the earth in my great strength and with my outstretched arm and I give it to whomever seems right to me. Now I have given all these lands into the hand of Nebuchadnezzar, king of Babylon, my servant, and all beasts of the field I have given him for his service and all the nations" (27:5–6; vs. 7 is perhaps correctly omitted by LXX, although its promise that Nebuchadnezzar's line will dominate the world for three generations accords well with Jeremiah's sense of the long but nevertheless limited do-

---

[89] The ineptness of Nebuchadnezzar's policy of deportation, which decimated the civil and military leadership and removed the property owners, leaving the official posts and the property to be fought over by the survivors, is commented on by Malamat, "The Last Wars of the Kingdom of Judah," *JNES* 9 (1950), 224.

[90] For the Asiatic campaign of Psamtik II see esp. J. Yoyotte, "Sur le Voyage Asiatique de Psammétique II," *VT* 1 (1951), 140–44, and additional brief notes by S. Sauneron and J. Yoyotte, "Sur la politique Palestinienne des rois Saïtes," *VT* 2 (1952), 135–36; also Kienitz, *op. cit.,* pp. 25–27.

minion of Babylon). The prophet admonishes that those who submit to "the yoke of the king of Babylon" will live peacefully but those who resist Nebuchadnezzar resist God himself and will be deported to perish away from their lands.

It is indeed a far-reaching conception at which Jeremiah has arrived. It springs, not from his conception of the covenant relations with Israel, but from his doctrine of creation. The mighty Creator wills the world rule of Babylon not merely to punish his apostate covenant people but to chastise the earth for its sins. Yet this chastisement is to be achieved in a more orderly and humane manner than that administered by Assyria—that is, if the subject peoples will realize that it is God's will for them "to serve" as faithful vassals of Nebuchadnezzar. The warnings against foreign alliances with Egypt and Assyria are not paralleled by warnings against vassal alliances with Babylon. *The ad hoc punishments of Assyria are now to be followed by an ordered world dominion which through vassal service will educate the nations and purge them of their arrogance and wantonness.* Nebuchadnezzar is even described by Yahweh as "my servant," a most unexpected term of intimacy if not of actual endearment. *Pax Babylonia is the plan of Yahweh.* To be sure, Nebuchadnezzar is not treated as an absolute novelty, for Jeremiah is aware that Yahweh has been in the habit of appointing world rulers to exercise world dominion, and apparently the prophet has former Assyrian and perhaps even Median rulers in mind. Nebuchadnezzar now stands in a special category; for a stated time his rule is to be absolute.

Isaiah, who most closely approaches this conception, regarded the various incursions of the Assyrians as part of the plan of Yahweh and stressed the futility of rebellion until God's hour of deliverance had arrived. He had not, however, called an Assyrian ruler "Yahweh's servant"; indeed, with the stress Isaiah gave to the willfulness and *hybris* of the Assyrian monarchs, it is doubtful that he would have found the title at all acceptable. Jeremiah came very close to an equation of Nebuchadnezzar's imperial administration and the educative punishment of Yahweh. In slaying the Jewish prophets who had incited revolt in Babylon, Nebuchadnezzar was carrying out Yahweh's will (29:

21–23). Such an ideology was fundamentally acceptable to Zedekiah. He was pleased to receive Jeremiah's encouragement to stand against the popular prophets who were insisting that the revolt would be successful (27:12–15). Furthermore, Jeremiah rebukes the priests for their facile belief that the temple appointments of metal which had been taken to Babylon would soon be returned. He suggests mockingly that they use their energies to dissuade Yahweh from sending the rest of the temple objects to Babylon, for the transfer of all the cult equipment to Babylon as war booty or tribute was in accord with Yahweh's plan and any contrary expectations were idle (27:16–22). To precisely this period in the prophet's life we should assign the powerfully reiterative passage in which Nebuchadnezzar is pictured as Yahweh's war club against the nations (51:20–23):

> You are my war club and battle weapon:
> > With you I shatter nations;
> > With you I shatter kingdoms;
> > With you I shatter horse and rider;
> > With you I shatter chariot and charioteer;
> > With you I shatter man and woman;
> > With you I shatter old and young;
> > With you I shatter young man and maiden;
> > With you I shatter shepherd and flock;
> > With you I shatter farmer and team;
> > With you I shatter governors and prefects.

As interpreter of Yahweh's will, Jeremiah felt a special obligation to rebut the specious prophecies of weal being bruited about by men like Hananiah, a Gibeonite prophet, who even went out of his way to accost Jeremiah and to rebuke and discredit him in public. While the prophet was wearing his wooden yoke in the temple court, Hananiah declared to his face: "I [Yahweh] have broken the yoke of the king of Babylon. Within two years I will return to this place all the appointments of Yahweh's house, which Nebuchadnezzar king of Babylon took from this place and transported to Babylon. I will bring back to this place Jeconiah the son of Jehoiakim, king of Judah [not Zedekiah!] and all the exiles from Judah who went to Babylon, says

Yahweh, for I will break the yoke of the king of Babylon" (28: 2–4). Formally, especially in the direct quotation of the words of Yahweh, this oracle was of one piece with Jeremiah's words. But the message was exactly antithetic: the contemplated revolt will be entirely successful and the legitimate Judean king, the Babylonian captives, and the temple equipment will be returned to Jerusalem within two years.

So sudden and emphatic was the frontal attack by Hananiah that Jeremiah was momentarily at a loss to reply and with unguarded frankness conceded that he should greatly prefer to agree with his colleague. Unfortunately he was obliged to disagree and with that he lectured Hananiah briefly on the criterion of true prophecy: "The prophets who came before me and you, prophesied war, famine, and plague to many lands and concerning great kingdoms. The prophet who will prophesy peace will be known to be truly from Yahweh when that thing transpires." Jeremiah makes two basic points: former prophets were largely prophets of doom[91] and prophets of peace must be tested by events. He presumably did not deny that prophets of doom will also be vindicated or discredited by the course of events, but the special need for testing prophecies of peace is that they are so much more easily delivered and are so readily received that they must be submitted to searching criticism. Inasmuch as conditions in Judah have not changed greatly since the time of the former prophets—and if at all, for the worse—those who have unlimited words of prosperity and victory should search both themselves and the times to see what it is that justifies this sudden change from doom to felicity. Yet this confrontation did not resolve the issue, either for the prophets or for the people and priests who looked on. *For this was the issue at stake: precisely what will forthcoming events reveal, a return from exile within two years*

[91] It is an altogether unjustified use of this intentionally extreme statement of Jeremiah to maintain that all hopeful passages in earlier prophets are late. The genuine hopeful passages of Hosea and Isaiah accord with Jeremiah's assertion for (1) they are only a small part of the prophetic preaching in each case; and (2) they always stand in conjunction with or beyond judgment and never—even Isaiah's "promise" of 701—as completely free and unconditional fulfillments of national hope in the manner preached by Hananiah.

or within seventy, if ever at all for those Jews who had come to accept life in Babylon?

Suddenly Hananiah decided on a symbolic action of his own —at the expense of Jeremiah. He seized the yoke bars from Jeremiah's neck and broke them as he solemnly declared over the split pieces: "Thus says Yahweh, just so will I shatter the yoke of Nebuchadnezzar king of Babylon from the neck of all nations within two years." So two could play the game of prophetic symbol-making. Jeremiah was taken aback. He could not at once conceive of a reply for such a perverse but nonetheless dramatically impressive distortion of his symbolic action. It would do no good merely to argue. Jeremiah needed time to ponder, so he withdrew.

Subsequently Jeremiah returned beneath a heavy load of *iron* yoke bars and, while amazed stares were fixed upon him, he declared: "You have broken wooden bars, but I will replace them with bars of iron. For this says Yahweh of hosts, the God of Israel: I have put upon the neck of all these nations an iron yoke of servitude to Nebuchadnezzar king of Babylon and they shall serve him. . . ." Jeremiah then charged Hananiah with false claims to be a prophet and pronounced Yahweh's judicial decree over him: "I will remove you from the earth. This year you shall die." Within a matter of months Hananiah was dead. There is no good reason to deny that Jeremiah spoke substantially these words (although "this year" may mean "soon" rather than a precise period of time) or to question the death of Hananiah as reported.[92] Certainly the story is told to vindicate Jeremiah and could hardly have accomplished its purpose if it were a false tale, especially inasmuch as it was one for which there was no special need since with the iron yoke Jeremiah had effectively established his point.[93]

[92] Cf. Rudolph, *op. cit.,* p. 153, and G. Widengren, *Literary and Psychological Aspects of the Hebrew Prophets,* 1948, p. 112.

[93] F. Giesebrecht, *Die Berufsbegabung der alttestamentlichen Propheten,* pp. 1–3, chose the incident of Hananiah's death as the starting point for his extended critique of A. Kuenen, *The Prophets and Prophecy in Israel,* 1877. When allowance is made for Giesebrecht's emotional reaction against Kuenen's rationalism, his argument is seen to be historically and psychologically sound.

At approximately the same time Zedekiah had occasion to send a letter to his Babylonian overlord. It is plausibly suggested that the purpose of the letter was to plead his non-participation in the western revolt and thus to free himself of charges of treason and to avert a campaign of reprisal against Judah.[94] This mission to Nebuchadnezzar in Babylon will have preceded the Syrian campaign of 594–593, in which a warning was served to all those states which had considered rebellion; some may actually have been attacked for carrying through their intention of revolt. It was doubtless this mission, and perhaps another slightly later in the year by the king in person, that averted military action against Judah.

Jeremiah took the opportunity to send a written message of his own which he entrusted to one of the messengers from the pro-Jeremianic family of Shaphan, in this case Elasah, and also to Gemariah son of Hilkiah. The letter was intended for the exilic community and was apparently circulated among the responsible councils of elders in the several Jewish communities in Babylonia. Whether the letter was approved by Zedekiah and the Babylonian representative at the Jerusalem court cannot be easily judged. Certainly its chief immediate counsel was congenial to both Zedekiah and the Babylonian authorities for both favored the political quietism which it inculcated, but if its promises of a later return to Palestine are genuine—although edited with non-Jeremian terminology in spots—it would not have been so favorably received by the Babylonians. For that reason it was probably carried secretly by the messengers to Babylon.

Jeremiah urged upon the exiles a policy of political compliance and of cultural accommodation. They were to participate wholeheartedly in Babylonian life, to acquire property, to intermarry, and in their prayers to remember the welfare of their new homeland. Negatively, they were to disregard the prophets who, like Hananiah in Jerusalem, were concocters of "dreams" and "lies," i.e., of the idea of an imminent restoration to Palestine. Obviously the infection of impending revolt was felt in Babylon, doubtless abetted materially by the army revolt, the reports of a new

[94] P. Volz, *Der Prophet Jeremia, Kommentar zum Alten Testament,* 1922, p. 267.

Asiatic-oriented pharaoh, and rumors of a widespread revolt in Syria and Palestine. Jeremiah identified two of the Jewish prophets, Ahab ben Kolaiah and Zedekiah ben Maaseiah (29: 21–23), whom he may have known in Jerusalem before 597 and of whose agitation he had recently learned either through letters or through verbal reports of Zedekiah's couriers. The prophet predicts that they will be burned to death by Nebuchadnezzar, possibly a fate reserved for political prisoners (cf. similar punishments in Dan. 3:6; II Macc. 7:3 ff.).[95] It did not matter that these prophets spoke in the name of Yahweh; they were opposing the immutable iron yoke of vassalage to Nebuchadnezzar and therefore they were utterly deluded as to the word of Yahweh. Judging by his so-called "confessions," Jeremiah blanched inwardly at the possibility that his inspiration was false, but in his public utterances there was no sign of uncertainty.

Although it was not the time to lay his major emphasis on the fact, Jeremiah nevertheless made it clear that Nebuchadnezzar's title to world dominion was limited. As Babylon's period of world rule he gives a span of seventy years (29:10). The number cannot be easily explained as a *vaticinium ex eventu*, if only because interpreters have never been able to agree as to which period he had in mind.[96] The seventy years do not correspond precisely to any period of historical importance in the late seventh and sixth centuries. *Certainly it must be stressed that the seventy years refer primarily to the time of Babylonian world dominion*

---

[95] The suggestion of E. Jenni, *Die politischen Voraussagen der Propheten*, p. 28, that the manner of death is not intended literally but is, instead, the result of a play on the similarity in sound between the name of Ahab's father Kolaiah-*Qolayah* (vs. 21) and the verb *qālām*, "he roasted them" (vs. 22), is not convincing. If this were the case, we should expect the proper name *Qolayah* to appear with Ahab in vs. 22 side by side with *qālām*.

[96] From the fall of Nineveh to the capture of Babylon by Cyrus was seventy-four years; from the Battle of Carchemish to the capture of Babylon, sixty-six years; from the deportation of Jehoiachin to the capture of Babylon, fifty-eight years; from the deportation of Zedekiah to the capture of Babylon, forty-seven years. The one exact seventy-year period, from the deportation of Zedekiah in 586 to the completion of the second temple in 516 (argued by C. F. Whitley, "The Term Seventy Years Captivity," *VT* 4 [1954], 60–72), founders on the clear claim of the text that the number refers not to Judean captivity but to Babylonian sovereignty (cf. A. Orr, "The Seventy Years of Babylon," *VT* 6 [1956], 304–6).

and not to the time of exile, as is often carelessly supposed. As an estimate of Babylon's domination of the ancient Near East it was a remarkably accurate figure, for from the Battle of Carchemish (605) to the fall of Babylon to Cyrus (539) was sixty-six years.[97] Yet, if a prophecy after the event, it is incorrect by four years, and if we conjecture that the addition was supplied late in the exile, then we must ask why the editor chose precisely the number of seventy. Any reason that we might assign to the unknown editor would appear to be as valid for the prophet himself. The point of Jeremiah's "prediction" was to specify a long period of time, some suggest the ideal life span (Ps. 90:10), and he was probably influenced by the notion of a mysterious world period with faint mythological overtones.[98] At any rate, a text in which Esarhaddon says that Sennacherib's destruction of Babylon was to last seventy years, according to Marduk's decree, seems sufficient evidence of the schematic religio-mythological character of the number and removes all necessity for eliminating it from the words of Jeremiah.[99]

Such a view of the exilic community was possible only because Jeremiah had severed Yahwism from the cult so completely that a group of Judeans could live in satisfactory relation with Yahweh while in a foreign land. *The important thing is not the place of residence but the attitude of the Judeans toward the community where they live and toward Yahweh himself. Toward the one there must be open acceptance (29:7) and toward the other there must be sincere intercourse typified in unrestricted prayer (29:12–13).* If these conditions are fulfilled, at the end

[97] This was already seen by Duhm, *op. cit.,* p. 230, and by Volz, *op. cit.,* p. 269; cf. also Orr, *op. cit.,* pp. 305–6, who argues, however, against Duhm and Whitley that Jeremiah 29:10 is original and that Zechariah 1:12 and 7:3 are based on it.

[98] See especially A. Bentzen, *Daniel,* 1937, p. 9, and 2nd ed., 1952, p. 29.

[99] The text cited by D. Luckenbill, *AJSL* 41 (1924–25), 166–67, has been recently commented on by E. Vogt, *Biblica* 38 (1957), 236, and by R. Borger, *JNES* 18 (1959), 74. All are agreed that the Assyrian text greatly strengthens the presumption of the authenticity of a seventy-year prophecy in Jeremiah. The objection of Volz, *op. cit.,* pp. 273–74, that Jeremiah expected a much earlier return because he excluded Shemaiah the false prophet from benefiting in it (29:32) is effectively rebutted by Rudolph, *op. cit.,* p. 168, who counters that the exclusion prophesied in vs. 32 refers not to Shemaiah but to his descendants.

of the Babylonian world dominion Yahweh will bring his people
back to their land, for "I know the thoughts I have for you, says
Yahweh, thoughts of peace and not of evil, to give you a future
[*'aḥᵃrîth*] and a hope [*tiqwāh*]." The same expression, in a
slightly different form, occurs in the oracles of hope which seem
to stem from the period of Gedaliah's rule after 587 B.C.: "there
is hope for your future" (31:17). The sense of the phrase as
"happy issue" is conveyed in its proverbial use (Prov. 23:18;
24:14, 20). There is no reason to think that Jeremiah here be-
trays his cultless spirituality. The return from exile is not represented as a return to the cult but rather as an extension of the
practice of prayer and of a people's natural love for their homeland with all of its ancient associations. *Thus, while Jeremiah's
piety was thoroughly "de-cultized" it was not totally "de-nation-
alized" in the ethnic and topographical senses.* Yahweh's people
could be perfectly at home in Babylon but they would be hap-
piest in their own land where the free life of prayer would replace the confining and deceptive cult.

After some months a letter was received from Shemaiah of
Nehelam, who claimed authority over the appointment of temple
personnel in Jerusalem, presumably with the approval of the
Babylonians. He wrote to Zephaniah ben Maaseiah, a priest currently "officiating over the temple," who had replaced Jehoiada,
who had presumably followed Pashhur ben Immer in turn
(20:1). Shemaiah rebuked Zephaniah for failing to suppress
Jeremiah, that "madman," if necessary by public punishment. It
is obvious that the epithet does not concern the prophet's ecstatic
inspiration but rather the content of Jeremiah's program for the
exiles. For the Judeans to adapt themselves to an indefinite future in Babylonia can only be described by a superpatriot as sheer
madness! Zephaniah read the letter to Jeremiah, probably in an
attempt to intimidate the prophet or, as Jeremiah had done to
Hananiah, to pronounce an effective curse upon him. Jeremiah
did not flinch but simply sent a reply to Shemaiah assuring him
that none of his descendants would live "to behold the good that
I will perform for my people" (29:32).

In this same year Jeremiah is represented as sending a scroll
to Babylon with words of future judgment upon the world em-

pire (51:59–64). The account thereof is intended as a description of the Sitz im Leben of the Babylon oracles in chaps. 50–51. Yet it is noticeable that 60b, which specifies the oracles of chaps. 50–51 as the contents of the scroll, is only loosely attached to the remainder of the passage,[100] and, of course, nearly all of the oracles of the preceding two chapters are indictments of Babylon written in a style more nearly like that of Deutero-Isaiah than that of Jeremiah. Yet the story must be judged by itself. The scroll is to be read by the courier Seraiah, apparently brother of Baruch (32:12), who accompanied Zedekiah to Babylon. An actual visit to Babylon by the king to clear his loyalty will not have been improbable.[101] The real difficulty is in the command to read the book at Babylon, to tie a stone to it, and to throw it into the Euphrates with the explanation, "So shall Babel sink, never to rise, because of the evil that I am bringing upon her."

Once we realize that this is not a piece of sympathetic magic but a prophetic symbolic action that had to be witnessed by someone to have any meaning, the problem of the audience becomes acute. For whom will a judgment upon Babylon in the far future have possessed any present meaning? The reading of the scroll to the community of exiled Judeans will have had the effect only of inflaming their disposition to revolt or to evade their obligation to build in the present rather than to dote on the past and to plot for the future. Having been at pains to dampen such sentiments in his letter to the exiles, the prophet will scarcely have sent them in the same year a scroll announcing Babylon's eventual total destruction. For Zedekiah the reading and casting of the scroll in the Euphrates will have had little point when the same thing could have been done in Judah and, most of all, he had not to be convinced of Babylon's final judgment since the effect of such an argument might well have been, as with the exiles, to encourage present defection from Babylon in an attempt to speed up Yahweh's timetable.

[100] Rudolph, *op. cit.*, pp. 275–77.

[101] In 672 B.C. Esarhaddon had summoned vassal kings from all parts of the empire to swear their loyalty in person to the crown prince Ashurbanipal (D. J. Wiseman, *Iraq* 20 [1958]). In this instance Zedekiah may actually have welcomed the opportunity to strengthen his position in Jerusalem by a fresh commission from Nebuchadnezzar.

Only if we can think of the scroll as addressed to Nebuchadnezzar can a satisfactory Sitz im Leben be given to the scroll. The purpose of such a frontal approach to the Babylonian king will have been to urge restraint upon him as the current world ruler. His days are numbered and so he must show himself a responsible servant of Yahweh by restraint and good sense in his treatment of vassals such as Zedekiah. That such frank words might have provoked the opposite reaction will not have deterred Jeremiah, who was not overly concerned about the psychological effects of his remarks. That the scroll was intended for Nebuchadnezzar is further suggested by the fact that the messenger who carried it was with Zedekiah and will have gone directly into the audience of the royal court. If this is the correct reconstruction of an admittedly somewhat baffling passage, Jeremiah carried his interpretation of the Babylonian king as Yahweh's "servant" to the extent of addressing him personally and taking to him a word from Yahweh just as he took messages to Judah and to other Babylonian vassals.

To the year of the contemplated revolt probably belong the portions of Jeremiah 48 which are original with the prophet. This threat against Moab shares a common body of tradition with Isaiah 15–16. Some of the poetic figures are altogether worthy of Jeremiah (e.g., vss. 11, 37b), but it is difficult to separate traditional sources from the prophet's contribution and from later amplifications. The purpose of the oracle as arranged by Jeremiah must have been to warn Moab against participation in an anti-Babylonian plot, and the spectacle of the ruin of Moab pictured by the ancient taunt song was suitable to this purpose. A strong argument for the pre-exilic origin of most, if not all, of the oracle is the fact that its attacks are almost exclusively political rather than religious. When Chemosh is derided it is chiefly in his role as representative and protector of his people, god and people being considered a unity (e.g., 48:7, 13, 46). An anti-idolatry animus, usual after the exile, is nowhere apparent in the oracle.[102]

[102] In an unpublished paper S. Talmon argues that the references to Chemosh in vss. 7b and 13 are late, the former being based on the Ammon oracle, in which Milcom is primary (Jer. 49:3). These verses belong to the

The Final Revolt and Aftermath (589–570)

The final revolt, siege, and capture of Jerusalem are documented in the book of Jeremiah by a series of unusually detailed narratives. They are particularly illuminative of the relations among king, officials, and prophet in the closing years of Judean independence. Unfortunately the Babylonian Chronicles are broken so that we have no information from them for the years 594–593 to 557–556. There are valuable historical data, however, in the Lachish Ostraca, which show the conditions in Judah toward the beginning of the revolt, c. 589–588.

The immediate causes and circumstances of the final revolt are hidden behind the one biblical sentence "And Zedekiah rebelled against the king of Babylon" (II Kings 24:20b). To this the Chronicler adds only the detail: "He also rebelled against King Nebuchadnezzar, who had made him swear by God" (II Chron. 36:13), indicating, as we should have guessed anyway and as Ezekiel tells us (17:13–15), that Zedekiah broke his vassal oath to Babylon. The pro-Egyptian and anti-Babylonian sentiment evidenced in the agitation for revolt in 594–593 must have grown stronger as the officials in Jerusalem saw an opportunity to cut all ties with Babylon. Doubtless they thought of this as a means of securing their official positions at the expense of the Judean leaders exiled to Babylon, who still claimed and hoped to return to their old posts. As long as Nebuchadnezzar controlled Judah there was always the possibility that some or all of the legitimate officials would be returned to their positions in Judah. This hope was not entirely baseless, for it is clear that the Babylonians did not treat their deportation of the Judeans with the finality that the Assyrians accorded their deportations.[103] Furthermore, Neb-

---

late stratum of Jeremiah 48:7–16, 25–28, (30), 39–41. The original Chemosh allusions are political, as demonstrated by vs. 46, which is a variant of Numbers 21:29. Whether it is possible to be so certain of the strata remains an open question, but Talmon is certainly correct in his conclusion that "these clauses are not concerned with the cultic or religious phenomenon Chemosh but with the socio-political aspect of the national god whose name is synonymous with the name of the country Moab."

[103] A. Alt, "Die Rolle Samarias bei der Entstehung des Judentums," *KS*, II, 325–29, demonstrates that the Babylonian exile was not a deportation

uchadnezzar himself seems to have recognized the legitimacy of the high office of the deportees, and such interferences in Judean affairs by these deportees as we glimpse now and then (Jer. 29: 24–28) must have been frequent enough to irritate the parvenus in Jerusalem.

Still the decision for revolt was not unanimous. Important officials not only opposed the insurrection but worked to undermine it. The assistance given Jeremiah by government leaders, particularly by members of the house of Shaphan, shows that opposition to the venture was not restricted to the prophet. The Lachish Letters reflect the divided feelings of the court, and the suspicions and rumors evidenced in this military correspondence indicate that certain officers were extremely doubtful about the revolt and even balked at carrying out orders.[104] Nebuchadnezzar's forces advanced from the coastal plain and laid siege to Lachish and Azekah on the western border of Judah. Letters from the Jerusalem court were sent to the army commander defending the western approaches to the capital, and en route they passed through an army post headed by a certain Hoshaiah, whose own correspondence with his superior at Lachish has been in part preserved on potsherds.[105] The commander at Lachish had received a letter from Zedekiah and also letters from "the princes," copies of which had been forwarded to Hoshaiah (apparently he was not permitted to read the originals when they

in the technical sense of the old Assyrian system but was instead political internment outside the home country in regions close to the central Babylonian regime. It is clear that the Jewish deportees were not settled in a region whose own upper class had been deported but were placed on old deserted sites (note occurrence of names compounded with *tel*—Ezra 2:59 = Neh. 7:61; Ezek. 3:15). It is also clear that no foreign aristocracy was established in Judah to fill the void, and such intrusions as occurred were from the neighboring province of Samaria and from immediate neighbors such as Ammon and Edom.

[104] This observation is not identical with the unfounded theory that the Lachish Letters were assembled in the military archives as evidence in a court-martial case against Hoshaiah, the writer of the letters.

[105] The editio princeps was by H. Torczyner, ed., *The Lachish Letters*, and, in revised form, *The Lachish Ostraca, Letters of the Time of Jeremiah*, 1940 (Hebrew). W. F. Albright's translation in *ANET*, p. 321, takes advantage of contributions by several scholars to a sounder reading of the sometimes difficult text than Torczyner was able to achieve alone in his first edition, although he accepted some new readings in his second edition.

passed through his post). Concerning these letters Hoshaiah re-
plies to the Lachish commander, "Behold the words of the
pr[inces] are not good, (but) to weaken our hands [and to
sla]cken the hands of the *m*[*en*] *who are informed about them*"
(Ostracon VI, *ANET,* p. 322). Hoshaiah advises his superior to
write to the princes as follows: "Why do ye thus [*even*] in Jerusalem? Behold unto the kings and unto [*his house*] are ye doing
this thing!"

It is evident that the king's letter and the letters from the
princes were at odds. Zedekiah, acquiescing in the revolt, apparently wrote words of encouragement to boost the morale of
the defenders of Lachish. The princes have written in such a way
as to discourage resistance, "to weaken our hands." Virtually the
same idiom is used by the officials who charge Jeremiah with
undermining the national security by urging Jerusalem's inhabitants to desert to the Babylonians (38:4). The suggested indictment, "Why do ye this in Jerusalem?" indicates that there
had been an explicit attempt to undermine the revolt against
Nebuchadnezzar. The pro-Babylonian faction, including the honored family of Shaphan and encouraged by Jeremiah, appealed
to the army to surrender to Nebuchadnezzar, probably on the
theory that better terms could be obtained from the Babylonians
early in the campaign than if they were required to take every
city by force.

Another letter came from Jerusalem, and Hoshaiah, who has
passed it on to Lachish, says of it: "And as for the letter of
Tobiah, servant of the king, which came to Shallum son of
Jaddua through the prophet, saying 'Beware!', thy servant hath
sent it to my lord" (Ostracon III, *ANET,* p. 322). "The
prophet" has sometimes been identified as Jeremiah[106] or Uriah
of Kiriath-jearim (Jer. 26:20–23),[107] but these identifications are

[106] See B. Chapira, "Les Lettres de Lakiš," *Revue des études sémitiques*
3 (1942–45), pp. 105–73.

[107] It was generally recognized from the start that the prophet of Ostracon
III was not Jeremiah, but in his first edition H. Torczyner advanced, and has
subsequently retained, the hypothesis that he was Uriah of Kiriath-jearim
(Jer. 26:20–23) and that the prophet's extradition from Egypt is referred
to in this letter (*op. cit.,* pp. 62–73, 112–13). He has not, however, been
followed in this theory by other scholars, who prefer to leave the matter of
identity open (e.g., R. de Vaux, *RB* 48 [1939], 181–206; S. Birnbaum, *PEQ*

virtually impossible since the letter came from an official of Zedekiah who supported the revolt, and the single word of its content reported ("Beware!") suggests that it was a warning by loyalists concerning action of the princes or concerning disaffection in the army ranks. It is likely, then, that the prophet of the Lachish letter was someone of the same stripe as Hananiah who felt that the revolt was Yahweh's way of delivering his people. It shows that Jeremiah continued to find prophetic opponents who were as willing to agitate politically *for* the revolt as he was *against* it.

On the strength of a reference in Ostracon IV to the probable capitulation of Azekah while Lachish is still holding out, these letters are perhaps to be dated in the summer or fall of 589 and slightly later than the incident recorded in Jeremiah 34:1–7, which occurred while Lachish and Azekah were both still resisting. Although this passage reports that Nebuchadnezzar and his army "were fighting against Jerusalem and all of its cities," the siege of Jerusalem had probably not yet begun. It was usual for an invader to reduce the smaller towns before attacking the capital. Of course a contingent of Babylonian troops may have blockaded Jerusalem and occasionally relayed terms of surrender from the king should Zedekiah change his mind. The prophet's promise of life to Zedekiah was apparently based on the analogy of Jehoiachin who was detained in Babylon in not-too-onerous circumstances (Jer. 34:3–5). Jeremiah's "promise" was doubtless premised on Zedekiah's capitulation.

The siege of Jerusalem began in earnest in January 588 with the concentration of the main body of Babylonian forces against the city. For months the blockade had cut off the food supply, and conditions within the city had deteriorated to the point that slave owners were no longer able to feed their charges. Furthermore, additional defenders for the city were badly needed. A general manumission of slaves would serve the double purpose of adding to the city's defenses and of discharging the owners from responsibility for the slaves' provisions. Together the king and the upper-class men covenanted to free the slaves (Jer. 34:

71 [1939], 20–28, 91–110; W. F. Albright, *BASOR* 82 [1941], 18–24; D. Winton Thomas, *JTS* 40 [1939], 1–15).

8–10). In a ceremony of animal sacrifice the slave owners passed between the halved parts of a calf, thus taking oath and calling upon themselves the fate of the calf should they break the covenant (vss. 18–19).[108] It is not certain that this general manumission was directly related to the command to release a Hebrew slave after six years (Exod. 21:2; Deut. 15:1, 12), for the decree makes no distinction between those who have served six years and those who have not but is based rather on the sweeping proposition "that everyone must release his Hebrew slaves, male and female, so that no one should inslave a Jew, his brother" (34:9).[109] Knowledge of the six-year limit must, however, have stung the consciences of the owners and moved them to an even more generous interpretation in the hope that Yahweh might be persuaded to show them his favor. The fate of the non-Hebrew slaves is not discussed, but probably all foreign domestics were pressed into labor gangs to strengthen the walls, to haul water, etc., until they were among the first to fall from the ravages of famine and disease.

Apparently even before the siege of Jerusalem had begun the chief officer of the Judean army, Coniah son of Elnathan,[110] traveled to Egypt to secure aid from the pharaoh (Ostracon III, *ANET*, p. 322). Zedekiah would not have committed himself to revolt without definite assurances of Egyptian aid and these were all the more certain since it seems that in 591 Jewish auxiliaries had strengthened the army of Psamtik in his campaign against

---

108 The similarity between this covenant ceremony and that by which the north Syrian king Mati'ilu of Bit-Agusi was bound to Ashurnirari V has been widely observed. Of a dismembered ram the treaty text says, "this head is not the head of a ram; it is the head of Mati'ilu. . . . If M. sins against this oath, as the head of this ram was cut off, . . . so will the head of M. be cut off" (cited in Rudolph, *op. cit.*, p. 190). The division of the body in halves is not, however, paralleled in the Assyrian ritual.

109 For a discussion of this incident in relation to the Hebrew laws on the freeing of slaves, see M. David, "The Manumission of Slaves Under Zedekiah," *OS* 5 (1948), 63–79. He does not think that the manumission was intended to cancel debt slavery once and for all but only to be applied to those currently enslaved.

110 The reading of Coniah, son of Elnathan, proposed by de Vaux, *op. cit.*, p. 193, and followed by Albright, *BASOR* 82 (1941), 19, has been accepted by Torczyner in place of his own reading of [Yi] kbaryahu, son of Elnathan, whom he formerly identified with the general named in Jeremiah as Elnathan ben Achbor.

Nubia.[111] Nevertheless a high-level military mission would be able to report on the strength and pattern of the Babylonian attack and the manpower and equipment of the defending army, and to advise as to the nature and timing of Egyptian help. In the spring or summer of 588 Pharaoh Hophra led out a force into Palestine which was aimed at releasing the Babylonian stranglehold on Jerusalem. The withdrawal of the Babylonian army from Jerusalem aroused elation in the city, but its intent was not to retreat to Mesopotamia but rather to meet Hophra's forces.

Jeremiah cautioned Zedekiah against thinking that the lifting of the siege was conclusive, for he insisted that the Babylonians would return: "Do not deceive yourselves, by saying, 'The Chaldeans will certainly stay away from us,' for they will not stay away, for even if you should defeat the entire Babylonian army which is fighting against you, and only their wounded remained, each in his tent, they would rise up and burn this city with fire" (37:9–10). The retort of Jeremiah shows how convinced he was that Babylon's yoke would remain upon Judah; Yahweh would see to that even if he had to use a band of wounded Chaldeans to do it! Judgment upon Jerusalem is inescapable. Taken by itself such a statement seems to make a complete separation between historical means and divine intentions, but the hyperbole should not be magnified out of proportion (cf. Lev. 26:36–37 for a similar figure of speech). Jeremiah sees Babylon as the world power instituted by Yahweh; therefore, Nebuchadnezzar will find sufficient forces to impose Yahweh's will on the nations. Even in seeming defeat or reversal, as was so often the case with Nebuchadnezzar's western policies, he will rise up with the necessary strength to put down rebels. Zedekiah's appeal for some word of the city's salvation echoes the similar appeals of Hezekiah to Isaiah some one hundred years earlier, and it is very likely that the prophet's hyperbolic reply contains an allusion to the tradition of the decimation of the Assyrian army in 701. To the contrary, however, in this instance an utterly decimated Babylonian

[111] Sauneron and Yoyotte, *op. cit.*, contend that reports of Jewish mercenaries aiding Psamtik II refer to the Nubian campaign of 591. They believe that these Jewish mercenaries may originally have gone to Egypt in the service of Ashurbanipal, who directed them to assist his vassal Necho.

army would still carry out Yahweh's unalterable decree. Then too, as the violation of the manumission decree followed so soon upon the withdrawal of the Babylonians and the citizens reclaimed their slaves, the patience of the prophet must have been sorely tried and his belief in the inevitability of judgment for such a people strengthened.

The release of nervous tension effected by the lifting of the siege also brought a sense of normalcy and an impulse to return to economic and social conditions which prevailed before the siege. Some, if not all, of the free citizens "reversed themselves" and reclaimed the slaves they had manumitted during the siege crisis. In an effective wordplay the prophet consigns them to their doom: "Therefore, because you have not obeyed me by proclaiming freedom to your fellows, behold I proclaim to you freedom—oracle of Yahweh!—to the sword, to the plague, and to famine" (34:17). The citizens must have smiled condescendingly at a prophet who had no feeling of relief at the deliverance of the city; yet we can well believe that inwardly they harbored secret apprehensions, for they had not simply the subjective impressions of Jeremiah to trouble them but also the clear knowledge that they had called down upon themselves the sanction of Yahweh in sealing the covenant and thus his vengeance in breaking it.

Shortly thereafter, while the siege was still lifted, Jeremiah attempted to leave the city "to go to the land of Benjamin *lah^{a}liq* there among the people" (37:12). The odd word is probably the infinitive, *l^{e}hahlîq*, "to take part in the division," which apparently refers to family inheritance.[112] The event must be distinct from the purchase of Hanamel's field, for at that time Jeremiah was imprisoned (32:1–2). Perhaps the prophet's father had died and it became necessary to dispose of the property according to the rights of the several sons. Jeremiah was stopped

[112] A. Malamat has suggested the possibility that *lah^{a}liq* is the Akkadian *halāqu*, which in one sense has the meaning "to escape, flee" and, of soldiers, "to desert" (*The Assyrian Dictionary of the Oriental Institute of the University of Chicago,* 1956, VI, 38). Possibly Jeremiah's biographer chose the word advisedly because of its double entendre: Jeremiah left the city to claim an ancestral plot of land but, in the authorities' eyes, he deserted to the enemy.

at the city gate by an officer who quite naturally concluded that the prophet was following his own advice to desert to the Babylonians.[113] He was arrested as a traitor and turned over to the high officials, beaten, and imprisoned in the house of Jonathan. Since the Babylonians had withdrawn it is not likely that Jeremiah would have chosen such an occasion to desert; in any case, he seems to have thought of his own role as one of counselor to Zedekiah to the very end. But the suspicions of his enemies were aroused and his departure from the city gave them an excellent opportunity "to frame" the prophet on plausible charges of treason. At the least his freedom of movement and right of agitation could be curtailed. At last Jeremiah seems to have made the mistake of crowning his treasonous words with treasonous deeds that could not go unpunished!

It is generally assumed that we have no record of the Egyptian-Babylonian encounter. Since the siege of Jerusalem was shortly resumed, it is thought that the Egyptians were defeated or fled without giving battle. In fact, however, the oracle in 46:13–24 seems to refer indirectly to the unsuccessful sally of Hophra against the Babylonians. The Egyptian forces, composed largely of mercenaries, "did not stand" but "turned and fled." The disheartened native troops said, "Up! Let us return to our people and to our birthplace." The derisive play on the pharaoh's name, *šā'ôn he'ĕbîr ham-mô'ēd,* "Loud mouth who misses his opportunity," strongly suggests that the boastful Hophra came forth boldly to battle but then equivocated until he lost the advantage of surprise and was forced to flee without a full test of arms. As a result, Zedekiah's hopes were nearly dashed. Nevertheless he felt compelled to seek some hopeful sign from Jeremiah (37:16–21). It is rather curious that the king should continue to seek consolation from one who so consistently preached a single message: "You shall be given into the hand of the king of Babylon." Zedekiah clung to the hope that Yahweh might re-

---

[113] Malamat, "The Last Wars of the Kingdom of Judah," p. 221, suggests that Benjamin early capitulated to the Babylonians, which accounts for the fact that Mizpah was not destroyed and also explains why Jeremiah was on his way to Anathoth to carry out a routine business transaction made possible by the political stability in that region.

lent at the last moment. In this he must have been abetted by prophets and officials who could not forget the marveolus rescue of the city from the siege of Sennacherib, for whatever the historical facts of 701, by now the most significant element in the tradition was the city's narrow escape from capture by the Assyrians. *Aside from its establishment as the city of David, Jerusalem was next remembered by Judeans of Jeremiah's time as the city spared by the bold prophecies of Isaiah.* The current prophets are discredited, Jeremiah insists, for just as their claim that Babylon would not come against the city had been dashed, so their declaration that the city would not fall was shortly to be proved fallacious.

Perhaps the most surprising element in this interview is Jeremiah's plea for his life. In Jonathan's house he faced death by starvation if not by maltreatment. In the "court of the guard" he could expect special care as a state prisoner. Jeremiah appears in a wholly atypical role when he turns suppliant. Except in God's presence the prophet did not customarily ask favors. The outcry here could well have sprung from fear of death, which had always hovered about the prophet but now tightened its grip upon him. At this one point the dreadful loneliness of the "Confessions" broke into public expression. Yet something more is expressed: the prophet's will to live long enough to see the judgment he had proclaimed, perhaps even to discover if—after all —Yahweh was to vindicate his word. The prophet felt the compulsion of a man with a mission who refuses to die until it is carried out. But to ask the favor of the very king whose doom he sealed in his prophecies was a strange if not incredible move. Nevertheless Zedekiah did not seem to regard the prophet's request as an impertinence. Jehoiakim, we can imagine, would have mocked him and perhaps even killed him as he had killed another critical prophet, Uriah of Kiriath-jearim. Zedekiah simply accepted the request as an entirely logical one and, even more surprisingly, granted it. He ordered Jeremiah moved to new quarters and commanded that a regular ration of bread be given him while the food supply lasted.

Zedekiah was obviously a pious Yahwist who believed that Jeremiah had a calling from God. He felt obliged to honor that call as best he could even while failing to understand its claims upon him and unwilling to obey those which he could understand. The minimum that he owed the prophet was to protect his life as long as he could, and with this sense of obligation went also the irrepressible hope that Jeremiah, like Isaiah of old, might yet prove to be the city's salvation. *Equally as the prophet of Yahweh and as a good luck piece for Jerusalem, Jeremiah must be protected by Zedekiah from harm.* Even to the very end Zedekiah does not seem to have subscribed to the natural belief that Jeremiah was weakening the city with his word of doom and surrender.[114] If such were the case, Zedekiah seemed willing to concede that it was Yahweh's work. *So the king slid toward disaster with a sense of religious fatalism, alternately seeking and rejecting the advice of the man he trusted most.*

In the midst of the gloom surrounding the final year of siege, an unusual thing happened to the prophet and of this strange circumstance Jeremiah made strange use. He was presented with the opportunity, indeed the obligation, to buy the field in Anathoth belonging to his cousin Hanamel. The circumstances of the worsening siege do not seem on the surface to accord with the conduct of business in a matter-of-fact way and thus the editorial introduction (32:1-5) which places the incident has been questioned. Yet nothing in vss. 6-15 speaks against the chronological notation and if vss. 16, 24-25 (26-28, 42-44?), are genuine the siege was definitely being pressed by the Chaldeans at the time of the business transaction (vs. 24). This being the case, Hanamel's approach to Jeremiah may well be explained as a desperate attempt to secure a sizable amount of silver to buy provisions. In siege conditions there are usually private speculators who have managed to hoard extra food or to obtain unsavory but edible

---

[114] It was the common feeling of Israelite kings that prophets must fill them with the spirit necessary to success. Therefore, the prophetic word of weal bore the king to victory and, conversely, the prophetic word of woe brought him down to defeat. This conception of the direct force of the word of a prophet stands behind all the stories of court prophets in the book of Kings (cf. esp. I Kings 22 and the remarks of J. Pedersen, *Israel,* 1925, I–II, 140–45). That Zedekiah did not simply adopt this interpretation and kill or at least utterly reject Jeremiah certainly speaks for a moral understanding above the average.

substitutes and who sell them at extortionist prices (e.g., II Kings 6:24–25). Hanamel was apparently driven to the extreme of sacrificing his landed property in order to get "hard cash." Obviously, not many in the besieged city would be interested in giving up their silver for a piece of property now in enemy hands. Knowing, however, that his prophet-cousin was supplied food by the king, Hanamel felt that he might be persuaded to part with some silver. All the more likely if he could appeal to the prophet to uphold the long-honored traditions of "redemption" of land within the family (cf. Lev. 25:25–28).

Jeremiah seems to have had some premonition of the proposal and he was prepared to accept it as an occasion to perform another dramatic symbolic action. Yet it was to be a symbolic action of a special kind, for it was one that involved the prophet's use of events initiated by others in contrast to events which he wholly or largely initiated (a parallel example is Ezekiel's symbolic use of the death of his wife,—Ezek. 24:15–24). The prophet went through all the details of purchase, many of which survived in Talmudic practice hundreds of years later, e.g., the signature of witnesses on the documents and the preservation of a bound or sealed deed and an open deed.[115] Since the prophet was still confined to the court of the guard he turned over the two deeds to Baruch his close friend and comanded him to put them "in a clay vessel that this may last for a long time. For thus says Yahweh of hosts, the God of Israel: 'Houses and fields and vineyards shall once again be bought in this land.' "

While the stages of the sale were being carried out the prophet's audience must have wondered at the paradox of Jeremiah, imprisoned for predicting the inevitability of the city's downfall and urging its surrender, using his confinement to buy real estate! Perhaps some shrugged it off as a kindly deed for the sake of a needy relative. Others probably laid it to the prophet's imbalance and thus were further confirmed in their suspicion that his judg-

---

[115] See L. Fischer, "Die Urkunden in Jer. 32:11–14 nach den Ausgrabungen und dem Talmud," *ZAW* 30 (1910), 136–42. Several real-estate deeds written on papyri in the Bar Cocheba period and similarly hidden away were found in the desert of Judah in the spring of 1961 by a Hebrew University expedition. The form and content of the deeds may provide parallels to the practice related in Jeremiah 32.

ment was erratic and impractical. Lest the prophet's point in buying the field be lost upon anyone, he added Yahweh's pithy pronouncement which made of the strange act a sacrament and a promise: "Houses and fields and vineyards shall again be bought in this land!" The essential kinds of immovable property in Judah will be owned and lived in, tilled and tended in the future. Jeremiah has not merely done a good turn for a relative out of gullibility or compassion. He has entered into a solid business deal. He has acquired a piece of property whose productivity someone in his family will eventually enjoy.

That such a hopeful interpretation was difficult even for the prophet to accept is apparent in those portions of 32:16-44 which appear to be reasonably authentic, especially vss. 24-25.[116] They express the prophet's incredulity at the prospect that normal social and economic life will ever return to Palestine. Presumably just such doubts assailed him between his first premonition of Hanamel's proposal (vs. 6) and the actual negotiation with his cousin (vs. 8). Again after the action was concluded and interpreted the prophet was swept by doubts: "Ah Lord God! Behold, the siege mounds have been raised against the city to take it and the city owing to sword, famine and disease has been given over to the Chaldeans who besiege it and behold thou seest it, yet thou hast said to me, 'Buy the field for money and get witnesses' —even though the city is given over to the Chaldeans." Jeremiah identifies the words of Hanamel as the words of Yahweh.

But a further divine reassurance is needed and it comes with the simple reminder: "Behold, I am Yahweh, the God of all flesh, is anything too difficult for me?" Since Yahweh is Lord of all men and has appointed Babylon and its ruler Nebuchadnezzar over the Fertile Crescent, it is also within his power to grant an ordered life once again to Judah. He can do so through a stable Babylonian administration, or he can do so when the Babylonian yoke will be broken in the future. It is interesting that the territory described in vs. 44 as eventually to return to normalcy is approximately that of the Judean state at the time of Jeremiah:

[116] Volz, *op. cit.,* p. 302, regards vss. 16, 17a, 24-29, 36a, 42-44 as genuine. Rudolph, *op. cit.,* p. 175, differs from Volz only in omitting 29b and 36a.

Jerusalem and environs, Benjamin on the north, the hill country southward to Hebron, the Shephelah on the west, and the Negeb in the far south.[117] Since approximately the same description appears in emphatically Deuteronomic contexts (Jer. 17:26; 33:13) it is possibly a later specification of Jeremiah's more general expression, "in this land," but in any case it originated before the actual restoration from Babylon.

The purchase of Hanamel's field seems to have remained an isolated event while the main force of the prophet's preaching continued to be relentlessly negative. His enemies grew more restive as the number of deserters increased alarmingly, encouraged in their desertion by the bold promise that "he who goes out to the Chaldeans shall live; he shall have his life for a prize of war and live" (38:2). His counsel was successful enough to arouse the bitter indictment of the princes, who appealed to Zedekiah: "Let this man be sentenced to death for he is weakening the hands of the soldiers who remain in this city, and the hands of all the people, by speaking such words to them. For this man does not seek what is good for this people but rather what is bad" (38:4). The further equivocation of the king was impossible. How could a public call to defection be permitted any longer? By all the standards of national security something had to be done, for wherever the prophet could find a listener he urged his case. Yet who should pronounce the death sentence? Not Zedekiah, who was inwardly convinced that the prophet was right and that in his dynastic aspirations one of his closest

---

[117] M. Noth, *JPOS* 15 (1935), 36, notes that the phrase "the mountains, the Shephelah, and the Negeb" is a fixed territorial expression which appears in combination with other geographical and political terms (e.g., the Arabah, the land beyond Jordan, the coastland). His contention, however, that in Jeremiah the *territorial* division (Shephelah, mountains, Negeb) overlaps with the *political-geographical* division of the kingdom of Judah (cities of Judah, Jerusalem, and land of Benjamin) is not applicable to Jeremiah 32:44. On the contrary, the order of the terms is such that the territorial terms form a parenthetic description of Judah outside of Jerusalem. The verse should then be understood: "the land of Benjamin, the environs of Jerusalem, and the cities of Judah, (consisting of) the cities of the hill country, the cities of the Shephelah, and the cities of the Negeb." The verse thus possesses a geographical logic lacking in Jeremiah 17:26 and 33:13 (and also in many of the other Deuteronomic verses cited by Noth) which perhaps argues for its originality.

supporters was Jeremiah.[118] Not the princes, for they did not wish innocent blood upon their hands, particularly the blood of one who came from an old priestly landowning family. Jeremiah was a radical from a conservative line but for the sake of the honored family he could not be touched. Furthermore, his calm courage was astounding and unnerving. And the deep superstition must have plagued the hostile princes that to cause Jeremiah's death would be to bring Yahweh's curse upon them. Yet they would do all they could to encourage his "natural death." They hit upon the idea of throwing him into an empty cistern in the hope that he would perish from starvation and exposure.

The deed could not be kept secret. It spread through the court, and a foreigner in the king's service, an Ethiopian called by the title Ebed-melech, "Servant of the King," interceded with Zedekiah and with the help of three men drew Jeremiah from the cistern (38:7–13). The promise of Jeremiah to Ebed-melech that his life would be saved at the city's fall is of particular interest since it shows that Jeremiah was free of ethnic or national arrogance and was even able to say to a foreigner on Yahweh's behalf, "you shall have your life as war booty, because you have trusted me" (39:18). The status of Ebed-melech in the Jewish community—whether he was a *gēr* with established rights or a hireling or appointee from Egypt during the rapprochement between Judah and that land after 605—is unknown. The latter seems the more likely since the title "the Ethiopian," rather than a family name, suggests a foreign officer (cf. Ittai the Gittite, II Sam. 15:19–20).

Of course Jeremiah was profoundly grateful to the man who had saved his life, but he need not have treated him as one who trusted in Yahweh unless he actually meant it. It is highly unlikely that Ebed-melech, as a foreign officer in the Judean court, was actually a Yahweh worshiper. Yet Jeremiah asserted that this man's adherence to the dictates of his conscience, his defiance of the princes, and his courage to intercede with the vacillating king were indeed signs of trust in Yahweh. Nebuchadnezzar, both as scourge and as imposer of discipline upon the nations,

[118] See Malamat, "Jeremiah and the Last Two Kings of Judah," pp. 81–87.

executed Yahweh's will without confessing his name. So another stranger to Judah, Ebed-melech, as deliverer of the prophetic interpreter of Yahweh's deeds, also performed Yahweh's will without owning Yahweh's name. Jeremiah's surprising doctrine of creation carries him unhesitantly to the claim that those who stand outside the covenant are "believers" in the covenant God whenever they are seen to obey the content of the covenant. To be sure, this remains an ad hoc insight and does not lead to proselytizing; rather it leaves the prophet open to recognize Yahweh's positive work, as well as his work of destruction, in the lives of non-Yahwists.

The final audience of Zedekiah with Jeremiah (38:14–23) is carried out in the utmost secrecy. The prophet repeats his counsel to surrender the city in order to escape death and to spare the city's destruction. The interview does not appear to be simply a repetition of the previous contacts between prophet and king. Zedekiah is wavering, but he is held back from surrender by the fear that Nebuchadnezzar will allow the Jews who have deserted to abuse him. While some commentators have regarded this merely as a lame pretext, it certainly was no idle fear. Among the defectors were many who detested the rebellion Zedekiah had permitted and who would gladly vent their spleen upon the surrendering king. Embittered compatriots would be more savage and sadistic than the Babylonians themselves. Jeremiah insisted, however, that Nebuchadnezzar would protect Zedekiah. There is no sign that the prophet had any immediate information—for example, in the form of surrender terms from Nebuchadnezzar— but he apparently was generally familiar with Babylonian imperial practice toward vassals, and Jehoiachin was a recent example. Vassals who surrendered could expect lenient treatment especially where it was evident that they had not initiated the revolt but were virtual hostages of a war party.

We are impressed with the sincerity of both men. Without evasion Zedekiah confesses his fear of torture and humiliation should he surrender. With equal directness Jeremiah insists that the worse fate awaits him if he does not surrender. Jeremiah shows a certain fear for his life at the hands of the king but it is not so much personal as vocational. The solemn oath of the king that he will not harm Jeremiah shows his piety, "As Yahweh lives who made our lives. . . ." So the audience ends without either man giving any ground, yet with Zedekiah much more inclined to act on the prophet's advice than Jeremiah was willing to accept the political reasoning which in the last analysis determined the king's course.

When the city was breached in July of 587 Zedekiah did make a bold bid to solve his dilemma. He decided to flee by night with an armed guard in the hope of getting across the Arabah into Gilead. The rugged wooded slopes and sequestered valleys of Gilead offered natural protection, and the Jewish Tobiad family of trans-Jordan was apparently already at this time strongly entrenched in its estates between the Jordan and Ammonite territory, thus presenting a splendid prospect of asylum.[119] The gamble failed, however, for the king and his troops were captured near Jericho and delivered to Nebuchadnezzar at his Riblah headquarters in southern Syria. His sons were slain and he was blinded before deportation to Babylon. The city itself was apparently sacked at once, but the systematic destruction of walls and the deportation of the populace occurred a month later when Nebuzaradan came to Jerusalem with direct orders from Nebuchadnezzar. The smaller number of deportees at this time (832 males or a total of approximately 2,500—52:28) suggests that the toll of the upper class during the siege had been heavy. Yet the depopulation was anything but complete, for high civilian and military officers were soon gathered around the provincial capital at Mizpah (40:7–8), and four years later Nebuchadnezzar carried off another group (745 persons, probably representing a total of 2,000–2,500 including families—52:30). The successive thinning out of the leadership from the time of Josiah had serious effects upon Judah for centuries to come.

Of the two accounts of the treatment accorded Jeremiah by the conquerors (39:11–14; 40:1–6), both of which agree that the prophet was given into the keeping of the new governor, the latter seems to contain the more likely outline of events. It is

[119] B. Mazar, "The Tobiads," *IEJ* 7 (1957), 233–35, assembles convincing evidence that the Tobiads held large estates in trans-Jordan from the eighth century onward—estates which were not expropriated by the Assyrians.

highly improbable that the first order of business for the Babylonians after capturing the city will have been to arrange for Jeremiah's future. It is more likely that the prophet was unrecognized until, as a company of deportees for Babylon was being assembled at Ramah, the new governor appealed to Nebuzaradan to allow Jeremiah to remain with him if he so desired. For the first time the Babylonians heard of the anti-revolutionary work of Jeremiah and they agreed that he would be a constructive influence in the new Judean administration. The actual speech attributed to Nebuzaradan in 40:2–5a is in the nature of a sermon summarizing Jeremiah's religio-political outlook and is typical of the tendency to put Yahwistic speeches in the mouths of sympathetic foreigners.

Nebuchadnezzar chose for his new administrator in Judah a certain Gedaliah, whose genealogy was a most impressive one. He was son of Ahikam, one of the pro-Babylonian princes who had saved Jeremiah's life by intervening on his behalf with an angry crowd of priests, prophets, and citizens who, having just heard the prophet's attack upon the temple, were about to kill him (26:24). This speaks for a high office and it is likely that Ahikam continued in the office of secretary which had been held by his father, Shaphan, in the days of Josiah (II Kings 22:3–14 *passim*). Shaphan had been one of the chief proponents of the Deuteronomic Reform. Judging by a seal of Gedaliah from Lachish, he held the chief civil post in Judah, that of royal steward, to which he, as a faithful pro-Babylonian, was probably appointed after the deportation of a pro-Egyptian steward in 597.[120] He did all that he could to restore economic and civil order to the badly ravaged and chaotic land. His highly regarded character and abilities soon drew to him many of the scattered Jewish

[120] See S. H. Hooke, *Palestine Exploration Fund Quarterly Statement,* 1935, pp. 195–97; H. G. May, *AJSL* 56 (1939), 146–48. Malamat's identification of the Gedaliah of the seal as the probable agent of Jehoiachin takes too much for granted since that position—insofar as crown lands were concerned—was apparently occupied after 597 by "Eliakim, servant of Jehoiachin," named on several Judean jar handles and it is inherently likely that Zedekiah's chief civil officer during the same years was Gedaliah ("Jeremiah and the Last Two Kings of Judah," p. 82).

leaders, including commanders of military units which had been operating as guerrilla forces or had gone into hiding during the final siege of Jerusalem. Also, many of the Jewish escapees to trans-Jordan began to return from Moab, Ammon, and Edom. All were assured of amnesty for previous acts against the Babylonian regime.

Gedaliah set up his administrative center at Mizpah a few miles north of Jerusalem, a central location that had been spared the destruction visited upon the capital. The precise status of the new leader is not clear from the records. It is simply stated that Nebuchadnezzar "appointed Gedaliah in the land" (40:7). Possibly he was governor for a separate Babylonian province; however, a province extending from north to south no more than twenty miles (and perhaps only ten)[121] and east to west not more than twenty-five miles was a very small province by Babylonian standards. Gedaliah may well have been a commissioner under the authority of the governor of Samaria and Judah may never have been a distinct Babylonian province.[122] With the tragic death of Gedaliah we hear of no further appointments. Nebuchadnezzar probably then decided to put the administration of Judah directly under the Samarian governor, presumably in 582 when the third deportation was made (52:30).

Jeremiah's role in the administration of Gedaliah is unspecified. It is indeed strange that the rather full narrative says nothing of the prophet from the time of his commitment to Gedaliah until after the latter's death. This may argue for a very short term of office for Gedaliah, no more than two months. In that case, Jeremiah had not the time to assert himself as a voice in the stable rule of the land. On the other hand, the report that the returned Jewish officers and fugitives settled down to agriculture and "gathered wine and summer fruits plentifully" suggests a period

---

121 Alt, *op. cit.,* p. 327, favors the view that the former Judean region from Bethlehem to Hebron was given over by the Babylonians to various non-Judean groups from the south, especially the Edomites. W. F. Albright, *JBL* 51 (1932), 105, regards the southern boundary of Judah as falling south of Beth-zur, thus extending approximately ten miles to the south of Bethlehem.

122 O. Procksch, *Theologische Literaturblatt* 53 (1932), 196.

at least from the fall of 587 to the late summer harvest of 586
(or from the fall of 586 to the late summer harvest of 585).[123]
Furthermore, the misplaced confidence of Gedaliah in his mur-
derer may be more readily understood if some months and even
years had passed during which Ishmael ben Nethaniah had
served the new order with every appearance of loyalty. Apparently then Jeremiah had time and opportunity to express himself positively in the political realm after so long a negative witness. For a man of his tender sensibilities it must have been a
tremendous relief. We shall not be wrong in imagining that
Gedaliah listened attentively to the advice of Jeremiah, who, as
in Jerusalem, served as a regular counselor to the head of state.

It is easy to conceive the prophet's urging upon the Judeans
the same program of peaceful subservience to Babylon and economic and social industry that he had urged upon the Babylonian
exiles (29:4–9). Jeremiah's prestige must have been high after
events had vindicated some of the chief elements of his message.
In particular, the lenience of Nebuchadnezzar in installing a local
prince of temperate qualities as commissioner was a pleasant surprise and showed that Jeremiah knew whereof he spoke when he
declared that the Babylonian yoke was for the peaceful discipline
of the subject peoples. Crops were bountiful and morale was returning. Some of Jeremiah's more hopeful oracles, marked by a
singing lyrical quality, seem to fit this happy period when he felt
prompted to announce the joyous reunion of the northern and
southern tribes (at least 31:2–6, 15–20; and perhaps 30:4–7,
10–15, 18–21; 31:21–22; also in this period belongs the prose
prophecy of the "new covenant," 31:31–34).[124] It is evident that,

---

[123] As S. Yeivin, "Families and Parties in the Kingdom of Judah," *Studies
in the History of Israel and Its Land,* pp. 292–93 (Hebrew), notes, it is possible to fit all the data into the late summer and fall of 586 [or 587]: the
city's fall in July, the late summer harvest of grapes in August-September,
and Gedaliah's murder in September. But the natural sense of the agricultural reference is that the vines and fruit trees had been tended at least
through one season, for it is unlikely that an extraordinary harvest will have
occurred without careful husbandry. On the present uncertainty as to whether
Jerusalem fell in 587 or 586 see D. N. Freedman in *The Bible and the
Ancient Near East* (ed. G. E. Wright), 1961, pp. 211–13.

[124] Among those who find a minimal number of Jeremianic oracles in
chaps. 30–31 are J. Skinner, *op. cit.,* chaps. XVI, XVIII (31:2–6, 15–16,

in spite of the centuries-old political friction between north and south, the pilgrimage of northerners to Jerusalem described in 41:4–5 attests the strong bonds felt between Yahwists in the two regions.

When Ishmael ben Nethaniah, "of royal seed,"[125] struck down Gedaliah (chap. 41) it was with a mixture of motives and with the complicity of Baalis, king of Ammon. Basically Ishmael hoped to restore the Davidic dynasty in Judah and to remove the stigma of Babylonian defeat, yet the chances for the success of his coup were so slim that he may in fact have been driven chiefly by a thirst for revenge against the Babylonians and those Jews who collaborated with them. The interest of Baalis was of another sort. A Babylonian-supported rule in Judah was a threat to independent trans-Jordan states, and, if Ishmael could seize power in Judah with Baalis' help, the latter stood to regain territory in southern Gilead which Judah normally claimed when strong enough and over which the government of Gedaliah probably exercised at least nominal authority.

The dastardly murder of Gedaliah, his officials, the Babylonian garrison or courier guard, and the pilgrims who happened upon the city shortly after the purge accomplished nothing for Ishmael and Baalis. On the other hand, at one stroke it wiped out the program of Judean reconstruction so ably begun under Gedaliah. How Jeremiah happened to escape the massacre is unknown. It

---

18–22, 31–34), and J. P. Hyatt, *IB*, V, 1023, 1037–38 (30:5–7, 12–15; 31:2–6, 15–22, 31–34; possibly 31:9c). P. Volz, *op. cit.*, pp. 281–97, regards 30:1–7, 10–15, 18–21a; 31:2–13, 15–22, 27b, 31–37, as genuine and W. Rudolph, *op. cit.*, pp. 159–74 follows him closely. Whereas Skinner and Hyatt date the prophecies during Gedaliah's term of office, Volz put them probably between 594 and 588 (possibly 604–597) and Rudolph placed them in Jeremiah's "silent period," i.e., during Josiah's reunion of north and south.

[125] Yeivin, *op. cit.*, pp. 282–83, proposes to identify Ishmael's grandfather Elishama (II Kings 25:25) with Elishama the scribe, in the days of Jehoiakim (Jer. 36:12), whose royal connection he finds attested on a seal "To Elishama son of the king" (published by D. Diringer, *Le iscrizioni antico-ebraiche Palestinesi*, 1934, pp. 232–33, Table XXI. 9). It remains, however, an open question as to whether the four persons identified in the Bible by the title "son of the king" were so in fact or were merely high officials (Joash, I Kings 22:26; II Chron. 18:25; Maaseiah, II Chron. 28:7; Jerahmeel, Jer. 36:26; Malchiah, Jer. 38:6).

is possible that just at this time he was visiting in his hometown of Anathoth. Or he may have been among the hostages taken by Ishmael and recaptured by Johanan ben Kareah. The latter will have been very likely since the possession of so highly touted a prophet might well have worked to the political advantage of Ishmael. To the demoralized survivors of the vicious attack there seemed to be only one thing to do: escape to Egypt for asylum. They feared Nebuchadnezzar's reprisal, for the blow was struck at Babylonian authority and had killed Babylonian troops either permanently stationed at Mizpah or serving as an armed guard for a diplomatic mission from Babylon or Samaria. As former Judean army officers, the refugees will have had strong ties with Egypt and may even have hoped to find employment there as mercenaries.[126]

Jeremiah's honored role as political adviser was respected to the extent that the people asked for Yahweh's judgment on the contemplated flight to Egypt. For ten days they awaited a reply from the prophet, who finally gave them a characteristic reply: stay in Judah for Nebuchadnezzar need not be feared. He will be lenient toward the surviving community but, if the survivors flee, it will be interpreted as an admission of guilt and the fate they seek to avoid will overtake them in Egypt. The memory of the prophet Uriah, who panicked, fled to Egypt, and was brought back for execution by Jehoiakim, may have played a part in Jeremiah's estimation of the prospects. He was satisfied that if the leaders did not flee or try to usurp Gedaliah's post, Nebuchadnezzar would take pains to establish the facts and thus spare the innocent. Perhaps the survivors, led by Johanan ben Kareah, were strongly swayed by the fear that no eyewitnesses of the murder acceptable to Nebuchadnezzar could be found, since all the Babylonians at Mizpah were apparently murdered. It would remain a question of Nebuchadnezzar's trust in the unsubstantiated word of a group of leaders who had previously strongly resisted Babylonian authority. Hostility of Samarian officials toward the Judeans will also have boded ill for a fair judgment, reinforced as it was by the senseless killing of the Samarian pilgrims.

[126] Yeivin, *op. cit.*, pp. 266–67.

The fact that the Babylonians deported a sizable number of Judeans in 582, probably shortly after the flight to Egypt,[127] seems to speak in favor of the assessment made by the Judean officials and against that of Jeremiah. Yet it is conceivable that precisely because all those able men who might have shared Gedaliah's frame of mind had been lost to the Babylonians Nebuchadnezzar, faced with hostile and doubtfully loyal leadership, decided to make a clean sweep of remaining malcontents before turning over the area to direct Samarian administration. Also, it is likely that in committing Judah to Samarian control he delivered over considerable properties to the Samarian upper class[128] and thus the ranks of the deportees of 582 were swelled by the expropriated. These included Judean parvenus and possibly also Ammonites, Moabites, and Edomites who had taken advantage of Gedaliah's removal to reach for some of the tempting Judean properties in trans-Jordan and southern Judah.

As feared by the prophet, the leaders rejected his counsel and elected to flee to Egypt. Much as they disregarded his advice and charged Baruch with manipulating the prophet for personal ends, they did not fail to take the prophet and his scribe with them as necessary protection against the hazards of life in a new land. They still considered themselves Yahwists and there was, furthermore, the practical consideration that it would be dangerous to leave Jeremiah and Baruch behind as possible informants against them. As to the fate of the Jews in Egypt, Jeremiah seems to have deepened his belief that Nebuchadnezzar would conquer Egypt and there rule over the few surviving Jews just as he had in Judah. His last recorded words are a symbolic action and a threat—both against Egypt.

In an intriguing symbolic act Jeremiah laid stones in a large public courtyard which he identified as the foundation supports for the royal canopy of Nebuchadnezzar when he should come to

[127] It is difficult to resist connecting the murder of Gedaliah with the deportation of Judeans in 582 (so Hyatt, *IB,* V, 1084, and Yeivin, *op. cit.,* p. 293). Rudolph, *op. cit.,* p. 281, claims that we have no notion of the occasion of the third deportation but he rejects deletion of vs. 30 and also the theory that the figures of the third deportation are a doublet of those for the second deportation.

[128] Alt, *op. cit.,* p. 329.

Egypt (43:8–13). The description contains some obscure technical terms,[129] and the identification of Tahpanhes as the pharaoh's capital seems to be incorrect since at this period the capital was at Sais in the western Delta.[130] Furthermore, the stress of the oracle on Egyptian idolatry instead of political crimes has opened it to suspicion. On the other hand, the palace named in the account may have been merely a government building chosen by Jeremiah because it was the first auspicious place reached by the Jews en route to their new home in Egypt. Probably not too much should be made of the fact that Jeremiah speaks not of a permanent occupation of Egypt but rather of a devastating raid by which Yahweh "shall clean the land of Egypt as a shepherd delouses his cloak" (vs. 12). When Josephus tells of an invasion of Egypt in 582 B.C. by Nebuchadnezzar, who killed one pharaoh and appointed another and led the Jews living in Egypt captive to Babylon (*Ant.* X. ix. 7), there is no apparent ground for the report other perhaps than a conjecture based upon the threatening oracles of Jeremiah. According to our present knowledge, there was no change of pharaohs in 582, as Josephus reports. A fragmentary neo-Babylonian text does tell us, however, that Nebuchadnezzar invaded Egypt in his thirty-seventh year (568–567) and fought Ahmose II, with results which the text does not make clear.

Shortly before this attack, in 570, according to Jeremiah 44: 29–30, the prophet predicted that Hophra would be given into the hands of "his enemies," which apparently refers to Hophra's death in a palace revolt rather than his delivery to Nebuchadnezzar. This passage revises an earlier belief of the prophet that the attack of Nebuchadnezzar would fall within the reign of

---

[129] In vs. 9 *melet*, "mortar," and *malbēn*, "bricked-terrace" (cf. W. Spiegelberg, *Aegyptologische Randglossen zum AT*, 1904, pp. 24, 38), and in vs. 10 *šaphrîr*, "state-tent" (Koehler, *LVTL*, p. 1006), or "throne carpet" (Delitzsch, *Prolegomena eines neuen hebraischen Woerterbuchs*, 1886, p. 126), or "sceptre" (H. Zimmern, *Akkadische Fremdwoerter*, 2nd ed., 1917, p. 8).

[130] William S. Smith, *Ancient Egypt as Represented in the Museum of Fine Arts, Boston*, pp. 137–38. Rudolph, *op. cit.*, p. 221, suggests that the text refers not to a palace but to a government building, a *byt mlk'*, of the sort mentioned in Elephantine (Papyrus Cowley No. 2:12), especially since Tahpanhes = Daphnae was, like Elephantine, a garrison town.

Hophra (46:13, 17). The last prophecy declares that Hophra, unlike Zedekiah, will *not* fall by the hand of Nebuchadnezzar.[131] This prophecy need not, however, be dismissed as a *vaticinium ex eventu,* for the troubles of Hophra with the army and his court official Amasis had been building up for some years and Jeremiah could easily have experienced a premonition of the outcome, all the more so if the Jews among whom he lived were mercenaries in the pharaoh's army. At any rate the impact of this prophecy, as of the symbolic action, was to disabuse the Jews in Egypt of any sense of security since Nebuchadnezzar's arm can also reach the Nile, and Pharaoh Hophra, who had busied himself with fending off the Babylonians in Palestine, will soon come to an unhappy end. Thus the final consequences of the judgment upon the kingdom of Judah and its accomplices were to be worked out and with them the prophecies of Jeremiah come to an end.

Four Undated Oracles

We have reserved comment until now on four oracles in Jeremiah touching upon the foreign nations, for their authenticity is disputed and, if genuine, they are not easily placed in the prophet's career. There is no serious obstacle to accepting at least three of these as authentic, and the fourth may contain a Jeremianic kernel. Two of the oracles speak of punishment on the states of Syria-Palestine in which Judah participates because, like the others, she is "uncircumcised in heart," i.e., impure of heart, although observing ritual circumcision (9:25–26). The nations surveyed—Egypt, Judah, Edom, sons of Ammon, Moab, the Arabs—may reflect simply a general summary of peoples who at various times in Jeremiah's ministry came under his criticism. It is, however, possible that the oracle is connected with the crisis of 602 in which Judah and the Arabs (?) broke away from Babylonian vassalage. At that time the trans-Jordan kingdoms assisted the Chaldeans against their neighbor Judah. If so, Jeremiah here condemns the accomplices in Judean revolt—Egypt and the Arabs—as well as the opponents of the revolt—Edom,

[131] H. M. Wiener, *The Prophets of Israel in History and Criticism,* 1923, p. 78.

Ammon, Moab. All have acted from motives which express their essential similarity as self-centered powers acting for momentary advantage and not on the basis of principles, which for Judah ought to be consistent with her covenant with Yahweh.

The oracle of Jeremiah 12:14–17 contains nothing fundamentally inconsistent with Jeremiah's outlook apart from some strange expressions which suggest that the oracle has been revised and given an introduction to suit a strong Judean self-consciousness and sense of superiority. The surrounding states are identified as "all my wicked neighbors who lay hold upon the heritage which I have granted my people Israel to possess"; and vss. 14b–15 speak of the exile of the neighbors of Judah and of Judah itself and of their return "each to his possession and each to his land." We are presented with something of the picture of Amos 1–2 and it seems compatible with the foreign prophecies of judgment which, as we have seen, may be in considerable measure assigned to Jeremiah. The last two verses seem less likely from the prophet. Elsewhere in the book "the ways of my people" is a condemnatory expression, but in vs. 16 it is a term of approbation since the heathen are invited to emulate "the ways of my people." The foreigners, converted to Yahwism, "will be incorporated in the midst of my people," in the editor's mind apparently as states in covenant with Judah, although how whole peoples are "to be built up into the midst" of Judah remains problematic and thus the verse has the appearance of having been originally addressed to individual converts. The final threat that Yahweh will destroy all the nations that do not convert to Yahwism is inconsistent with the prophet's generosity toward other peoples and even admiration of their religious fidelity, however misguided (cf. 2:11). Therefore, vss. 14b–15 may safely be attributed to the prophet, while vss. 16–17 must remain doubtful.

The other two oracles envision a participation of the other peoples in Israel's faith without their political dissolution and perhaps even without the total surrender of their own religious beliefs and practices. The prophecies are cast in such traditional language that their precise import is not clear. In the future Jerusalem is to be called "the throne of Yahweh . . . (and) all nations shall assemble to Yahweh's name at Jerusalem and shall no more obstinately follow their own evil heart" (3:17). This seems to refer not so much to conversion from idolatry as to surrender of false political pretensions. Perhaps, after Babylonian rule, the theocratic rule of God will be recognized by a confederation of separate peoples. This idea accords closely with that in Isaiah 2:2–4.

Another passage closely connects the repentance of Israel with its influence on the nations (4:1–2). If Israel will expunge itself of idolatry and live by the truth, justice, and righteousness of Yahweh, "then nations shall bless themselves in him and in him shall they rejoice." The latter is an obvious recollection of the promise to Abraham (Gen. 12:1–3) and suggests that the prophet here purposely disassociates himself from extreme national-militaristic interpretations of Israel's relation to the nations. Not through conquest but through fidelity to its own religious tradition Israel will succeed in attracting the nations. That the same promise was connected with the Davidic dynasty is clear from Psalm 72:17, and for that very reason Jeremiah seems at pains to clarify the terms of international recognition of Israel's uniqueness.

The sole reference to a future purified Davidic line in 23: 5–6 = 33:15–16 may be from Jeremiah, particularly since it closes with an effective wordplay on *Ẓedekiah,* "Yah(weh) is righteous," whereas the coming ruler will be called *Yahweh Ẓidqēnû,* "Yahweh is our righteousness." The reconstitution of Judah and Israel was close to Jeremiah's heart. He was probably aware that the Judean exiles in Babylon had made contact with some of their fellow Yahwists from the northern kingdom who had been scattered in Mesopotamia by the Assyrians in 722. Of course to get a fair picture of Jeremiah's feeling toward the monarchy we must consider his bitter condemnation of Jehoiakim and Jehoiachin, which includes the assertion (22:30):

> Record this man [Jehoiachin] as childless,
>   a man who shall not prosper in his days;
> for none of his offspring shall prosper
>   in sitting on the throne of David,
>   and ruling again in Judah.

Yet this would not necessarily be incompatible with having someone of the Davidic line take the throne. Even so, the restored life
of Israel in Palestine does not appear to depend heavily upon a
king, and 33:17–18 with its categorical assertion of Davidic kings
and Levitical priests as the future leaders of Israel is hardly from
the prophet.

*It seems, nonetheless, from probably authentic oracles of prom-
ise in chap. 30 that room must be allowed in Jeremiah's outlook
for a civil leader of some authority, whether of the Davidic line
or not.* The prophet declares that "the palace will stand where it
formerly was" (30:18) and the new leader will be chiefly distinguished by his modesty and subservience to religious standards
(30:21):[132]

> Their prince ['addîr] shall be from their own number,
>   and their ruler [mōshēl] from among them shall come forth;
> I will bring him near and he shall approach me,
>   For who would dare to come near me of his own accord?

Perhaps there is a purposeful omission of *melek* or a reference to
David. Certainly the whole conception is that of a king chastened
and limited in powers and aspirations (similar to the conception
of Deut. 17:14–20 and of Ezek. 45:7–17; 46:1–8, 16–18, with
the important exception that Jeremiah does not even tentatively
mark off the ground of leadership between the monarchy and
the priesthood, as is defined in the other passages). It seems that
this passage should be the touchstone for interpreting the traditional formulation of a Davidic king in 23:5–6.

"Prophet to the Nations"

To a pre-eminent degree among pre-exilic prophets Jeremiah
deserves the epithet "prophet to the nations." *Beginning with an
interest in Babylon and Egypt as contenders for the balance of
power in Syria-Palestine, his concern grew to include all the
nations allied with or opposed to them.* He insisted that powerful

---

[132] On the authenticity of the passage and the limited view of the monarchy it expresses, cf. Volz, *op. cit.*, pp. 281, 287, and Rudolph, *op. cit.*, p.
163, although Volz's limitation of the passage to the northern kingdom
does not commend itself.

Mesopotamian forces were destined to replace the Assyrians as "the northern foe." From the reign of Jehoiakim he opposed all dependence on Egypt as futile since the new master was to be Babylon. He foresaw and proclaimed the utter defeat of Egyptian forces that for several years had been fighting sporadically against the neo-Babylonians in upper Syria and Mesopotamia. And with the defeat of Egypt at Carchemish he asserted the world plan of Yahweh to be the submission of all Near Eastern peoples to the empire of Babylon.

In the following years the course of Nebuchadnezzar's campaigns was followed by the prophet. He uttered threats against the Philistines and Phoenicians (603–602?), the Arabs (599), and Elam (596–595) for stirring up resistance against Babylon and he denounced Ammon (601) for its seizure of Judean territory in Gilead, even though it acted in the name of Babylon. To an assembly of ambassadors from Tyre, Sidon, Edom, Moab, and Ammon, gathered in 594–593 at Jerusalem to plan revolt, he reaffirmed and detailed his conviction of Nebuchadnezzar as the Yahweh-appointed world ruler under whose yoke all nations must serve until Yahweh had disciplined them sufficiently. Moab, perhaps leader of the revolt, was attacked in a hard-hitting oracle built on traditional anti-Moabite taunts. In the same year he seems to have sent a message of warning to Nebuchadnezzar to the effect that the king must rule with discretion and humility inasmuch as Babylon is not an eternal empire but will itself one day perish. Hophra's attempt to divert the Babylonian army from its siege of Jerusalem was condemned as a futile gesture. In Egypt the prophet continued his claim of Nebuchadnezzar's world dominion.

Although Jeremiah lacks the explicit references to the plan of Yahweh which appear often in Isaiah, his thought was similarly dominated by an intense conviction of Yahweh's unalterable purpose for the nations. *He saw that purpose as unfolding through the appointment by Yahweh of a series of world empires and rulers. In the present age Nebuchadnezzar of Babylon was Yahweh's "servant." He could be cautioned and advised but not opposed by revolt for he operated under Yahweh's decree.* It is clear that the subtle dialectic of Isaiah's thought is not reproduced in the same manner by Jeremiah. The dialectic is not absent. No matter how emphatically Babylon serves as Yahweh's agent in the present time, her term of dominance is not unlimited for she too will fall under judgment. But the judgment is pushed farther into the future, beyond the lifetime of any of the prophet's listeners. Isaiah stressed the rapine and brutality of an Assyria that had gone beyond its commission from Yahweh and was ripe for judgment. Jeremiah stressed the reasonableness and orderliness of a Babylon that would pacify and chastise the unruly sinful peoples of the ancient Near East with restraint.

Objectively there seems to have been some basis for this contrast in viewpoints. The Assyrians under Tiglath-pileser, Shalmaneser, Sargon, and Sennacherib had carried out a vast and cruel program of plunder and deportation on a scale previously unknown in the ancient world. The neo-Babylonians showed less of a disposition merely to terrorize and to plunder. Terrorize and plunder they did, but with less frequency and savagery, and they seem not to have imposed their own administration and culture on conquered regions in so thoroughgoing a manner as the Assyrians used. At best the contrast, however, is merely relative and does not account altogether for the different attitudes of Isaiah and Jeremiah. Subjectively, there was a very different sense of "times" in the two prophets. In his later years Isaiah saw with increasing clarity that there was to be a "time" of Assyrian defeat in punishment for its reckless arrogance and rapine. Jeremiah saw by contrast a "time" of Babylonian hegemony in punishment and discipline for the peoples' sins. While neither prophet forgot the complement to the facet of world dominion which he stressed, there was an emphatic difference in the predominant attitudes they held toward the world powers of their day.

With this went the firm conviction of Jeremiah that his was the "time" of the destruction of Judah as a political entity and its radical alteration as a religious entity. Isaiah had proclaimed a "time" of terrible punishment and, at the beginning of his ministry, his point of view did not differ noticeably from Jeremiah's teaching after his call. Yet the two prophets developed along different lines. Increasingly Isaiah sensed that a margin of time for conversion was being offered to Judah, that a full end to the political and religious institutions of the kingdom had not yet been decreed by Yahweh. From 705 onward his prevailing summons was for Judeans to pay attention to and to make wise use of the time of grace being granted them by Yahweh. Events disappointed him in a way which Jeremiah's dimmer outlook avoided. Jeremiah did not look for repentance and was not disappointed when he elicited none. He knew that a radical alteration in Judean life would be necessary before something new emerged as the chrysalis of Judean faith. Although it is not accurate to set the two prophets against one another in opposition, there is a striking difference in their conceptions of the timing and process of Yahweh's world program. *Isaiah hoped to salvage Judah while Assyria was punishing and being punished. Jeremiah felt that the punishment of Judah must be pursued to the bitter end and that Babylon's punishment must be dealt with as an entirely separate matter and at a much later date.* Isaiah had the advantage of a more plastic dynamic view, of a greater sensitivity to wrong wherever it existed. Jeremiah had the advantage of seeing the international situation more realistically and of focusing with unrelenting courage and agony upon the wrongs that were really the concern of Judah, namely, Judah's wrongs.

Jeremiah showed a remarkable detail and accuracy in his prophecies. He predicted the defeat of Egypt at Carchemish, the seventy-year dominion of Babylon in the ancient Near East, the impending death of his prophet opponent, Hananiah, the execution of two Jewish prophet-agitators by Nebuchadnezzar, and the temporary nature of the lifting of the siege of Jerusalem. Needless to say, none of these predictions has the character of soothsaying; each can be "explained" from the combination of the prophet's knowledge of international affairs and his deep insight into the content of the souls of men and peoples which activated the ever-unfolding events of political history. Even so, a prophet so willing to be specific in his prophecies inevitably suffered "errors." The vividly conceived "foe from the north" was a long time in coming. Jehoiakim was presumably not dishonored in death as the prophet had anticipated. Nebuchadnezzar's punitive invasion of Egypt did not develop in Hophra's reign and, in fact, was never on the scale envisioned by Jeremiah. *Yet the prophet's predictive "score" was astonishingly high and in no important matter did he fail. All of his "errors" could be compensated for by slight reinterpretation.* If not immediately after 609, then within four years the Babylonians would strike from the north. If Jehoiakim was not assassinated, his policy at any rate ended in the capture of Jerusalem. If Nebuchadnezzar was slow to invade Egypt and if his attack was not after all so devastating, it was nevertheless sufficient to keep Egypt in an entirely secondary position in ancient Near Eastern affairs.

The pro-Babylonian spirit of the prophet seems to have been traitorous and impossibly passive. There is no blinking the fact that he saw the kingdom of Judah as doomed and, if the king would not act accordingly, individual Judeans should take matters into their own hands and surrender. This view was astonishing in the light of the ancient conception of a corporate body and shows that there is much to the view that Jeremiah stressed the individual responsibility of Yahweh believers, even though his "individualism" has frequently been misrepresented. By all recognized political standards Jeremiah was a traitor and would have been so regarded in any nation in the world, then or now, whether or not the actual legal machinery was invoked to judge and to sentence him. But his motives were very different from those usually detectable in traitors. He was not seeking any personal advantages from the Babylonians. He was not acting in the belief that it would be better to live under a Babylonian regime than under a Judean one. He simply believed that obedience to Yahweh, the world deity, which alone distinguished his people from other peoples, was to be best served by surrendering to the Babylonians. *No political entity as such could possibly understand his motives or logic but he had very clear support in the religious traditions of his people, and in his own mind there was no doubt sufficient to deter him from his unrelenting course.* That he was no wild eccentric is plain enough from the fact that he influenced wide sections of the ruling class in Judah. Zedekiah himself was strongly persuaded by the prophet's arguments although officially he resisted the course of action which he privately sensed to be right.

Accordingly, Jeremiah preferred to suffer the social and physical abuse of a traitor than to suffer the inward shame of being a traitor to the message he had received from Yahweh. By the same token he was quite oblivious to the fact that this position was favored and "used" by pro-Babylonians and by Babylonians for their own purposes, that he could be viewed as a collaborator or "a fellow traveler." He who had urged desertion to the Babylonians seemed surprised and indignant when his own departure from the city was interpreted as desertion. Since for himself that course had been so far from his mind, he could not readily see how others could entertain the suspicion of him. The chain of political causality, the congeries of hate and fear that inflame men in groups to intense chauvinism were very distant from his mind. He knew these realities for they had often enough buffeted and bruised him, but he could not understand them or think in their terms. He was thus in a real sense politically naïve despite the immense knowledge of affairs which he had at his grasp, not because of abstract utopian concepts, but because his own nature was not subject to the wild irrationalities of political life. In spite of his sensitivity to popular feelings and opinions, and his really deep love for his homeland, he could not in the last analysis grasp the motive or the meaning of human sacrifice upon the altar of nationalism. Yet even this deep irrationality of men could be used of Yahweh and would be.

The prophet understood the community of Yahweh worshipers in chiefly non-political but not non-collective terms. *The individualism of Jeremiah means only that one by one Yahweh believers will pass through the collapse of the old institutions and on the other side band themselves in new forms of community, but the community will endure.* One form was emerging in exile and another in Judah. These communities might or might not have independent political rulers. What was important was their fidelity to the ancient Yahwistic conceptions of social righteousness and an intimate life of prayer. Temple and sacrifice were quite immaterial. Particular forms of political order were also dispensable. Mizpah in Benjamin would serve as the religious center of Judah as easily as Jerusalem. Gedaliah, a Babylonian commissioner, was as acceptable as a Davidic prince. There is an astonishing plasticity to Jeremiah's view of the future. He picks up certain strains of Isaiah's thought and looks distantly toward the coming of the nations to a confederated faith in Yahweh. But because this will presumably occur at the end of the Babylonian world dominion it does not assume urgent proportions in his thought. His ability to call Nebuchadnezzar Yahweh's "servant" and his confidence that a foreigner in Judean government service "trusted in Yahweh" when he did what was right suggest that Jeremiah saw no limit to Yahweh's positive relations to people outside the covenant with Judah.

Ezekiel

Ezekiel straddles the fall of Judah in 587 with one foot in the sphere of Judean independence and the other in the realm of exile. His prophecies about and against the foreign nations reflect this fact by their double character, for they declare the nations to be both instruments of Yahweh's judgment of his people and oppressors of Israel and mockers of Israel's God. The arrogance of the foreigner so deeply felt by Isaiah and Habakkuk is expressed in Ezekiel as an affront to the honor of God, especially in the persons of the merchant-king of Tyre and the god-king of Egypt. Yet Ezekiel shares with Jeremiah an essentially favorable attitude toward Babylonia, which he too regards as the great imperial chastiser and pacifier of the nations. There are, in fact, no oracles against Babylon incorporated in the book of Ezekiel analogous to those appended to the book of Jeremiah.

The prophet's political knowledge was ample. He surveyed the previous two centuries of Israelite and Judean relations with Egypt, Assyria, and Babylonia. He was aware of Zedekiah's defection from his sovereign Nebuchadnezzar. He knew of an Ammonite rebellion in 589 paralleling Judah's revolt and of the advance of Nebuchadnezzar's army in the west. He heard of the defeat of Hophra's troops during the siege of Jerusalem. He was familiar with the destruction of the Ammonite and Moabite states in 582 by Babylonia and he expected the same fate for Edom. He was acquainted with the long struggle of Nebuchadnezzar to capture island Tyre. He knew of civil turmoil in Egypt and the consequent uprising of Ahmose, who replaced Hophra, and he reflects knowledge of the invasion of Egypt by Nebuchadnezzar. Although the last certainly dated oracle in the book is 570, it is likely that he knew of the action of Awel-Marduk in 562–561 in releasing Jehoiachin from Babylonian detention and placing him in a favored court position (as reported in II Kings 25: 27–30).

There is nothing in the prophet's knowledge of political developments in the western provinces which he could not have learned in Babylon, nor did his symbolic actions require a Judean rather than an exilic audience. As Jeremiah was well advised on exilic affairs by means of letters and oral messages, so Ezekiel was similarly informed on Palestinian affairs (cf. Jer. 29). The prophet's political knowledge and activity contain no objection to the plain sense of the text that Ezekiel carried out his entire ministry in Babylon.[133]

Political Allegories and Symbolic Acts

In two allegories Ezekiel applies the imagery of the husband-wife relations to Israel's international relations. In 16:1–43 Jerusalem is pictured as a foundling girl of bastard origin whom Yahweh befriended and married. In time, however, the wedding gifts he had lavished upon her were invested in idolatrous worship (vss. 15–22) and squandered upon foreign nations (vss. 23–29). Judah's relations with Egypt in the reign of Hezekiah, with Assyria under Manasseh, and with Babylonia in the reign of Jehoiakim and Zedekiah are described as "engaging in harlotry" (*wattiznî 'el,* vss. 26, 28). Sennacherib's transfer of Judean territory to the loyal Philistine cities in 701 B.C. is alluded to as the punishment for harlotry with Egypt (vs. 27).[134]

[133] For the main outlines of the argument in favor of the Babylonian ministry of Ezekiel, cf. N. K. Gottwald, *A Light to the Nations,* 1959, pp. 381–84. For supporting details, cf. C. G. Howie, *The Date and Composition of Ezekiel* (*JBL* Monograph Series, IV), 1950, pp. 5–26; C. J. Mullo Weir, "Aspects of the Book of Ezekiel," *VT* 2 (1952), 97–112; and G. Fohrer, *Die Hauptprobleme des Buches Ezechiel,* 1952, pp. 203–59.

[134] O. Eissfeldt, "Ezechiel als Zeuge fuer Senherib's Eingriff in Palaestina," *PJ* 27 (1931), 58–66.

In 23:1–35, the prophet treats Samaria and Jerusalem as
sisters (cryptically named *Oholah,* "her tent" [?] and *Oholibah,*
"tent in her" [?]; but cf. *Oholibamah,* "tent of the high place,"
Gen. 36:18). The erotic symbolism is heightened by franker descriptions of sexual play. The sisters "lust after" the handsome
Assyrian and Babylonian warriors and officials. The pro-Assyrian
reigns of Menahem and Hoshea in the north and of Ahaz, Hezekiah, and Manasseh in the south are roundly condemned, as are
the pro-Babylonian policies of more recent years.

The Assyrians are described rather schematically as "troops
dressed in purple, governors [*paḥôth*] and officials [*sᵉgānîm*], all
of them attractive young men on horseback" (vss. 5, 12, 23).
The description of the Chaldean officers whom Jerusalem "saw
pictured upon the wall, the likenesses . . . drawn in red, girded
with waistcloths, with draped turbans on their heads," is more
detailed, but we have insufficient independent knowledge of neo-
Babylonian dress to understand exactly the prophet's delineation.
Brilliantly colored murals of Assyrian kings, officers, and gods do
bear some resemblance to this description.[135] Perhaps the prophet
is describing murals he saw in Babylon or in Jerusalem before
his deportation. It is possible that among the idolatrous therio-
morphic pictures said to have been painted in the temple area
there were portrayals of Babylonians (cf. 8:10). The peoples
Pekod, Shoa, and Koa may be the Aramean tribes known respectively as the Paqadu, the Sutu, and the Qutu, who lived east
of the Tigris,[136] although the lack of a letter *t* in the Hebrew
names makes the latter two identifications doubtful.

*In these allegories, Ezekiel carries through the most sustained
application of the husband-wife imagery in the Old Testament.*
Political harlotry is the primary sin which he attacks, although
idolatry is not excluded and it seems that the tendency of the
editor who supplemented the basic allegories was to stress the

---

[135] See the reproduction of a wall painting from Dur-Sharruken in Mazar,
ed., *Views of the Biblical World,* III, 179. In 16:24–28, the *gav* (RSV,
"vaulted chamber," but perhaps "altar molding") and *rāmāh* ("elevated
place") may refer to masonry structures shown on relief scenes from the
temple of Ishtar at Ashur in the thirteenth century (Eissfeldt, "Hesekiel
Kap. 16 als Geschichtsquelle," *JPOS* 16 [1936], 286–92).

[136] H. G. May, *IB,* VI, 192.

religious apostasy of the sisters (cf. 16:44–63; 23:36–49). Hosea had previously exploited the political possibilities of the husband-wife imagery. The foreign nations with whom Israel sought alliance may be in the prophet's mind when he speaks of "lovers" (Hos. 2:5, 7, 12), and her agricultural produce is "the harlot's price" that they have paid the "lovers." Yet at best this is only a secondary consideration, a possible double entendre in the passage, for the chief emphasis is upon Baal as the paramour and agricultural bounty as his gift to Israel rather than as an exaction from Israel. When the more explicitly political dimensions of Hosea's prophecy are treated, new figures are employed and Israel becomes "a silly dove" (Hos. 7:11) or "a lone ass" (Hos. 8:9) or "an overheated oven" (Hos. 7:4, 6).

Ezekiel seizes upon the sexual imagery in order to extract political meanings. He sees the course of Israel's and Judah's international involvement as one of thoughtless infatuation, hurled this way and that by baseless whims and erotic seductions. Israel has been guilty of faddism, of pursuing the momentarily pleasurable at the expense of the abidingly productive. In a clever manipulation of his imagery he pictures Jerusalem as lower than a harlot for, instead of receiving gain for her services, she has flung herself at her lovers and has given bribes in order to receive their attentions! The heady draughts of international power politics have unbalanced her emotionally and she has ceased to calculate or to weigh what is best for her. This sweeping indictment is not altogether fair as a characterization of the entire course of Hebrew foreign policy. There were in truth occasions when the nations sought Judah and were apparently willing to pay a good price or at least to offer fair service or advantage in return, e.g., Merodach-baladan in 704 B.C. and the rebel Palestinian states in 594 B.C. But more often Judah, as a small power, was in the position of the suppliant, and the total effect of her foreign policy had been to deplete the country rather than to augment it economically.

Another facet of sexual experience is superbly employed by the prophet, namely, the ambivalence of sexual attraction and sexual revulsion. The pro-Babylonian and anti-Babylonian sentiments are seen to have something of the same irrational and unstable emotional intensity. The polar political loves and hates have an inner connection so that one extreme proclivity gives rise to its opposite. Unrequited hopes in a foreign alliance leave a sense of bitter disappointment which awakens counterforces impelling Judah toward hasty alliance against a former ally. Allies become enemies and enemies become allies, almost at will, for the bitter frustration following upon the failure of one alliance pattern gives rise to new but equally unstable configurations. Emotional release is sought by identifying the former love as an object of disdain and vice versa. The psychological penetration of the prophet is noteworthy.

In the allegory of the two vultures (Nebuchadnezzar and Hophra [?]), the cedar cutting (Jehoiachin), and the seedling vine (Zedekiah) Ezekiel sets forth contemporary events (17: 1–21). Nebuchadnezzar's transfer of Jehoiachin to Babylon is pictured as a beneficent action which preserves the Judean royalty. Zedekiah, the new Babylonian appointee, rebels against his sovereign by seeking aid from Egypt. This despicable action is precisely described by the prophet as "holding the [vassal] oath in contempt" [*bāzāh 'ālāh*, vss. 16, 18] and "frustrating the [vassal] covenant" [*lᵉhāphēr bᵉrîth*, vs. 18]. The expected help from the pharaoh will not materialize, and Zedekiah will be carried to Babylon where he will suffer his just punishment. The present form of the interpretation clearly connects the incident with the rebellion of Zedekiah in 589 and his dependence upon Pharaoh Hophra (cf. especially vs. 17). This seems the most natural view, although some see the allegory as originally referring to Pharaoh Psamtik in 592–591.[137] The allegory is rambling and syntactically vague at points. The conjecture that the reference to the pharaoh was entirely lacking in the original allegory is, however, unfounded.[138]

The severity of Ezekiel in condemning Zedekiah's breach of the vassal oath is unparalleled in prophecy. It is not true to say

[137] M. Greenberg, "Ezekiel 17 and the Policy of Psammetichus II," *JBL* 76 (1957), 304–9; in footnote 2 Greenberg cites other scholars who have made the same identification and he is followed by W. Zimmerli, *Biblische Kommentar*, 1958, p. 381.

[138] L. P. Smith, "The Eagle(s) of Ezekiel 17," *JBL* 58 (1939), 43–50; W. A. Irwin, *The Problem of Ezekiel*, 1943, pp. 110–18.

that *only* Ezekiel opposed violation of political oaths, for earlier prophets had appealed to Hebrew kings not to join in rebellions against their overlords. But never was the judgment upon revolt so pointed and absolute, as is underlined by the identification of the broken covenant and oath with the very demand of Yahweh, for "As I live, I shall repay him [Zedekiah] for my oath which he held in contempt and my covenant which he frustrated" (vs. 19). This undoubtedly reflects accurately the fact that Zedekiah had been made to swear allegiance to Nebuchadnezzar in the name of Yahweh as well as in the name of the Babylonian gods —apparently the typical Babylonian practice in the western provinces or at any rate perhaps in keeping with ancient Hittite practice.[139] The Chronicler also correctly notes the practice: "and he [Zedekiah] also rebelled against Nebuchadnezzar who had made him swear by Elohim" (II Chron. 36:13).

Two factors account for the fierce intensity of the prophet's condemnation of Zedekiah. One is the uncompromising standards of individual conduct which the prophet urged upon men as the basis of their "living" or "dying" (chap. 18).[140] A Judean king was not thought to be exempt from these stipulations. It is true that the moral requirements mentioned in chap. 18 do not include prohibition of oath-breaking, but such lists are merely exemplary and not exhaustive; furthermore, fidelity to the oath was an ancient ingredient of Yahwistic morality, which it shared, in fact, with general Semitic antiquity (cf., e.g., Gen. 21:22–23 and Josh. 9:19–20 for collective oaths, and Num. 30:1–2 and Zech. 8:17 for individual oaths). To regard the P condemnation of oath-breaking in Leviticus 5:4 as the immediate occasion of

---

[139] G. Mendenhall, *BASOR* 133 (1954), 30, note 16; Zimmerli, *op. cit.*, p. 386. Whether the Assyrians required their vassals to swear fealty in the name of the local gods is a matter of dispute. G. E. Mendenhall, *Law and Covenant in Israel and the Ancient Near East,* p. 60, definitely and D. J. Wiseman, "The Vassal Treaties of Esarhaddon," *Iraq* 20 (1958), apparently deny it, while M. Tsevat, "The Neo-Assyrian and Neo-Babylonian Vassal Oaths and the Prophet Ezekiel," *JBL* 78 (1959), 199–200, and E. F. Weidner, the original editor and commentator on the treaties of Esarhaddon with Baal of Tyre and Ashurnirari VI with Mati'ilu of Bit-Agusi (*Archiv fuer Orientforschung* 8 [1932,] 17–34) affirm it.

[140] Tsevat, *op. cit.*, pp. 203–4, and esp. W. Zimmerli, " 'Leben' und 'Tod' im Buche des Propheten Ezechiel," *TZ* 13 (1957), 494–508.

the prophet's attack upon Zedekiah is, however, highly doubtful.[141] That verse speaks of "hidden" or inadvertent violations of an oath, and Zedekiah's action was certainly deliberate. In any case, that the prophet was able to apply an uncompromising moralism to the nation as well as to individual Judeans is no surprise in the light of the prophetic "whole view" of societal responsibility and in the light of the emphatic moralism of Ezekiel.

A second factor influencing the prophet's savage judgment upon the king was his belief that the special status of Judah since 597 might have continued to the benefit of the Hebrews had not Zedekiah upset the arrangement. Judah was semi-independent. Her actual king Jehoiachin was in custody in Babylon while his regent Zedekiah presided in Jerusalem. A sizable portion of the upper classes was interned in Babylonia, and a new ruling class had risen in Judah to surround the regent. The deportation had been intended not to destroy Judean sovereignty but to limit and insure it by removing rebellious elements and deterring further revolt. An aside in the allegorical interpretation notes that "the leaders of the land he [Nebuchadnezzar] had removed in order that the kingdom might be humbled and not arrogantly self-assured, and that by observing his treaty [Nebuchadnezzar's] it might endure" (17:13–14). Now, unfortunately, this policy of pacification by limited deportation and detention was jeopardized. It seemed that Zedekiah had learned nothing, and the loss of Judean independence was thus sealed by his intrigue with Egypt.

Ezekiel was deeply disappointed by this decision of Zedekiah for he shared Jeremiah's belief that cooperation with Babylon might permit a limited Judean monarchy to continue, whereas insubordination would only lead to loss of independence. It may seem inconsistent for the same prophet who announced the withdrawal of Yahweh from Jerusalem and its utter destruction because of its citizens' sins to have held the king responsible for this destruction. But to Ezekiel the king's sin was of one piece with the people's sins and was all the more culpable since the king

[141] Tsevat, *op. cit.,* p. 203. Against the interpretation is the fact that Leviticus 5:4 refers to an *inadvertent* breach of oath and one could scarcely break a vassal oath without knowing it.

acted with special responsibility for the whole people. When the king broke his vassal oath to Nebuchadnezzar, he only confirmed the prophet's dim view of Judean corruption. Strictly speaking, the punishment envisioned is the deportation and arraignment of Zedekiah for treason in Babylon and the destruction of his bodyguard (reading *mibhhārāw*, "hand-picked," instead of *mibhrāhāw*, "fugitives," in vs. 21, in accordance with several Hebrew manuscripts, Syriac, and Targum).[142]

Doubtless, at the same time, however, the collective sins of the Judean people will conspire to bring destruction upon them. The catastrophe is not the result of the sins of the few or even of the king alone, yet all the guilty will receive their punishment and the righteous few will somehow be spared (cf. 9:4–6). The seeming unrealism of this view of a collective guilt compounded of innumerable individual guilts, each to be requited, is, nevertheless, thoroughly understandable as a serious effort by the prophet to combine the predominant collective guilt theory with a sharp re-emphasis and heightening of an equally ancient belief in individual responsibility.[143] *It is not that Ezekiel first introduces "individualism" but rather that he reasserts individual guilt in company with collective guilt as two ways of seeing the same truth.*

In the allegory of the lioness (Judah) and her two whelps (Jehoahaz and Jehoiachin), Ezekiel pictures the facile confidence of the Judeans in the two young rulers, who reigned only three months each and who shared similar fates (19:1–9). Jehoahaz, who followed his father Josiah to the throne in 609 (or 608), was taken to Egypt as a political prisoner by Necho and replaced on the throne by Jehoiakim, his half-brother. The latter's son, Jehoiachin, succeeded to the throne in 598 just as the Babylonian army was on its way to quell the Judean revolt. Jehoiachin was taken to Babylon in the spring of 597. These events are par-

---

[142] See esp. the textual note in Zimmerli, *op. cit.*, p. 376.

[143] The relation between the collective and individual modes of thought in ancient Israel is currently being re-examined, as, e.g., by W. Eichrodt, *Man in the Old Testament*, 1951, pp. 9–20, who finds a radical moral personalism in the most ancient Hebrew laws, and J. Scharbert, *Solidaritaet in Segen und Fluch*, 1958, I, 223–28; cf. also T. C. Vriezen, *An Outline of Old Testament Theology*, 1958, pp. 324–25.

tially mirrored in the allegory. Much of the language is a purely figurative endeavor to carry out the lion imagery in a consistent manner,[144] but the fact that the kings are each chosen by their own people and each carried into exile makes their identification unmistakable. As to why the intervening king Jehoiakim has been omitted, we can perhaps only conjecture that the youthfulness and promise of two briefly reigning monarchs reflect a pathos which the prophet wishes to emphasize.

The one historical detail possibly supplied by this lament is the reference to the *sûgar* (Akkadian *šigarū*, "cage") in which the Assyrians on occasion put captive kings and which the neo-Babylonians seem to have imitated in carrying Jehoiachin into captivity.[145] The presumed domestic ravages of Jehoiachin posited by the English translations of vs. 7 are based on a difficult text which upsets the lion imagery and in itself cannot be used either to contradict the identity of the king or to supply additional historical knowledge concerning Jehoiachin. It is of course possible that the youthful Jehoiachin, faced with an advancing Babylonian army and contending factions at home, took swift action in suppressing his internal opponents and that civil strife contributed to the quick capitulation of Jehoiachin to Nebuchadnezzar; but it would be shaky exegesis to conclude such only from Ezekiel's enigmatic allegory.

Among the vivid symbolic actions of Ezekiel is his miming of Nebuchadnezzar at the Syrian crossroads in the act of determining by means of divination which rebel city to attack first—Rabbath-Ammon or Jerusalem (21:18–24; Hebrew 21:23–29). The king stands at a road fork in southern Syria in the Litani Valley or in the vicinity of Damascus. He knows that both Judah and Ammon have revolted and he consults the occult powers in order to draw up his battle plan; he is obliged "to consult the omens; he shakes the arrows, he inquires of the teraphim, he examines the liver. Into his right hand comes the omen [lot?] for Jerusalem . . ." (vss. 21b–22a). The prophet portrays the elaborate divinatory paraphernalia carried by Mesopotamian kings

---

[144] May, *op. cit.*, pp. 164–65.

[145] G. A. Cooke, *ICC*, p. 208, and Mazar, *Views of the Biblical World*, III, p. 174.

when they went on military campaigns.[146] Arrow divination by shooting and striking the ground was known in Israel (II Kings 13:15–19), and arrows with names inscribed on them were used as lots among the Arabs.[147] Teraphim, apparently small household images, are frequently associated with consultation of oracles and necromancy in the Old Testament, but the exact mechanics of teraphim divination are unknown (Judg. 18:14, 17, 20; I Sam. 15:23; II Kings 23:24; Zech. 10:2; Hos. 3:4). Liver examination, unmentioned in the Bible, was a common Babylonian practice which required considerable skill in mastering the anatomy of the liver and the omen code based upon variations in the color and formation of the liver.[148] Clay liver models divided into sections with the omens written on them are known from Babylon and even from Megiddo and Hazor.[149]

Whether "the omen [or lot?]" (*qesem*) which comes into the king's hand is a general summary statement for the answer given by all three means of divination or whether it refers to an oracular answer obtained from only one, perhaps from the teraphim, cannot be judged. For the sake of keeping his symbolic action simple and to the point, the prophet represents only the king as divining; but in actual fact he would have been surrounded by divining priests whose technical knowledge was indispensable for getting the proper results from the oracles.

Oracles Against Tyre

The oracles against Tyre in the book of Ezekiel have a distinctive character not closely paralleled anywhere in the Old

[146] J. M. Munn-Rankin, *Iraq* 18 (1956), 70–74, discusses the religious and cultic aspects of warfare and diplomacy, especially among the Amorites.

[147] Cooke, *op. cit.,* p. 232.

[148] The origin, character, and historical worth of the Mesopotamian omen texts are discussed by A. Goetze, "Historical Allusions in Old Babylonian Omen Texts," *JCS* 1 (1947), 253–65. The texts describe the types of events which can be expected to happen if a particular configuration of the animal liver, or viscera generally, is observed.

[149] In 1958 an inscribed clay liver model from the fifteenth century was found in a Canaanite temple at Hazor (Y. Yadin, *BA* 22 [1959], 7–8; color photograph in Mazar, *Views of the Biblical World,* III, p. 176). Earlier an uninscribed liver model was found at Megiddo (G. Loud, *Megiddo,* 1935, vol. II, pl. 255).

Testament. The style is pleasantly felicitous in a book which is so often turgid reading. Canaanite mythological motifs are used in an effective symbolic manner.[150] The most difficult problem for the exegete is a determination of the date and even the number of the neo-Babylonian sieges of Tyre. The basic data in Josephus (*Contra Apionum* I. 21) and in Ezekiel (26; 29: 17–20) do not permit of any certain reconstruction. Josephus declares that a thirteen-year siege of Tyre began in the seventh year of Nebuchadnezzar, i.e., 598–586. If this is the same siege described by the prophet in chap. 26 and placed in the eleventh year of exile, i.e., 586, his prophecy of disaster for Tyre seems rather ill timed inasmuch as the long siege was drawing toward its close, presumably in Babylonian frustration. There is the further difficulty that 26:2 implies the fall of Jerusalem but, according to 33:21, the prophet did not yet know of the city's fall until the twelfth year of exile, i.e., 585. In addition, an oracle of the prophet in 570 speaks of the siege of Tyre as though it were a fairly recent event and not an operation completed sixteen years earlier (29:17–20).

Various plausible but inconclusive proposals to meet these difficulties have been put forward. By understanding Josephus to have meant the seventh year of Ittobaal of Tyre's rule rather than Nebuchadnezzar's, the siege may be placed beginning in 586 and thus synchronized with Ezekiel 26:1.[151] Or, by reading the *seventeenth* year of Nebuchadnezzar instead of the seventh, the siege will have opened in 588–587.[152] The date in Ezekiel 26:1 is "the twelfth year" in LXXA, which, if accepted, permits a better synchronization with 33:21, since word of the fall of Jerusalem will in that case have reached the prophet in 585 *before* his tirade against Tyre. The most novel suggestion is to assume that Josephus was correct in dating one unsuccessful siege of Tyre 598–586 but that there was a successful siege at a later

---

[150] S. B. Frost, "Eschatology and Myth," *VT* 2 (1952), 79–80, and J. L. McKenzie, "Mythological Allusions in Ezek. 28:12–28," *JBL* 75 (1956), 322–27.

[151] O. Eissfeldt, "Das Datum der Belagerung von Tyrus durch Nebukadnezar," *Forschungen und Fortschritte* 9 (1933), 421–22.

[152] W. F. Albright, "The Seal of Eliakim and the Last Pre-exilic History of Judah," *JBL* 51 (1932), 94–95.

date which accounts for the contemporary interest in Tyre in 570 and its association with an attack on Egypt[153] (Ezek. 29: 17–20). This also explains why in 557 and 553 Tyrians had to send to Babylon for a prince (governor?) since they were by then subject to Babylon.[154] The second siege might be placed between 574–572 and 570–569 (or even as late as 565), following Pharaoh Hophra's conquest of Phoenicia in 581 or slightly later and preceding Nebuchadnezzar's invasion of Egypt in 568. This theory fails, however, to deal illuminatingly with the oracle against Tyre dated 586 (or 585) according to 26:1, nor does it account for the fact that Tyre is reported to have sent emissaries to a revolutionary council meeting in 594 at Jerusalem (Jer. 27:3), at a time when, on Josephus' date, the city of Tyre was under siege.

No hypothesis concerning the siege of Tyre is entirely satisfactory beyond the general recognition that, after a lengthy siege (or perhaps two), the city was finally subjected to Babylon. And the subjection of the city may well have occurred before 570 for the statement that "neither he [Nebuchadnezzar] nor his army got any wage for the service he performed against it" (Ezek. 29:18) does not necessarily mean that the city had not been captured but may only signify that, whenever captured, the booty was insufficient compensation for the long and costly siege.

The mocking lament over the ruin of the ship Tyre by a sudden squall is superbly executed (27:2–9a, 25b–36). The imagery is disturbed in vss. 9b–25a by a shift in concept from Tyre as a ship to Tyre as the great city to which come "all the ships of the sea." It is true that the list of peoples trading with Tyre is a sixth-century inventory of Phoenician colonies and Near Eastern peoples which can hardly be later than the rise of the Persian empire.[155] It is also possible to argue that the labored itemizing of peoples and products is a device for illustrating the fabulous wealth of Tyre.[156] The supposed parallel instances of lists in the

[153] M. Vogelstein, "Nebuchadnezzar's Reconquest of Phoenicia and Palestine and the Oracles of Ezekiel," *HUCA* 23 (1950–51), 197–220.
[154] *Ibid.*, p. 204.
[155] R. H. Pfeiffer, *Introduction to the Old Testament*, 1941, pp. 533–34.
[156] S. Smith, "The Ship Tyre," *PEQ* 85 (1953), 100.

midst of poetry are not quite parallel, however, since they are drawn from extended epics whereas in this instance the prose is about as long as the lament. Ezekiel may have been the author of the commercial catalog but its prophetic function is not at all apparent. On balance, it seems to be a learned insertion which arose during the exile and which was supplied here to underscore the vast commercial connections of Tyre. The poem alone reflects a considerable knowledge of the select materials and the skills used in shipbuilding, although nothing in it presupposes that the author had visited Tyre. That men of Arvad and Sidon are represented as "rowers" of the ship Tyre correctly reflects the mercantile and political prominence of Tyre in the sixth century.[157]

Two additional poems over Tyre, both mocking laments, although only one is specifically called a *qinah*, make skillful use of old north Canaanite mythological motifs. In one the prince of Tyre is derisively described as "wiser than Daniel," the ancient sage-king, father of Aqat, known from a fourteenth-century Ugaritic text[158] and mentioned also by Ezekiel in 14:14, 20 (28: 2–10). It seems clear that this is a north Canaanite version of the primeval garden myth uninfluenced by the Hebrew version in Genesis 3–4.[159] Certain similarities in the story suggest an ul-

[157] *Ibid.*, p. 107; for discussion of the positions of Arvad and Sidon in the sixth century, see Cooke, *op. cit.*, pp. 298–99.

[158] Most commentators see at least indirect dependence on the Ugaritic myth of Danel (A. Bertholet, *HZAT*, 1936, p. 53; G. Fohrer, *HZAT*, 1955, pp. 78–79; M. Noth, "Noah, Daniel und Hiob in Ezechiel 14," *VT* 1 [1951], 251–60). May, *op. cit.*, pp. 137, 217–18, inclines toward *denying* an allusion to the Canaanite Daniel in chap. 14 and *affirming* it in chap. 27; the latter he believes to be "a revision of an original Ezekelian allusion to Danel . . . in the light of the Daniel of the Hebrew tradition" (pp. 217–18). For the Ugaritic myth cf. C. Gordon, *Ugaritic Literature*, 1949, pp. 84–103, and *ANET*, pp. 149–55.

[159] H. Stocks, "Danel, die suedbabylonische und die nordpalaestinisch-phoenikische Ueberlieferung," *ZDMG* 97 (1943), 125–49, followed by Fohrer, *HZAT*, p. 162. M. Pope, *El in the Ugaritic Texts*, 1955, pp. 97–100, sees a myth of the expulsion of El from the Ugaritic pantheon but, in the opinion of J. L. McKenzie, *op. cit.*, p. 325, the absence of the palace and rivers of Paradise motifs in Ezekiel invalidates Pope's argument. McKenzie believes that Ezekiel 28 is a condensed form of an alternate Hebrew Paradise story in which only a man appeared who was famed for his wisdom (pp. 326–27).

timate common origin (e.g., the garden is called Eden, it is the source of precious materials, a guardian cherub expels the fallen man), but there are significant variations (e.g., the garden is located on a holy mountain, the precious materials are stones rather than metals, the cherub is appointed initially to protect the man, there are no trees). Since the old myth is only used illustratively, as Milton used classical mythology, it is impossible to reconstruct the exact form of the original.

The sins with which the city (or the prince, clearly representing the city Tyre)[160] is charged are forcefully stated. Tyre has thought itself "the very perfection of beauty" (27:3; 28:11), has "pretended to have a mind equal to that of a god" (28:2, 6), and "has exalted its heart (in pride)" because of its wealth and beauty (28:2, 5, 17). Its undoubted skill in commerce has led to violent wrongs and overweening pride; an original wisdom, i.e., commercial skill, has been "spoiled" by its abuse (28:16–17). Illustrative of its distorted commercialism is the glee with which Tyre greets the news of Jerusalem's destruction: "Ha, the gate of the peoples is smashed, it has swung open for me; I shall be filled (now that) she is laid to waste" (26:2). Tyre thinks only of her own trade advantage when other peoples are destroyed. The allusion to Jerusalem as "the gate of the peoples" is exaggerated, to be sure, but Jerusalem, like Damascus, was in a position to control the trade routes from Arabia to the Phoenician coastlands.[161] By exacting tribute from the overland caravans, the prices of goods were inevitably raised in the Phoenician ports. When Israel or Judah had strong kings (most recently Josiah), Tyre no doubt felt the commercial disadvantage—unless she could manage to enter a covenant with her competitor, as she did in the reigns of David and Omri-Ahab.

The sin then with which Tyre is charged is nationalistic egocentricity, which leads to an excessive self-regard, an insensitivity

---

[160] G. Hoelscher, *Hesekiel, der Dichter und das Buch,* 1924, pp. 140–43, and I. G. Matthews, *Ezekiel* (An American Commentary on the OT), 1939, p. 106, believe that Ezekiel refers only to the city, the king in vs. 12a being editorial, but the clear presence of the king in a similar passage, Isaiah 14, argues for the originality of the reference to royalty (May, *op. cit.,* p. 220).

[161] C. F. Whitley, *The Exilic Age,* pp. 102–3.

to her own limitations and impermanence, and a callousness toward other peoples in distress. An originally desirable and admirable talent for trade has been corrupted by a people who forgot its place among the nations and even came to boast in effect: "I am a god" (28:2, 9). *The prophetic sense of evil as rebellion and arrogance rather than utter depravity and malevolence is superbly expressed.*[162] At the same time we see how remote the prophet's idea is from that of the reactionary Nazirite or Rechabite groups. Mercantalism is not an intrinsic evil but rather the occasion for temptation to inordinate pride, to violence of hand and hardness of heart. The implication is that an authentic national life based upon commerce would be possible if men once fully accepted their ontological and moral limitations.

Oracles Against Egypt

The book of Ezekiel contains seven oracles against Egypt, of which five are dated in the years 587–585 (29:1–16 [January 6, 587]; 30:20–26 [April 19, 586]; 31:1–18 [June 11, 586]; 32:1–16 [March 3, 585]; 32:17–32 [April 16, 585]), one in 570 (29:17–20 [April 16, 570]), and one is undated (30:1–19).[163] There may, in fact, be more than seven oracles against Egypt, for chapter 30 appears to be composed of three separate oracles: vss. 1–9, 10–12, 13–19. In other instances the original oracles appear to have been supplemented by the prophet or an editor (29:6–9, 11–16; 31:14–18)[164] and elsewhere two versions of an oracle seem to have been combined (30:20–26; chap. 32—cf. vss. 4 and 5–6, 9 and 10, 11b–12 and 13–14).[165] Serious doubts about the integrity of the oracles have been expressed repeatedly, especially with respect to 30:1–19; 32:1–16; and 32:17–32. It is easy to share these doubts for, in any case, the style of the

---

[162] O. Procksch, *Theologie des Alten Testaments,* 1950, pp. 632–42.

[163] The dates are those given by May, *op. cit.,* p. 59, on the basis of R. A. Parker and W. H. Dubberstein, *Babylonian Chronology 626 B.C.—A.D. 45,* 1942, pp. 25–26. The dating assumes that the Hebrews at this time were following an autumnal rather than a vernal calendar.

[164] May, *op. cit.,* pp. 223, 233.

[165] J. Plessis, *Les prophéties d'Ézéchiel contre l'Égypte (XXIX–XXXII),* pp. 83–84, 87–88.

oracles is repetitious and bombastic; but the style is so uniform that the identification of additions or the transition from prose to poetry is extremely subjective. There are no clear historical allusions that require a time later than Ezekiel, nor are there theological beliefs or motifs which necessitate a much later age. There are inconsistencies of imagery and sharp transitions in the themes which suggest editing but it is not to be ruled out that the prophet is responsible for some or all of these incongruities.

In the first oracle the pharaoh is conceived as the *tannîn* or crocodile (possibly "dragon" or "water monster") who will be hauled onto land along with the fishes clinging to him (the Egyptian people) and left to be devoured by beasts and birds (29:1–16). The object of particular disdain is the pharaoh's presumption to be Creator, for he says: "My Nile is mine: I made it" (vss. 3, 9).[166] Vss. 6–9a intrude into this imagery by employing the earlier figure of Egypt as an unreliable reed staff (cf. Isa. 36:6). In vss. 11–16 the destruction of Egypt is limited to a forty-year desolation, after which Yahweh will restore its fortunes. The future Egyptian kingdom will, however, be limited to Pathor or Upper Egypt, which is correctly described as "the land of their origin," for it was from southern Egypt that the united kingdom arose under Menes.[167] This limited kingdom will be so diminished that it will never again be a threat to the nations. The oracle may be from Ezekiel; its modest hope for Egypt is reminiscent of Isaiah 19:18–25, although very differently expressed.

The fact that the oracle of Yahweh in 30:1–19 is undated may reflect the miscellaneous character of the words within it. All three sections may be from the prophet's hand, but, apart from the reference to an invasion of Egypt by Nebuchadnezzar in vs. 10, the historical data are virtually nil. The presumed references in vs. 5 to the various peoples serving as mercenaries in the Egyptian army are undermined by the doubtful text.[168] The cities named in vss. 13–18 as the targets of a punitive invasion are listed in a highly erratic pattern.[169] Memphis appears first, fol-

---

[166] Read *ᵃsîthiw* with Syria (LXX *ᵃsîthîm*) instead of MT *ᵃsîthinî;* cf. Cooke, *op. cit.*, pp. 326, 330.

[167] *Ibid.*, p. 328; Fohrer, *HZAT*, p. 169.

[168] Plessis, *op. cit.*, pp. 29–30; Cooke, *op. cit.*, pp. 332, 336.

[169] Plessis, *op. cit.*, pp. 33–39; Cooke, *op. cit.*, pp. 333–34.

lowed by Zoan in the Delta linked with Thebes in Upper Egypt, another Delta city Pelusium joined to Thebes (the pair repeated), and finally the three Delta cities of On, Pibeseth, and Tehaphnehes. The prominence of Delta cities corresponds to the expectation of an invasion from western Asia, but the absence of reference to the capital under Hophra's dynasty, namely Sais, suggests that the list is simply a schematic description of invasion and widespread destruction. It is possible that the allusions reflect the Egyptian campaign of Ashurbanipal almost a century earlier when he passed through the Delta and captured Memphis and Thebes.[170]

In the extremely verbose oracle of 30:20–26 there is a wordplay on the "arms" of the kings of Egypt and Babylon. Hophra's one arm had been broken when he went out to aid Jerusalem in 587 but soon both of his arms will be broken. Into Nebuchadnezzar's strengthened arms will go the sword of Yahweh to punish Egypt.

The allegory of the cedar of Lebanon employs the world-tree motif (31:1–18; cf. Dan. 4:1–37; Mark 4:30–32).[171] The figure was especially appropriate for pharaoh since from ancient times Egypt had obtained cedars from Byblos in Lebanon for building and ceremonial purposes.[172] The cosmic religious significance of the tree is shown in the two cedar trunks girdled by copper bands which stood on either side of the temple portals at Sargon's capital of Dur-Sharruken.[173] The Masoretic reading *'aššûr 'erez*, "Assyria was a cedar" (31:3), may easily be read as *'ašûr 'erez*, "I will consider a cedar"—without any consonantal change in the text. The imagery is carried through very effectively as far as vs. 13, but vs. 14 is an admonitory side glance at other arrogant trees, and vss. 15–18 mixes the world-tree and Sheol images in a none-too-felicitous manner. The essential sin

[170] H. R. Hall, *The Ancient History of the Near East*, pp. 500–503.

[171] G. Widengren, *The King and the Tree of Life in Ancient Near East Religion*, esp. pp. 56–58, believes that the originally separate motifs of the Tree of Life and the Cosmic Tree have been joined in Ezekiel 31:2–9 and in Daniel 4:7b–9; cf. also A. J. Wensinck, *Tree and Bird as Cosmological Symbols in Western Asia*, pp. 25–35.

[172] H. Kees, *Ancient Egypt. A Cultural Topography*, pp. 108–9.

[173] H. Frankfort, *Cylinder Seals*, 1939, pp. 205–7.

of excessive pride ("his mind was exalted in its pride"—vs. 10)
tallies aptly with the judgments on the prince of Tyre. The similar use of a mythological motif, including mention of "the trees
of Eden" located "in the garden of God" shows how well stocked
in traditional Canaanite symbols was the mind of the prophet.

In the *qinah* of 32:1–16 it is impossible to trace a consistent
3/2 lament meter and there are signs of a double recension.[174]
The dragon imagery of vss. 1–8 is given up in vss. 9–12, which
dwell rather upon the punishment of Egypt by the sword of the
king of Babylon. The apparent doublet of vss. 11 and 12 has been
connected with Cambyses II's invasion of Egypt in 525[175] but
this link is gratuitous. Vss. 13–16 cease to address Egypt in person
and describe rather the inhabitants of the land desolated by Yahweh. Oscillation between the king as head of a country, on the
one hand, and the land with its many inhabitants, on the other,
is a familiar biblical phenomenon and cannot of itself prove the
lament's disunity.[176]

Egypt's descent to Sheol where she is to lie prostrate with the
defeated peoples of Assyria, Elam, Meshech and Tubal, Edom,
and Sidon affords a valuable glimpse into ancient ideas of the
underworld. It seems, however, to have been revised considerably
and, if anywhere, the prophet's words are probably behind vss.
18–21. The *gibbôrîm*, the mighty legendary warriors of Sheol,
"shall speak of them [the multitudes of Egypt]" (vs. 21), but in
vs. 27 the *gibbôrîm* are entombed and silent. Ashur, Elam, Meshech and Tubal are assigned a place in Sheol apart from the
legendary *gibbôrîm* because these more recent inhabitants of the
underworld are "uncircumcised" and "slain by the sword" (vss.
26–28). The use of the epithet "uncircumcised" is curiously imprecise. It is incorrectly applied to Egypt,[177] and the assignment

---

[174] Plessis, *op. cit.,* pp. 87–88.

[175] Hoelscher, *op. cit.,* pp. 158–59.

[176] A. Jeffrey, *IB,* 1956, VI, 460–61, has shown convincingly that in interpreting the beasts and the Son of Man in Daniel 7 it is not necessary
to choose between an individual (king) and a collective (kingdom) since
both connotations are present.

[177] J. P. Hyatt, "Circumcision," *IDB,* I, 629, and cf. Mazar, *Views of the
Biblical World,* I, 57, for reproduction of a tomb relief illustrating a circumcision rite in the Sixth Dynasty of ancient Egypt.

of circumcised peoples, Edom and Sidon, to graves among the uncircumcised will hardly have been an ignominy for those people. In fact the constant coupling of "uncircumcised" and "slain by the sword" suggests that for the writer the former simply means "ritually defiled," i.e., having died an unnatural death.[178]

If the date over the oracle is accurate (585), neither Edom nor Sidon is correctly described as a lifeless people in Sheol for Edom was independent until 582 and Sidon seems to have gained a new commercial power after the diminution of Tyre's strength. Meshech and Tubal (the Akkadian Musku and Tabal of Asia Minor) are mentioned elsewhere in passages not attributable to the prophet (27:13; 38:2-3; 39:1). Internal evidence thus inclines rather decisively against authenticity, but the conception of Sheol as a place of utter desolation and silence depicted here is an ancient one, perhaps even more primitive than the more activistic view of Isaiah 14 and Ezekiel 31.[179] The arrangement of the tombs with the personified land in a central position surrounded by the graves of "all its multitude" suggests the royal circle graves of Mycenae in Greece.[180]

The last dated oracle in the book of Ezekiel is the promise that Nebuchadnezzar, who got no booty from Tyre, will plunder Egypt (29:17-20). It tacitly confirms the long siege reported by Josephus, for the efforts of Babylon against Tyre are described as "a great service" and, after exhausting siege efforts, there were insufficient goods to pay the wages of the army. This may mean that the siege was a failure and Tyre was not taken, or it may simply mean that during the course of the siege the inhabitants had sent away their treasures and consumed their food supplies so that nothing remained for the conquerors. The firm belief of the prophet that Nebuchadnezzar "serves" Yahweh by attacking

---

[178] O. Eissfeldt, "Schwerterschlagene bei Hesekiel," *Studies in Old Testament Prophecy Presented to T. H. Robinson,* 1950, pp. 73–81.

[179] For conception of Sheol, see R. Martin-Achard, *From Death to Life,* 1960, pp. 31–46, and J. Pedersen, *Israel; Its Life and Culture,* 1926, I, 460–70, and, for a contrary view, E. F. Sutcliffe, *The Old Testament and the Future Life,* 1946, pp. 36–81.

[180] A. J. B. Wace, *Mycenae. An Archaeological History and Guide,* 1949, pp. 59–63, plates 22, 77.

Tyre and Egypt is consonant with his other statements about the Babylonian king, as it is with the conviction of Jeremiah.

The extraordinary emphasis of Ezekiel upon the destruction of Tyre and Egypt may seem out of historical proportion. Why should the fate of these places be of such importance, especially now that the city of Jerusalem had fallen and there could no longer be doubt that Nebuchadnezzar had the will and the means to annul Judean independence? *Yet precisely this was still in question: could Nebuchadnezzar maintain his position in the west against the union of Egypt and the Phoenician cities?* Hophra, to be sure, had been repulsed on land in 587, but his navy seems to have been more successful along the Phoenician coast[181] and the long siege of Tyre may have been due to pharaoh's supply of the island city. The naval power of Egypt was a strong factor against the neo-Babylonians, who, like their Mesopotamian forebears, had no skills in seamanship. The Medes, who had maintained an uneasy peace with Babylonia ever since the defeat of the Assyrians, were waging victorious wars in Asia Minor. Nebuchadnezzar had good reason to fear that they might turn southward into Syria.[182] *The Jewish community in Babylon, augmented by the deportees of 587, will have been restive under such circumstances, eager to grasp at any sign of Babylonian weakness in the west.*

To this wistful optimism Ezekiel opposed himself by launching prophecy after prophecy against the two major threats to Babylon in Syria-Palestine: Tyre and Egypt. His words were not pointless simply because neither Tyrians nor Egyptians heard them directly. They were, as in the case of all oracles against foreign nations, intended in the first instance for the Jewish people. *They were intended to show that the exile would continue*

---

[181] Kienitz, *Die politische Geschichte Aegyptens* . . . , p. 29.

[182] The Medes pressed the Lydians as far as the Halys River but had to settle for it as a boundary (R. C. Thompson and D. G. Hogarth, *Cambridge Ancient History*, 1925, III, 214–15, 512). It is of interest that some Old Testament prophecies envision a Media strong enough to attack Babylon; cf. Isaiah 13:17–19; Jeremiah 51:11, 28, although it is possible that Media is confused with Persia in these passages, as apparently also happened in the book of Daniel. *IB*, VI, pp. 387–88.

for some time to come and that the expectation of a Phoenician-Egyptian axis against Babylon was a chimera. There was still considerable unfinished business to be taken care of by Babylon in behalf of Yahweh. Tyre and Egypt were arrogant states which needed to be chastised by Nebuchadnezzar and to have their commerce and agriculture destroyed before they would learn humility.

Oracles Against Judah's Near Neighbors

The oracles of chap. 25 which are directed against Ammon, Moab, Edom, and the Philistines in succession probably belong to the period just before Nebuchadnezzar's attack upon Ammon and Moab in 582. It is true that the prose is disappointing, but unless one assumes that Ezekiel was only a poet,[183] there is insufficient ground to deny him all of the oracles. There are no manifestly late ideas in the Ammonite and Moabite oracles; on the contrary, the situation in Palestine in 587–582 seems accurately reflected in them.[184] These peoples have harassed the depopulated regions of Judah and mocked the suffering of the Jews. The Ammonites "rejoiced with all the contempt within (them) over the land of Israel" (vs. 6), and the Moabites said, "Lo, like all the nations is the house of Judah!" The former expresses an affront against the suffering of Judah and the latter an affront to Judah's God, who refuses to be classified among the national gods and therefore to be thought of as defeated in the political defeat of Judah.

The chastisement of these peoples will be at the hands of the *benē qedem,* "the eastern tribes" from the adjacent desert, who will sweep into the cultivated sections of trans-Jordan and de-

---

[183] So largely G. Hoelscher, *op. cit.,* pp. 13–25, who found less than 170 verses from Ezekiel in 21 passages, 16 of which were poetic. W. Irwin, *op. cit.,* pp. 283–86, isolated fragmentary poetic units from 251 verses embedded in editorial prose. G. Fohrer, *Die Hauptprobleme des Buches Ezechiel,* pp. 60–66, by ignoring parallelism of members, purported to find poetry in what most commentators regard as prose.

[184] Vogelstein, *op cit.,* p. 203; Van Zyl, *The Moabites,* p. 25; Pfeiffer, *op. cit.,* p. 551.

nude it (vss. 4, 10).[185] Although this is to be the sad end of the Ammonites and Moabites, the initial attack appears to be expected not from the desert but from the northeast across the Jordan. Moab's high tableland will be invaded ("I will cut open the shoulder of Moab, from the cities along its frontier, the glory of the land, Beth-jeshimoth,[186] Baal-meon,[187] and Kiriathaim").[188] The sites generally proposed are located northeast of the Wadi Arnon along the edge of the cultivated plateau just as it plunges toward the Dead Sea and the Jordan Valley.[189] From this direction the punitive attack of Nebuchadnezzar in 582 no doubt came and, once the fortifications and armies of Ammon and Moab were laid waste, it was an easy thing for the bedouins from the desert to disrupt all sedentary life. For some reason, probably difficulties in Mesopotamia, Nebuchadnezzar was forced to withdraw before he had taken similar punitive measures against Edom.

The remaining two oracles in chap. 25 are not so vivid as the first two. They share a common emphasis upon "the vengeance" of the Edomites and Philistines against Judah and Yahweh's determination to visit his "vengeance" upon them, for the which "I will stretch out my hand against (Edom/the Philistines) and I will cut off . . ." (vss. 13, 16). Particularly dubious is the clear statement of vs. 14 that "I will put my vengeance upon Edom

---

[185] The area occupied by "the sons of the East" may be connected with the region of Safa eastward from Jebel Hauran to the eastern edge of the Harra (O. Eissfeldt, "Das Alte Testament im Licht der safatenischen Inschriften," *ZDMG* 104 [1954], 88–118). Other biblical references to the *bᵉnē qedem* occur in Genesis 29:1; Judges 6:3, 33; 7:12; 8:10; I Kings 4:30—Hebrew 5:10; Isaiah 11:14; Jeremiah 49:28; Job 1:3.

[186] Beth-jeshimoth may be Tell el-Azeimeh, twelve miles west-northwest of Medeba (N. Glueck, *BASOR* 91 [1943], 23–25, and Van Zyl, *op. cit.*, pp. 89–90).

[187] Baal-meon is apparently modern Ma'in, five and one-half miles southwest of Medeba (*IDB*, I, 332; Van Zyl, *op. cit.*, p. 87).

[188] Kiriathaim may be el-Qereiyat, twelve miles south-southwest of Ma'in (Glueck, *AASOR* 18–19 [1937–39], p. 131), but many doubt the identification (*IDB*, I, 37; Van Zyl, *op. cit.*, p. 83).

[189] May, *op. cit.*, p. 202, observes that the three sites named formed part of the "well-planned chain of fortresses, often within sight of each other, on the hilltops at the extreme edge of the fertile areas of the Moabite plateau."

by the hand of my people Israel." Elsewhere in the book, the foreign oppressors are always pictured as punished by another power, Nebuchadnezzar or the sons of the East. If the oracle is from Ezekiel, it can hardly come from the same period as the first two in the chapter for at that time he expected the Judean exile to continue. He will hardly have been thinking of an attack by the few hundred men around Gedaliah at Mizpah before 584, for the campaign envisioned is far more than a clearing out of encroaching Edomites from southern Judah. Rather it is a sweeping devastation of Edom. The final unit does not say that Judah will bring vengeance upon Philistia but, since in many respects the oracle is formally similar to the word against Edom, it too probably belongs to a later period.

Chaps. 35–39 form prophecies of the restoration and the establishment of Judah in Palestine and of the humiliation and the enfeeblement of the nations so that Judah will no more be molested by them. Except for the Gog of Magog prophecy in chaps. 38–39, the materials are largely from the prophet, allowing for possible occasional supplementation (e.g., 34:17–31; 36:33–38). *The return of Judah from the grave of her exile by a miracle of the divine Spirit* (37:1–14) *will be accompanied by a vindication of Yahweh before the nations.* Only in the unauthentic chaps. 38–39 is Israel's triumph accompanied by a universal destruction. Otherwise, the emphasis falls upon a manifestation of Yahweh's holiness by the resurrection of Israel. Insofar as there is to be destruction it is directed chiefly against Edom, addressed as Mount Seir (35), corresponding to the oracle of hope "to the mountains of Israel" (36), which in turn is coupled with the much earlier oracle of doom upon the "mountains of Israel" (6).

The doom/salvation oracles in chaps. 35 and 36 are to be dated after 582. The declaration "In my blazing anger I spoke against the remnant (*še'ērîth*) of the nations and against all Edom . . ." (36:5) and the even more precise "because they desolated you, and oppressed you from all sides, so that you became the possession of the remnant of the nations . . ." (36:3) show that the Edomites are still independent and a threat to the returning Jews. On the other hand, Ammon and Moab (and perhaps Philistia?), former oppressors of the Judeans, have suffered a military attack and deportation.[190] The term "remnant" is applied to these nations collectively and they lose their identity alongside Edom. It is clear from other biblical usages of *šeʾērîth hag-gôyim* that the phrase refers not to all nations of the ancient Near East but to Israel's immediate neighbors (cf. Jer. 25:20 [Ashdod]; 47:4 [island of Caphtor]; Ezek. 25:16 [Philistines]; Amos 9:12 [Edom]).[191]

After the fall of Jerusalem, the Edomites are known to have pressed into southern Judah in considerable numbers and to have formed elements later reckoned to the tribe of Judah (cf. I Chron. 2:9 ff.; 4:18 ff.). Unfortunately we do not know precisely when they came although, on the assumption that they were in part driven by the advancing Nabatean Arabs, the main movement is normally placed in the post-exilic period.[192] It is likely, however, that shortly after 582 the Edomites began to move more and more into southern Judah and that the Nabatean incursion into Edom was under way in the sixth century.[193] The devastation of much of trans-Jordan by the neo-Babylonians and the weakening of the Jewish population in Palestine following the murder of Gedaliah will have tempted the Edomites to occupy the Judean hill country around Hebron. The intensification of feeling against Edom in chap. 35, as against 25:12–14, may reflect the growing threat of Edom to Judah. If it was written after Nebuchadnezzar's attack on Egypt in 568, Edom may indeed have been the last serious threat to Judah in the West.

[190] Vogelstein, *op. cit.,* pp. 203–4, 208, who suggests that Nebuchadnezzar failed to conquer Edom in 582 because Hophra moved into Palestine and diverted his forces.

[191] *Ibid.,* p. 208; J. Morgenstern, "The Rest of the Nations," *JSS* 2 (1957), 225–31, seems accurate in his exposition of *šeʾērîth hag-gôyim,* but his further claim that Ezekiel 36 should be dated in 479 and referred to contingents of these peoples who were decimated in the defeat of Xerxes' campaign against Greece suffers a complete lack of convincing evidence.

[192] M. Haller, "Edom im Urteile der Propheten," *Marti Festschrift,* 1925, pp. 115–16; S. Cohen, "Edom," *IDB,* II, 26.

[193] The suggestion is based on the admittedly tenuous evidence of Herodotus' report that Cambyses had the aid of Arabs adjacent to Egypt (*History* III. 4, 9). This may be taken to mean that shortly after 587 the Nabatean Arabs were in Edom, which also may be hinted at in Malachi 1:3 ff. (Vogelstein, *op. cit.,* pp. 209–10).

Yahweh's Vindication Before the Nations

In the prophet's expectation of return from exile ("they will shortly come"—36:8) there is a strong sense of Yahweh's desire to vindicate his work with Israel in the sight of the nations. "The reproach of the nations" has fallen upon Israel but now Yahweh swears "that the nations surrounding you shall suffer reproach" (36:7). What is this despicable reproach above all else? It is the jeer against the God of Israel, "These are the people of Yahweh; yet from his land they were expelled!" (36:20b). This cry is perfectly consistent with the "people-oriented" religious thinking of the ancient world. Every god has a land and the people occupying it are just as secure as their god is strong. If a people fails and loses its land, its god loses all status in the international community. Inevitably Yahweh is a defunct deity, only to be laughed at.

Ezekiel cannot imagine Yahweh's merely brushing aside this unenlightened reasoning. His terrible jealousy is aroused. In an astonishing anthropopathism the prophet represents God as saying, "I will take pity upon my holy name which the house of Israel defiled among the nations to which they came" (36:21). And what was Israel's defilement of Yahweh? Not that they sinned grievously in exile, but only that they were in exile. They were living signs of the failure of Yahweh, or so the nations reckoned. How then can the reputation of God be restored among the nations? Nor merely by punishing the nations, any more than it was sufficient to punish Israel. To be sure, the peoples must be humbled as Israel was humbled. But since this work of punishment is largely completed, Yahweh will rebuild the community of Israel in Palestine, for "I shall be hallowed among you before their very eyes" (36:23). *The restored Israel will exist as a constant demonstration to the nations that Yahweh is Lord. Precisely for this reason the nations are not to be destroyed, for dead men cannot acknowledge the honor of Yahweh.*

Once restored to Palestine, the survivors of the two Hebrew kingdoms will form one people under a single king. Purged of their idolatry and lawlessness, they will join in covenant with

Yahweh and worship at their rebuilt sanctuary. The symbolic action of the joining of the two sticks labeled "For Judah and the Israelites with him" and "For Joseph and the Israelites with him" (37:15–28) anticipates in embryo the plan for the new temple and the new Jerusalem sketched in chaps. 40–48. The oracle closes with the sanctuary (*miqdāš*) posited as the epitome of the purified worship of Israel, which shall be a sign to the nations that God sanctifies (*meqaddēš*) Israel.

The nations thus play a crucial role in Ezekiel's conception of judgment and salvation. On one level they suffer punishment for their own wanton pride and cruel attitude toward Judah. On another level they shall reap the bitter fruit of their mockery of God's people, for in mocking Israel they mock God. Conversely, the delivery of Judah into exile has afforded Yahweh the opportunity to work the miracle of his grace. It has become clear that the Judeans have not merited the least of his favors, nor are they at all strong enough to demand his assistance. They are corpses—in fact only bleached bones which he must resurrect, to the astonishment of the house of Israel and to the utter amazement of the nations. *The exile serves to bear the reality of Israel's impotence and sin to all the nations and at the same time it serves to manifest the unmerited grace and incomparable power of Yahweh.* Nations serve Yahweh only indirectly for they do not participate in the salvation of Israel (except perhaps for Egypt), but they are the indispensable backdrop for fulfilling Israel's salvation. Yahweh as the God of all peoples desires their adulation, and to give it unstintingly they have had to know of the wonder of his work with Israel.

The Prophet's Hope of Restoration

There arises in connection with these last prophecies of Ezekiel the problem of their date. Chaps. 34–37 are undated but they seem, without question, among the latest in the book. Certainly they were written later than the neo-Babylonian attack upon Ammon and Moab in 582, and one is inclined to think that they were written after 568, when the consuming interest of the prophet in Egypt may have receded following Nebuchadnezzar's punitive raid upon the land of the Nile. *In fact the hopeful spirit which pervades these chapters must have had some basis. The steady insistence upon judgment which informs the oracles dated in the 580's, and even one as late as 572, has given way to a new atmosphere.*

What is the new factor? Is it the prophet's expectation of Babylon's overthrow? To the contrary, there is not so much as a hint in the book of Ezekiel that the prophet expected or desired the downfall of Babylon. He has not breathed so much as the seventy-year qualification for the rule of Babylon introduced by Jeremiah. This can only mean that the restoration of Judah was to take place under the aegis of Babylon. Nevertheless, why should he suddenly expect that Babylon would re-establish the Jews in Palestine? The answer may lie in the stabilization of the empire which Nebuchadnezzar managed to achieve in his last years. The attack on Egypt, while apparently in no sense a total defeat for the pharaoh, was sufficient to prevent further Egyptian meddling in Asiatic politics. With the chief troublemakers in Syria and Palestine sufficiently pacified, it seemed a likely prospect that the aged Nebuchadnezzar would begin a program of rebuilding in the west (see Maps 11 and 12). By returning the Jews to their homeland he could work for economic recovery in Palestine, and an effective buffer against renewed Egyptian adventures would be established at the same time.

Further attestation to this interpretation is the hopeful appendage to the oracle against Egypt dated in 572, which says, "In that day I will cause a horn to spring forth for the house of Israel and to you [Ezekiel] I will give freedom to speak in their midst and they shall know that I am Yahweh" (29:21).[194] This is not a strict messianic passage but it does foretell the political rebuilding of Israel and the prophet's ability to communicate with his people (in contrast to 33:30–33). The prophet may in fact have been a laborer for the restoration of his people, representing his ideas to the Jewish elders and to the Babylonians as he had opportunity. And if the date of 40:1 gives at least the

[194] Vogelstein, *op. cit.*, pp. 211–15; the verse is widely regarded as authentic (May, *op. cit.*, p. 228; Cooke, *op. cit.*, p. 330; Fohrer, *HZAT*, p. 170).

time for the first form of the vision of the new temple, he was already in 572 engaged in sketching the plan for a division of civil and religious authority in the restored community.

The enigmatic "thirtieth year" of the superscription (1:1) has been plausibly referred to an edition of the book of Ezekiel in the year 567, just as the prophet's hopes in a restoration were coming to a head. It is apparent that nothing immediate came of those hopes, perhaps because the king seriously doubted the loyalty of the exiles or found no suitable Jewish leader to whom he could entrust the project. Then again, renewed difficulties with the Medes may have cautioned him against ventures of uncertain outcome.

Perhaps Ezekiel lived long enough to witness the astounding action of Awel-Marduk, Nebuchadnezzar's son, who in 562 "lifted up the head of Jehoiachin king of Judah from prison; spoke pleasantly to him, and seated him higher than the kings who were with him in Babylon" (II Kings 25:28). This royal preferment for Jehoiachin may have buoyed the hopes of the prophet as it did the Deuteronomist's. It is noticeable that the ration tablets from Babylon describing the portions of captured kings for the years 594–569 list Jehoiachin as receiving the largest amount. The initial favor was now followed by an increased ration and admission to the king's presence at mealtime. This seems to have heralded a decision of Awel-Marduk to restore the Jews but his early assassination in 560 by Neriglissar cut the prospects short. It may be, however, that this brief period of promise afforded the occasion for Ezekiel to introduce or sharpen passages in his book which spoke of the purified Davidic dynasty as the civil arm of Yahweh in the restored community.[195] *So within twenty-five to thirty years after the deportation of 598 Ezekiel was beginning to look for the return of the Jews under the patronage and protection of a still enlightened Babylonian world empire.*

[195] E. Hammershaimb, "Ezekiel's View of the Monarchy," *Studia Orientalia. Ioanni Pedersen,* pp. 130–40, surveys the vacillation in use of the terms *nāsî'* and *melek,* on which he is unable to throw much light, but he concludes that the role of king is not rejected by Ezekiel but degraded or restricted to that of a "secular leader" (p. 139).

Isaiah of the Exile

The unknown author of Isaiah 40–55, and perhaps of portions of 56–66, continued the broad interest in the nations shown by his namesake, Isaiah of Jerusalem. He lived at the end of the age of Babylonian suzerainty in the Near East prophesied by Jeremiah. Expectations for a return of the Jews to Palestine, which had proved premature in 570–568 B.C. when Ezekiel first nourished them, were heralded with confidence some twenty-five years later by this ardent prophet. Not Babylon but its imperial successor, Persia—a power from the Iranian highlands east of Mesopotamia—was to be the restorer of the Jews. Babylon's punishment was declared imminent. Decisive in the prophet's outlook was his overriding soteriological outlook on the nations. The partial and sporadic hopes of earlier prophecies (e.g., Isa. 2:2–4; 19:18–25) suddenly broaden into a tide of joy at the prospect of the conversion of the peoples of the world to Yahwism. *The whole history of Israel is interpreted as a* praeparatio evangelica *for the salvation of the nations.*

The Impotence of the Nations

Apparent inconsistencies in the prophet's attitude toward the nations may be explained in part by the traditional poetic imagery he employs[196] but primarily by the several purposes his writings serve. He sometimes depreciates and mocks the nations in order to exalt Israel's faith in the power of her God and to maintain a firm belief in his control over history vis-à-vis the worthless idols. He sometimes appeals to nations to accept Yahweh's dominion and to Israel to orient her message toward the nations in order to extend the redemptive power of Yahweh beyond the limits of Israel. *Depending on whether the prophet seeks to deepen the exiles' faith in God or to move them to a wider view of their task, he stresses respectively the* impotence *of the nations before God or the* preciousness *of the nations to God.*

---

[196] C. C. Torrey, *The Second Isaiah: A New Interpretation,* pp. 128–30, 387–88.

Just as the glorification of Yahweh among his people Israel necessitates the terrible punishment of exile, so the glorification of Yahweh among the nations will be preceded by punishment of the oppressing Babylonians.

Any just assessment of the unknown Isaiah's view of the nations requires, therefore, a careful consideration of his respective motives: punishment for oppressing nations, encouragement of Israel's faith in Yahweh, conversion of the nations to Yahweh. It cannot be claimed, however, that the order and interconnection of these motives are casual for they belong together as a totality which reaches its culmination in the final stage of a universal Yahwistic faith. All that is said about the impotence and wickedness of the nations is preliminary to the good news of their conversion to Yahweh, just as all that is said of the weakness and apostasy of Israel is preliminary to the joy of her restoration as Yahweh's mode of mediation to the other Near Eastern peoples.[197]

The opening and closing poems of the primary literary unit, Isaiah 40–55, contain the contrasting prophetic attitudes toward the nations. In exalting the power and wisdom of Israel's God, the prophet declares (40:15, 17):

> Lo, the nations are as a drop in a bucket
>> And are regarded as a film of dust on the scales. . . .
> All the nations are as nothing over against him.
>> And as nothing and formlessness he accounts them.

Before the Creator all the inhabitants of the earth are as locusts (vs. 22) and the special power of God over history is seen in his removal of political rulers who are "barely planted, barely sown, and barely is their root set in the soil, when he blows on them and they are dried up and the storm-wind carries them off like stubble" (vss. 23–24). It is clear that this is not chiefly a statement about the nations but about God. It does not draw a distinction between Israel and the nations but asserts God's om-

[197] That the prophet thinks much more of Israel's priestly mediating function than of a missionary role in the modern sense has been well stated by R. Martin-Achard, *Israël et les nations. Perspective missionnaire de l'Ancien Testament.*

niscience and omnipotence over that wider world which Israel was likely to deny to him in fact if not in theory. Furthermore, as a theological assertion magnifying divine power, it does not pretend to a complete description of God's attitude toward the other peoples of the world. It does in fact assert nothing at all—positive or negative—about the divine love toward Israel and the nations. The immediate practical aim of the passage is to strengthen Israel in her trust in Yahweh's intent and power to complete his work with his people. That he has further purposes with other peoples is not affirmed or denied.

In the apparent finale to the original work, the prophet summons the exiles to accept the unrestrained forgiveness and mercy of God so that "an everlasting covenant" may be established, thereby giving effect to "the sure mercies of David" (55:3). As David was given to be "witness" and "prince and command-giver" to the peoples of the earth, so now nations previously unknown to Israel will be called by her and will run to her (vss. 4–5). It is seen as an integral part of the purpose of the divine word in history that the covenant with Israel shall incorporate the nations. So it is clear that the brusque opening allusions to the nations are not the prophet's decisive words, for God aims to include many peoples—if not actually all—in his salvation. *Judgment upon the nations, as upon Israel, is provisional. Salvation for the nations, as for Israel, is ultimate.*

To say only this much is not, however, to appreciate the depth and subtle nuances of the prophet's insights. To understand the nature of the universal salvation contemplated, the precise anticipated relation between Israel and the converted nations, and the means of conversion, it is imperative to enter into the substance of the poetry and attempt to isolate the relevant data. Accordingly, we shall give particular attention to the prophet's views of Cyrus, his occasional chauvinistic expressions, the restoration of the Jews to Palestine, and Israel conceived as the Servant of Yahweh.

The Role of Cyrus as "Messiah"

The prophet is fascinated by the career of Cyrus, the Persian, whose phenomenal rise to power as the lord of a vast empire extending from Asia Minor to India occurred within the space of three years (see Map 13). In 550 Cyrus was still a petty prince in one of the small Iranian states which formed the Median empire. After overthrowing Astyages, he effectively extended the domain of the Iranians eastward toward India and westward by the conquest of Croesus of Lydia in 547. Not only is the poet filled with admiration and astonishment at the conqueror but he identifies him as one specifically chosen of God, indeed, "his anointed" (45:1), to carry out the divine will to destroy Babylon as a political power, to restore the Jewish exiles to Jerusalem, and to lay the political basis for the universal religion of Yahweh.

Cyrus is depicted as one roused and sent on his mission of conquest by Yahweh. The prophet vividly sketches the conqueror's irresistible charismatic and military impact throughout the Near East. Resistance avails nothing; all the former territories of Media and Babylon will be joined in his dominion. Amid the poetic descriptions, occasional historical details are observable. The allusions to Cyrus' coming "from the east" (41:2) and "from the north" (41:25) perhaps indicate two stages in his western campaign, first against Croesus of Lydia in Asia Minor and second against Syria-Palestine. The rejoicing of "the desert and its cities," specifically Kedar and Sela (42:11), may reflect military action by Cyrus against the Babylonians in north Arabia.[198] It becomes increasingly evident that Nabonidus' ten-year stay at Tema, the Arabian oasis located approximately 500 miles southwest of Babylon and 300 miles southeast of the Dead Sea, put him in a fertile, thriving region of Arabia which stood at the crossroads of trade routes between south Arabia, Egypt, and Babylon (see Map 12).[199] Overland traffic in Arabia was greatly stimulated in the first millennium B.C. by the increase of trade with Africa and the Far East, the silting up of the lower Tigris-

[198] S. Smith, *Isaiah Chapters XL–LV. Literary Criticism and History*, pp. 61–62.

[199] Our knowledge of Nabonidus' reign, and especially of the reasons for and the circumstances of his stay at Tema in Arabia, has been measurably increased by the Harran inscriptions (C. J. Gadd, *Anatolian Studies*, 8 [1958], 79–89). Earlier assessments of Nabonidus, such as S. Smith, *Isaiah . . .* , pp. 37–40, and R. P. Dougherty, *Nabonidus and Belshazzar. A Study of the Closing Events of the Neo-Babylonian Empire,* must now be materially altered.

Euphrates Valley with consequent difficulty of navigation, and the domestication of camels, which allowed for more dependable desert travel.

Some of the prophet's references to the desert may be more than *typological* allusions in line with his conception of a new Exodus into wilderness, or *geographical* references to the area to be traversed by the returning exiles. The prominence of the desert in Isaiah 40–55 may partially reflect the great economic and political importance of Arabia to the neo-Babylonian and Persian kingdoms. Indeed, it is plausible that the communities of Jews known in north and south Arabia in Islamic times had their origin as early as the exile when Jewish colonists followed Nabonidus to Tema and its adjacent oases.[200] If so, we would have an analogy to the Jewish military colony at Elephantine which served the Persians in Upper Egypt, probably also as early as the sixth century B.C.

It is well known from ancient sources that a considerable pro-Cyrus and anti-Nabonidus campaign was carried on in Babylon in order to discredit the last Babylonian king and to picture Cyrus as the true defender of Babylonian cultural and religious interests. Especially tendentious is the so-called "Verse Account of Nabonidus,"[201] but even the clay cylinder of Cyrus likewise lauds the Persian at the expense of his impious predecessor.[202] It has been proposed that certain alleged striking parallels between the Babylonian and Hebrew verse descriptions of Cyrus, or between the prose cylinder text and the work of the prophet, show that the prophet had read the secular political documents.[203]

One clear difficulty with the theory seems to be that the extra-biblical texts in question were not written until Cyrus had cap-

[200] Gadd, *op. cit.*, pp. 82–83.

[201] Published by S. Smith, *Babylonian Historical Texts Relating to the Capture and Downfall of Babylon*, pp. 27 ff.; *ANET*, pp. 312–15.

[202] H. C. Rawlinson, *The Cuneiform Inscriptions of Western Asia*, 1884, V, 35; *ANET*, pp. 315–16.

[203] M. Haller, "Die Kyros-Lieder Deuterojesajas," *Gunkel Festschrift*, pp. 269–70, 274. In actuality the royal motifs and clichés in Deutero-Isaiah can be paralleled from widely divergent areas of the Near East and are not specifically Babylonian or Persian; cf., e.g., the Hittite seal showing the god Muwatallis holding the hand of the king Tudhaliyas IV in accord with Isaiah 45:1 (Mazar, *Views of the Biblical World*, III, 70).

tured Babylon, whereas there is no sign in Isaiah 40–55 that Babylon had as yet fallen. It is of course quite possible that the pro-Cyrus sentiments of the Marduk priesthood and other factions in Babylon which later found literary expression were well known to the prophet in the years before the city's capture. The parallels are such, however, that they can be accounted for by a common milieu rather than direct acquaintance, for they concern figures of speech such as the destructive wind (Verse Account vi. 19: Isa. 40:24), the release of prisoners (Verse Account vi. 25; Isa. 42:7), and the grasping of a king's or servant's hand (Cyrus Cylinder; Isa. 42:6). Even in these instances the biblical passages do not clearly involve Cyrus.

Indeed, the prophet's entire outlook on Cyrus is untouched by the imperial propaganda which was employed at Babylon, and perhaps elsewhere, to legitimate the Indo-European monarch's appropriation of the venerable Semitic heritage of the Crescent. All the alleged connections are nothing more than the facts available to any intelligent Babylonian, such as that Cyrus was not a practicing Yahwist but that he showed a broad toleration of local religious customs and beliefs and was more humane than previous Near Eastern rulers. His specific premonition that Cyrus would repatriate the Jews to Jerusalem and rebuild the temple was not dependent on the pro-Cyrus Marduk priesthood but rather on a combination of the prophet's assessment of Cyrus' prevailing imperial policy and his deep belief in the guiding purpose of God for his exiled people.

Another conceivable source of the prophet's sympathy for Cyrus is the Persian's adherence to a non-idolatrous religion. As a prince of Anshan, Cyrus was a devotee of Mithraism; as heir of the Median empire, he was a Zoroastrian. The fact that both Mithraism and Zoroastrianism at this stage of their development were free from idolatry (Herodotus, *History,* I, 131) may serve to account for the prophet's confidence in Cyrus and in Cyrus' favoritism toward the Jews.[204] Yet our evidence is meager and cuts both ways. The most that such an affinity between Iranian and Jewish faiths might have suggested was an imperial syncre-

[204] M. Jastrow, *Religion of Babylonia and Assyria,* 1898, pp. 61, 288–90.

tism whereby elements of both religions would be joined or whereby Zoroastrianism was to be practiced in the Indo-European parts of the empire and Yahwism in the Semitic parts. There is, however, no hint of syncretism by the prophet but rather the opposite; repeatedly he insists that no deity is to share the stage of nature and history with Yahweh.

The notion that in certain articles of his belief the unknown Isaiah has been influenced by Zoroastrianism is impalpable and unprovable. The assertion that Yahweh creates "prosperity and calamity" (*šālôm* and *raʿ*, 45:7) is a flat monotheistic claim and has nothing to do with the Zoroastrian belief in the good god Ahura Mazda and the evil god Ahriman. It is not necessarily a polemic against Zoroastrian dualism.[205] It is rather an assertion sufficiently rooted in Israelite understanding of God (cf. Deut. 32:39) so that it could be made by one who had no knowledge of Iranian religion. The suggestion that the prophet's use of the key theological terms "glory" (*kābhôd*) and "righteousness" (*tsedek*) is indebted to the Zoroastrian *hvareno* and *Khshathra vairya* has even less to commend it.[206] In short, we can assume that the prophet knew Cyrus to be the practitioner of a non-Babylonian religion but we have no secure basis for making any further claims to the effect that the prophet was familiar with Zoroastrianism—its dualism, its system of intermediaries, or its aniconic character.

What is emphatically clear in Isaiah 40–55 is that the role of Cyrus in the new era is strictly political and formal. There is no attribution of extraordinary cultural, humanitarian, or religious motives to Cyrus such as those with which the Marduk priesthood of Babylon sought to glorify him. It is certain that all of Cyrus' work to date has been by one who does not know Yahweh to be the sole God, for "I name you . . . I equip you for war, but you do not know me" (45:4–5). Yet the prophet anticipates the monarch's conversion, for "he shall call on my name" (41:

---

[205] Wade, *The Book of the Prophet Isaiah*, p. 293; J. Muilenburg, *IB*, V, 524–25.

[206] C. E. Simcox, "The Role of Cyrus in Deutero-Isaiah," *JAOS* 57 (1937), 158–71; A. F. Von Gall, "Die Reich-Gottes-Hoffnung im Parsismus," *Basileia tou Theou*, pp. 83–163.

25). Whether his conversion is thought of as the precondition of his restoration of the Jews is not known.

Cyrus is to go about his work as deliverer of captive peoples and royal sponsor of international Yahwism. The first servant song (42:1–4), which extols the patient work of the servant in the instruction of nations and the execution of justice, does *not* refer to Cyrus. There are no demonstrated political allusions in the obscure imagery of the song. *The functions of the servant there described are precisely those functions of religious teaching that mark all the servant songs and distinguish the task of Israel as the universal spiritual counterpart to the universal political dominion of Persia.* The wide horizons of the song do not point to Cyrus but only to the conditions created by Cyrus which will allow Israel to complete its divine mission. Cyrus' work for Yahweh is solely to create the imperial structure within which the restored Jews will be commissioned to propagate their religion. Although called by Yahweh "my shepherd" and "my anointed," Cyrus is as secular a ruler as the Hebrew could conceive. As king, he has no covenantal relation with Yahweh. He is to have no part in the cult. He will presumably rule his empire on the foundations of such legal and diplomatic praxis as he has traditionally at hand. His relation to Yahweh as a worshiper will be through his acknowledgment of Israel as the priesthood of God.

By stressing the formal political task of Cyrus, in accordance with the sparse data of the text, we remove the supposed difficulty that the ruler who is so prominent in chaps. 40–47 is absent from chaps. 48–55. The mere shift away from preoccupation with Cyrus proves nothing beyond the fact that once the prophet had established that the historical foundation was to be laid by Cyrus it was possible to concentrate increasingly upon the special calling of Israel. It is thus unnecessary to assume that an early naïve confidence in Cyrus as a devout Yahwist led to disillusionment and turning from a political deliverer to a suffering spiritual deliverer, i.e., the Servant of the last three songs.[207] At least no simple antitheses may be drawn. From the start the prophet was clear about the essential but limited work of Cyrus and there

[207] Haller, *Gunkel Festschrift*, pp. 261–77; W. E. Barnes, "Cyrus as the Servant of Yahweh," *JTS* 32 (1931), 32–39.

was no danger of his confusing the king's task with Israel's task. They were always two entirely different responsibilities—Cyrus as the enlightened imperialist and sponsor of Yahwism, Israel as the dedicated priestly enclave and propagator of Yahwism within the world empire.

Of course it was envisaged by the prophet that Cyrus would become a Yahwist and use his office to establish Yahwism as the official faith of his empire. Although the unknown Isaiah would have rejoiced at the return of his people to Palestine with Cyrus' permission, he would have been saddened at the Persian's failure to convert to Yahwism and to establish it as the imperial religion. Furthermore, Cyrus' astute avowal of Babylonian religion in order to pacify the Babylonian population would have shocked and revolted but scarcely embittered the prophet. The conditional must be used in the above sentences, because it is not at all clear that the prophet lived to see the fall of Babylon and the consequent religious politicking practiced by Cyrus. No references in his poems require or even suggest a date later than 539 B.C.[208] Moreover, the final servant song suggests that it should be understood, at least in part, as an account of the martyrdom of the prophet.[209] To this we must return, but for the moment we must emphasize our impression that the prophet never lived to know that Cyrus remained a Zoroastrian in his homeland and became a Marduk worshiper in Mesopotamia.

Yet even had the prophet experienced that disappointment, it would not have been a fundamental blow to his faith. There would have been no need to transfer soteriological functions from

---

[208] The contention of S. Smith, *Isaiah . . .* , p. 181, n. 81, that Isaiah 52:11–12 could have been written only after Cyrus' edict and 45:11–13 and 55:12–13 only after the fall of Babylon appears to disregard the character of "the prophetic perfect" in Hebrew.

[209] What I mean to suggest is that the prophet's experience of opposition and persecution enabled him to describe the Servant's death empathetically, and later, by his own death, he became a kind of symbolic action mirroring the earlier prophecy. This is not to accept the outright autobiographical interpretation of the Servant figure, even as most recently modified by S. Mowinckel, *He That Cometh,* 1956, pp. 246–55. The view that the prophet was consciously describing himself or was deliberately described in the servant songs has, in my opinion, been effectively rebutted by C. R. North, *The Suffering Servant in Deutero-Isaiah. An Historical and Critical Study,* 1948, pp. 195–99.

Cyrus to Israel for the simple reason that he had never attributed any to the Persian ruler. What was within Cyrus' power to do, namely, to put the world state at the disposal of Yahwism, Israel could not do. The most that the prophet could have done would have been to transfer the functions of Cyrus as a patron of Yahwism to a later Persian king or to a ruler of some other state. The prospect of Israel's own monarch assuming Davidic powers over so vast an empire would hardly have been entertained. But Israel's teaching function on behalf of Yahweh could go forward now from a base in Palestine, greatly facilitated if a beneficent world monarch should arise but carried on steadily and patiently even without him.

The Preciousness of the Nations

Against such a reading of the unknown Isaiah, it is possible to muster passages which on the surface appear to be assertions of Israelite political supremacy in the ancient Near East. Israel is addressed as a sharp-toothed threshing sledge which will pulverize the mountains and valleys into chaff to be carried off by the wind (41:15–16a), a common agricultural figure for destruction of nations (cf. Amos 1:3; Mic. 4:13; Hab. 3:12; and Isa. 25:10). The wealth of Egyptians and Ethiopians and Sabean slaves will "pass over" to Israel and serve her (45:14). God declares to his servant, "self-despised, abhorred by nations," but nonetheless "servant of rulers," that kings and princes will take note of him and pay homage for the sake of Yahweh (49:7). The nations will repatriate the Jewish captives to Palestine, kings and queens will serve as guardians and nurses; with "faces to the ground, they shall bow to you and the dust of your feet they shall lick" (49:22–23). Israel will expand until "her seed will possess the nations and will dwell in desolated cities" (54:3).

These nationalistic statements must be judged in part as instances of poetic exuberance or as typical diplomatic phraseology for expressing homage.[210] When they are weighed, however, in the total context of the prophet's words, they give no evidence

[210] Torrey, *op. cit.*, pp. 387–88.

whatsoever that he envisioned Israelite military or political dominion. Nevertheless, it is equally mistaken so to emphasize his internationalism that Israel's specially reserved position among the nations is obscured. Only the establishment of a Yahweh community in Palestine, universally acknowledged and thus given political status, can properly implement the mission of Israel to the nations. *The particular historical center of Yahweh's revelation to Israel is strongly asserted while the perimeter of his revelation is extended out to the limits of Cyrus' world empire.* This systole and diastole of the faith in Yahweh is brilliantly asserted in the confession of the Gentiles as they awesomely declare to the Jews (45:14b–15):

God is with you alone and there is none other, no god beside.
Indeed you are a God who hides yourself, Israel's God, Savior!

The poet-prophet thus maintains the unique Yahwistic dialectic of the unity of the nations and the particularity of Israel in the purpose of God. In historical terms this allows for various nuances and phases in the work of God. Babylon has executed Yahweh's will upon sinful Israel but has exceeded her mandate. Now she is to be punished (47; 49:25–26), yet the very Babylonians who were Zion's "destroyers" and "wasters" will all assemble and come to Yahweh (49:18). Under Persian aegis, the nations will give up their captives (43:14), and not only from Babylon but from Arabia, Phoenicia, and Egypt the scattered Jews will be assembled in Palestine. To be sure, the formerly sinful Jews are still far from fully obedient to Yahweh; nonetheless his action in restoring Israel means that he does not wait for human perfection but goes ahead "for his righteousness' sake" (42:21), "for my own sake" (43:25; 48:11), or "for my name's sake" (48:9). Thus the image of Yahweh as having no helper does not mean primarily that he worked without human means but rather that he worked without the full understanding of men who served him unwittingly (45:1–7).

Without the return of Israel to Palestine there can be no calling of the nations. Yahweh's word will not fall to the ground; he resolves to recall his people because in their regathering

Yahweh has exposed his holy arm
before the eyes of all the nations;
And all the ends of the earth
shall see our God's salvation.

(52:10)

In a series of court scenes the idols of the nations are called to
account and assigned to impotence and oblivion (41:21–29;
43:8–13; 44:6–8; 45:20–25).[211] On the other hand, the peoples
who have trusted in the idols, once delivered from them, will
truly worship Yahweh—quite unprejudiced by the fact that they
were pagans or oppressors of Israel. In short, there is no projection of Israelite vengeance into the relations among the peoples
in Cyrus' kingdom. Even the threat "the nation and kingdom
which refuses to serve you shall perish" (60:12)—whether the
prophet's own words or not—is based not upon past differences
but upon the new imperial situation in which deviations from the
imperial religion will be punished by Cyrus or his successor.
There is not the slightest suggestion that because of prior Egyptian, Assyrian, or Babylonian oppression of Israel those people
were to be excluded from Yahweh worship or were to suffer
special disabilities at the hands of the Persian overlords. The old
situation was past.

The Role of Israel as "Mediator-Servant"

The superiority of Israel's religion is uncompromisingly insisted
upon by the prophet, and thus he maintains a steady claim that
Israel is to retain its identity within the world empire as a teacher
and priest of the nations. *It is regrettably difficult to judge from
the poetic generalities exactly what relation Israel is to have to
the nations.* Some features of the expected religious union of the

---

[211] H. Gunkel and J. Begrich, *Einleitung in die Psalmen*, 1933, pp. 364–
65, recognized the two types of lawsuits, the one in which God is plaintiff
(chiefly in pre-exilic prophets) and the other in which he is judge (chiefly
in the exilic Isaiah). The main features of the two types have been helpfully schematized by H. B. Huffmon, "The Covenant Lawsuit in the
Prophets," *JBL* 78 (1959), 285–86; but esp. see L. Koehler, *Deuterojesaja
stilkritisch untersucht,* pp. 111–20, which characterizes the formal and ideological features of the *Streitgespräch.*

nations may be discerned, however, especially if attention is paid
to certain of the poems in the final chapters of the book of Isaiah.

It appears that the oracles of Isaiah 60–62 either are by the
poet of chaps. 40–55 or contain many quotations from his
work.[212] The prospect of the nations' supporting a Yahweh cult
at Jerusalem is sketched in conformity with the views of Deutero-
Isaiah and in somewhat greater detail. Nations will gather to
honor Yahweh at Jerusalem and will lavish upon his people gifts
of herds and flocks, timber, spices, and precious metals. Jerusalem, rebuilt by royal patronage, will be maintained by the innumerable gifts of surrounding lands, so that it may be said to
her (60:16),

> You shall suck the milk of nations,
> You shall suck the breasts of kings.

If any nation or kingdom fails to serve Israel, i.e., fails to honor
and support the Yahweh cult, "those nations shall be utterly laid
waste" (60:12). In spite of the undeniably one-sided, non-
syncretic exaltation of the religion of Yahweh there is no inkling
in these chapters that Israelite political power is involved in the
least. The punishment to be administered to non-complying nations is apparently exclusively the responsibility of the Persian
authorities, who shall take the pains to re-establish the Jewish
religious community as the religious center of the empire.

The description of the relation between the foreigners and the
Judeans in 61:5–7 is of particular value for our purposes. It appears that Gentiles will have various pastoral and agricultural
assignments in Palestine by way of direct support of the temple,
for the reference here seems to imply more than the tribute and
sacrifices brought from far countries. The poetic allusion does
not permit, however, any direct comparison of these foreign at-
tendants of the cult with those mentioned by Ezekiel (44:7–9)
or with those described as "the descendants of the slaves of
Solomon" and the Nethinim ("given" or "appointed" ones) who
returned from captivity and had menial tasks in the temple cult
(Ezra 2:43–58; Neh. 7:46–60).[213] At any rate, all of these al-

---

[212] Muilenburg, *op. cit.*, pp. 383–84, 697.

[213] G. H. Davies, "Nethinim," *IDB*, III, 541; M. Haran, "The Gibeonites,

lusions belong to about the same period of time and that Deutero-Isaiah thought of a corps of foreign slaves serving the Jerusalem cult is further supported from his mention of the large-framed African slaves who "shall come over to you [Israel] and be yours" (45:14).

Whatever precisely the roles conceived for the foreigners—if indeed the prophet himself had any clearly formulated idea—on one point the text is clear: *Israel will be the priestly benefactor of the nations.* The same foreigners who with Israel acknowledge the suzerainty of Cyrus and his dynasty will, in religious matters, hail the Judeans as "the priests of Yahweh" and "the ministers of our God" (61:6).

It seems reasonable to apply this fuller description of the imperial Yahweh cult in chaps. 60–62 to the somewhat more cryptic allusions in the contexts of the Servant songs, especially in 42:5–9 and 49:1–12. Those who believe that the Servant songs belong to the work of Deutero-Isaiah and that they must be interpreted with reference to Israel, whether as allegories[214] or on the principle of corporate personality,[215] seem to provide the soundest presuppositions for understanding the Servant motif in this prophet of the exile. Certainly, this interpretation does not rule out the individualizing traits of the Servant as contributed by many great leaders in Israel's history,[216] nor does it neglect the

---

the Nethinim and the Sons of Solomon's Servants," *VT* 11 (1961), 159–69. For slavery as a social, economic, and political institution, see I. Mendelsohn, "Slavery in the O.T.," *IDB,* IV, 383–90, and *Slavery in the Ancient Near East.*

[214] J. Lindblom, *The Servant Songs in Deutero-Isaiah.*

[215] O. Eissfeldt, "The Ebed-Jahwe in Isa. XL–LV in the Light of the Israelite Conception of the Community and the Individual, the Ideal and the Real," *ET* 44 (1932), 261–68; *Der Gottesknecht beim Deuterojesaja (Jes. 40–55) im Lichte der israelitischen Anschauung von Gemeinschaft und Individuum;* H. W. Robinson, *The Cross of the Servant;* "The Hebrew Conception of Corporate Personality," *Werden und Wesen des Alten Testaments,* 1936, pp. 49–62. Their views are summarized by C. R. North, *op. cit.,* pp. 103–10. See now also the penetrating study by O. Kaiser, *Der koenigliche Knecht: Eine traditionsgeschichtlich-exegetische Studie ueber die Ebed-Jahweh-Lieder beim Deuterojesaja,* which sees the Servant as exiled Israel who takes over the role of the king and embodies a prophetic function.

[216] Especially by Jeremiah; cf. F. A. Farley, "Jeremiah and 'The Suffering Servant of Jehovah in Deutero-Isaiah,'" *ET* 38 (1927), 521–24, and Sheldon Blank, "Studies in Deutero-Isaiah," *HUCA* 15 (1940), 1–46. It must be

deep experience of personal sacrifice by which the prophet has come to his own costly understanding of Israel's Servant task.[217] It does say that the various parts of the prophecy may be taken to illuminate one another and, in the last analysis, the Servant figure signifies something crucial about Israel's constitution as the people of God which is not so esoteric as the unending debates about the identity of the Servant have sometimes seemed to imply.[218]

If we begin with such an understanding, the specification of the Servant as *berîth 'ām* (42:6; 49:8) and *'ôr gôyim* (49:6) is altogether consonant with the picture we have drawn largely from chaps. 60–62. Israel is to be "a confederation of peoples"[219] (preferable to "covenant to the people") and "a light for the nations." Standing as the terms do in poetic parallelism, they are to be taken as synonyms for the priestly mediatorial work of Israel among the nations of the Persian empire. As has been noted, this is hardly the evangelizing, missionary commission which has traditionally been assigned to the prophet.[220] Israel does not proselytize. Rather she capitalizes on the largesse of Cyrus in turning the peoples politically subject to him to support of the Yahweh cult. This does not imply that it is wholly a matter of political coercion, since the nations—or at least many of them— may be expected to appreciate the lordship of Yahweh over history once they see the restoration of his cult in Jerusalem. *The establishment of the universal Yahweh cult will be a triumph of imperial policy and of national conversion. The conversion will, however, not be due so much to what Israel says as to what Israel is.* To the prophet it means that the combination of what Israel has undergone both as a decimated people and as a re-

---

stressed, however, that such individualizing features were greatly diffused; cf. Gottwald, *Studies in the Book of Lamentations,* chap. 2, for a discussion of the exilic mixture of literary types, the archetypal role of Jeremiah, and the individual/collective polarity in Lamentations and Deutero-Isaiah.

[217] See note 209.

[218] Muilenburg, *op. cit.,* pp. 408–13, provides a particularly penetrating theological analysis of the Servant figure; for the deep biblical roots of the Servant image, cf. C. Lindhagen, *The Servant Motif in the Old Testament.*

[219] Lindblom, *The Servant Songs . . . ,* pp. 21–22.

[220] See note 196 and contrast with H. Rowley, *The Missionary Message of the Old Testament,* 1945, pp. 83–84.

stored people will awaken a recognition of Yahweh's lordship among the peoples of the empire.

The suffering *Servant and the* triumphing *Servant are one and the same Servant, and this Servant's inner spiritual history and outer political destitution in exile and quasi-political re-establishment in Palestine are all parts of the same vindicating action of Yahweh.* There is little possibility of segregating the poems according to whether they are more or less "nationalistic" or "universalistic," "materialistic" or "spiritual," "coercive" or "persuasive," "retributive" or "sacrificial." All such antinomies are to some extent caught up within the historical action which the prophet declares to be unfolding before the unbelieving eyes of outsiders and insiders to the Yahweh faith.

The organic totality of the universal saving action of God is well expressed in the way the Servant's task to be a "confederation of peoples" and a "light for the nations" necessitates his firm establishment in Palestine. The tribes of Jacob must be raised up, the rescued Israelites restored (49:6), the land established, the desolate heritages reapportioned (49:8).[221] *In short, the Israelite community must be restored in Palestine. This is not a task separate from Israel's mediatorial calling. It is the implementation of her mediatorial work.* The restoration does not occur at the expense of or to the exclusion of Israel's "missionary" task. Israel's mission is not to go out and lose herself indiscriminately among the nations so that she is no longer seen or heard. It is her mission to focus her attention and energy upon her own calling as God's people, to revive and maintain the prophetic morality and the priestly cult by which all the nations will be claimed.

The *descending* and *negating* rejection and death of the Servant in exile was the necessary demonstration both to Israel and to the nations that Yahweh is God alone. But now the *ascending*

[221] S. Smith, *Isaiah* . . . , pp. 70, 174, seems correct in regarding 49:6a, 8 as references to "re-establishing national organization of the land according to the old tribal divisions, obliterated by the foreign regime." The indecisiveness of the neo-Babylonian deportation policy and provincial reorganization, as compared with those of the Assyrians, had kept open the prospect of restoration to Palestine (A. Alt, "Die Rolle Samarias bei der Entstehung des Judentums," *KS* II, 325–29).

and *affirming* exaltation and resurrection of the Servant to his homeland is the necessary demonstration to Jew and Gentile that Yahweh has not left his creation but provides for all people an everlasting means of order and peace under the twin rule of Persian emperor and Jewish priestly enclave.

The Servant then is rightly interpreted as a non-political figure only if we carefully discriminate between Israel as an independent state and Israel as a definite religious community politically supported. The former is decidedly not the expectation of Deutero-Isaiah; the latter emphatically is. Nothing in the desolating fate of the Servant of the fourth song and in the spiritual depth of the nations' confession should be understood to rule out the denouement of ethnic and religious triumph which the prophet insists upon. In fact the culmination of the poem in the Servant's "portion with the great" and "spoil with the strong" (53:12) shows that the "death" of the confessional lament was preliminary to the historical vindication of the exilic community. It is ironic that generations of Christian interpreters have lauded Deutero-Isaiah's sacrificial, missionary spirit without conceding that it is indestructibly rooted in the restored Jewish community. The same interpreters would be troubled at the suggestion that the best way the early Christians could have celebrated the resurrection of Christ was to disband their churches.

CHAPTER V

Israelite Prophecy and International Relations in the Ancient Near East

We began our study with a brief survey of the growth of empire and of the basic patterns of international relations in the ancient Near East. Against that backdrop, the heart of our inquiry has been devoted to the references to international relations in Hebrew prophecy during the period of Israelite independence, with some attention to the preceding age of the tribal league and to the subsequent exilic age. This method allowed us to examine a series of prophets from Balaam at the close of the thirteenth century to Isaiah of the exile in the sixth century. While bearing in mind the widely different historical settings in which these prophets worked, we have noted that most of them demonstrated a strong persisting interest in the relations of nations as a primary sphere for the activity of Israel's God.

The decisive religious character of the prophetic interest in the nations inevitably posed for this study crucial questions of scope and method. To insure precision and focus it was decided to restrict the study almost exclusively to the portions of prophecy which directly allude to the relations of states, both those which give fresh or supplementary information of value for reconstructing ancient Near Eastern history and those which illustrate current diplomatic and military practice. We have not failed to note, in fact, the many points at which our increased knowledge of the ancient Near East, materially and epigraphically, has thrown significant light upon the biblical text.

Nevertheless, in order properly to grasp the essential purpose of prophecy in concerning itself with the nations, we were obliged to sacrifice any narrow restriction of treatment. It has been necessary to set international relations, as seen prophetically, within the context of prophecy's deep belief in a God-directed destiny for the nations. To overlook or to minimize that factor would be to disregard the compelling reason that prophetic writings relate such a kaleidoscope of historical, diplomatic, and military information. In all its far-ranging variety, this fascination with international political activity is in reality only a commentary upon the acts of God for his people Israel and for the salvation of the world. The prophet has in view a public, international sphere for God's work which has no safely predictable limits, even though the range of vision in any particular writing may be less than universal. Thus we have deliberately enlarged our consideration, especially from Isaiah onward, to include passages that show how the prophets foresaw the relations among nations in the future when Yahweh will have more perfectly shaped history to his will. Nevertheless, it is hoped that even in these more general, so-called "eschatological" passages it has been possible to sense the firm historical ground beneath the prophet's feet and to realize that his highest flights never go far from the scenes of international conflict and cooperation known so well to him.

In this concluding chapter we shall deal with three aspects of the subject in ascending order: first, a brief *summary of the data concerning foreign relations in the strict sense;* second, *the political role and destiny of Israel against the background of a spirited modern debate over the nature of prophetic politics;* and lastly, *the prophetic models for conceiving international relations.* It is precisely in the rich interconnection and interpenetration of these motifs that prophetic literature stands forth with a dimensional reality, allowing us to see the living organism of ancient Israelite belief and, especially, to sense the prophetic commitment to a living God of men and nations. In particular we shall attempt to show the way in which knowledge of God arose within the sphere of political knowledge and gave structure to it. We shall stress the way in which the modes of international affairs in the ancient Near East have shaped the prophetic parables about the nations in the end time. One would perhaps not think that a study of what prophets have to say about such matters as warfare and treaty-making would lead to a profound assertion of the lordship of Israel's God. To underline this initially surprising connection as sharply as possible is the immediate intent of this concluding chapter.

International Relations in Prophecy from Balaam to Isaiah of the Exile

We have seen that nearly all of the salient aspects of international relations in the ancient Near East are documented in the prophetic writings, either as elements in the relation between Judah or Israel and the nations or as aspects of the relations between non-Hebrew states.

War is commented on by the prophets as the crude adjudicator of disputes and the ready instrument of aggrandizement. They attest to the fact that by late Assyrian times the imperial armies were heavily supplemented by mercenaries and units of conquered troops. Treaties are recognized by them as the accepted means for securing desired national behavior, whether to bind a vassal to his superior or to pledge equals.

The provincial organization of the Assyrian empire and its successors was noted as the standard method for incorporating subject peoples. Moreover, the punitive military campaigns of the overlord against rebellious segments of his empire are described with special brilliance, forming in fact one of the most characteristic threats in Hebrew prophecy. The onerous annual tribute and the crushing indemnity for revolt are observed, and the prophets are particularly pointed in their references to the hated practice of deportation of peoples, which they describe either by premonition or as an accomplished fact.

Prophetic oracles are permeated frequently with the tense atmosphere of political intrigue and revolt. Notable are the descriptions of Assyrian and neo-Babylonian punitive campaigns and raids against Syria and Palestine. Often the information related by the prophets is of help in visualizing events and placing them in a framework supplied by extra-biblical sources such as the Assyrian annals and the neo-Babylonian Chronicles. Treason is stigmatized as a serious crime but faithfulness to God is put above fidelity to human notions of national loyalty. The shifting balance of power among Palestinian states—and also between the powers at the two termini of the Fertile Crescent—is well attested in the prophetic oracles.

Obviously the prophets do not supply a complete or connected self-explanatory description of diplomatic and military practice in the ancient Near East. They do contain an astonishing fullness of reference which becomes increasingly understandable as more extra-biblical information is made available. This fact gives us reason to believe that with further light it will be possible to understand additional prophetic political allusions which at present are cryptic or ambiguous. Without being a handbook of international relations, the prophetic collection of the Old Testament presents information, in the course of pursuing its own special interests, which acquires historical and cultural significance when it is placed in a wider Near Eastern context.

The Prophetic Political Orientation

Theories About Political Prophecy from Winckler to Kraus

What did the prophets intend to accomplish in political affairs? This was a question scarcely asked as long as the prophets were subordinated as one phase of an orthodox religious schema. Ancient Israelite politics, which were of course known from the Old Testament account, were so subjected to the working out of the divine plan in Scripture that they were little more than curious debris carried along on the flood tide of divine purpose. To be sure, interpreters inclined at times toward a starkly literal respect for the concreteness of the biblical political directives, but normally this position was only to stress the remarkable prophetic "predictions" as one of the signal proofs of the inspiration of Scripture. Or, if the situation in Israel was examined, it was seen almost exclusively in the guise of the Deuteronomic judgment upon monarchy, namely, the faith or unfaith of politicians. The precarious political situation facing a prophet and his contemporaries was not sufficiently sensed to lead to a careful examination of the prophet's political orientation.

This attitude of orthodox opaqueness toward prophetic politics was altered by the achievement of nineteenth-century German biblical scholarship, which succeeded in illumining the prophets as authentic and truly protean historical figures. At last, it seemed, the way was open for the full force of the prophetic politics to be borne in upon the interpreter because the distinctiveness of each prophet had been accented by a keen-eyed historico-critical exegesis, and the discreteness of their several "messages" was grasped. Furthermore, the realization of the historical development of the canon led to the insistence that the prophet had to achieve his own political viewpoint and to convince his contemporaries without either his or their having the benefit of a written norm to guide them.

The apprehension of the live, variegated, precarious political activity of prophecy was, however, by no means wholly won at the close of the nineteenth century. Such apprehension was retarded, it must be noted, by a too simple—and even basically erroneous—interpretation of the prophets as religious teachers whose instructions accumulated harmonistically from generation to generation. Because their ordered teachings about the nature of God and man were superior to the ravings of the lesser prophets, a psychological distance was thought to stand between canonical prophecy and false prophecy. The failure to see both ecstatic elements in canonical prophecy and orderly teaching elements in non-canonical prophecy was at least in great measure a result of the new orthodoxy of "prophetic ethical monotheism" which tended to replace the earlier theological orthodoxy.

Thus the climate at the turn of the century which made it possible to pose the question about the political intention of prophecy was not an unambiguous gain for a true understanding of prophecy. It was certainly an advance of exegetical and theological science that fuller scrutiny of the political, social, and religious aspects of prophecy was encouraged. The deficiencies in the answers were very largely due to the one-sided understanding of prophecy as the teaching activity of rationally religious (or should we say religiously rational?) men. As a result, *the course of the discussion of the purpose of political prophecy has been a curiously circumscribed one. It has been a discussion marked by extremes of viewpoint which have been rather fruitlessly re-asserted over against one another—often without searching anal-ysis of differences of principle.* It is difficult to escape the im-pression that the way the question was originally framed doomed the discussion to frustrating fights between extremes which were all, to one degree or another, wide of the mark. This claim will be clearer after an examination of the discussion but it is made now because a proper formulation of the question and a con-sequent sound method must be the starting point for fresh at-tempts to assess political prophecy.

The latter half of the nineteenth century had seen some aware-ness of the political role of prophecy. A. Dillmann had published a lecture on "The Prophets According to Their Political Effec-tiveness" (1868). There had been a lively debate on the question of the patriotism of Jeremiah, with M. Duncker (1875) and G. Maspero (1877) impugning it and K. H. Graf (1862) and A. Koehler (1893) defending it.[1] But it was not until Hugo Winckler's programmatic sketch of the prophets in 1903 that the issue really came to life and a continuing debate was provoked.[2] Winckler interpreted the prophets as politicians first and fore-most. They were, in his judgment, professional agitators who re-ceived their directions from foreign powers: Elisha from Damas-cus, Amos from Judah, Isaiah from Assyria, Jeremiah from Babylon. Their severe domestic attacks and threats of foreign occupation were the result of a deliberate program to undermine the morale of the populace and to subject the independent He-brew states to vassalage. The prophets may have had some gen-uine religious interest but it was wholly secondary to their work as foreign agents.

[1] Cited in F. Wilke, *Die politische Wirksamkeit der Propheten Israels,* p. 5.

[2] H. Winckler and H. Zimmern, eds., *Die Keilinschriften und das Alte Testament* (von E. Schrader).

In spite of the superficiality and incredibility of Winckler's thesis, it was a comprehensive conception which placed politics at the very center of prophetic concern. It was bound to provoke rebuttal and, more significantly, to encourage a radical assessment of the problems Winckler had merely skirted in drawing his ingenious conclusions. In a study of Isaiah's political outlook, F. Kuechler, in explicit contradiction to Winckler, insisted that political decisions were met by the prophet entirely from a religious point of view.[3] Concerning the question of the political feasibility of Isaiah's advice, Kuechler frankly said that it was untenable and that it was justly disregarded by the king and people. Over against this he placed prophetic universalism, which was brought to its culmination in Jesus. The contradiction between the prophetic advice about foreign relations which should have been disregarded and the prophetic proclamation of universalism which should have been heeded was not seen by Kuechler, as it has not been seen by many subsequent interpreters. He might have said that the deliberate hardening of Israel's heart so that its political independence was doomed made possible the later extension of universalism, but Kuechler did not draw this conclusion. In countering Winckler's extremities, he succeeded only in underlining the ineptness and irrelevance of prophetic politics.

Two interpreters before the First World War sought to oppose Winckler's distorted theory of political prophecy not by denying that the prophets were politicians but by showing that they were politicians with a primarily religious orientation. W. Staerk wrote on the prophetic assessment of the Assyrian empire but stressed that the prophet had "a sharp political view" and "a sound sense of reality."[4] Staerk's book is perceptive in that he rejected many of the *religionsgeschichtliche* positions that were in vogue, such as, for example, the theory that the prophets were the creators of monotheistic faith. He stressed that they labored publicly as a deliberate part of their religious conception and thus were catapulted inevitably into the midst of social and political turmoil and controversy. Coupled with their religious calling, they pos-

[3] F. Kuechler, *Die Stellung des Propheten Jesaja zur Politik seiner Zeit.*
[4] W. Staerk, *Das assyrische Weltreich im Urteil der Propheten,* pp. 1–4.

sessed areas of political perception of a clear-headed and wise order. The prophets' contribution to Israel was to point up the contrast between *Weltreich* and *Weltreligion*. By seeing the nature of Assyrian empire they were enabled rightly to point Israel away from political empire to universal religion. Staerk thereby creates the picture of the prophet balancing religious and political factors and coming to a prudential decision in which religious factors prevailed but served political ends at the same time.

In 1913 F. Wilke, who had earlier written a valuable book on Isaiah and Assyria,[5] made a substantial contribution to the discussion.[6] His method had the virtue of attacking the questions of the political stance and motives of the prophets directly and systematically, rather than touching upon them in an introduction or summarizing them in a conclusion to an otherwise chronological survey of prophetic history or teaching. Wilke found that the prophets had a positive relation to politics but he more emphatically subordinated that interest to the religious motives than had Staerk; he saw the political concerns of prophecy contained within and defined by its religious outlook.

His examination of the prophetic attitude toward foreign alliances is typical of Wilke's approach.[7] Religious motives fixed certain boundaries for their attitude, since the prophets opposed all alliances and armaments that led to such an exaggerated development of external power that Israel was alienated from its task as the people of Yahweh. But this was only a relative or shifting boundary, for "the prophets only appeared to be in outspoken opposition to armaments" when, in fact, they permitted defensive use of arms. Yet within the limits, to be determined according to the given context, they allowed other motives to operate in opposition to or qualification of proposed alliances. National motives militated against the introduction of foreign personnel or foreign practices which might result from treaties. Social motives chafed against the heavy burdens of taxation and military draft required by an expansive military policy. All these

[5] F. Wilke, *Jesaja und Assur. Eine exegetisch-historische Untersuchung zur Politik des Propheten Jesaja,* 1905.

[6] F. Wilke, *Die politische Wirksamkeit des Propheten Israels,* 1913.

[7] *Ibid.,* chap. 3.

motives combined in varying patterns depending upon the specific historical circumstances. These remarks of Wilke are in some ways still the fullest and often the most suggestive ever written on prophetic politics. Yet in the contrast between a legitimate political life and a political autonomy in which faith in Yahweh was disregarded, as also in the tension between the uncoordinated "religious" and "practical" motives, Wilke was left with an uneasy separation of spheres beyond which the study of prophetic politics was unable to proceed fruitfully for many years.

To this point Winckler's thesis that the prophets were professional political agitators for foreign powers had been rejected by all writers on the subject, but the debate about the actual political concern of the prophets which he had set in motion had failed to come to any clear conclusion. Suddenly a new factor was introduced in the debate, namely, a vigorous espousal of the view that the prophets were in no meaningful sense politicians but were in fact "utopians." In 1916 E. Troeltsch set forth the utopian conception of prophecy as boldly as Winckler had stated the opposite,[8] and this conception was elaborated by F. Weinrich in a monograph in 1932.[9] Precisely because until recently this has been the only alternative view of prophetic politics spelled out with the precision of Winckler's untenable analysis, and also because it is a view widely circulated in studies of prophecy, the utopian hypothesis must be defined as sharply as the views of Troeltsch and Weinrich will allow.

In the title to his work Weinrich significantly enclosed two key words in quotation marks: *Der religiös-utopische Charakter der "prophetischen Politik."* Similarly, Troeltsch found any genuine prophetic politics excluded by their emphatic renunciation of power and their firm trust in miracle as a substitute for power. In his opinion prophetic utopianism sprang from the inmost nature of prophetic teaching, for such politics as it implied were built on the ancient faith in "the unshakeable, merely enigmatic certainty of the essential relation of Israel and Yahweh and the

[8] E. Troeltsch, "Das der hebraeischen Propheten," *Logos* 6 (1916), 1–28.
[9] F. Weinrich, *Der religiös-utopische Charakter der "prophetischen Politik."*

unconditional indestructibility of Israel so long as it was true."[10] Consequently it was necessary to reject all that was foreign; in this way the sole work of Yahweh for his people was manifested. Israel must submit to whatever other nations will do to her and, in these events, God will do as he pleases for the sake of his people. This can only be called politics in the purely formal sense that the prophets gave their views on the affairs of the polis. It was, however, wholly negative inasmuch as there was no assessment of actual conditions; rather, by means of a religious dogma an impossible attempt was made "to stop the course of cultural development and the course of political necessities."[11]

Weinrich attempted to be even more precise in his analysis of prophetic utopianism. "The question of men face to face with Yahweh, the only one which they ask, is as follows: how can I discharge my duty before Yahweh? but not the question: can I endure if I discharge it?"[12] It is scientifically correct to use the term "utopian" to describe this belief that "before Yahweh a cultural stream and a world politics of great conquerors will stand still when the people who obey him walk in his ways, the faith that religious-social life can avert a catastrophe, the faith that God in a great miracle (sometimes in the Messianic form) can turn the fate of this world."[13]

Nevertheless, Weinrich is explicit in rejecting any suggestion that the prophet had a program or a system of rules by which he determined his political response in advance. He stood rather at the point where the traditional magic-demonic faith in the covenant with Yahweh presented itself as a religious-ethical force in the immediate prophetic ecstasy, a type of inspiration from which all preliminary asceticism and mystical absorption were excluded. This immediate appropriation of the ancient faith meant that "the prophet is politically dangerous, domestically as well as internationally,"[14] for at the point where others employ prudential political considerations the prophet has only the be-

[10] Troeltsch, *op. cit.,* p. 10.
[11] *Ibid.,* p. 22.
[12] Weinrich, *op. cit.,* p. 21.
[13] *Ibid.,* pp. 21–22.
[14] *Ibid.,* pp. 17–18.

lief in the possibility of Yahweh's doing all things. "The content of the prophetic preaching is purely religious."[15] Because of their belief in the purely transcendental source of "prophetic politics" it is understandable that Troeltsch and Weinrich should have chosen the term "utopian" to describe it. Yet in their own description there is a fundamental incompatibility between the term and the referent, for both interpreters stress that the prophets excluded all those programmatic conceptions which have been the stock in trade of utopian schemes.[16]

In his conclusion, Weinrich sharply formulates the dualism running throughout this utopian analysis.

Prophecy has pointed out two fundamentally different worlds, *bāsār* and *'ēl*. The prophet lives in and on the basis of the world of *'ēl*, which for him is the only "true" world; insofar as this people Israel and also other peoples are determined by the "true" world, just so far all earthly-human (*'ādām*) matters have their pivot therein, and from it their "Life." The world of *bāsār* as such, taken in itself, is for him a false world.[17]

The world of flesh over against the world of God can only be negated or saved; the two worlds cannot comfortably "co-exist." Although Weinrich struggles manfully to do justice to the prophetic estimate of the world, his terms are misleadingly drawn for they imply a dualistic dogmatism. The claim that "religious" (other-worldly) factors wholly replaced "political" (this-worldly) factors in prophetic thought is an undemonstrated assertion. In fact, certain valuable insights in Troeltsch and Weinrich, especially the latter's suggestions about the relation of tradition and ecstasy[18] and his idea of "the two circles" in which prophetic ethos moved,[19] are not given proper context. In short, the frame-

---

[15] *Ibid.,* p. 19.

[16] For description and illustration of the utopian trust in visionary reform which fails to recognize defects in human nature and operates with a priori principles, cf. *Encyclopaedia Britannica,* 14th ed., vol. 22, p. 915; J. O. Hertzler, *History of Utopian Thought,* 1923, part II and esp. chap. X on "The Limited Perspective of the Utopians;" and K. Mannheim, *Ideology and Utopia,* 1949, chap. IX, esp. pp. 173–77.

[17] Weinrich, *op. cit.,* pp. 66–67.

[18] *Ibid.,* pp. 11–16.

[19] *Ibid.,* pp. 20–21.

work of their analyses remains highly rationalistic and ill suited to prophecy.

Explicit criticism of this utopian analysis of prophetic politics was undertaken by Karl Elliger. He took sharp exception to an overemphasis upon the supposed dogmatic traditions which led the prophets to a naïve rejection of political means and a too-simple belief in God's miraculous intervention.[20] Elliger accuses Troeltsch and Weinrich of failure to perceive the original force of "the special experiences" of the prophets on the basis of which they actually reshaped the traditions. If received Israelite dogma had it that Israel would be saved, Amos saw only the slightest possibility of salvation in his situation (5:14 f.) and Isaiah gave up all hope (6:9 f.). The direct experience of God led them against tradition to assert a virtually unqualified disaster. "The old faith lies alongside the new, and in struggle with the special experience of the prophets, and there is no doubt as to which is the stronger."[21] The certainty of woe is primary with the prophets and was only secondarily associated with religious-moral factors in the life of the people. It derived directly from "a completely *sui generis* experience" which fell upon them from above, without historical explanation.

The prophetic experience had a remarkable double character. First, it created "a genuine prevision" of future events, such as the failures of the Syro-Ephraimite alliance against Jerusalem, the Ashdod revolt against Assyria, and the Assyrian attack upon Jerusalem. The prophet's knowledge was of the actual course of political events and it was "a knowledge resting upon a secret experience."[22] Isaiah predicted that Jerusalem would not fall in 701, not because of some dogma of the city's inviolability or because of the sin of the Assyrians, but because the knowledge that it would not fall was granted him by divine intuition. Elliger seems to say that, prior to all theoretical notions, the prophet on occasion by momentary insight discovers what will happen and,

---

[20] K. Elliger, "Prophet und Politik," *ZAW* 53 (1935), 3–22, and, by way of reply to J. Hempel, *Gott und Mensch im Alten Testament*, 2nd ed., 1936, pp. 321–22, in "Nochmals 'Prophet und Politik,' " *ZAW* 55 (1937), 291–96.

[21] Elliger, *ZAW* 53 (1935), 8.

[22] *Ibid.*, p. 12.

upon further reflection, gives it an incidental moral-religious explanation.

Second, the unique prophetic experience passes from the *"actus* of being included in the divine counsel to the *habitus* of being taken into the sphere of deity as the possession of the Holy Spirit."[23] This intimacy with God contributes an amazing sobriety and objectivity of outlook on all human matters, politics included. Isaiah warns against subjecting Judah to Assyria in order to lift the Syro-Ephraimitic siege because he knows that Assyria will do so anyway (chap. 7); he seeks to prevent rebellion against Sennacherib by pointing out the need of the weary Judeans for rest (28:12); and he notes the loss of national assets through payment of tribute to Egypt (30:6 f.). Concludes Elliger,

> It is not to be disputed that the politics of the prophets is religious. But this religion is in its essence no system, no dogma, no sum of received elements of faith and moral commands which thrust themselves between God and his elected servant. Rather it is an immediate state of communion (*Verbundensein*) with the living God, and this state of communion translates itself directly, as in other functions of human life, also into politics, and precisely in politics of an unheard-of objectivity.[24]

Such a prophetic outlook, insists Elliger, should not be called religious utopianism but *pneumatic Realism.*

Elliger closes his study by rebutting the three specific utopian elements which Troeltsch and Weinrich had found in the prophets: (1) rejection of foreign alliances; (2) rejection of military force; (3) dependence on divine miracle. Of the first he insists that "opposition to one alliance and even opposition to a whole series of alliances is still not utopianism,"[25] since all depends upon the reasons for opposition. The prophet does not oppose alliances because of a principled rejection of all alliances but because of his feeling of inner and outer security through trust in the definite word of God. As to the second, many verses (e.g., Isa. 5:27 ff.; 9:5; 22:1 ff.; 28:6), Elliger finds, indicate that the prophets did

[23] *Ibid.,* p. 13.
[24] *Ibid.,* p. 15.
[25] *Ibid.,* p. 16.

not renounce military action per se. Finally, confidence in the supposed miracle turns out, on analysis, to be no more than a manner of speaking which really describes human actions as the means of God to punish and to redeem his people.

Unquestionably the central objection of Elliger is well taken, namely, that the utopian understanding of prophecy derives from an a priori interpretation which disregards the special historical reality of prophecy. His attempt to state the uniqueness of the prophetic viewpoint on all matters as the outgrowth of the communion between the prophet and God is a laudable one. Elliger's observations on the practical character of many prophetic political judgments are reminiscent of Wilke's earlier arguments.

Regrettably Elliger's substitute conception of pneumatic Realism is not satisfactory, for its several elements are questionable in themselves and are not successfully related to one another. The bold claim, against the tide of scholarly opinion, that prophets foresaw the future is not in itself as disturbing as the way in which the foresight is suspended in isolation from the other elements of the prophetic activity. Elliger appears to believe that the utterly unexplicable foreknowledge of an event is rationalized by the prophet when the latter supplies religious and moral causes from national life. This is a weird rationalization which sunders event and interpretation, leaving only the arbitrary constructions of the prophetic mind to bridge the gap between them.

Furthermore, the two aspects of the prophetic experience, i.e., the prevision of future events and the sustained objectivity due to Spirit possession, are not intelligibly related. Aside from the few examples given, there are no hints as to how we are to distinguish between insights which came over the prophet by prevision and those which dawned upon him within a complex situation as a result of his marvelous objectivity. Although he does not say so explicitly, Elliger seems to believe that the former kind of insight simply came to the prophet as a singular inexplicable datum, while the other was an insight which he deduced and was prepared to defend in all its interconnections as a part of his total trust in God. This may seem like a slight distinction, but we may well wonder, for example, if there is not quite a difference between counseling against armaments because it is *known* for a fact that a particular campaign or alliance will fail and counseling against armaments because in that situation it is *probable* that trust in this form of human means will result in serious damage to other aspects of God's work with his people, e.g., through loss of political independence, neglect of internal wrongs, and economic privation. These two views might be combined but Elliger does not suggest a way to do it. Finally, granted that Troeltsch and Weinrich overplayed the prophetic reliance on miracle, one wonders if Elliger doesn't practice sleight of hand when he explains the miracle hope of the prophets entirely as a manner of speaking. In short, it seems necessary to grapple more seriously with the way the divine action is manifested politically. All in all, Elliger presents us with a series of uncoordinated parts which do not in fact produce a satisfying synthesis.

Martin Buber has consistently stressed the unified field of prophetic thought and experience.[26] Under the divine *melek* Israel exists as his citizen-subject whose every decision is "theopolitical" and who hears the prophetic word not as a political inference from a religious principle but as a single word. This word defines at one and the same time the nature of God and the nature of Israel and, therefore, the presently demanded response of Israel. Any attempt to understand prophetic politics apart from the whole prophetic understanding of Israel as the embryonic Kingdom of God is misconceived. In Isaiah's struggle against covenant politics, his theopolitics is concerned "to establish a certain people in a certain historical situation under the divine sovereignty, so that this people is brought nearer the fulfilment of its task, to become the beginning of the Kingdom of God."[27] "Religious" as well as "political" factors enter into the protest against an alliance which "puts the people under obligations and in a position of dependence, contrary to that one such relationship which is true" and at the same time jeopardizes its political and economic independence by involving it in foreign wars and exposing it to extinction.

The "communal existentialism" of Buber should also be stressed, since he sees Israel with tremendous potential for sway-

[26] M. Buber, *The Prophetic Faith.*
[27] *Ibid.,* p. 135.

ing the course of the future, for in each theopolitical moment Israel decides for or against God. In fact, "to be a *nabi* means to set the audience, to whom the words are addressed, before the choice and decision, directly or indirectly."[28] The future is shaped by the community decision of the present. "I emphasize 'community' for even where he [the *nābî'*] is mentioning individuals, the main purpose is the realisation in the whole of public life."[29] *Buber's understanding of prophetic politics is based upon what H.-J. Kraus calls "theological Monism," since the Kingdom of God must come to fulfillment in this empirical Israel. Buber largely succeeds in imparting to the political directives of the prophets an integral connection with their leading theme of the kingship of Yahweh.*

Buber's analysis of the precise relation between "religious" and "political" factors is, however, less acceptable. It is even surprising that he should make this distinction in speaking of Isaiah's motives for attacking alliance politics. When he explains the former in this way, "He who has dealings with the powers renounces the power of powers, that which bestows and withholds power, and loses its help,"[30] we wonder how his view would really be distinguished from the utopian view of prophecy. Buber has perhaps come closer than any to grasping the total "theopolitical" reality of prophecy, but insofar as he considers the motives of the specific political judgments of prophets he is not more helpful than others who have failed to break through the religious/secular and subjective/objective dichotomies which constantly haunt interpreters. This limitation does not obscure, however, several significant insights of Buber which should be followed up, such, for example, as his recognition that prophetic foreign policy "is not merely a negative program, if we take it in connection with all the prophetic teaching about the right ordering of community life,"[31] and his note that Isaiah counsels "keeping still" as "the imitation of divine attributes" (18:4).[32]

[28] *Ibid.*, p. 2.
[29] *Ibid.*, p. 3.
[30] *Ibid.*, p. 137.
[31] *Ibid.*, pp. 135–36.
[32] *Ibid.*, pp. 136–37.

H.-J. Kraus has set himself the task of finding out whether Israel should be thought of as a "state" (and therefore politically) and of determining the authority and purpose of the prophet when he stepped into politics.[33] He proceeds against the backdrop of a critical analysis of previous answers which he believes were all in one way or another vitiated by rationalistic or idealistic orientations that ended up with untenable dualisms or false objectifications. Even Buber's monistic approach is criticized for relying too heavily on *"tōrāh"* as the medium of prophetic communication and for asserting too immediate a connection between God's kingdom and the Israelite community.

Kraus traces the formative elements of prophetic politics in a fuller manner than is used in any of the earlier studies, with the exception of Buber's. He finds that the Israelite amphictyony was a sacral order of a pre-political rather than a genuinely political character, and the central notion of that sacral order was the kingship of Yahweh. The monarchy was in its charismatic beginning a continuation of the amphictyony, but its new political features were the acclamation of the king by the people and his rule by "royal law" which turned charismatic warfare into enforced military service. In David the double character of monarchy is even sharper for he incorporates the amphictyonic religious symbols in his Jerusalem cult but also rules as the especially elected representative of Yahweh in dynastic perpetuity. Politics has the ambiguous character of faithlessness to Yahweh and of acknowledgment of his lordship in the state. Monarchy produced a type of state prophecy which was also ambiguous in that it proclaimed the righteous rule of Yahweh through his regent but also tended to detach the king's charisma from his close personal obedience to Yahweh and to make it into an independent good which cultic technique could augment and maintain. Monarchy becomes autonomous, free from genuine Yahwistic conditions.

The "true prophets" were messengers of the divine king who drew their self-image from the amphictyonic conception of Yahweh enthroned over the ark. "The prophets of Israel stand in the

---

[33] H.-J. Kraus, *Prophetie und Politik.*

service of the kingship of God, as it decisively emerged in the amphictyonic central sanctuary in the pre-political form of Israel's life."[34] They set themselves against the falsification of the state prophets by proclaiming the Rule of God in history. They saw their own words as effecting history so that the Hebrew kingdoms were to come to an end before the demand of God's Rule. "The elected are now the accused" and within the context of Israelite political life no repentance is possible. The end in which repentance and return will be possible will also be the end of politics. "The heart of the plan of salvation is the end of the old,"[35] in opposition to cultic state prophecy, which in contemporizing salvation secularizes it at the same instant. The prophet is thus not a political adviser nor is he the defender of a higher political idea or utopia. Rather his task is "consistently eschatological." In contrast to the previous "gropings" after the proper understanding of political prophecy, Kraus affirms,

> Old Testament prophecy exposes all political errors of the elected king and his state in order to announce the end of the old polis in threat and to promise the beginning of a new polis. The encouragement and demand of this new polis pressing upon history permit human politics no more time to pursue its own goals.[36]

It is proper to share Kraus's disappointment with the previous history of the discussion of prophetic politics. By resisting the idealistic and utopian dualisms of earlier conceptions, he stands with Buber in a sounder tradition. Unfortunately, by his sharp contrast between the present and future, between Israel and the Kingdom of God, he has introduced an eschatological dualism that leaves something to be desired. The prophetic word about politics seems to be an exclusive "no," and the power of repentance to turn the tide of history is renounced in such a way that on this issue Kraus is absolutely opposed to Buber. *To say that the authority of prophecy derives formally from amphictyonic elements seems valid but to say that prophecy intended to bring Israelite politics to a complete end is doubtful in the ex-*

34 *Ibid.,* p. 39.
35 *Ibid.,* p. 77.
36 *Ibid.,* p. 82.

treme. It is a generalization that does not fare much better than earlier generalizations by Winckler, Troeltsch, and Elliger.

The Prophetic Political Consciousness: A Synoptic View

We must now attempt to trace the political facets of the totality experience of the prophet so that we may ground his "politics" precisely where it is at home, i.e., in the unified field of the knowledge of God and man. We must make a particular effort to avoid the misleading dichotomies (subject/object, cause/effect, utopian/prudential, ideal/real, religion/politics) which have repeatedly lured interpreters into one-sided or superficial reconstructions.

The prophet lives his life in communion with the God of Israel. His life in God is analogous to Israel's life in God. The community and its leaders maintain distinct identities but they receive their entire vitality and meaning in close personal association with God. At the heart of the prophet's understanding of himself and his people is the distinctive incorporation of God and man in a common life which flows from the side of the living God and forms the very basis of human life. As a specially called and sent one, the prophet attests to the incorporating act of God which continually forms the people as the people of God while it forms him as the man of God. The self remains a genuine self but is caught up into the Selfhood of God so that neither God nor man can be known except in their communion in a marvelous creative unity in duality,[37] a communion which completely by-passes the false antinomies of pantheism and supernaturalism.

Innumerable are the ways of stating the incorporation of God and man which maintains the distinction of the Person from the persons but holds them in a vital communion stronger than any natural community. It is permissible to describe the communion as an "encounter/decision" pattern, as a "revelation/response" motif, as a "grace/faith" relationship, as "the engendering deed" and "the engendered response"—depending upon the angle from

[37] H. Knight, *The Hebrew Prophetic Consciousness,* 1947, pp. 109–20.

which the communion is viewed.[38] What is at stake in the biblical imagery for the relation (king/subject, father/son, husband/wife), as also in the systematic theological reflections, is *the delicate but crucial balance in a communion which is* unnatural *and, therefore, not inevitable* (thus the value of the king/subject, encounter/decision, revelation/response concepts) *but which is simultaneously* internal *and* personal *and, therefore, not merely juridical* (thus the value of the father/son, husband/wife, grace/faith, engendering deed/engendered response concepts).

In this communion, with its dynamic unity in duality, lurk seemingly unfathomable implications for prophetic politics. Israel and the prophet locate the starting point for their self-understanding and the impetus for their task only in their communion with God. At the same time the locus of the communion with God is the totality of life in the communal body, with its past focused upon a present that is equally open to the future. The communion with God must be realized in just this existing historical and communal body for there is no other point of intersection and formation. Elliger's claim that *prophetic Realism* properly describes prophetic politics instead of the religious utopianism of Troeltsch is correct in one important sense, namely, that the prophet really meets God in these concrete circumstances and therein actually comes to his knowledge of God. The prophet's life in the community of Israel is indeed a communion with and a discovery of God rather than a purely secondary sphere for the application and illustration of the knowledge of God. If Elliger had fully appreciated this he would not have replaced programmatic utopianism with the mystique of the prophet's "special experience."

In an exactly analogous manner, Israel meets her God and knows his will for her in the peculiar life that she must live—and politically this means vis-à-vis the great and the small nations of the Near East. In the course of Israel's living, with all that entails, God's will becomes visible to his people and in his people. All life has potential for communicating direct knowledge of God, and the powerful formative knowledge of God is given

[38] J. Sittler, *The Structure of Christian Ethics,* 1958, pp. 24–26.

in just this concrete way, through what has been called "the important principle of mediation."[39]

Regrettably, the failure to see that a living communion is involved in prophetic faith marked the error of the utopian interpretation of the prophets' political "message." The initial assumption of divine and human realms which communicate with one another through a moral-religious nexus led inevitably to assessing prophetic ethics as a *transfer* of transcendent ideals or principles into more or less satisfying *applications* in society and politics. This ideal-real dualism is clearly expressed in Weinrich's assertion: "Thus the prophetic ethos operates within two circles: one encloses God, the other Men (the people of Yahweh). All prophetic assertions recur in both circles: it is a question of the religious moral relation of men to God."[40]

The "two circle" hypothesis, which might have been employed to describe the communion of God and man, discloses its misunderstanding of prophecy in that the circles do not touch but are connected only insofar as the lower human sphere reflects or is made to copy the patterns and principles of the higher divine sphere. The deity is "the formative life principle." A demand from God orients the prophet in the right direction, and he in turn demands something similar of his people. "The defection from Yahweh is also apostasy from moral norms. . . . Yahweh forms the 'metaphysical' background of all life and happenings."[41]

In spite of its comprehensive view, the utopian reading of prophecy is not comprehensive enough to grasp the prophetic totality experience. It remains an account of the earthward-directed life of God which becomes a model or incentive for human life but does not actually form that life in intimate communion. Although the utopian view is organic in a measure, it is an organic conception of two fixed dualities, the lower constantly trying to shape itself by the example of the higher but with no real basis for communication between the two inasmuch as the

---

[39] Knight, *op. cit.*, p. 115.
[40] Weinrich, *op. cit.*, p. 20.
[41] *Ibid.*, p. 21.

principles of the higher world cannot formatively penetrate the unreceptive real world. On such a view politics can only be a practice at considerable remove from religious influence, a practice that is deductive and rationalistic and always uncomfortably caught in juggling the incompatible ideals and realities.

The public life of Israel stands in relation to Israel's call from God as does the prophet's life in relation to his call. The whole visible life of people and prophet is a context within which to receive and to embody God's calling. The relation of the hidden center of the call and the public sphere is not the relation between admonition and application, or even between speaking and hearing, but between form as entelechy and substance that is shaped in accordance with the form. The "hearing" of the word must be the embodiment of the seminal word of God in society and history so that it bears its fruit in the structures of life. The impact of God upon man's far-flung life in history is not like that of a stone thrown into a pool so that the waves are progressively weaker as they extend from the center. It is rather more like a pool steadily fed by deep springs.

Having known moments of extraordinary communion with God in vision and audition, the prophet also communes with him in the begetting and naming of his children symbolically, in the public actions which teach Israel by the senses, or by actually presenting his life and conduct as a parable that will be instructive and life-nourishing for the entire community. In the course of his ministry the prophet actually does things whose significance he learns only in the course of doing them or even thereafter, e.g., Jeremiah's purchase of Hanamel's field. Having known the high moments of redemptive and covenantal communion with God, the people also communes with him in the ordering of its social and political life in accordance with what he continues to reveal of his will, and even on occasion presents its life as a sign of this ever-present action of God which may become instructive for all nations. In her history Israel actually does things (or things are done to her) whose significance she learns only in the course of doing them or even thereafter, e.g., the occupation of Canaan and the Babylonian exile.

We must be as exact as possible. It is not that in call vision and in covenant ceremony prophet and people learned all that was necessary to know of God and subsequently "applied" it to life. No, for then Israel and the prophet would be religious technicians, learning something from one realm of discourse which they transfer, with necessary modifications because of the changes in contexts and materials, to another realm. Rather, prophet and people are themselves formed by a stream of divine life which articulates its source and direction in the paradigm of call and covenant. But the paradigms are not typological patterns which so stand to the rest of life that they become deductive instruments for categorizing life. The call and the covenant are a part of the life existing for prophet and people as they let themselves be formed in a manner that has become familiar through God's previous dealings with them but that occurs now in a fresh and unpredictable context. *The paradigmatic form and the novel context are inseparable factors in the prophetic politics.* Isaiah's directive to desist from the Syro-Ephraimite alliance and from an alliance with Assyria and his namesake's proclamation of Cyrus as messiah were as direct and "theological" as their celebrations of God's holiness and glory and of man's sinfulness and frailty. In this sense Buber is justified in speaking of "theopolitics," i.e., a politics formed not alone or primarily by predetermined political rules or by religious ideals but by Israel's communion with God.

Fundamental to the dynamic of the community's life is the imitation of the divine life by allowing that life to form and to re-form the community. The entelechy of the community, as distinct from its mere potential existence, is realized insofar as the divine life determines the life of the community. Otherwise, the community is threatened by formlessness or complete redefinition as a community which has realized its entelechy in full, i.e., as the Kingdom of God on earth. True imitation of the divine life cannot be articulated as a system. "System is proper to the inorganic; the living has a characteristic *style*."[42] *The "style" of*

---

[42] Sittler, *op. cit.,* p. 50.

Israel's faith is that of the imitation of God through conformance to his life which as Word and Spirit works within the life of Israel.

The answers concerning God's nature and will are not known systematically in advance, although the records of what men once knew of God (e.g., Moses and former prophets) create a certain expectation for the present. While Isaiah may have opposed alliances throughout his entire lifetime, it was never because he was obligated to an inflexible principle but solely because of loyalty to what God was revealing in the organic context of the latter part of the eighth century in Judah. What appears to us as an inflexible rule of resistance to foreign alliances on examination dissolves before the variety of the contexts and the special force and coloring with which the position of Judah vis-à-vis the nations is seen. The warning against foreign alliances may, for example, attest to the growing power of Assyria or, later, may assure fearful Judah of Assyria's downfall. It is clear that Jeremiah urged the surrender of Jerusalem to Nebuchadnezzar not because he was against killing or because he wanted to save his life but because he thought it the then necessary step in Israel's life to assure her of further formation under God. It was a step in the imitation of God and of walking in the way which he opens toward the future; only this gave the prophet the power to declare his message without bitterness or fatalism.

Thus we cannot speak sensibly of "utilitarian" prophetic ethics any more than we can speak of "utopian" prophetic ethics. The presuppositions and proofs of utilitarianism in the prophets are lacking. To be sure, they engaged in a remarkably far-ranging participation in public life and they were politically informed beyond the average. Their political comment is startlingly extensive, and it can also be shown that on many occasions they counseled in a manner which prudent statesmen might regard as politically sound. Nevertheless the prophets did not select their counsels by balancing the elements of the situation in terms of consequences. *It is true that the prophet was "prudential" in his resolute openness toward what God was actually forming in the social and political life, but that is better described as "theological pragmatism."* He surveyed politics without detailed foreknowledge of events—although prediction of the future was not to be ruled out—and not in order to shape a calculating ethic or to find a field for the application of his principles. He looked intently at politics in order to see what Yahweh was doing and therefore what Israel must do. Consequences were considered not as rewards or proofs but as vindications of God's way by means of the enhancement of life through its further formation in accord with the divine life. Therefore, mere calculation and stern duty cannot understand the prophet's attentive watching and obedient action.

It is somewhat frustrating to conclude that all attempts to sort out the factors operative in prophetic political judgments into a system are open to serious doubt. *The alternative to rigid utopianism, which would have compelled prophets to prejudge events, was not a heterogeneous bundle of prudential factors, which added together formed a certainty no stronger than the motives were individually strong.* It is of course probable, as Wilke and Elliger recognized, that many elements and factors grasped within prophetic realism's field of vision coincided formally with a calculating political outlook. The prophets saw clearly, for example, the devastating domestic effects of wars and alliances which drained the land of means and manpower and fostered barbarism and vanity in men. Yet all these were ingredients of the totality experience of what God was doing among men and what he required of them. Within the total form the prophet saw the self-destructive factors, but he did not induce the form of God's action from the sum total of separate disintegrating forces. No absolute judgment on the basis of preconceived principles and no calculation of outcome could serve to fill for a moment the space occupied in the prophetic consciousness by the ever-engendering action of God, who appears to and with Israel and gives shape to his people within the events created and suffered by them.

Precisely because foreign policy tended to dominate Israel's consideration, the prophets spoke with special sharpness and with a savage negation on that subject. If we can account for this attitude on the ground of their totality experience of Yahweh's incorporation of Israel in communion with him, it certainly lies in the emotional nationalistic excitation produced by wars and rumors of wars, which had the serious effect of diverting Israel's attention from the total formation of her life. *Under such circumstances foreign policy was likely to be a diseased growth in the body of Israel.* Foreign policies of fear and grandeur, with a sincerely applied Yahwistic veneer, tended to fill deep psychic needs, and their makers could always appeal to a venerable theology of the holy war by way of support of the adventurous pursuit of status and security among the nations.

The prophet insisted—prosaically from a nationalist point of view—that the total incorporation of the people by Yahweh be kept in view; so, while cautioning on foreign adventures and defensive alliances, he counseled domestic development and redress of social wrong. The prophet reached his conclusion, not through calculation of the probable success of policies, but through the absolute apprehension of Yahweh's deed among his people in the great wasteland of internal social, economic, and political life. Genuine involvement and responsibility had been drained from public life by individual aggrandizement and by national defensiveness or aggressiveness toward other peoples. Isaiah reminded his people that "by means of foreign lips and with an alien speech the Lord will speak to his people" but this was only because they had long since ceased to hear the clarion call, "This is rest; give rest to the weary; and this is repose" (28:11–12).[43] *A people formed solidly from within need not fear comparison or rivalry with other peoples.* Elliger was correct when he insisted that Isaiah's "Be still" does not mean to fold the hands and to wait, and Buber was correct when he stressed that such stillness was Israel's imitation of the patience of God. "Be still" meant to work within the scope of historical life carved out by what Yahweh was actually forming, first among his own people Israel but ultimately throughout the cosmos.

Prophetic politics are not based upon any particular monarchic or anti-monarchic ideologies. It is true, as Kraus demonstrates, that the amphictyonic style of "pre-political" life in Canaan has contributed important formal elements to the prophetic attitude toward the state. Clearly the prophets reject particular kings as

[43] S. H. Blank, *Prophetic Faith in Isaiah,* p. 24.

faithless leaders of the people. Nevertheless, as A. Johnson and von Rad have shown, Isaiah depends very heavily upon the concept of Jerusalem as the holy city and the king as the guardian and executor of its traditions of peace and righteousness.[44] In fact, just as we can clearly see a distinction between the blunt anti-cultural stand of the Rechabites and Nazirites and the critique of the prophets which sought to transform culture, so *we can distinguish between regional or amphictyonic rejection of the kingdom and the political critique of the prophets which sought to re-form the kingship in keeping with God's formation of his people.* For the prophet, God's work in Israel was not ideologically dependent upon the elimination of kingship nor upon the cessation of all foreign relations nor upon the revival of ancient amphictyonic practices such as the holy war in place of a professional army. The prophetic advice against foreign alliances and in favor of passivity toward the enemy cannot, therefore, be explained as springing from an ideological insistence that the political entities of Israel and of Judah be destroyed. *The realization of God's purpose for Israel merely presupposed the faithful use of the existing political structures.*

The striving of God to form Israel and her recalcitrance result in an eschatological orientation of prophecy but it cannot be said with Kraus that this meant the end of the state as the sphere of God's action. To put it in that way is to make the end of Hebrew politics a *sine qua non* of God's work and in effect to define God's formation of his people in terms of opposition to some particular political order. Prophetic eschatology does of course entail the belief that God's incorporation of Israel in communion with him is not bound by any specific political form. Yet even Jeremiah seems to have believed that the repentance of Zedekiah could have spared the Judean state, and Ezekiel envisioned the return of Jews to Palestinian statehood within thirty years of the first deportation. We are therefore obliged to heed the dialectic of prophetic thought about the state, which is "transpolitical" in that God may dispense with or alter any particular political form, even kingship, but which is also thoroughly "po-

[44] A. Johnson, *Sacral Kingship in Ancient Israel*, pp. 27–46; G. von Rad, *Old Testament Theology*, 1962 (trans. of 1957 German ed. with revisions), I, 46–48.

litical" since it holds no communal forms under necessary suspicion but looks within them all for the forming work of God.
There is a danger in replacing the spatial dualism of utopian
interpretation of the prophets with a temporal eschatological dualism which separates the sinful present from the restored future
so that the connection between the two is effectively cut. The
prophetic "end," whether of judgment or renewal, does not so
much annul or neutralize the present as enhance it by calling
forth new understanding of the formative communion between
God and his people.

It would be wrong to close with the impression that because
there is no prophetic system of faith and ethics there was complete arbitrariness in the prophet's discovery and appropriation
of the will of God. Clearly, the powerful organizing center of the
prophet's personal experience of God always served as a lode-
stone to the truth. Equally clearly this experience was not a
merely untested private opinion, for the prophet did not fear to
match his vision of God with the best in the traditions of Israel.
In fact he felt an obligation to the continuing revelation of God
to locate his own place within a larger company of speakers for
God. The received reports of what earlier Israelites knew of God,
whether in parabolic form or in the hortatory instruction form,
created certain expectations for the present knowledge of God.
Whatever precise forms of the early narratives and laws of Israel
were known to the pre-exilic prophets, it is abundantly evident
that they relied upon the traditions in such a way as to avoid all
impression of being innovators.[45] Their "innovation" was to call
for uncompromising obedience in the unlikely present, to draw
upon the ancient truth without imitating the forms of the past.

From our standpoint it is possible to see whole dimensions of
the truth of God which the prophets articulated for the first time.
We may conclude that in some important ways they were "in-

---

[45] For discussion of the extent and nature of the prophetic dependence
upon tradition, written or oral, cf. O. Procksch, *Geschichtsbetrachtung und
Geschichtsueberlieferung bei den vorexilischen Propheten;* K. Galling, *Die
Erwaehlungstraditionen Israels,* 1928, pp. 5–37; G. H. Davies, "The Yahwistic Tradition in the Eighth-Century Prophets," *Studies in Old Testament
Prophecy Presented to T. H. Robinson,* 1950, pp. 37–51; H.-J. Kraus, *Die
prophetische Verkuendigung des Rechts in Israel,* 1957.

novators." But when we inquire into the structure of their own thought, of the mechanism by which they worked through to their intense convictions, we must conclude that they themselves experienced a remarkable correspondence between their compelling intuition of God and their far-ranging knowledge of Israelite traditions. *In this sense we may speak of a prophetic pattern or style for ascertaining the will of God, a style which involved an oscillation between the depths of psychic communion with God and the manifold communal traditions.* For Isaiah this meant that his profound shuddering before the holiness of God was associated with the long-standing tradition of God's judgment of his people, and especially of his city Zion, because of the righteousness that lies insistently at the heart of divine holiness. For Jeremiah it meant that his awesome awareness of the dereliction of Israel was matched by the recollection that prophets of old, such as Micah, also had to declare repeatedly the doom of their people rather than their facile redemption.

The accompanying diagram is an attempt to represent *the dynamics of the prophet's political consciousness.* To arrive at

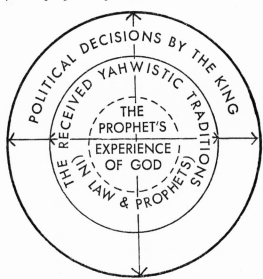

The Prophet's Political Consciousness

the "outer" political decisions it was necessary for the prophet to find a sure "inner" center of communion with God, which was enriched and reinforced by the received Yahwistic traditions. Instead of rejecting the body of mores and customary law in Israel, the prophets employed it to strengthen their case. With few exceptions, the prophet stops short of making the decision for Israel. That is the task of the king and his officials. The prophet supplies the weight of Yahwistic custom and insight against the tendency to see political issues in terms of limited and immediate goals.

Similarly, *the dynamics of the king's political consciousness* is represented in our second diagram. At the heart of the king's

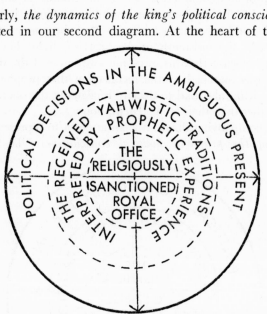

The King's Political Consciousness

obligation is his calling to an office of leadership which is sanctioned by religious traditions; he is the "servant" of Yahweh and the "shepherd" of his people, possessed of his own calling and inner responsibility.[46] The king's vocation must be seen through

---

[46] For balanced treatments of the religious basis of the Israelite kingship see C. R. North, "The Religious Aspects of Hebrew Kingship," *ZAW* 50 (1932), 8–38; M. Noth, "Gott, Koenig, Volk im AT," *Gesammelte Studien*

the received Yahwistic traditions as interpreted by the contemporary prophetic insight. The king cannot make decisions for his people merely by paying attention to the technical functions of his office as domestic administrator, military leader, and judge. He must rather see his office in its Yahwistic depth and totality, and for this vision he needs the prophet. Only the king can make the political decisions but he can make them wisely only with the prophetically expounded traditions of his people in mind.

Prophetic Models for International Relations

One of the decisive evidences for the traditional orientation of the prophets is the manner in which their treatment of international relations follows certain patterns. They tend to conceive of the nations as related to one another along the lines determined in certain periods of Israelite history.[47] *It is possible to examine their various "models" or "constructs" of international relations with an eye on the historical circumstances that shaped them.* These models do not, however, merely appear successively in history, to be dropped when the historical conditions that inspired them have passed. To the contrary, the models form a continuing body of traditional concepts upon which the prophets draw freely, and it it not uncommon for the same prophet to present two or more models or to combine elements from logically inconsistent constructs. The result is a very considerable measure of variety and freedom within the context of a rather solidly fixed body of traditions.

Some of the models are largely concerned with the present relations among the nations. Others are descriptive of future "redeemed" relations. To be sure, a line of separation between present and future cannot always be clearly maintained, and it is further noteworthy that the various "eschatological" models

---

zum Alten Testament, 1957, pp. 188–229; Johnson, *op. cit.,* pp. 27–44; S. H. Hooke, ed., *Myth, Ritual and Kingship. Essays on the Theory and Practice of Kingship in the Ancient Near East and in Israel.*

[47] H. Gross, *Weltherrschaft als religioese Idee im Alten Testament,* pp. 124–50, correctly argues that the concept of world dominion in Israel grew out of its own experience but he does not sufficiently stress the contribution of Israelite foreign relations to the formation of the religious motifs.

of international relations are drawn from historical examples, however much heightened or transformed. Perhaps the most instructive distinction is between models already well developed and merely used by the prophets and models which they were largely effective in creating.

Traditional Models

Israel defeated by or subject to another power. This model is the primary one shaping the thought of the pre-exilic prophets. The people of God is chastised by God through the instrumentality of the foreign power.[48] There can be no doubt that this is one of the oldest traditional beliefs of Israel. It was inherent in the theocratic constitution of the amphictyony that when Israel deserted her God she was bound to be punished by military disaster and political vassalage. This concept is not restricted to the Deuteronomic framework for the stories of Judges, inasmuch as a careful reading of the stories proper shows that the disciplinary defeat and subjection of Israel to other peoples is not only pre-Deuteronomic but pre-prophetic and pre-monarchic. *When Israel "sins" against the foundation of the amphictyony and violates Yahweh's interests by moral or cultic sin, she is "punished" until she repents.*

In pre-prophetic thought the enemy was mainly those smaller Palestinian peoples with whom the amphictyonic tribes had to do: Moabites, Midianites, Canaanites, and Philistines. However, larger and more distant powers could on occasion be involved. The prophets retained the assumption that the smaller neighbors could be Israel's chastisers but, in accord with the changing historical scene, they increasingly regarded the great imperial powers—Assyria and Babylonia in particular—as the agents of divine chastisement. It is obvious that the prophets did not have to think twice about espousing the deeply rooted belief of their people that God used other nations to "punish" and to "reward"

[48] H. Frederiksson, *Jahwe als Krieger. Studien zum alttestamentlichen Gottesbild,* 1945, esp. pp. 23–27; G. von Rad, *Der heilige Krieg im alten Israel.*

the people in covenant with him. In this they were completely traditional.

Nevertheless the prophets very significantly altered the model of disciplinary action by one state against another. For one thing they tended to see a broader canvas of international relations. Of course even this vision of the nations under Yahweh was to some extent anticipated in the pre-prophetic or "extra-prophetic" Israelite cult, but in the cult that vision had become highly formalized and archaic and its consequences for contemporary life were not very readily seen by most Israelites. *Although the prophets used the old cult models for reviewing the sinful nations and for asserting Yahweh's judgment, they filled them with a live, completely contemporary content and stressed always the importance for Israel of faithful and obedient response to God.* Thus from one angle Amos could view Israel as simply one of several small Palestinian states that had disregarded Yahweh, and Jeremiah could regard all the states of the Near East, Judah included, as subject to the divinely commissioned rule of Nebuchadnezzar, Yahweh's "servant." Such a broad leveling outlook on the nations was a very significant enlargement of the view of the old amphictyonic league.[49]

The most revolutionary modification in this disciplinary model was the prophetic belief that Israel could be so subjected to punishment that she would either cease to exist or would be drastically altered. According to the older theocratic conception, Israel might be administered a crushing defeat and even be dominated for a long period of time. It was nevertheless understood that, at the end of the time of trial, Israel would emerge again as an independent entity, essentially unchanged. Amos shattered this stability by declaring the dissolution of the Israelite state and the scattering of its populace. Later prophets were not so categoric in their assertions of doom; in fact some even held out various kinds of hope. Even so, all later prophets assumed radical alterations in the visible Israel. They expected the deportation of leadership and the loss of political independence in so drastic a form

[49] W. Cossmann, *Die Entwicklung des Gerichtsgedankens bei den alttestamentlichen Propheten,* esp. pp. 3–24.

that the new Israel which should arise would be very different from the present Israel.

Punishment of Israel was not merely to be temporary; it had a deep continuing effect upon the political structure of the state and thus upon the Israelite state's relations to other nations. In other words, with the prophets the old theocratic view of an Israel virtually sealed off from the rest of the nations was abolished, or at any rate very thoroughly revised. *Israel was now among the nations and she could perish as a separate state without losing her religious interests. The prophetic form of the model of Israel's defeat and vassalage was, therefore, a much more flexible concept than the amphictyonic original.* It allowed for political development and modification of institutions. It could even permit the abolition of an independent Hebrew state in the conviction that true belief in Yahweh could be carried on by general social institutions. This, of course, implied a degree of separation between political and social institutions which was well in advance of the ancient Near East.

Israel as the head of an empire. If the notion of Israel's chastisement by other nations was formulated largely from amphictyonic experience, the anticipation of Israel's political domination of the Near East was formulated with the united empire in mind.[50] Only in the tenth century had Israel been the dominant power in the region between the Nile and the Tigris-Euphrates valleys; at that time she was in some respects the equal of—perhaps even stronger than—the then quiescent Egyptian and Assyrian empires.[51] Before the united empire, as a vigorous but decentralized league of tribes, and afterward, as two kingdoms

[50] Gross, *op. cit.*, pp. 63–97, usefully surveys the references to Israelite world dominion, the king, and David redivivus, but he does not sufficiently take into account the powerful effect of the united monarchy in all formulations of world dominion and not merely in those which name David. Gross wisely discounts the supposed operation in Israel of a general Near Eastern *Hofstil* which carried with it developed eschatological concepts (pp. 18–21).

[51] A. Malamat, "The Kingdom of David and Solomon in Its Contacts with Egypt and Aram Naharaim," *BA* 21 (1958), 96–102; M. Noth, *The History of Israel*, pp. 193–98, 205–6.

often at odds with each other, Israel was either politically effete or only relatively strong vis-à-vis surrounding states.

Even the period of the united kingdom should be more precisely narrowed to the age of David. Saul had only begun to repel the Philistines. Solomon added no new territory to the empire by conquest and actually lost some. It was David who had expanded Israelite sovereignty over an area that included most of the cultivable territory between Egypt and the great bend of the Euphrates, the only significant exceptions being the regions immediately along the Mediterranean coast in the Philistine Plain on the south and in Phoenicia to the north. Commercial arrangements with the Phoenicians, and possibly also with the Philistines, overcame this lack of control over the coast as a serious obstacle to the Davidic empire.

It is therefore thoroughly understandable that salvation for Israel should be understood politically on the model of what David had accomplished. In the prophets, wherever this notion of a vast Israelite empire is in view, it is generally connected explicitly with a ruler of the line of David. This David is obviously not the David of the court history, the fatuous father and incompetent administrator who lost his earlier steady grip. *The David of the model of Israelite empire is the David celebrated in the royal cult.*[52] He is the ruler appointed (or "adopted") by Yahweh to establish "peace" and "righteousness" in Israel and throughout the earth. He is a benevolent despot who can be completely trusted because he obeys perfectly the will of God.

While it has been plausibly argued that the pre-exilic prophets at any rate had no sympathy with this conception of a Davidic ruler as the bearer of divine blessing, it cannot be ruled out, as we have seen, that they employed the conception even though they did not make it their major model—no doubt just because it was so easily subject to misunderstanding. It is certain that the ninth-century prophets Elijah and Elisha were not simply antimonarchic, and, with the possible exception of Hosea, none of the prophets of Israel regarded monarchy as itself a corrupt in-

[52] See the historically cautious sketch of the Davidic cult drawn by A. Johnson, *op. cit.*

stitution. Isaiah even builds one of his basic models of the future on the notion of a purified Davidic dynasty, which he sees as drawing its strength and its criteria from the appointment of Zion as the place where Yahweh is to fix and to maintain his righteousness in the world.

Israel surviving while the nations are destroyed. This conception is never very fully developed in Israelite prophecy. It becomes a significant model only with Israelite apocalyptic[53] and is first fully presented in the Gog of Magog passage of Ezekiel 38–39, which is apparently post-exilic. The notion does, however, appear in a less dogmatic form in some of the prophets. The actual origin of this conception was probably the severe blow which Yahweh dealt the Egyptians during the Exodus. The spectacle of Yahweh employing natural phenomena to terrorize and defeat the enemy was a definite article of amphictyonic belief (Judg. 5; Ps. 68) and remained a feature of Israelite liturgics (Hab. 3; Isa. 64:1–7). Isaiah expects the destruction of Assyria while Israel, although humbled, will continue. Ezekiel is emphatic in his repeated declarations of doom for the nations but he promises that Israel will be restored to her homeland. Although his position is not systematically propounded, it is easy to see why the Gog of Magog oracle was developed among Ezekiel's later disciples.

Yet the notion of a total obliteration of the nations is one that depends upon a kind of absolute thinking that was not usual in ancient Israel. It was much more natural to think of the defeated nations existing as vassals. Only as the relative weakness of Israel as a political force was fully accepted, so that it could not ever be envisioned as a world conqueror, did it become feasible to think of a destruction of the hostile nations either by natural means or by human means not under Israel's control. Also, the destruction of the hostile nations was anticipated only at a time when sufficient chastisement was thought to have been administered to Israel. Only Isaiah, at the close of the eighth century,

[53] The elaboration of the theme in intertestamental thought is given in considerable detail by P. Volz, *Die Eschatologie der juedischen Gemeinde in neutestamentlichen Zeitalter,* 2nd ed., 1934, pp. 280–83.

and Nahum, in 612, seem to have thought in such terms before the exile.

Newly Created Models

Three "eschatological" models seem to have been developed specifically by the prophets.

Israel as the refuge and gathering point for individual converts from the nations round about. This was foreshadowed by the ancient practice of granting asylum in Israel to outsiders (the *gērîm* or "resident aliens").[54] Such foreigners were granted virtually the full rights of citizenship in Israelite society and were permitted, with few disabilities, to participate in the religious privileges of Israel. The *gērîm* did not come to Israel, however, primarily as converts. They did not prefer Israelite religion to other religions. They came in various capacities, as fugitives or refugees, as mercenaries or merchants; and when by necessity they settled in Israel they came to accept Israel's religion in accordance with the unwritten rule of the ancient Near East: to each people its own deity.

When the Deutero-Isaianic disciples (Isa. 56–66) and Zechariah anticipate the gathering of converts to Jerusalem, they have in mind the deliberate choice of Israel's religion by foreigners. Naaman had been a convert of a sort to Yahwism but he returned to practice Yahwism in Damascus and in the course of his duties as a high official had also to participate in rites which honored Aramean deities (II Kings 5). *The situation to which these early post-exilic prophets point is apparently an idealized projection of what was already taking place at Jerusalem.* Among the Jews who returned to Jerusalem and took part in the restored cult there were apparently a considerable number of foreigners who "joined themselves to Yahweh" (*nilwāh;* Isa. 56:3, 6). They were assured of equal status with Jews by birth, so long as they observed the covenant requirements. In fact, the temple is

---

[54] A. Bertholet, *Die Stellung der Israeliten und der Juden zu den Fremden,* pp. 27–50; M. Guttmann, "The Term 'Foreigner' (נכרי) Historically Considered," *HUCA* 3 (1926), 1–20.

even described lyrically as "a house of prayer for all peoples" (56:7). Perhaps only some of the most bitterly despised of Israel's neighbors, who had taken advantage of her at the fall of Jerusalem—Edomites, Moabites, and Ammonites—were excluded from the Jewish community.[55]

It is of interest that we read of "a mixed multitude" of people accompanying the Israelites at the time of the Exodus from Egypt (Exod. 12:38), suggesting that a number of non-Israelites had joined the escaping tribes. Similarly it is understandable that at the restoration of the Jewish community to Palestine in 538 serious inquirers into Yahwism decided to join the returning Jews. The ardent proclamation of Israel's religion as a world faith by men of the persuasion of Deutero-Isaiah probably had considerable effect upon some non-Jews, particularly on other captive peoples who had been torn up from their moorings and transplanted in Babylon. It would not be surprising if captive Arameans from the western part of the empire, who had already heard of Yahweh and could converse with his adherents, were persuaded to accompany the returning Jews. No doubt, also, foreign adventurers living in Palestine at the time of the restoration were impressed by the Persian patronage of the Jewish cult and decided to become worshipers. That such non-Jewish adherents are not spoken of in the work of the Chronicler is not an insuperable objection for by this time, a century later, the memory of these non-Jewish converts had probably been lost and, with increasing hostility between the Judean community and the Samaritans and non-Jews of the land, the number of

[55] The evidence on this point is not easily interpreted. Already in Deuteronomy 23:3–8, Ammonites and Moabites were prohibited from Yahweh worship while Edomites and Egyptians were specifically admitted. Ezekiel 44:9 excludes all foreigners from temple worship but whether that proscription included the resident aliens (*gērîm*) is not certain. By the late fifth century, Samaritan Jews or other half-breeds were forbidden participation in the Jerusalem cult (Ezra 4:3; Neh. 13:7–9, 30). All intermarriage with Philistines, Ammonites, and Moabites was forbidden (Neh. 13:23–27). But none of these proscriptions seems to have excluded the taking in of converts, and even of proselytizing, provided that the newcomers did not intermarry until some generations had passed. For the relation between the older *gēr* and the later proselyte, cf. M. Weber, *Ancient Judaism*, pp. 362–64, 418–21.

converts probably declined—if not wholly ceased. At any rate, it is evident from Isaiah 56:8 that some Jews thought of an indefinite enlargement of the restored community through conversion of foreigners:

> Thus says Yahweh Elohim,
>   who gathers the outcasts of Israel,
> I will gather yet others to him
>   besides his gathered ones.

Israel as one partner in an international federation of major powers. The prophet on occasion seems to have in view the joining together in treaty obligations of several powers which in good faith agree to arbitrate their differences by means of the religious traditions of Israelite Yahwism. In one sense, all of the peoples so allied worship the same God, although in every instance it is not clear that the prophet excludes all local and national forms of worship from the non-Israelite members of the federation. This conception has its parallel in the Greek Amphictyonies, especially the Delphic League, which served to arbitrate differences among the member states and to limit the wars that did occur.[56] *Of course the Hebrew prophet looks at the federation not from the viewpoint of its organization and functions but from that of its primary Yahwistic allegiance. He asserts it as a promise rather than describes it as a program to be carried out.*

As with other prophetic models of international relations, this model of an international federation is rooted in Israel's past. It appears to be an extension of the structure of the old Israelite amphictyony into international affairs. The league had provided for certain common religious, military, and judicial interests but the tribes retained their autonomy in most matters. The prophetic mind seems to envision a similarly loosely organized league, allowing Assyria, Israel, and Egypt, for instance, to keep their own

[56] H. G. Liddell and R. Scott, *A Greek English Lexicon*, rev. ed., 1940, p. 92, entry on *amphiktyones;* M. Noth, *Das System des Zwoelf Staemme Israels*, 1930.

special political and social forms, joining only to submit their foreign policies to the judgment of the league officials in the person of the Hebrew prophets (Isa. 2:1–4; 19:19–25). Yet the model implies more than mere prevention of open conflict among nations; it implies a strong loyalty among the member states which creates a fellow feeling based upon solid trust. In such an atmosphere it is possible for Yahweh, without stirring national jealousies, to say, "Blessed be Egypt my people, and Assyria the work of my hands, and Israel my heritage" (Isa. 19:25).

Although Isaiah was the first prophet to think along the lines of this model explicitly, there were certainly strains of prophetic "universalism" which prepared the way for such federal concepts. The Yahwist knows of a promise to the sons of Abraham that "in you all the families of the earth will be blessed [or will bless themselves]" (Gen. 12:3), a promise which makes a very large claim without specifically showing how the narrator thought the blessing would be communicated.[57] Amos is emphatic in claiming that divine providence controlled the migrations not only of Israel but of her most hated enemies, the Philistines and the Arameans (9:7). Such strong "universalist" sentiments must be given great weight, even though Amos does not conceive of an international confession of Yahwism, primarily because he focuses upon the apostate kingdom of Israel, which is soon to collapse.

The federal model agrees with the model of Israelite imperialism in two important ways: For one thing, both expect a universal acknowledgment of Yahweh as the God of the nations. "Universal" in this context means of course only the known effective political environment, i.e., the ancient Near East. For another, both expect that Yahwism will be maintained by political means. But here the paths separate. In the model of Israelite imperialism the means are primarily the imposition of Israel's will upon other nations. In the model of international federation the means are primarily the free consent of the several nations to limit their sovereignty in obedience to the standards of Yahwism. *In one case Israel is first among the nations as an imperial power;*

[57] G. von Rad, *Genesis. A Commentary,* 1961 (trans. of 1956 German ed.), pp. 148–50, 155–6; Gross, *op. cit.,* pp. 61, 64–65.

in the other case Israel is one among several allied states. As a political entity she has no special prerogatives. As the home of the Yahwistic center Jerusalem, whose religious leaders are the keepers of Yahwistic traditions, she possesses a pre-eminence which is exerted by moral authority.

Israel as the priestly enclave in a single world empire. This conception is in one sense a modification of the model of international federation adjusted to the conditions of the sudden growth of the Persian empire. One sovereign political authority will replace all the sovereign states of the Near East, including the Jewish state. This model has the advantage of removing the conflict of interests and indecisiveness of action always latent in a federation. It also has the effect of removing the ambiguity between Israel as a political entity and Israel as a religious community. Israel ceases to be the former and becomes wholly the latter. Her political significance is simply that of a province within the Persian empire, but her religious significance is that of the religious capital of the entire empire. Israel both loses and gains in significance.

In projecting this conception of the redemption of the world, Deutero-Isaiah seems to build upon the model of Israelite imperialism, which he has radically revised by transferring the messianic leadership from an Israelite native prince to Cyrus as the head of the Persian empire (41:2–4, 25–29; 44:28; 45:1–7). *This bold transfer of authority from a Jewish messianic figure to a Persian messianic figure is much more than a concession to an existing situation; it is an attempt to free Israel for her special world-wide task, which she could never accomplish as long as she was burdened with the obligations of an independent kingdom.* No longer having to worry about her own affairs of state, she could serve the Kingdom of God. This model goes as far as Hebrew thought ever reaches in separating the religious and the political, the sacred and the secular; and even here it must be carefully noted that political and secular matters remain of great concern to Yahweh, who assures their proper care by putting them in the hands of his "messiah" Cyrus.

Conclusions

Without attempting to describe each prophet, we may offer certain general conclusions:

1. *The prophets were well informed about political issues but they were informed largely as intelligent laymen.* Some were close advisers of kings or officials, such as Isaiah and Jeremiah, but none was an official in the sense that he had to take responsibility for political decisions.

The rich knowledge of political events which we find in their writings has come almost exclusively from the prophets' general familiarity with current events rather than from official records. The few instances of official records—for example, in the historical extracts from Kings, or from a common source, in Isaiah 36–39 and Jeremiah 52—have been drawn into the prophetic books not by the prophets but by their editors.[58] Nevertheless the prophetic understanding of the power realities of the ancient world was impressive. When they advised against alliances they were well informed about the political and military prospects. When they foretold the defeat of this or that nation their threats were normally fulfilled. Many oracles previously thought to be inserted by later editors can now be explained within the lifetimes of the original prophets. For example, the publication of the Babylonian Chronicles makes it very likely that the oracle of Jeremiah against Kedar (49:28–33) belongs to the year 599 and the oracle against Elam (49:34–39) to the year 596.

Of course we must do justice to the formal and therefore exaggerated character of prophetic writing. Allowance must be made for predictions of total destruction which in many instances were not carried out. Where we can check their "predictions," however, the prophets scored rather well, chiefly because they knew the power realities and had a sense of the tides of political feelings, the rise and fall of morale, the impact of propaganda and terror.

2. *The prophets expressed their political concern by using old Israelite literary forms and religious motifs.* They do not seem

[58] R. B. Y. Scott, *IB*, V, 155–56; J. P. Hyatt, *IB*, V, 1137.

to have originated any single literary form, unless the invective or reproach (often beginning with *hôy*, "woe!") and the threat (beginning with *lākhēn*, "therefore") are so considered.[59] The majority of their forms of speech came from the cult, the law court, and the royal court. They achieved freshness in content and in the way they combined the forms. The process of combination came to a climax in Deutero-Isaiah (chaps. 40–55), who created a great tapestry woven from the strands of many separate literary forms. More than literary form was involved. The actual themes of early Israelite and general Semitic culture were used. When Isaiah or Jeremiah attacked a foreign nation he did so in a traditional way. He spoke of the nation as sinning and deserving divine punishment and as about to be totally destroyed. There is a severity and absoluteness to the prophecy of punishment which is traditional, as, for example, in the Egyptian execration texts[60] or in the seal of Sennacherib used on Esarhaddon's vassal treaty.[61] To be sure, the prophets put the traditional motifs to many unconventional uses, as when they judged Israel and Judah even more severely than other nations, when they condemned foreigners for violations of right rather than simply because they were anti-Israelite, and when they held out a generous hope for the unity of the human family.

3. *The prophets adopted neither a purely practical nor a purely utopian attitude toward the relations of nations; their position was instead an experiential and contextual one, provided that "experience" and "context" are interpreted in the light of the historic Yahwistic traditions and the overpowering apprehensions of God experienced by the prophets.*[62] A long discussion

[59] The form and setting of the threatening speeches of the prophets have been helpfully explored, but with sometimes conflicting or unrelated results, by E. Balla, *Die Droh- und Scheltworte des Amos*, 1926; E. Wuerthwein, "Der Ursprung der prophetischen Gerichtsrede," *ZTK* 49 (1952), 1–16; H. B. Huffmon, "The Covenant Lawsuit in the Prophets," *JBL* 78 (1959), 185–95; and E. Gerstenberger, "The Woe-Oracles of the Prophets," *JBL* 81 (1962), 249–63. Perhaps the best all-around form-critical analysis of prophetic literature is C. Westermann, *Grundformen prophetischer Rede*, 1961.

[60] *ANET*, pp. 328–29.

[61] D. J. Wiseman, "The Vassal-Treaties of Esarhaddon," *Iraq* 20 (1958).

[62] See *supra*, pp. 365–77.

as to the basis of prophetic political thought has found extremes in those, on the one hand, who said that the prophets were foreign agents in the service of Assyrian and Babylonian kings and in those, on the other hand, who said that they were completely religious in interest and utterly naïve in their belief that historical forces could be stopped or reversed by faith in God. The discussion has sometimes presupposed that the prophets were bound by ideological forms, that they were, for instance, either consistently prudential or consistently moralistic. It is a great mistake, however, to think that the prophets had a closed and finished system of thought and knew exactly how they would react to every political situation. The contrary was true. Their strong experience of God was decisive and from this they faced current social and political realities. They were flexible and adjustable to new situations according to their understanding of God's word. The will of God was not an abstraction or a general rule that could be applied without struggle. It had to be found in each new context. This explains why they could at one time speak of a foreign power's military victory as the will of God and at another time speak of the same nation's defeat as the will of God. What was important was not logical consistency but sensitive obedience to the will of God, who fixes the times and means of historical action. The result was that the prophets succeeded in giving political relations a personal bearing which has to a very large extent disappeared today.

4. *The prophets regarded political institutions, including sovereign states, merely as instruments in the plan of God.* They had a temporary but not a final value. The states of Israel and Judah were treated as provisional along with all the other states of the ancient Near East. There is of course variety in view, ranging from Amos and Jeremiah, who insisted that the Hebrew states would be utterly obliterated, to Zechariah and Haggai, who prophesied the revival of the Davidic kingdom. In the main, however, the prophets regarded particular political forms as immaterial to the fulfillment of God's purpose for Israel. It is certainly clear that they thought in collective ethnic terms, but mainly in non-political or, perhaps we should say, trans-political terms. So too for other peoples they could envision the breakup

of states and the death of rulers without an impairment of authentic national life.

The outstanding example of the prophets' trans-political views was their attitude toward the exile, which they considered absolutely necessary to the discipline of Israel. For the sake of religious fidelity Israel must cease to exist in any recognizable political form. Israel would survive in a religio-cultural sense. Yet an ambiguity remained in prophetic thought that was never resolved. An official interpretation was given to the fall of the kingdoms of Judah and Israel. They were destroyed because of the sins of the people against God. However, no similarly clear interpretation was given to the restoration of Israel and to its relation to other nations. The prophets shifted between thought of the future political supremacy of Israel and thought of Israel's role as teacher of the nations, perhaps in the form of a priestly enclave within the nations. This ambiguity is striking in the later prophets. Zechariah and Haggai expected the political triumph of Judah over the nations accompanied by her religious triumph. Deutero-Isaiah, however, expected that the religious triumph of Israel would occur at the same time that the Jews were political subjects of the Persian empire. Ezekiel held still another position; he believed that the foreign powers would be destroyed as threats to Israel but not with the help of a strong Jewish state, for Judah was in fact to remain a relatively small nation.

We conclude that whereas the prophets succeeded in giving a uniform religio-political interpretation to events of the past, they did not in a similar manner impress a uniform interpretation upon Israel's future. It remained an open question whether Israel was to have political identity, and if so, whether it would be imperialistic. Consequently the expected relations with other peoples ranged from the view that Israel would conquer them to the view that Israel would be conquered by them, and embraced in some instances the view that Israel would be in confederation with other states and serve them as a kind of priestly class. Often these views are mixed in the same prophetic writing.

This ambiguity sprang partly from the lack of logical consistency in prophetic thought, but much more from the prophets' strong involvement in the community. They did not transcend it sufficiently to give a unified plan for the future, but only to form unified conceptions of the past. *The prophets were influential enough to effect the survival of a community,*[63] *but not powerful enough to give it a single distinctive form vis-à-vis the state.* Even had they done so, it is not certain that the community would have followed them, for history has a way of overturning the best plans of men. *But that the prophets were able to think of a communal view of life outlasting the two ancient states of Israel and Judah was itself remarkable. Also, that they were able to envision the acceptance of that view of life by other states on equal terms was quite unusual in ancient thought.*

The prophets' interpretation of the relations between states rose on religious grounds informed by a high degree of political knowledge. They laid the foundations for internationalism in their view of a single God related to all states and not only to the peoples in special covenant with him. Many urgent contemporary problems cannot be solved from the prophetic traditions —for example, the structure of an international organization to bring about effective disarmament and the adjudication of disputes among nations. Even in fundamental matters it is necessary often to decide which prophetic view is most helpful for today. Nevertheless, there is no other point in human history where a group of men so combined hard knowledge of political life with high vision of man's responsibilities. Their sketch was rough and unfinished, but we do not seem to have progressed so far in international relations that their limitations make the prophets incapable of teaching us many things.

[63] See esp. N. K. Gottwald, *Studies in the Book of Lamentations.*

Bibliography

Bibliography

I. *Ancient Near Eastern Politics, History, and Culture*

Albright, W. F., "Historical Adjustments of Political Authority in the Near East," *History, Archaeology and Christian Humanism,* 1964, pp. 177–94.

——, "Notes on Ammonite History," *Miscellanea Biblica B. Ubach,* 1954, pp. 131–86.

——, "A Votive Stele Erected by Ben-Hadad I of Damascus to the God Melcarth," *BASOR* 87 (1942), 23–29.

Alt, A., "Hohe Beamte in Ugarit," *KS,* 1959, III, 186–97 (originally published 1953).

——, "Die Syrische Staatenwelt vor dem Einbruch der Assyrer," *KS,* III, 214–32 (originally published 1934).

——, "Voelker und Staaten Syriens im Fruehen Altertum," *KS,* III, 20–48 (originally published 1936).

Anspacher, A., *Tiglath-Pileser III,* 1912.

Atkinson, K. M. T., "The Legitimacy of Cambyses and Darius as Kings of Egypt," *JAOS* 76 (1956), 167–77.

Authority and Law in the Ancient Near East, Supplement 17 *JAOS* (1954) : J. A. Wilson on Egypt, E. A. Speiser on Mesopotamia, H. G. Gueterbock on Hittites, and I. Mendelsohn on Canaan-Israel.

Bengtson, H., *Einfuehrung in die alte Geschichte,* 3rd rev. ed., 1959.

Bibby, G., *Four Thousand Years Ago. A World Panorama of Life in the Second Millennium B.C.,* 1961.

Boehl, F. M. T., *King Hammurabi of Babylon in the Setting of His Time,* 1946.

Breasted, J. A., *A History of Egypt from the Earliest Times to the Persian Conquest,* 1935.

——, "The Predynastic Union of Egypt," *Bulletin de l'institut français d'archéologie orientale* 30 (1930), 709–24.

Buckler, F. W., "The Oriental Despot," *Anglican Theological Review* 10 (1928), 238–49.

Buhl, F., *Geschichte der Edomiter,* 1893.

Cameron, G. C., "Darius, Egypt, and 'The Lands beyond the Sea,' " *JNES* 2 (1943), 307–13.

———, *Early History of Iran*, 1936.

Contenau, G., *Everyday Life in Babylonia and Assyria*, 1954.

Cooke, G. A., *A Text-book of North Semitic Inscriptions: Moabite, Hebrew, Phoenician, Aramaic, Nabatean, Palmyrene, Jewish*, 1903.

Deimel, A., "Die sumerische Tempelwirtschaft zur Zeit Urukaginas und seiner Vorgaenger," *Analecta Orientalia* 2 (1931), 71–113.

Dentan, R. C., ed., *The Idea of History in the Ancient Near East*, 1955.

Dougherty, R. P., *Nabonidus and Belshazzar. A Study of the Closing Events of the Neo-Babylonian Empire*, 1929.

Drioton, E., and Vandier, J. *L'Égypte*, 3rd ed., 1952.

Duhm, B., *Die Edomiter*, 1893.

Dupont-Sommer, A., *Les Araméens*, 1949.

———, "Sur les débuts de l'histoire araméenne," Supplement 1 *VT*, 1953, 40–49.

Eddy, S. K., *The King Is Dead, Studies in the Near Eastern Resistance to Hellenism*, 1961.

Edgerton, W. F., "The Government and the Governed in the Egyptian Empire," *JNES* 6 (1947), 152–60.

Eiselen, F. C., *Sidon: a Study in Oriental History*, 1907.

Elliger, K., "Sam'al und Hamat in ihrem Verhaeltnis zu Hattina, Unqi und Arpad," *Eissfeldt Festschrift*, 1947, pp. 69–108.

Faulkner, R. O., "Egyptian Military Organization," *Journal of Egyptian Archaeology* (1953), pp. 32–47.

Fish, T., "The Cult of King Dungi during the Third Dynasty of Ur," *BJRL* 11 (1927), 322–28.

———, "Some Aspects of Kingship in the Sumerian City and Kingdom of Ur," *BJRL* 34 (1951–52), 37–43.

Fleming, W. B., *The History of Tyre*, 1915.

Forrer, E., *Die Provinzeinteilung des Assyrischen Reiches*, 1920.

Friedell, E., *Kulturgeschichte Aegyptens und des alten Orients. Leben und Legende der Vorchristlichen Seele*, 4th ed., 1953.

Friedrich, J., *Staatsvertraege des Hatti-Reiches in Hethitischer Sprache* (*Mitteilungen der vorderasiatisch-aegyptischen Gesellschaft* 31.1 [1926]; 34:1 [1930]).

Frye, R. N., *The Heritage of Persia*, 1962.

Gadd, C. J., ed., *The Fall of Nineveh*, 1923.

————, "The Harran Inscriptions of Nabonidus," *Anatolian Studies* 8 (1958), 35–92.

————, *Ideas of Divine Rule in the Ancient East,* 1948.

Gelb, I. J., "The Early History of the West Semitic Peoples," *JCS* 15 (1961), 27–47.

————, *Hurrians and Subarians,* 1944.

Glueck, N., "The Boundaries of Edom," *HUCA* 11 (1936), 141–57.

Goetze, A., *Das Hethiter-Reich (Der Alte Orient,* 27), 1928.

————, "Historical Allusions in Old Babylonian Omen Texts," *JCS* 1 (1947), 253–65.

Gueterbock, H. C., "Die historische Tradition und ihre literarische Gestaltung beim Babyloniern und Hethitern," *Zeitschrift fuer Assyriologie* 42 (1934), 1–91.

Gurney, O. R., *The Hittites,* rev. ed., 1961.

Hall, H. R., *The Ancient History of the Near East,* 8th rev. ed. by C. J. Gadd, 1932.

Hardy, R. S., "The Old Hittite Kingdom: a Political History," *AJSL* 58 (1941), 177–216.

Helck, H.-W., *Der Einfluss der Militaerfuehrer in der 18. aegyptischen Dynastie (Untersuchungen zur Geschichte und Altertumskunde Aegyptens,* 14), 1939.

Hjelt, A., *Die Chronik Nebopolassars und der syrische Feldzug Nechos (BZAW,* 41), 1925.

Huart, C., *Ancient Persian and Iranian Civilization,* 1927.

Hunger, J., *Heerwesen und Kriegfuehrung der Assyrer auf der Hoehe ihrer Macht,* 1911.

Jacobsen, T., "The Assumed Conflict between Sumerians and Semites in Early Mesopotamian History," *JAOS* 49 (1939), 485–95.

————, "Primitive Democracy in Ancient Mesopotamia," *JNES* 2 (1943), 159–72.

Jeremias, C., *Die Vergoettlichung der babylonisch-assyrischen Koenige (Der Alte Orient,* 19), 1919.

Johns, C. H. W., *Assyrian Deeds and Documents,* 2nd ed., 1924.

Kees, H., *Ancient Egypt. A Cultural Topography,* 1961.

Kienitz, F. K., *Die politische Geschichte Aegyptens vom 7 bis zum 4 Jahrhundert vor der Zeitwende,* 1953.

King, L. W., and Hall, H. R., *Egypt and Western Asia,* 1910.

————, *History of Babylon,* 1919.

————, *History of Sumer and Akkad,* 2nd ed., 1916.

Klauber, E., *Assyrisches Beamtentum nach den Briefen aus der Sar-gonidenzeit* (*Leipziger Semitische Studien*, pt. V. 3), 1910.

Koehne, C., "Die Bevoelkerungspolitik in der Gesetzgebung Koenig Hammurabis," *Zeitschrift fuer Soziale Wissenschaft* (1918), pp. 46–68.

Koenig, F. W., *Aelteste Geschichte der Meder und Perser,* 1934.

Korošec, V., *Hethitische Staatsvertraege. Ein Beitrag zu ihrer juris-tischen Wertung* (*Leipziger Rechtswissenschaftliche Studien,* 60), 1931.

Labat, R., *Le caractère religieux de la royauté assyro-babylonienne* (*Études d'Assyriologie,* 2), 1939.

Landes, G. M., "The Material Civilization of the Ammonites," *BA* 24 (1961), 66–86.

Laqueur, R., "Formen geschichtlichen Denkens im alten Orient und Okzident," *Neue Jahrbuecher fuer Wissenschaft und Jugend-bildung* 7 (1931), 489–506.

Leuze, O., *Die Satrapieneinteilung in Syrien und im Zweistromlande von 520–320* (*Schriften der Koenigsberger Gelehrten Gesellschaft,* 11.4), 1935.

Lewy, J., *Forschungen zur alten Geschichte Vorderasiens* (*Mitteil-ungen der vorderasiatisch-aegyptischen Gesellschaft,* 29.2), 1925.

Macalister, R. A. S., *The Philistines, Their History and Civilization,* 1911.

Manitius, W., *Das stehende Heer der Assyrerkoenige und seine Organisation,* 1910.

Martin, W. J., "Tribut und Tributleistungen bei den Assyrern," *Studia Orientalia* 8 (1936).

Meissner, B., *Koenige Babyloniens und Assyriens,* 1926.

Mendelsohn, I., *Slavery in the Ancient Near East,* 1949.

Mercer, S. A. B., *The Oath in Babylonian and Assyrian Literature,* 1912.

Meyer, E., *Geschichte des Altertums,* 2nd ed., 1909.

———, *Gottesstaat, Militaerherrschaft und Staendewesen in Aegypten* (*Sitzungsbericht der Berliner Akademie*), 1928.

Munn-Rankin, J. M., "Diplomacy in Western Asia in the Early Sec-ond Millennium B.C.," *Iraq* 18 (1956), 68–110.

O'Callaghan, R. T., *Aram Naharaim,* 1948.

Olmstead, A. T., "Assyrian Government of Dependencies," *Ameri-can Political Science Review* 12 (1918), 63–77.

———, *Assyrian Historiography: a Source Study,* 1916.

———, *History of Assyria,* 1923.

———, *History of the Persian Empire*, 1948.

———, "Oriental Imperialism," *American Historical Review* 23 (1918), 755–62.

———, "Shalmaneser III and the Establishment of the Assyrian Power," *JAOS* 41 (1921), 345–82.

Oppenheim, J. J., "The City of Ashur in 714 B.C.," *JNES* 19 (1960), 133–47.

Pallis, S., *The Antiquity of Iraq. A Handbook of Assyriology*, 1956.

Pancritius, M., *Assyrische Kriegfuehrung von Tiglath-pileser bis auf Samsi-adad III*, 1904.

Parker, R. A., "Darius and His Egyptian Campaign," *AJSL* 48 (1941), 373–77.

Poebel, A., "Der Konflikt zwischen Lagaš und Umma zur Zeit Enannatums I und Entemenas," *Paul Haupt Anniversary Volume*, 1926, pp. 220–67.

Pritchard, J. B., ed., *Ancient Near Eastern Texts Relating to the Old Testament*, 2nd ed., 1955.

———, ed., *The Ancient Near East in Pictures Relating to the Old Testament*, 1954.

Proosdij, E. A., "Der sogenannte orientalische Despotismus," *P. Koschaker Festschrift*, 1939, II, 235–46.

Saggs, H. W. F., *The Nimrud Letters*, 1952.

Sauneron, S., and Yoyotte, J., "Sur la politique Palestinienne des rois Saïtes," *VT* 2 (1952), 131–36.

Scharff, A., and Moortgat, A., *Aegypten und Vorderasien im Altertum*, 1950.

Schmoekel, H., *Geschichte des Alten Vorderasien*, 1957.

Sethe, K., "Die Einsetzung des Vezirs unter der 18. Dynastie," *Untersuchungen zur Geschichtes Aegyptens*, 1909, pt. V. 2.

Smith, M., "The Common Theology of the Ancient Near East," *JBL* 71 (1952), 135–47.

Smith, S., *Babylonian Historical Texts Relating to the Capture and Downfall of Babylon*, 1924.

Smith, W. S., *Ancient Egypt as Represented in the Museum of Fine Arts, Boston*, 3rd ed., 1952.

Soden, W. F. von, *Herrscher im alten Orient*, 1954.

Steindorff, G., and Seele, K. C., *When Egypt Ruled the East*, 2nd ed., 1956.

Tadmor, H., "The Campaigns of Sargon II of Assur," *JCS* 12 (1958), 22–40, 77–100.

Thomas, D. W., ed., *Documents from Old Testament Times*, 1958.

Ungnad, A., "Der Gottesbrief als Form assyrischer Kriegsberichter-stattung," *Orientalische Literaturzeitung* 21 (1918), 72–75.

Van der Meer, P., *The Chronology of Ancient Western Asia and Egypt,* 2nd rev. ed., 1955.

Van Zyl, A. H., *The Moabites,* 1960.

Vaux, R. de, "La chronologie de Hazaël et de Benhadad III rois de Damas," *RB* 43 (1934), 512–18.

Weidner, E. F., *Politische Dokumente aus Kleinasien (Boghazkoï Studien,* 8–9), 1923.

Wiseman, D. J., *Chronicles of the Chaldaean Kings (626–556 B.C.) in the British Museum,* 1956.

———, "The Vassal-Treaties of Esarhaddon," *Iraq* 20.1 (1958).

Yadin, Y., *The Art of Warfare in Biblical Lands,* 2 vols., 1963.

II. *Palestinian and Hebrew Politics, History, and Culture*

Abel, F.-M., *Géographie de la Palestine,* I (1933), II (1938).

———, *Histoire de la Palestine depuis le conquête d'Alexandre jusqu'à l'invasion Arabe,* 1952.

Ackroyd, P., "Two Old Testament Historical Problems," *JNES* 17 (1958), 13–27.

Aharoni, Y., "The Date of the Casemate Walls in Judah and Israel and Their Purpose," *BASOR* 154 (1959), 35–39.

———, *Erez-Israel in the Biblical Period. A Historical Geography,* 1962 (Hebrew).

Albright, W. F., "The Chronology of the Divided Monarchy of Israel," *BASOR* 100 (1945), 16–22.

———, "Dedan," *Geschichte und Alte Testament* (ed. G. Ebeling), 1953, 1–12.

———, "King Joiachin in Exile," *BA* 5 (1942), 49–55.

———, "An Ostracon from Calah and the North-israelite Dias-pora," *BASOR* 149 (1958), 33–36.

———, "The Seal of Eliakim and the Last Pre-exilic History of Judah," *JBL* 51 (1932), 77–106.

Alt, A., *Israel und Aegypten. Die Politischen Beziehungen der Koenige von Israel und Juda zu den Pharaonen,* 1909.

———, "Die Rolle Samarias bei der Entstehung des Judentums," *KS,* 1953, II, 316–37 (originally published 1934).

———, "Das System der assyrischen Provinzen auf dem Boden des Reiches Israel," *KS,* II, 188–205 (originally published 1929).

———, "Die territorialgeschichtliche Bedeutung von Sanheribs

Eingriff in Palaestina," *KS*, II, 242–49 (originally published 1930).

Avi-Yonah, M., ed., *Sepher Yerushalayim*, 1956 (Hebrew).

Baly, D., *Geographical Companion to the Bible*, 1963.

———, *The Geography of the Bible*, 1957.

Barnett, R. D., "The Siege of Lachish," *IEJ* 8 (1958), 161–64.

Begrich, J., *Die Chronologie der Koenige von Israel und Juda und die Quellen des Rahmens der Konigsbuecher*, 1929.

Boehl, F. M., *Kanaanaeer und Hebraeer*, 1911.

Bonkamp, B., *Die Bibel im Lichte der Keilsschriftforschung*, 1939.

Borger, R., "Das Ende des aegyptischen Feldherrn Sib'e = סוא ," *JNES* 19 (1960), 49–53.

Bowman, R. A., "Arameans, Aramaic and the Bible," *JNES* 7 (1948), 65–90.

Bright, J., *A History of Israel*, 1959.

Campbell, E. F., Jr., "The Amarna Letters and the Amarna Period," *BA* 23 (1960), 2–22.

David, M., "The Manumission of Slaves Under Zedekiah," *OS* 5 (1948), 63–79.

Dhorme, P., "Les pays bibliques et L'Assyrie," *RB* 7 (1910), 54–75, 177–99, 368–90, 501–20; 8 (1911), 197–218, 346–65.

Diringer, D., "The Royal Jar-Handle Stamps," *BA* 12 (1949), 70–86.

Donner, H., "Der Freund des Koenigs," *ZAW* 73 (1961), 269–77.

Dougherty, R. P., "Sennacherib and the Walled Cities of Judah," *JBL* 49 (1930), 160–71.

Driver, G. R., "Jehoiakin in Captivity," *ET* 56 (1945), 317–18.

Ebeling, E., *Aus dem Leben der juedischen Exulanten*, 1914.

Eissfeldt, O., "Israelitisch-philistaeische Grenzverschiebungen von David bis auf die Assyrerzeit," *ZDPV* 66 (1943), 115–28.

———, *Philister und Phoenizier (Der Alte Orient*, 35), 1936.

Fensham, F. C., "Malediction and Benediction in Ancient Near Eastern Vassal-treaties and the Old Testament," *ZAW* 74 (1962), 1–9.

Feuillet, R., "Les villes de Juda au temps d'Ozias," *VT* 11 (1961), 270–91.

Fohrer, G., "Israels Staatsordnung in Rahmen des Alten Orients," *Osterreichische Zeitschrift fuer offentliches Recht* (1957), 129–48.

———, "Der Vertrag zwischen Koenig und Volk in Israel," *ZAW* 71 (1959), 1–22.

Forrer, E. O., "The Hittites in Palestine," *PEQ* 68 (1936), 190–209; 69 (1937), 100–115.

Fraine, J. de, *L'aspect religieux de la royauté israélite*, 1954.

Fuller, L. E., *Reign of Manasseh*, 1912.

Galling, K., "Die Exilswende in der Sicht des Propheten Sacharja," *VT* 2 (1952), 18–36.

———, *Die israelitische Staatsverfassung in ihrer vorderorientalischen Umwelt* (*Der Alte Orient*, 28.3/4), 1929.

———, *Syrien in der Politik der Achaemeniden bis zum Aufstand des Megazybos 448 v. Chr.* (*Der Alte Orient*, 36), 1937.

———, "Von Naboned zu Darius," *ZDVP* 69 (1953), 42–64; 70 (1954), 4–32.

Ginsberg, H. L., "Judah and the Transjordan States from 734 to 582," *Alexander Marx Jubilee Volume*, 1950, pp. 347–68.

Gordis, R., "Sectional Rivalry in the Kingdom of Judah," *JQR* 25 (1934–35), 237–59.

Gordon, C., "The Origins of the Jews in Elephantine," *JNES* 14 (1955), 56–58.

Gottwald, N. K., *Studies in the Book of Lamentations* (*Studies in Biblical Theology*, 14), rev. ed., 1962.

Graham, W. C., and May, H. G., *Culture and Conscience. An Archaeological Study of the New Religious Past in Ancient Palestine*, 1936.

Gray, J., "Canaanite Kingship in Theory and Practice," *VT* 2 (1952), 193–220.

Gressmann, H., *Der Messias*, 1929.

Hallo, W. W., "From Qarqar to Carchemish: Assyria and Israel in the Light of New Discoveries," *BA* 23 (1960), 34–61.

Haydn, H. M., "Azariah of Judah and Tiglath-Pileser III," *JBL* 28 (1909), 182–99.

Henry, K. H., "Land Tenure in the Old Testament," *PEQ* 86 (1954), 5–15.

Honeyman, A. M., "The Evidence for Regnal Names Among the Hebrews," *JBL* 67 (1948), 13–25.

Honor, L. L., *Sennacherib's Invasion of Palestine. A Critical Source Study*, 1926.

Hooke, S. H., ed., *Myth, Ritual, and Kingship. Essays on the Theory and Practice of Kingship in the Ancient Near East and in Israel*, 1958.

Hoppe, H., "Aegypten und das Alte Testament," *Neue Kirchliche Zeitschrift* 30 (1919), 485–509.

Hyatt, J. P., "New Light on Nebuchadnezzar and Judean History," *JBL* 75 (1956), 277–84.

Jack, J. W., *Samaria in Ahab's Time. Harvard Excavations and Their Results*, 1929.

Janssen, E., *Juda in der Exilszeit. Ein Beitrag zur Frage der Entstehung des Judentums*, 1956.

Jepsen, A., "Israel und Damaskus," *Archiv fuer Orientforschung* 14 (1941–42), 153–72.

———, *Nabi. Soziologische Studien zur alttestamentlichen Literatur und Religionsgeschichte*, 1924.

Jirku, A., *Der Kampf um Syrien-Palaestina im orientalischen Altertum* (*Der Alte Orient*, 25.4), 1926

Johnson, A. R., *Sacral Kingship in Ancient Israel*, 1955.

Junge, E., *Der Wiederaufbau des Heerwesens des Reiches Juda unter Josia*, 1937.

Kittel, R., *Geschichte des Volkes Israel*, 6th ed., 1923–29.

Kraeling, E., *Aram and Israel*, 1918.

———, "The Death of Sennacherib," *JAOS* 53 (1933), 335–46.

Lehmann-Haupt, C. F., *Israel. Seine Entwicklung in Rahmen der Weltgeschichte*, 1911.

Lewy, J., "Les textes paléo-assyriens et l'Ancien Testament," *Revue de l'histoire des Religions* 110 (1934), 29–65.

Lurje, M., *Studien zur Geschichte der wirtschaftlichen und sozialen Verhaeltnisse im israelitisch-juedischen Reiche*, 1927.

Maisler (Mazar), B., "The Historical Background of the Samaria Ostraca," *JPOS* 21 (1948), 117–33.

Malamat, A., "Aspects of the Foreign Policies of David and Solomon," *JNES* 22 (1963), 1–17.

———, "Doctrines of Causality in Hittite and Biblical Historiography," *VT* 5 (1955), 1–12.

———, "The Kingdom of David and Solomon in Its Contacts with Egypt and Aram Naharaim," *BA* 21 (1958), 96–102.

———, "The Last Wars of the Kingdom of Judah," *JNES* 9 (1950), 218–27.

———, "A New Record of Nebuchadrezzar's Palestinian Campaigns," *IEJ* 6 (1956), 246–56.

May, H. G., "Three Hebrew Seals and the Status of the Exiled Jehoiakim," *AJSL* 56 (1939), 146–48.

Mazar, B., "The Aramean Empire and Its Relations with Israel," *BA* 25 (1962), 98–120.

————, "The Campaign of Pharaoh Shishak to Palestine," Supplement 4 *VT* (1957), 57–66.

————, "The Tobiads," *IEJ* 7 (1957), 137–145, 229–238.

McCarthy, D. J., *Treaty and Covenant,* 1963.

Medico, H. E. de, "Armées et finances dans l'Ancien Testament," *L'Ethnographie* (1944), pp. 3–53.

Meek, T. J., *Hebrew Origins,* rev. ed., 1950.

Meissner, B., *Die Achaemeniden-Koenige und das Judentum (Sitzungsberichte d. Preuss. Akademie d. Wissenschaft),* 1938.

Mendelsohn, I., "Samuel's Denunciation of Kingship in the Light of the Akkadian Documents from Ugarit," *BASOR* 143 (1956), 17–22.

Mendenhall, G. E., "The Hebrew Conquest of Palestine," *BA* 25 (1962), 66–87.

————, *Law and Covenant in Israel and the Ancient Near East* (reprinted from *BA* 17 [1954], 26–46, 49–76), 1955.

Meyer, E., *Die Israeliten und Ihre Nachbarstaemme,* 1906.

Morgenstern, J., "Jerusalem—485 B.C.," *HUCA* 27 (1956), 101–79.

Mowinckel, S., "Die Chronologie der Israelitischen und Juedischen Koenige," *Acta Orientalia* 10 (1932), 161–277.

Murphy, R. E., "Israel and Moab in the Ninth Century B.C.," *CBQ* 15 (1953), 409–17.

North, C. R., "The Old Testament Estimate of the Monarchy," *AJSL* 48 (1931–32), 1–19.

————, *The Old Testament Interpretation of History,* 1946.

Noth, M., "Beitraege zur Geschichte des Ostjordanlandes," *PJ* 37 (1941), 50–101.

————, "Beitraege zur Geschichte des Ostjordanlandes," *Beitraege zur bibl. Landes u. Altertumskunde* 68 (1949), 1–50.

————, "La Catastrophe de Jérusalem en l'an 587 et sa signification pour Israel," *RHPR* 33 (1953), 82–102.

————, "Die Einnahme von Jerusalem in Jahre 597 v. Chr.," *ZDPV* 74 (1958), 133–57.

————, *Gesammelte Studien zum Alten Testament (Theologische Bucherei,* 6), 1957.

————, "Gilead und Gad," *ZDPV* 75 (1959), 14–73.

————, *The History of Israel,* 2nd ed., 1960.

————, "Israelitische Staemme zwischen Ammon und Moab," *ZAW* 19 (1944), 11–57.

————, "Das Krongut der israelitischen Koenige und seine Verwaltung. Die samarischen Ostraka," *ZDPV* 50 (1927), 211–14.

————, *Die Welt des Alten Testament,* 3rd ed., 1957.

Olmstead, A. T., *History of Palestine and Syria,* 1939.

————, "Western Asia in the Reign of Sennacherib," *Proceedings of the American Historical Association,* 1909.

Parrot, A., *Babylon and the Old Testament (Studies in Biblical Archaeology,* 8), 1958.

————, *Nineveh and the Old Testament (Studies in Biblical Archaeology,* 3), 1955.

————, *Samaria—the Capitol of the Kingdom of Israel (Studies in Biblical Archaeology,* 7), 1958.

Pfeiffer, R. H., "Assyria and Israel," *Rivista degli studi orientali* 32 (1957), 145–54.

Rad, G. von, *Der Heilige Krieg im alten Israel,* 3d ed., 1958.

Rainey, A., "Administration in Ugarit and the Samarian Ostraca," *IEJ* 12 (1962), 62–63.

Rinaldi, G., "Quelques remarques sur la politique d'Azarias (Ozias) de Juda en Philistie (2 Chron. xxvi. 6ss.)," Supplement 9 *VT* (1963), 225–35.

Rosenthal, E. I. J., "Some Aspects of Hebrew Monarchy," *Journal of Jewish Studies* 9 (1958), 1–18.

Rothstein, J. W., *Juden und Samaritaner,* 1908.

Rowley, H. H., "Sanballat and the Samaritan Temple," *BJRL* 38 (1955), 166–98.

Rudolph, W., "Zum Feldzug des Sanheribs," *PJ* 25 (1929), 59–80.

Schedl, C., "Textkritische Bemerkungen zu den Synchronismen der Koenige von Israel und Juda," *VT* 12 (1962), 88–119.

Schrader, E., *The Cuneiform Inscriptions and the Old Testament,* 2nd ed., 1885–88.

Segal, J. B., "An Aramaic Ostracon from Nimrud," *Iraq* 19 (1957), 139–45.

Simons, J., *The Geographical and Topographical Texts of the Old Testament,* 1958.

————, *Jerusalem in the Old Testament,* 1952.

Slousch, N., "Representative Government among the Hebrews and Phoenicians," *JQR* 4 (1913–14), 303–10.

Smith, J. M. P., "Traces of Emperor Worship in the Old Testament," *AJSL* 39 (1922), 32–39.

Speiser, E. A., " 'People' and 'Nation' of Israel," *JBL* 79 (1960), 157–63.

Tadmor, H., "Azriyahu of Yaudi," *Scripta Hierosolymitana* 8 (1961), 232–71.

Thiele, E. R., *The Mysterious Numbers of the Hebrew Kings,* 1951.

Todd, J. C., *Politics and Religion in Ancient Israel,* 1904.

Torczyner, H., ed., *The Lachish Letters,* 1938.

———, *The Lachish Ostraca, Letters of the Time of Jeremiah,* 1940 (Hebrew).

Unger, M. F., *Israel and the Arameans of Damascus,* 1957.

Ungnad, A., "Die Zahl der von Sanherib deportierten Judaer," *ZAW* 59 (1942–43), 199–202.

Vogt, E., "Die Neubabylonische Chronik ueber die Schlacht bei Karkemisch und die Einnahme von Jerusalem," Supplement 4 *VT* (1957), 67–96.

Wainwright, G. A., "Some Early Philistine History," *VT* 9 (1959), 73–84.

Weber, M., *Ancient Judaism,* 1952 (trans. of German ed., 1921).

———, *Sociology of Religion,* 4th rev. ed., 1956 (English trans. 1963).

Whitley, C. F., "The Deuteronomic Presentation of the House of Omri," *VT* 2 (1952), 137–52.

———, *The Exilic Age,* 1957.

Wilson, J. A., "The Assembly of a Phoenician City," *JNES* 4 (1945), 245.

Wolf, C. U., "Traces of Primitive Democracy in Israel," *JNES* 6 (1947), 98–108.

Wright, G. E., ed., *The Bible and the Ancient Near East. Essays in honor of W. F. Albright,* 1961.

———, *Biblical Archaeology,* 2nd ed., 1961.

Wright, J. S., *The Date of Ezra's Coming to Jerusalem,* 1946.

Yadin, Y., "The Fourfold Division of Judah," *BASOR* 163 (1961), 6–12.

———, "Recipients or Owners. A Note on the Samaria Ostraca," *IEJ* 9 (1959), 184–87.

———, "A Further Note on the Samaria Ostraca," *IEJ* 12 (1962), 64–66.

———, "Some Aspects of the Strategy of Achab and David," *Biblica* 36 (1955), 322–51.

Yeivin, S., "Families and Parties in the Kingdom of Judah," *Studies in the History of Israel and Its Land,* 1959, pp. 250–93 (Hebrew).

III. *Israel's View of the Nations: Particularism and Universalism*

Bertholet, A., *Die Stellung der Israeliten und der Juden zu den Fremden,* 1896.

Blank, S., "Studies in Postexilic Universalism," *HUCA* 11 (1936), 159–91.

Cadbury, H. J., *National Ideals in the Old Testament*, 1920.

Caspari, W., "Der biblische Friedensgedanks nach dem Alten Testament," *Biblische Zeit- und Streitfragen* 10 (1916).

———, "Vorstellung und Wort Friede im Alten Testament," *Beitraege zur Foerderung Christlicher Theologie* 14.4 (1910).

Causse, A., *Israël et la vision de l'humanité*, 1924.

Eichrodt, W., *Die Hoffnung des ewigen Friedens im alten Israel*, 1920.

Gross, H., "Die Idee des ewigen und all-gemeinen Weltfriedens im Alten Orient und im Alten Testament," *Trier Theol. St.* 7 (1956).

———, *Weltherrschaft als religioese Idee im Alten Testament*, 1953.

Martin-Achard, R., *Israël et les nations. Perspective missionnaires de l'Ancien Testament*, 1959.

May, H. G., "Theological Universalism in the Old Testament," *JBR* 16 (1948), 100–107.

Peisker, M., *Die Beziehungen der Nichtisraeliten zu Jahwe* (*BZAW*, 12), 1907.

Schmoekel, H., *Jahwe und die Fremdvoelker* (*Breslauer Studien zur Theologie und Religionsgeschichte*), 1934.

IV. *Selected Aspects of Prophecy*

Childs, B., "The Enemy from the North and the Chaos Tradition," *JBL* 78 (1959), 187–98.

Cossmann, W., *Die Entwicklung des Gerichtsgedankens bei den alttestamentlichen Propheten* (*BZAW*, 29), 1915.

Dunkerly, R., "Prophecy and Prediction," *ET* 61 (1949–50), 260–63.

Fohrer, G., "Remarks on Modern Interpretation of the Prophets," *JBL* 80 (1961), 309–19.

———, *Die symbolischen Handlungen der Propheten*, 1953.

Giesebrecht, F., *Die Berufsbegabung der alttestamentlichen Propheten*, 1897.

Gray, J., "The Kingship of God in the Prophets and Psalms," *VT* 11 (1961), 1–29.

Haller, M., "Edom im Urteile der Propheten," *Marti Festschrift*, 1925, pp. 105–17.

Hempel, J., "Jahwe-Gleichnisse der israelitischen Propheten," *ZAW* 1 (1924), 74–104.

Hentschke, R., *Die Stellung der vorexilischen Schriftpropheten zum Kultus (BZAW,* 75), 1957.

Lauha, A., *Zaphon. Der Norden und die Nordvoelker im Alten Testament,* 1943.

Micklem, N., *Prophecy and Eschatology,* 1926.

Procksch, O., *Geschichtsbetrachtung und Geschichtsueberlieferung bei den vorexilischen Propheten,* 1908.

Quell, G., *Wahre und falsche Propheten (Beitraege zur Foerderung Christlicher Theologie,* 46.1), 1952.

Rad, G. von, "Die falschen Propheten," *ZAW* 51 (1933), 109–20.

Wolff H. H., "Das Thema 'Umkehr' in der alttestamentlichen Prophetie," *ZTK* 48 (1951), 129–48.

Wuerthwein, E., "Der Ursprung der prophetischen Gerichtsrede," *ZTK* 1 (1952), 1–16.

V. *The Political Role and Outlook of Prophecy*

Allen, E. L., *Prophet and Nation,* 1947.

Buber, M., *The Prophetic Faith,* 1949.

Eberharter, A., *Das soziale und politische Wirksamkeit des alttest. Prophetentum,* 1924.

Elliger, K., "Nochmals 'Prophet und Politik,' " *ZAW* 55 (1937), 291–96.

———, "Prophet und Politik," *ZAW* 53 (1935), 3–22.

Hempel, J., *Die Mehrdeutigkeit der Geschichte als Problem der prophetischen Theologie,* 1936.

———, *Politische Absicht und politische Wirkung im biblischen Schriftum (Der Alte Orient,* 38.1), 1938.

Jenni, E., *Die politischen Voraussagen der Propheten (Abhandlungen zur Theologie des Alten und Neuen Testaments,* 29), 1956.

Kraus, H.-J., *Prophetie und Politik (Theologische Existenz Heute,* N.F. 36), 1952.

McCown, C. C., *The Genesis of the Social Gospel,* 1929.

Procksch, O., *Der Staatsgedanke in der Prophetie,* 1933.

Staerk, W., *Das assyrische Weltreich im Urteil der Propheten,* 1908.

Troeltsch, E., "Das Ethos der hebraeischen Propheten," *Logos* 6 (1916), 1–28.

Weinrich, F., *Der religiös-utopische Charakter der "prophetischen Politik,"* 1932.

Wilke, F., *Die politische Wirksamkeit der Propheten Israels*, 1913.

Winckler, H., and Zimmern, H., eds., *Die Keilinschriften und das Alte Testament* (von E. Schrader), 3rd ed., 1902–3.

VI. *Politics and International Relations in Particular Prophets*

A. *Pre-Writing Prophets*

Albright, W. F., "Oracles of Balaam," *JBL* 63 (1944), 207–33.

Alt, A., "Das Gottesurteil auf dem Karmel," *KS*, 1953, II, 135–49 (originally published 1935).

Ap-Thomas, D. R., "Elijah on Mt. Carmel," *PEQ* 92 (1960), 146–55.

Daiches, A., "Balaam—a Babylonian *baru*," *Hermann Hilprecht Anniversary Volume*, 1909, pp. 60–70.

Diman, M. (Haran), "An Archaic Survival in Prophetic Literature," *Yedi'oth hahebrah lehaqirat Eretz-Yisrael we'atiqotheha* 13 (1947), 7–15 (Hebrew).

Erbt, W., *Elia, Elisa, Jona. Beitrag zur Geschichte der 9 u. 8 Jahrhundert*, 1907.

Fohrer, G., *Elia*, 1957.

Galling, K., "Der Gott Karmel und die Aechtung der fremden Goetter," *Festschrift fuer Alt*, 1953.

Junker, H., *Prophet und Seher in Israel*, 1927.

Malamat, A., "History and Prophetic Vision in a Mari Letter," *Eretz-Israel* 5 (1958), 67–73 (Hebrew).

Meyer, E., "Der Krieg gegen Sihon und die zugehoerigen Abschnitte," *ZAW* 5 (1885), 36–52.

Mowinckel, S., "Der Ursprung der Balaamsage," *ZAW* 48 (1930), 233–71.

Napier, B. D., "The Omrides of Jezreel," *VT* 9 (1959), 366–78.

Noth, M., "History and the Word of God in the Old Testament," *BJRL* 32 (1950), 194–206.

——, "Numeri 21 als Glied der 'Hexateuch' erzaehlung," *ZAW* 58 (1940–41), 161–89.

Parzen, H., "A Chapter of Israelitish History," *Bibliotheca Sacra* 85 (1928), 188–223.

——, "The Prophets and Omri's Dynasty," *HTR* 33 (1940), 69–96.

Soden, W. von, "Verkuendigung des Gotteswillens durch prophetisches Wort in den altbabylonischen Briefen aus Mari," *Die Welt des Orients* 5 (1950), 397–403.

B. *Amos*

Beek, M. A., "The Religious Background of Amos II.6–8," *OS* 5 (1948), 132–41.

Bentzen, A., "The Ritual Background of Amos I.2—II.16," *OS* 8 (1950), 85–99.

Budde, K., "Zu Text und Auslegung des Buches Amos," *JBL* 43 (1924), 46–131; 44 (1925), 63–122.

Duerr, L., "Altorientalisches Recht bei dem Propheten Amos und Hosea," *Biblische Zeitschrift* 23 (1935-36), 150–57.

Kapelrud, A., *Central Ideas in Amos*, 1956.

Maag, V., *Text, Wortschatz und Begriffswelt des Buches Amos*, 1951.

Malamat, A., "Amos 1:5 in the Light of the Til-Barsip Inscriptions," *BASOR* 129 (1953), 25–26.

Marti, K., "Zur Komposition von Amos 1:3—2:3," *Baudissin Festschrift*, 1917, pp. 323–330.

Neher, A., *Amos. Contribution à l'étude du prophétisme*, 1950.

Rieger, J., *Die Bedeutung der Geschichte fuer die Verkuendigung des Amos und Hosea*, 1929.

Seesemann, O., *Israel und Juda bei Amos und Hosea*, 1898.

Wuerthwein, E., "Amos-Studien," *ZAW* 62 (1950), 10–52.

C. *Hosea*

Alt, A., "Hosea 5:8—6:6. Ein Krieg und seine Folgen in prophetischer Beleuchtung," *KS*, 1953, II, 163–87 (originally published 1919).

Elliger, K., "Eine verkannte Kunstform beim Hosea," *ZAW* 69 (1957), 151–60.

Ginsberg, H. L., "Hosea's Ephraim; More Fool than Knave. A New Interpretation of Hosea 12:1–14," *JBL* 80 (1961), 339–47.

Humbert, P., "La logique de la perspective nomade chez Osée et l'unité d'Osée, 2:4–22," *Festschrift Karl Marti*, 1925, pp. 158–66.

Nyberg, H. S., *Studien zum Hoseabuche*, 1935.

Peters, N., *Hosea und die Geschichte*, 1924.

Sellin, E., "Die geschichtliche Orientierung der Prophetie des Hosea," *Neue Kirchliche Zeitschrift* 36 (1925), 607–58.

Snaith, N., *Mercy and Sacrifice*, 1953.

Tadmor, H., "The Historical Background of the Prophecies of Hosea," *Yehezkel Kaufmann Jubilee Volume*, 1960, 84–88 (Hebrew).

D. *Isaiah of Jerusalem*

Alt, A., "Jesaja 8:23—9:6. Befreiungsnacht und Kroenungstag," *KS*, 1953, II, 206–25 (originally published 1950).

Avigad, N., "The Epitaph of a Royal Steward from Siloam Village," *IEJ* 3 (1953), 137–52.

Blank, S. H., *Prophetic Faith in Isaiah*, 1958.

Burrows, M., "The Conduit of the Upper Pool," *ZAW* 70 (1958), 221–27.

Crook, M. B., "A Suggested Occasion for Isa. 9:2–7 and 11:1–9," *JBL* 68 (1949), 213–24.

DeBoer, P. A. H., "Notes on Text and Meaning of Isaiah 38:9–20," *OS* 9 (1951), 170–86.

Fichtner, J., "Jahwes Plan in der Botschaft des Jesaia," *ZAW* 63 (1951), 16–33.

Fullerton, K., "The Interpretation of Isa. 8:5–10," *JBL* 43 (1924), 253–89.

———, "Isaiah 14:28–32," *AJSL* 42 (1925–26), 86–109.

———, "The Problem of Isa., chap. 10," *AJSL* 34 (1918), 170–84.

———, "The Stone of the Foundation," *AJSL* 37 (1920), 1–50.

Ginsberg, H. L., "An Unrecognized Allusion to Kings Pekah and Hoshea of Israel (Isa. 8:23)," *Eretz-Israel* 5 (1958), 61–65.

Gottwald, N. K., "Immanuel as the Prophet's Son," *VT* 8 (1958), 36–47.

Graham, W. C., "Isaiah's Part in the Syro-Ephraimite Crisis," *AJSL* 50 (1934), 201–216.

Hallo, W. W., "Isaiah 28:9–13 and the Ugaritic Abecedaries," *JBL* 77 (1958), 324–38.

Hayes, J. H., "The Tradition of Zion's Inviolability," *JBL* 82 (1963), 419–26.

Irwin, W., "The Attitude of Isaiah in the Crisis of 701," *JR* 16 (1936), 406–18.

Jones, D. R., "The Tradition of the Oracles of Isa. of Jerusalem," *ZAW* 68 (1955), 226–46.

Junker, H., "Die messianische Verkuendigung des Buches Isaiah,"

RB 48 (1938), 189–93; 49 (1939), 5–11, 240–51, 279–85, 338–46; 50 (1940), 5–11.

Katzenstein, H. J., "The Royal Steward (asher 'al ha-Bayith)," *IEJ* 10 (1960), 152–55.

Kuechler, F., *Die Stellung des Propheten Jesaja zur Politik seiner Zeit*, 1906.

Kuschke, A., "Mitteilungen zu Jes. 30:1–5," *ZAW* 64 (1952), 194–95.

Liebrich, Y., "The Agricultural *Mashal* in Isa. 28:23–29," *Tarbiz* 24 (1955), 126–28 (Hebrew).

Lindblom, J., "Der Eckstein in Jes. 28:16," *Festschrift S. Mowinckel*, 1955, pp. 123–32.

———, *A Study in the Immanuel Section in Isaiah, Isa. 7:1—9:6*, 1958.

Quell, G., "Jesaja 14:1–23," *Festschrift F. Baumgaertel*, 1959, pp. 131–57.

Rudolph, W., "Jesaja XV–XVI," *Hebrew and Semitic Studies presented to G. R. Driver*, 1963, pp. 130–43.

Vogt, E., "Filius Tab'el (Isa. 7:6)," *Biblica* 37 (1956), 263–64.

Whitley, C. F., "The Call and Mission of Isaiah," *JNES* 18 (1959), 38–48.

Wildberger, H., "Jesajas Verstaendnis der Geschichte," Supplement 9 *VT* (1963), 83–117.

———, "Die Voelkerwallfahrt zum Zion, Jes. II.1–5," *VT* 7 (1957), 62–81.

Wilke, F., *Jesaja und Assur. Eine exegetisch-historische Untersuchung zur Politik des Propheten Jesaja*, 1905.

E. *Micah*

Beyerlin, W., *Die Kulttraditionen Israels in der Verkuendigung des Propheten Micha*, 1956.

Crook, M. B., "The Promise in Micah 5," *JBL* 70 (1951), 313–20.

Elliger, K., "Die Heimat des Propheten Micha," *ZDPV* 57 (1934), 81–152.

Graham, W. C., "Some Suggestions toward the Interpretation of Micah 1:10–16," *AJSL* 47 (1931), 237–68.

Kapelrud, A., "Eschatology in the Book of Micah," *VT* 11 (1961), 392–405.

Nielsen, E., *Oral Tradition (Studies in Biblical Theology*, 11), 1954, pp. 79–93.

F. *Zechariah 9:1–8*

Delcor, M., "Les allusions à Alexandre le Grand dans Zach. 9:1–8," *VT* 1 (1951), 110–24.

Elliger, K., "Ein Zeugnis aus der juedischen Gemeinde im Alexanderjahr 322 v. Chr.," *ZAW* 62 (1949–50), 63–115.

Jones, D. R., "A Fresh Interpretation of Zech. IX–XII," *VT* 12 (1962), 241–59.

Kraeling, E., "The Historical Situation in Zech. 9:1–10," *AJSL* 41 (1924), 24–33.

Malamat, A., "The Historical Setting of Two Biblical Prophecies on the Nations," *IEJ* 1 (1950–51), 149–54.

G. *Zephaniah*

Cales, J., "L'authenticité de Sophonie 2,11 et son contexte primitif," *Recherches de Science Religieuse* 10 (1920), 355–60.

Ferguson, H., "The Historical Testimonies of the Prophet Zephaniah," *JBL* 3 (1883), 42–59.

Gerleman, G., *Zephanja: textkritisch und literarisch untersucht*, 1942.

Hyatt, P., "The Date and Background of Zephaniah," *JNES* 7 (1948), 125–33.

Smith, L. P., and Lacheman, E. R., "The Authorship of Zephaniah," *JNES* 9 (1950), 137–42.

Sullivan, K., "The Book of Sophonias," *Worship* 31 (1957), 130–39.

H. *Isaiah 19:16–25*

Feuillet, R., "Un sommet religieux de l'Ancien Testament. L'oracle d'Isaïe XIX (vv. 16–25) sur la conversion de l'Égypte," *Recherches de Science Religieuse* 39 (1951), 65–87.

I. *Nahum*

Allis, O. T., "Nahum, Nineveh, Elkosh," *Evangelical Quarterly* 27 (1955), 67–80.

Arnold, W. R., "The Composition of Nah. 1:2—2:3," *ZAW* 21 (1901), 225–65.

Graham, W. C., "The Interpretation of Nah. 1:9—2:3," *AJSL* 44 (1927), 337–48.

Haldar, A., *Studies in the Book of Nahum,* 1947.

Haupt, P., "The Book of Nahum," *JBL* 26 (1907), 1–53.

Humbert, P., "Essai d'analyse de Nahoum 1:2—2:3," *ZAW* 3 (1926), 266–80.

———, "Le problème de livre de Nahoum," *RHPR* 12 (1932), 1–15.

———, "La vision de Nahoum II.4–11," *Archiv fuer Orientforschung* 5 (1928), 14–19.

Lods, A., "Trois études sur la littérature prophétique," *RHPR* 11 (1931), 211–19.

Mihelic, J. L., "The Concept of God in the Book of Nahum," *Interpretation* 2 (1948), 199–215.

J. *Habakkuk*

Albright, W. F., "The Psalm of Habakkuk," *Studies in Old Testament Prophecy Presented to T. H. Robinson,* 1950, pp. 1–18.

Brownlee, W. H., "The Placarded Revelation of Habakkuk," *JBL* 82 (1963), 319–25.

———, *The Text of Habakkuk in the Ancient Commentary from Qumran* (*JBL* Monograph Series, 11), 1959, pp. 45–49.

Budde, K., "Habakuk," *ZDMG* 84 (1930), 139–47.

Cannon, W. W., "The Integrity of Habakkuk, Ch. 1, 2," *ZAW* 43 (1925), 62–90.

Delcor, M., "La geste de Yahve au temps de l'Exode et l'espérance du psalmiste en Habacuc III,'" *Miscellanea Biblica B. Ubach,* 1954, 287–302.

Gruenthauer, M. J., "Chaldeans or Macedonians?" *Biblica* 8 (1927), 129–60, 257–89.

Humbert, P., *Problèmes du livre d'Habacuc,* 1944.

Irwin, W., "The Psalm of Habakkuk," *JNES* 1 (1942), 10–40.

Mowinckel, S., "Zum Psalm des Habakuk," *TZ* 9 (1953), 1–23.

Nielsen, E., "The Righteous and the Wicked in Habaqquq," *Studia Theologica* 6 (1952), 54–78.

Schmidt, H., "Ein Psalm im Buche Habakuk," *ZAW* 62 (1950), 52–63.

Staerk, W., "Zu Habakkuk 1:5–11, Geschichte oder Mythos?" *ZAW* 51 (1933), 1–28.

Stenzel, M., "Hab. 2:1–4, 5a," *Biblica* 33 (1952), 506–10.

K. *Jeremiah*

Albright, W. F., "The Nebuchadnezzar and Neriglissar Chronicles," *BASOR* 143 (1956), 28–33.

Bardtke, H., "Jeremia der Fremdvoelkerprophet," *ZAW* 53 (1935), 209–39; 54 (1936), 240–62.

Budde, K., "Ueber die Kap. 50 und 51 des Buches Jeremia," *Jahrbuecher f. Deutsche Theologie* 23 (1878), 428–70, 529–62.

Fischer, L., "Die Urkunden in Jer. 32:11–14 nach den Ausgrabungen und dem Talmud," *ZAW* 30 (1910), 136–42.

Ginsberg, H. L., "An Aramaic Contemporary of the Lachish Letters," *BASOR* 140 (1948), 24–27.

Malamat, A., "The Historical Setting of Two Biblical Prophecies on the Nations," *IEJ* 1 (1950–51), 149–59.

———, "Jeremiah and the Last Two Kings of Judah," *PEQ* 83 (1951), 81–87.

Orr, A., "The Seventy Years of Babylon," *VT* 6 (1956), 304–6.

Rost, L., "Jeremais Stellungnahme zur Aussenpolitik der Koenige Josia und Jojaqim," *Christentum und Wissenschaft,* 1929, pp. 69–79.

Rowton, M. B., "Jeremiah and the Death of Josiah," *JNES* 10 (1951), 128–30.

Schwally, F., "Die Reden des Buches Jeremia gegen die Heiden, XXV, XLVI–LI," *ZAW* 8 (1888), 177–217.

Thieme, K., "Jérémie, traître à sa patrie ou apôtre de la paix?" *Dieu Vivant* 19 (1951), 17–36.

Thomas, D. W., "The Age of Jeremiah in the Light of Recent Archaeological Discovery," *PEQ* (1950), 8–13.

———, *"The Prophet" in the Lachish Ostraca,* 1946.

———, "Again 'The Prophet' in the Lachish Ostraca," *Von Ugarit nach Qumran (Festschrift O. Eissfeldt),* 1958, pp. 244–49.

Whitley, C. F., "The Term Seventy Years Captivity," *VT* 4 (1954), 60–72.

———, "The Seventy Years Desolation—a Rejoinder," *VT* 7 (1957), 416–18.

Wilke, F., *Das Skythenproblem im Jeremiabuche (Beitraege zur Wissenschaft vom Alten Testament, 9),* 1913.

L. *Ezekiel*

Barnes, W. E., "Ezekiel's Denunciation of Tyre, Ez. 26 bis 28), *JTS* 35 (1934), 50–54.

Berry, G. R., "The Date of Ezekiel 38:1—39:20," *JBL* 41 (1922), 224–32.

Bevan, A., "The King of Tyre in Ezekiel," *JTS* 4 (1903), 398–411, 500–505.

Cheminant, P., *Les prophéties d'Ézéchiel contre Tyr (XXVI— XXVIII.19)*, 1912.

Eissfeldt, O., "Das Alte Testament im Licht der safatenischen Inschriften," *ZDMG* 104 (1954), 88–118.

————, "Das Datum der Belagerung von Tyrus durch Nebukadnezar," *Forschungen und Fortschritte* 9 (1933), 421–22.

————, "Ezechiel als Zeuge fuer Senherib's Eingriff in Palaestina," *PJ* 27 (1931), 58–66.

————, "Hesekiel Kap. 16 als Geschichtsquelle," *JPOS* 16 (1936), 286–92.

————, "Schwerterschlagene bei Hesekiel," *Studies in Old Testaent Prophecy Presented to T. H. Robinson*, 1950, pp. 73–81.

Fohrer, G., *Die Hauptprobleme des Buches Ezechiel*, 1952.

Foster, R. S., "A Note on Ezekiel XVII:1–10, 22–24," *VT* 8 (1958), 374–79.

Greenberg, M., "Ezekiel 17 and the Policy of Psammetichus II," *JBL* 76 (1957), 304–9.

Gronkowski, W., *Le Messianisme d'Ézéchiel*, 1930.

Guthrie, H. H., "Ezekiel 21," *ZAW* 74 (1962), 268–81.

Hammershaimb, E., "Ezekiel's View of the Monarchy," *Studia Orientalia. Ioanni Pedersen*, 1953, pp. 130–40.

Lods, A., "Le sort des incirconcis," *Comptes rendus de l'Académie des Inscriptions et belles-lettres*, 1943.

May, H. G., "The King in the Garden of Eden: a Study of Ezekiel 28:12–19," *Israel's Prophetic Heritage. Essays in Honor of J. Muilenburg* (eds. B. W. Anderson and W. Harrelson), 1962, pp. 196–207.

McKenzie, J. L., "Mythological Allusions in Ezek. 28:12–28," *JBL* 75 (1956), 322–27.

Millard, A., "Ezekiel 27:19: the Wine Trade of Damascus," *JSS* 7 (1962), 201–3.

Morgenstern, J., "The Rest of the Nations," *JSS* 2 (1957), 225–31.

Myres, J. L., "Gog and the Danger from the North in Ezekiel," *Palestine Exploration Fund Quarterly Statement for 1932*, pp. 213–19.

Plessis, J., *Les prophéties d'Ézéchiel contre l'Égypte (XXIX– XXXIII)*, 1912.

Reventlow, H., "Die Voelker als Jahwes Zeugen bei Ezechiel," *ZAW* 71 (1959), 33–43.

Smith, S., "The Ship Tyre," *PEQ* 85 (1953), 97–110.

Stocks, H., "Danel, die suedbabylonische und die nordpalaestinisch-phoenikische Ueberlieferung," *ZDMG* 97 (1943), 125–49.

Tsevat, M., "The Neo-Assyrian and Neo-Babylonian Vassal Oaths and the Prophet Ezekiel," *JBL* 78 (1959), 199–204.

Vogelstein, M., "Nebuchadnezzar's Reconquest of Phoenicia and Palestine and the Oracles of Ezekiel," *HUCA* 23 (1950–51), 197–220.

Wensinck, A. J., *Tree and Bird as Cosmological Symbols in Western Asia*, 1921.

Widengren, G., *The King and the Tree of Life in Ancient Near East Religion*, 1951.

Zimmerli, W., " 'Leben' und 'Tod' im Buche des Propheten Ezechiel," *TZ* 13 (1957), 494–508.

M. *Isaiah of the Exile*

Barnes, W. E., "Cyrus the servant of Jehovah," *JTS* 32 (1931), 32–39.

Blank, S., *Prophetic Faith in Isaiah*, 1958.

———, "Studies in Deutero-Isaiah," *HUCA* 15 (1940), 1–46.

Buckler, F. W., "Firdausī's Shāhnāmah and the Genealogia Regni Dei," Supplement 1 *JAOS* (1935), 1–21.

Eissfeldt, O., "The Ebed-Jahwe in Isa. XL–LV in the Light of the Israelite Conception of the Community and the Individual, the Ideal and the Real," *ET* 44 (1932), 261–68.

———, *Der Gottesknecht beim Deuterojesaja (Jes. 40–55) im Lichte der israelitischen Anschauung von Gemeinschaft und Individuum*, 1933.

———, "The Promises of Grace to David in Isa. 55:1–5," *Israel's Prophetic Heritage. Essays in Honor of J. Muilenberg*, 1962, pp. 166–76.

Farley, F. A., "Jeremiah and 'The Suffering Servant of Jehovah in Deutero-Isaiah,' " *ET* 38 (1927), 521–24.

Haller, M., "Die Kyros-Lieder Deuterojesajas," *Gunkel Festschrift*, 1923, pp. 261–77.

Kaiser, O., *Der koenigliche Knecht: Eine traditionsgeschichtlich-exegetische Studie ueber die Ebed-Jahweh-Lieder beim Deutero-jesaja*, 1959.

Kittel, R., "Cyrus und Deuterojesaja," *ZAW* 18 (1898), 149–62.

Koehler, L., *Deuterojesaja stilkritisch untersucht,* 1923.

Lindblom, J., *The Servant Songs in Deutero-Isaiah,* 1951.

Lindhagen, C., *The Servant Motif in the Old Testament,* 1950.

North, C. R., "The Interpretation of Deutero-Isaiah," *Festschrift S. Mowinckel,* 1955, pp. 133–45.

————, *The Suffering Servant in Deutero-Isaiah. An Historical and Critical Study,* rev. ed., 1956.

Robinson, H. W., *The Cross of the Servant,* 1926.

Simcox, C. E., "The Role of Cyrus in Deutero-Isaiah," *JAOS* 57 (1937), 158–71.

Smart, J. D., "A New Interpretation of Isa. 46:1–6," *ET* 46 (1934–35), 420–24.

Smith, S., *Isaiah Chapters XL–LV. Literary Criticism and History,* 1944.

Torrey, C. C., *The Second Isaiah: A New Interpretation,* 1928.

Von Gall, A. F., "Die Reich-Gottes-Hoffnung im Parsismus," *Basileia tou Theou,* 1926, pp. 83–163.

General Index

Index of Authors

Index of Biblical References

The books are listed in their order in the English versions.

440

Index of Foreign Terms

Index of Foreign Terms: Akkadian, Egyptian, Hebrew, Persian